William Henry Whitmore

The Colonial Laws of Massachusetts

Reprinted from the Edition of 1660, with the Supplements to 1672 - Containing

also, the Body of Liberties of 1641

William Henry Whitmore

The Colonial Laws of Massachusetts
Reprinted from the Edition of 1660, with the Supplements to 1672 - Containing also, the Body of Liberties of 1641

ISBN/EAN: 9783337154646

Printed in Europe, USA, Canada, Australia, Japan

Cover: Foto ©Suzi / pixelio.de

More available books at **www.hansebooks.com**

THE COLONIAL LAWS OF MASSACHUSETTS.

REPRINTED FROM THE EDITION OF

1660,

WITH THE SUPPLEMENTS TO 1672.

CONTAINING ALSO,

THE BODY OF LIBERTIES OF 1641.

PUBLISHED BY ORDER OF THE CITY COUNCIL OF BOSTON, UNDER THE SUPERVISION OF WILLIAM H. WHITMORE, RECORD COMMISSIONER.

WITH A COMPLETE INDEX.

BOSTON:
1889.

DISTRICT RAILWAY.
* BEST & DIRECT ROUTE FOR ATTRACTIVE POINTS OF THE THAMES. *
LONDON
RIVERSIDE STATIONS,
Wapping, Rotherhithe,
MONUMENT (for London Bridge)
MANSION HOUSE (CITY),
BLACKFRIARS, TEMPLE,
CHARING CROSS, WESTMINSTER,
HAMMERSMITH,
SHAFTESBURY ROAD, TURNHAM GREEN,
AND PUTNEY BRIDGE (FULHAM).
Passengers are Booked Through
TO AND FROM
KEW BRIDGE, BRENTFORD,
RICHMOND, TWICKENHAM,
Teddington, Kingston,
WINDSOR, TAPLOW,
MAIDENHEAD (for Great Marlow),
TWYFORD (for Henley),
Reading, &c.

TABLE OF CONTENTS.

PREFACE.

By authority of the City Council of Boston I am enabled to make accessible to the public two books of great rarity, which possess a great value in the history of our laws. These are the Body of Liberties of 1641, and the Revised Laws of the Colony issued in 1660. Taken in connection with the Colonial Laws of 1672 and Supplements, which were reprinted last year under the sanction of the City Council, it is now possible for every lawyer to study conveniently the progress of legislation from the foundation of the colony.

Although the State has published the Records of the Massachusetts Colony from 1629 to 1686, these do not supply the necessary information in regard to the laws. The entire code known as the Body of Liberties was enacted in 1641, but not entered on the Records. Again in each Revision changes were made in codifying and condensing, and of course such revision superseded the older forms of the separate acts. Hence it is most desirable to have easy access to copies of the Laws of 1660, because from that date onward they embodied all the active general legislation. It must be conceded that any law of a general nature which was not included by Secretary Rawson and the committee in such codification, must be considered as repealed and null after that date.

Owing to the scarcity of copies of the Laws of the Colony and Province, the Legislature, in 1812, appointed Nathan Dane, William Prescott, and Joseph Story a committee "at the expense of the Commonwealth to collect the Charters and the public and general Laws of the late Colony and Province of Massachusetts Bay; and . . . . to add in an appendix any other documents or laws which they may deem proper to explain the jurisprudence of this Commonwealth." One thousand copies were issued at the public expense, and this is the volume so often quoted in decisions as "Ancient Charters and General Laws."

Useful as this compilation has proved, it will be of necessity entirely superseded by recent publications. The State has commenced and nearly concluded the publication of all the General Laws of the Province from 1692 to the Revolution, a work which is enriched with every kind of illustrative notes gathered by the industry of the indefatigable editor, A. C. Goodell. It has also published all of the Records of the Great and General Court and the Assistants, prior to 1686, carefully reproduced under the care of the late Dr. N. B. Shurtleff. Now the City of Boston has supplemented these by these two volumes of Laws, viz., the Liberties of 1641 and Revision of 1660, and the Revision of 1672 and Supplements.

The student will therefore have, in print, everything which the Commissioners of 1812 had to use mainly in manuscript. One suggestion indeed is made with the utmost diffidence by the present editor. In the Preface to Ancient Charters the editors say: "A number of colony acts of importance, especially in a historical view of our laws, have been found in the original records, not included in the edition of 1672; these have been selected and printed in this volume wherever found to have remained a material part of the colonial system."

In other words, the committee of 1812 did not reprint either the edition of Laws of 1660 or of 1672 complete, but they made a new compilation with a new arrangement of chapters, and inserted such general laws, evidently, as they considered "to have remained a material part of the colonial system."

With the utmost deference to the honored memory of Dane, Prescott, and Story, it is certain that we now know much more of the history of Massachusetts as a colony than was known in 1812. Such antiquaries as Farmer, Savage, Winthrop, Palfrey, Trumbull, Dexter, and Ellis, with the innumerable lesser historians, have added immensely to the true knowledge of the events of that period. Hence it may not be presumptuous to suggest that the selections made in 1812, even by such eminent lawyers, were not always wise, and by no means complete.[1]

---

[1] One instance may be cited. The present editor, after the Laws of 1672 was issued, received an inquiry from a prominent lawyer, asking for the reason for the omission of Section 19 of Chapter XVIII., of Ancient Charters. It will be found therein on p. 61, and refers to the punishment for Blasphemy. Now, it will be found that in 1641, Liberty No. 94, § 3, gave the first simple act punishing blasphemy. In 1646 (Records, II., 176–177), this Section 19 was passed as printed. But in 1660 (and presumably in 1649), the Revised Statutes cut down the act to the form printed as Section 3 of this very chapter in Anc. Char., p. 58. The editors in 1812 reprinted the first Act of 1646 as well as the revised form, but surely thereby they darkened counsel instead of aiding the student, who would suppose this §19 to be a different and continuing statute. — W. H. W.

The editors of 1812 pointed out that the Revision of 1672 is little more than an extension of that of 1660; and it is probable that the first Revision of 1649, of which no example has survived, was the prototype of that of 1660. It is certain that the Body of Liberties of 1641 was incorporated, almost without change, into the Revision of 1660.

It was also pointed out, in 1812, that the marginal notes, both in 1660 and 1672, of the style "A. 46," "A. 54," etc., are abbreviations for "Anno 1646," etc. Other side-notes in both were apparently almost inexplicable. I refer to those of the form "L. 1, p. 8;" "L. 1, p. 49;" "L. 2, p. 1;" "L. 2, p. 8," etc. Of course these are Liber 1 and 2, respectively, and their identification is discussed later. The manuscript volumes of the Records from 1628 to 1686, now preserved at the State House, are five in number, whereof volume three is a duplicate for the years 1644–1657, containing only the proceedings of the House of Deputies. There are various consecutive marginal numbers in these volumes, but none to be identified with those used in the printed Laws. I find references in the latter to Liber 1, pp. 2, 4, 9, 14, 15, 16, 22, 23, 24, 28, 30, 31, 32, 35, 36, 38, 45, 46, 47, 49, 50, 51, 52, 53, 57; to Liber 2, pp. 1, 3, 4, 5, 6, 7, 8, 9, 10, 11, 12, 13, 14, 15, 16, 17, 24, 31, 32; and one reference to Liber 3, p. 5, which may be a misprint.

As to the Body of Liberties, I have devoted much time to it, as it has hitherto not received the recognition to which its importance entitles it. This Code was first rediscovered by the late Francis Calley Gray, and printed by him in 1843. But being published only in a volume of the Collections of the Massachusetts Historical Society, a knowledge of it has been confined to very few persons. I have merely followed out Mr. Gray's line of unanswerable arguments proving the certainty of the identification of his copy of this Code, but I have added a Table of Contents, Index, and Notes, which may assist the student in using it.

The Laws of 1660 are reproduced by the same process of photo-electrotyping which was used so successfully in the reprint of those of 1672. The exemplar used was the fine copy preserved in the State Library; — other copies were kindly tendered me by the Boston Athenæum and the Massachusetts Historical Society.

For the Supplements from 1660 to 1672 I am indebted to the courtesy of the American Antiquarian Society, of Worcester. They own the copy which belonged to Secretary Edward Rawson, and the supplementary leaves seem to be nearly complete, lacking only a final page. No other copy known to me has any considerable portion of these pages, and I esteem it a most fortunate chance that this perfect volume has been preserved, a fit companion to the Hutchinson copy of the edition of 1672. I need hardly state that copies are extremely rare, and that the price of one is estimated at three to five hundred dollars. This reprint is made not on account of the cost of the original however, but in view of the intrinsic value of the work to lawyers and antiquaries, which renders it desirable that a reasonable number of copies should be distributed in this community. In the Introduction and Notes I have endeavored to give only facts, and to cite the authorities in full.

The indexes were prepared by F. E. Goodrich, Esq.

It is reasonable to think that the ground covered by these two volumes is now completely covered, even should some fortunate chance restore to us a copy of the edition of 1649. But there is room, and almost a necessity, for some qualified person to work up this material into a concise and well-digested history of the jurisprudence of Massachusetts. A thorough consideration of the Body of Liberties will prove that our ancestors were far more enlightened than their English contemporaries, and that the influence which they sent forth has continued to affect most powerfully our laws, customs, and thoughts to the present time.

Especially to be forever remembered, for their pious care and intuitive perception of the value of these records, are Edward Rawson, Elisha Hutchinson, and Francis Calley Gray.

THE PRINTED RECORDS.

In 1853 (Resolves, chap. 63) the Governor was directed to have printed one hundred copies of the first two volumes of the General Court's Records. By chap. 5 of Resolves of 1854, eleven hundred more copies were ordered, and twelve hundred copies of Volumes III., IV., and V. The work was done under the supervision of the late Dr. N. B. Shurtleff, the first two volumes bearing the imprint 1853, and the others that of 1854.

In 1855 (Resolves, chap. 19) the Governor was directed to have printed five hundred additional copies of the first volumes of said Records.

In 1856 (Resolves, chap. 9) the Secretary was empowered to allow the State printer to publish an edition for public sale, as a private enterprise, the permission being for three years from June 4th. (Resolves, chap. 87, 1856.)

In the "Boston Daily Advertiser" for March 6, 1865, Dr. Shurtleff published a letter in regard to certain changes made by him in the stereotype plates after the first edition was issued. The following extracts cover the main point: —

"Soon after the issue of the edition ordered by the Legislature in 1853, my excellent friend, Col. Thomas Aspinwall, came back to his American home, bringing, with his historical treasures collected during a lóng residence in London, a manuscript copy of the first volume of the old records, and of a portion of the second volume, extending, I think, to the year 1646. This manuscript contained a large portion of the lost records, namely, a portion of the proceedings of the 23d of March, 1628–9, the proceedings of the 30th March, 2d, 6th, 8th, 13th, 16th, 27th, and 30th of April, 1629, and also portions of the proceedings of the 10th of December, 1641 (being part of Volume I.), and the commencement of the record of the General Court of Elections, commencing on the 13th of May, 1642, being the beginning of Volume II."

"Fortunately the succeeding Legislature passed an order for the issue of another edition of Volumes I. and II.; and, consequently, an opportunity was afforded for completing the printed volumes of records from the material furnished so opportunely by Colonel Aspinwall's copy. *The stereotype plates were revised, and the lost parts of the original records were artistically supplied*, so that the second impression from the stereotype plates contains all that exists of the old colonial records of Massachusetts."

Dr. Shurtleff proceeds to copy a note in the Aspinwall manuscript, showing that it had been in the possession of Gov. Thomas Hutchinson. He adds: "The manuscript is not so old as the year 1653, but is in a later style of chirography."

Subsequently this precious manuscript was purchased by Hon. Samuel L. M. Barlow, of New York city, in whose extensive and valuable library it now remains.

It appears that the changes made in the stereotype plates after the first edition was printed were as follows: In Volume I. ten pages were inserted, marked 37 *a* to 37 *j*, inclusive, and on p. 346 enough was added to complete that page. In Volume II. (which begins, in the first edition, with p. 3), two whole pages were inserted, numbered 1 and 2, and the first half of page 3. The former page 3 was cancelled, the two bottom lines (concerning one Gregory Taylor) being carried over to page 4, and the spaces on page 4 being readjusted, so that page 4 ends alike in both editions.

I believe that I am correct in saying that no change was made in the title-pages to this second edition of Volumes I. and II., that no notice was given of the corrections and additions (except a short note on p. 344 of Volume I.), and that no alterations were made in the Index of either volume.

As to the additions made in the first volume, their value is merely antiquarian. But the pages added in the second volume contain the organization of the government for 1642, an order about votes in the General Court, and a law respecting constables, (which is in the Code of 1660, the first clause of section 2, and not cited in the margin as passed in 1642, the whole section being referred to Anno 1646). There are also two laws, one relating to the pay of the Elders when employed by the General Court, and the other empowering any Court having two magistrates to admit church members to be freemen: both laws copied into the Code of 1660.

For these two laws I spent many hours in fruitless search, till I learned the fact of there being two editions. In the lack of any definite information of the number of copies printed by the State printer under his license, I conclude that fully two-thirds of the copies of the first two volumes of the Records now in circulation and use are defective. The stereotype plates of these books were destroyed in the great fire in Boston in 1872, and I have therefore reproduced the four pages, one (p. 346) of Volume I., and three pages of Volume II., in order that any one who wishes to verify my citations, and who is unfortunately the owner of the first edition only, may have the full copy before him.

It is useless to criticise Dr. Shurtleff's peculiar method of altering the plates of such an important book. Any one taking up a copy of State Records issued by authority of the Legislature naturally relies upon its entire accuracy. I am sorry to say that this reliance is misplaced in many small matters of textual correctness, as I have discovered; but the fact that three or four pages of proceedings are to be found in one edition, and not in another, is one which calls for the greatest publicity. I fear that many of the highly valued copies of the first edition were placed in public libraries, and are the only ones accessible to many students.

The legislation of the Andros or Inter-Charter period remains still in manuscript, and deserves to be printed as the only missing link in the chain of entire continuity from A.D. 1629 to the present time.

WILLIAM H. WHITMORE.

CITY HALL, BOSTON, February, 1889.

ADDITIONS MADE IN THE SECOND PRINTED EDITION OF THE RECORDS OF MASSACHUSETTS,

AND NOT TO BE FOUND IN THE FIRST EDITIONS.

[P. XIII. is p. 346 of Volume I.]

[Pp. XIV.-XVI. are the beginning of Volume II.]

1641. 10 December. Mrs Winthrope 3000 ac's.

Mrs Marg^t Winthrope hath her 3000 acres of land formerly granted her, to bee assigned about the lower end of Concord Ryver, near Merrimack, to bee layde out by Mr Flint & Leift Willard, wth Mr Oliver, or some other skilfull in measuring, so as it may not hinder a plantation; & any pt thereof they may purchase of any Indians that have right to it./

Upon the petition of Mr Willi: Tynge, it was ordered, that Mr Bartholomew, George Giddings, & John Whipple should set a dewe valuation upon the house & ground wch Willi: Whitred did effeose to Mr Tyng aforenamed./

It was ordered, that Sara, the late wife of James Hubberd, should have fourty pound of the estate of her said late husband, & the use of the childrens stock till they come to the ages mentioned in the will, & then the eldest sonne./

At this Court, the bodye of laues formerly
sent forth amonge the ffreemen, &c,
was voted to stand in force, &c./

[The last paragraph is in the handwriting of Governor Winthrop. The following is restored from an early copy of the records in the possession of Thomas Aspinwall, Esq.]

Mr Hoffes 400 acres.

Mr Atherton Hoffe is graunted foure hundred acres of land in regard of fiftie pounds disburssed in the ioint stocke.

Wm Davies.

Mr Davies was denied libertie to sell drinke, or ale, or to keepe a cookes shopp, because there are others sufficient in the towne of Boston, and his carriage hath bin formerlie offensiue.

Mr Dunster farme.

Mrs Dunster is graunted hir farme with the bondaries from Sudburie bounds, a straite line running south easterlie and north westerlie to the great ponnd over against that place, where the river issueth outt of itt on the other side, the line cutting ye said pond over unto the said issue, then following the streames vnto the place where Sudburie cutteth againe the river, & soe along by the river within Sudburie line, as itt is agreed betweene the towne of Sudburie and hir: the line lying in forme is described in the plott subscribed by Mr Thom Flintt & Thom Mayhewe.

Mr Sam: Mavericke fine remitt.

Mr Samuell Mavericke is remitted 40li of his fine of 100li, formerlie sett vpon him, if hee pay ye remaining 60li in due valuation.

Mr Mayhewe his accounts were referred to the Treasuror & Mr Duncum; & for the bridge by the mill over the Charles River, the Co'rt doth conceiue itt to belong to the towne or townes in wch itt lyeth.

Military officers.

Thomas Bartlett is appointed leivetenant & Hugh Mason ensigne to Captaine Jeanison, Watertou.

MASSACHUSETTS RECORDS.

THE RECORDS OF THE COLONY OF THE MASSACHUSETTS BAY IN NEW ENGLAND.

[The manuscript of the second volume of the Massachusetts Colony Records commences on the third page, at the place indicated by an asterisk. The first portion of the volume is lost, and the first eighteen pages of what remains are in a very decayed condition. By the aid of ancient transcripts of the volume, made apparently very early, and by a duplicate leaf in the handwriting of the Secretary who wrote the volume, the decayed portions have been restored. The volume is mainly in the chirography of Secretary Nowell, although occasionally passages, and sometimes pages, are in that of Mr. Edward Rawson, who succeeded Mr. Nowell as Secretary in 1650.]

[*The Generall Court of Elections, the 18th Day of yᵉ 3d Monᵗʰ, 1642.* 1642.

18 May.

PRESENT, The Governoʳ, The Depᵗⁱᵉ Governoʳ, Mʳ Dudley, Mʳ Bellingham, Mʳ Saltonstall, Mʳ Bradstreet, Mʳ Staughton, Mʳ Flintt, Mʳ Increase Nowell.

Deputies ꝑsent:

Wᵐ Hilton,
Wᵐ Walderne,
Wᵐ Hayward,
John Saunders,
Edward Rawson,
Matthew Boyse,
Maximi: Jewett,
Mʳ Sam: Simonds,
John Whipple,
Mʳ Ema: Downing,
Edm: Batter,
Edw: Hollioke,
Robert Bridges,
Mʳ Wᵐ Ting,
Captˡ Edw: Gibbons,
Ralph Sprague,
Thomas Line,
Captˡ Geo: Cooke,
Mʳ Nat: Sparhawke,
Captˡ Wᵐ Jeanison,
Mʳ Simon Eyres,
Symon Willard,
Peter Noyse,
Edw: Allen,
Elea: Lusher,
Wᵐ Heath,
Wᵐ Parkes,
Mʳ John Glover,
Mʳ Nat: Duncum,
Alex: Winchester,
Wᵐ Cheesborough,
James Parker,
Edw: Bates,
Jos: Pecke,
Edm: Hubberd.

JOHN WINTHROPP, Esqʳ, was chosen Governoʳ for this yeare and till new bee chosen, and tooke his oath. Governʳ

John Endicott, Esq, was chosen Depᵗˡᵉ Governoʳ, & tooke his oath. Dep. G.

Thom: Dudley, Esqʳ, was chosen an Assistant, & tooke his oathe. Assistants.

Rich: Bellingham, Esqʳ, was chosen an Assistant, & tooke his oath.

THE RECORDS OF THE COLONY OF

1642. 18 May. Rich: Saltonstall, Esqr, was chosen an Assistant, & tooke his oath.

Mr Symon Bradstreet was chosen an Assistant, & tooke his oath.

Mr Increase Nowell was chosen an Assistant, & tooke his oath.

Mr Israell Staughton was chosen an Assistant, & tooke his oath.

Mr John Winthrop was chosen an Assistant.

Mr Wm Pinchen was chosen an Assistant, and tooke his oath.

Mr Thomas Flintt was chosen an Assistant, and tooke his oath.

Treaurer. Mr Tyng was chosen Treasurer.

Deputye. It was ordered that a warrant should bee sentt to Salem for a new election of a new deputie to be ioined with Mr Downing, because the Court is doubtfull of ye choyse, & Mr Edmund Batter was sent.

Mr Staughton & Mr Ting, Treasuro^{r}, were appointed a comittee to advise Goodman Johnson aboutt ye amunition.

Pressinge of horses. An order was made for the ꝑssing 4 horses, to goe wth Mr Collecott and his companie (if they cannot hire wthout ꝑssing) to helpe them to carrie necessaries to run the south line.

Gloster. Cape Anne is to bee called Gloscester; John Sadler is chosen constable thereof, and tooke his oath.

John Sadler had comission to traine the men att Gloscester.

Obadiah Brewen is appointed Surveyer of ye Armes att Gloscester.

George Norten is appointed to keepe an ordinarie att Gloscester.

Gibson. Richard Gibson was comitted to the marshall for his seditious practises, & vpon his submission & acknowlegement of his fault vnder his hand hee was dismissed with an admonition.

Waterton. Watertowne delivering in a transcript of thier lands, nott being perfect was lent them backe againe.

Shawsin. Leivetenant Symon Willard & Edward Converse are appointed to view Shawshins, & to certifie whether the land that is free bee fitt for a village or nott.

South line. Goodman John Johnson had order to lend six carabines to Mr Collecott & his companie wch are to run the south line.

487. Charges. Itt was ordered, that the Treasuro^{r} should defray the charges of the elders, when they are imployed vpon anie speciall order from the General Co^{r}t.

20 May. Lawes. The lawes were read over the 20th of the 3^{d} month.

Pembleton. John Pemberton was bound in 20^{li} to appeare att the nextt Court att Ipswich.

488– Flaxeseed, 12^{s} bush. Repeale. The order for hempe & flax seed to passe att twelve shillings the bushell is repealed.

The orders for restraint of wheat are repealed.

489– Freemen, admission. There is power given to everie Co^{r}t wthin o^{r} jurisdiction y^{t} hath two magistrates to admitt anie church members that are fitt to bee free, & to give them the freemens oath, & to certifie thier names to the Secretarie att the next Generall Courtt. 1642. 20 May.

The order formerlie made for writeing things before they bee voted, is declared nott to concerne matter of forme, butt to bee meant of things that are to bee matters of record. 490- Votes in Courts. Repeale.

Phillip White, for drunkenesse, was fined 10s, & for misdeamenor, wch 10s Richard Wayte vndertooke for White. White.

The Deputy Governor, Mr Staughton, Capt Gibbons, Captaine Jeanison, Capt Cooke, Mr Rawson, Leivetent Willard, & Mr Parker, these or the greater number of them, are appointed to putt the countrey in a posture of warre. Posture of Warre.

Itt is ordered, yt when anie person shall bee tendred to anie officer of this jurisdiccōn by anie constable or other officer belonging to anie forreigne jurisdiction in this countrey, or by warrant from anie such authoritie, hee or shee shall bee presentlie receiued and conveyed forthwith from constable to constable till the partie bee brought to the place to which hee or shee is sentt, or before some magistrate of this jurisdiction, who shall soe dispose of the partie as occasion & the justice of the cause shall require, & thatt all hew and cryes shall bee dilligentlie receuived & pursued to full effect.] 491- Officers duly to receiue forraine prisoners. Hue & cry.

Whereas the country is put to great charge by the Courts attendance vpon suites cōmenced or renewed by either appeales, petition, &c, it is ordered, that in all such cases, if it shall appeare to the Cort that the plaint in any such action of appeale, petition, &c, in any Cort, hath no iust cause of any such proceeding, they shall take order that the said plaintiff shall beare all the charges of the Cort wch they shall iudge to have beein expended by his occation, & may further impose a fine vpon him if the merrit of the cause shall so require; & if they shall finde the defendant in fault, they shall impose the charges vpon such defendant./ [*1.] 492- Ord' about hue encry.

William Aspinwall, upon his petition & cirtifficat of his good carriage, is restored againe to his former liberty & freedome./

The Court left it to the liberty of the townes to send but a deputy a peece, if they please, to the next session of this Court./

The marshall hath leave to go to Cōnecticut, leauing a deputy./

The beaver tradrs are appointed to bring in what is due to the countrey at the next session./

Edward Bendall hath liberty to make vse of any of the cables, & other things belonging to the worke, as he needeth, alowing for the hurt of them./

Gregory Taylor, being chosen constable of Water Towne, tooke his oath to discharge that place./

INTRODUCTION.

THE history of the published Laws of the Colony of Massachusetts is naturally divided into four periods. First, the publication of the Body of Liberties in 1641; secondly, the issue of the first collection of Laws, in 1649; thirdly, the revision of 1660; fourthly, the further revision of 1672, with its supplements through 1686.

Having already been able to reprint the edition of the Laws of 1672, with its supplements, I now have the satisfaction of presenting in this volume two of the other earlier documents, namely, the Body of Liberties of 1641 and the revision of the Laws as printed in 1660. The other edition, that of 1649, is doubtless hopelessly lost, no copy being now known. We may, however, conclude that its title was the same as the first part of that prefixed to the edition of 1660; and we are assured by the preface to the last-named book that the edition of 1649 was arranged "in an alphabetical order," that it had a preface or "epistle" telling "there would be need of alterations and additions." It is also clear that the editions of 1660 varied from that of 1649 by the omission of such laws as had been repealed and the addition of such laws as had since been enacted. Those which were omitted cannot be recovered, but by comparing the Body of Liberties with the edition of 1660, and by striking out of the latter also all the laws dated after 1649, it would still be possible to reconstruct the edition of 1649 in almost perfect form.

It is perhaps as well to state here that for a long time a spurious Code of Laws has been cited as the genuine Body of Liberties of 1641. I refer to the pamphlet issued in 1641 in London, which was undoubtedly the work of Rev. John Cotton. It was reprinted there in 1655 under the care of William Aspinwall, and has in later years been reprinted, in 1798, in the fifth volume of the first Series of the Collection of the Massachusetts Historical Society, and, in 1844, in the third volume of Force's Tracts. It was also printed in Hutchinson's Collections of Papers (Boston, 1769), and reprinted with notes in the re-issue of that book by the Prince Society (Albany, 1865).

Although, as will be shown, the evidence is conclusive that Cotton's Code was only *proposed* and never accepted, while a totally different set of laws was actually enacted in 1641, this error has obtained in many quarters, and needs to be authoritatively denied and disproved.

Reverting therefore to the facts which can be ascertained, it is well to remember that our system of making laws by a representative body was not coincident with the settlement of the colony of Massachusetts. The Charter of March 4, 1629, provided for a governor, a deputy-governor, and eighteen[1] assistants to be chosen from time to time out of the freemen of the company, whereof seven assistants, together with the two officers, were to be a quorum. They were to meet once a month or oftener at their pleasure, and four times in each year, viz., upon every last Wednesday in Hilary, Easter, Trinity, and Michaelmas terms, were to hold a Great and General Court. In the General Court new members could be admitted, and at that time they could "make laws and ordinances for the good and welfare of the said Company, and for the government and ordering of the said lands and plantation and the people inhabiting and to inhabit the same, as to them from time to time shall be thought meet. So as such laws and ordinances be not contrary or repugnant to the laws and statutes of this our realm of England." (Records, p. 12.)

In fact, for several years after the settlement here the powers of the General Court were allowed to lie dormant. The Court of Assistants met from time to time, as seemed necessary, but the General Court met only as follows: —

1630.	October 19.	(Records,	i. p. 79, printed edition.[2])
1631.	May 18.	"	i. p. 86.
1632.	May 9.	"	i. p. 95.
1633.	May 29.	"	i. p. 104.
1634.	May 14.	"	i. p. 116.

The Records as preserved show both the extent of the powers exercised by the Assistants, and the insignificance of the action of

[1] This number was not observed until 1680. Before this twelve was the highest number actually serving, and eight or nine more usual. — W. H. W.

[2] I cite Savage's edition of Winthrop. Boston. 1853; and in all cases the printed edition of the Records, issued by the State. — W. H. W.

the body of freemen assembled in the annual General Court. The Assistants acting as a Court had during these three years inflicted fines, whippings, and imprisonments, had levied taxes and granted lands. In fact, at the first General Court on Oct. 19, 1638, it was voted "by the general vote of the people and the erection of hands," that the Governor and Deputy Governor with the Assistants, "should have the power of making laws and choosing officers to execute the same." (Records, p. 79.)

Winthrop indeed records (Hist. i. 84) that in February, 1631–2, the settlers at Watertown objected to paying £8 as their part of a rate for £60 for fortifying the new town, on the ground that the government was like that of a mayor and aldermen. But they were convinced by the Governor and Council "that this government was rather in the nature of a Parliament."

In 1634, however, the freemen of the colony showed a desire to take a part in the government. Winthrop (i. 152–3) thus introduces the matter: —

"Notice being sent out of the General Court to be held the 14th day of the third month called May, the freemen deputed two of each town to meet and consider of such matters as they were to take order in at the same General Court; who having met, desired a sight of the patent, and, conceiving thereby that all their laws should be made at the General Court, repaired to the Governor to advise with him about it, and about the abrogating of some orders formerly made, as for killing of swine in corn, &c. He told them, that when the patent was granted, the number of freemen was supposed to be (as in like corporations) so few, as they might well join in making laws; but now they were grown to so great a body, as it was not possible for them to make or execute laws, but they must choose others for that purpose: and that howsoever it would be necessary hereafter to have a select company to intend that work, yet for the present they were not furnished with a sufficient number of men qualified for that business, neither could the company bear the loss of time of so many as must intend it. Yet this they might do at present, viz. they might at the General Court make an order, that once in the year, a certain number should be appointed (upon summons from the Governor) to revise all laws, &c. and to reform what they found amiss therein; but not to make any new laws, but prefer their grievances to the Court of Assistants; and that no assessment should be laid upon the country without the consent of such a committee, nor any lands disposed of."

At the meeting of the General Court, May 14, 1634, there were present, besides the Governor, Deputy, and six other assistants, twenty-four deputies, undoubtedly sent by Newtown (*i.e.*, Cambridge), Watertown, Charlestown, Boston, Roxbury, Dorchester, Saugus (*i.e.*, Lynn), and Salem; three from each place.[3]

This regular Legislature proceeded to vote (Records, i. 117), that none but the General Court had power to choose and admit freemen, nor to make and establish laws, to appoint or remove officers and fix their duties, nor to raise money and taxes, nor to dispose of lands. It was also ordered (p. 118), that there should be four General Courts yearly, to be summoned by the Governor, and not to be dissolved without the consent of the major part of the Court. Lastly, they ordered that the freemen of every town might choose two or three men to prepare business to be submitted to each Court, — a provision which was soon neglected, — and also the following system which has continued ever since.

> "Such persons as shall be hereafter so deputed[4] by the freemen of the several plantations, to deal in their behalf in the public affairs of the commonwealth, shall have the full power and voices of all the said freemen, derived to them for the making and establishing of laws, granting of lands, &c., and to deal in all other affairs of the commonwealth wherein the freemen have to do, the matter of election of magistrates and other officers only excepted, wherein every freeman is to give his own voice."

From this time on, the records of the General Court show that this body exercised its powers vigorously and extensively, but at the beginning without much idea of theoretical legislation. General laws were often passed, but they related to special subjects, often to trivial ones. No constitution and no general code of system of laws was enacted, though of course the laws of England were supposed to be the authority on which all orders or sentences were founded.

In 1635 a step was taken as follows: At a General Court held at New Town, May 6, 1635, it was voted (Records, i. 147): —

> "The Governor [John Haynes], the Deputy Governor [Richard Bellingham], John Winthrop and Thomas Dudley, Esquires, are deputed by the Court to make a draught of such laws, as they shall judge useful for the well ordering of this Plantation, and to present the same to the Court."

---

[3] Savage (Winthrop, i. 154) writes that he identified the residences of all but one or two. He adds, that Ipswich sent deputies on March 4, 1635, Weymouth in September, 1635, Hingham in May, 1636, Newbury in September, 1636, and Concord in April, 1637. — W. H. W.

[4] "At first the deputies were chosen for each General Court; from 1639 to 1640 they were chosen semiannually; and in 1642 and ever since that time they have been elected once a year." — *F. C. Gray.*

Winthrop (History, i. 191) confirms this as follows: —

"6th of 3d month (May) 1635. The deputies having conceived great danger to our state in regard that our magistrates, for want of positive laws, in many cases, might proceed according to their discretions, it was agreed, that some men should be appointed to frame a body of grounds of laws, in resemblance to a Magna Charta, which being allowed by some of the ministers and the general court, should be received for fundamental laws."

At the General Court for March 3d, 1635–6 (Records, i. 169, 170), the system of Courts to be held by the magistrate was settled; and it was ordered that only two General Courts should be held annually, one in May for elections and other affairs, and one in October for making laws and other public occasions. It was also provided that, since there might be differences in the General Courts between the magistrates and the deputies,

"No law, order, or sentence shall pass as an Act of the Court, without the consent of the greater part of the magistrates on the one part, and the greater number of the deputies on the other part; and for want of such accord, the cause or order shall be suspended, and if either party think it so material, there shall be forthwith a committee chosen, one-half by the magistrates, and the other half by the deputies, and the committee so chosen to elect an umpire, who together shall have power to hear and determine the cause in question."

At the General Court, May 25, 1636, it was ordered as follows (Records, i. 174–5): —

"The Governor [Henry Vane], the Deputy Governor [John Winthrop], Thomas Dudley, John Haynes, Richard Bellingham, Esquires, Mr. Cotton, Mr. Peters and Mr. Shepherd are entreated to make a draught of laws agreeable to the word of God, which may be the Fundamentals of this Commonwealth, and to present the same to the next General Court. And it is ordered that in the mean time the magistrates and their associates shall proceed in the Courts to hear and determine all causes, according to the laws now established, and where there is no law, then as near the law of God as they can; and for all business out of Court for which there is no certain rule yet set down, those of the standing council [5] or some two of them, shall take order by

[5] This refers to a curious experiment made in 1636, in the form of a council for life. March 3, 1635–6 it was voted that the General Court should, from time to time, elect a certain number of the magistrates for the term of their lives as a Standing Council, to be removed only for crime, insufficiency, or other weighty cause; the Governor always to be president of the body, and the power to be such as the General Court might indue them with. May 25, 1636, Gov. Winthrop and Thomas Dudley were so chosen; May 17, 1637, John Endicott was elected; but none others were ever added. The scheme was connected with certain proposals by Lord Say and

their best discretion, that they may be ordered and ended according to the rule of God's word, and to take care for all military affairs until the next General Court."

We have seen that in May, 1636, Mr. Cotton, Mr. Peters, and Mr. Shepherd were asked to assist in preparing a code, and Winthrop gives this further information (Hist., i. 240), under date of Oct. 25, 1636: —

"Mr. Cotton being requested by the General Court, with some other ministers, to assist some of the magistrates in compiling a body of fundamental laws, did, this Court, present a copy of Moses his judicials, compiled in an exact method, which were taken into further consideration till the next General Court."

There is nothing to show that any action was taken on Mr. Cotton's draft of laws, nor, indeed, that anything was done by the committee of 1635 and 1636.

At the General Court, begun March 12, 1637-8, however, a vigorous show of work was made. The following order was then passed (Records, i. 222): —

"For the well ordering of these Plantations now in the beginning thereof, it having been found by the little time of experience we have here had, that the want of written laws hath put the Court into many doubts and much trouble in many particular cases, this Court hath therefore ordered, that the freemen of every town (or some part thereof chosen by the rest) within this jurisdiction, shall assemble together in their several towns, and collect the heads of such necessary and fundamental laws, as may be suitable to the times and places, where God in his providence hath cast us, and the heads of such laws to deliver in writing to the Governor for the time being before the 5th day of the 4th month, called June, next, to the intent that the same Governor [John Winthrop] together with the rest of the standing council, and Richard Bellingham Esquire, Mr. Bulkeley, Mr. Phillips, Mr. Peters and Mr. Shepherd, elders of several churches, Mr. Nathaniel Ward, Mr. William Spencer, and Mr. William Hawthorne, or the major part of them, may, upon the survey of such heads of laws, make a compendious abridgement of the same by the General Court in Autumn next, adding yet to the same or detracting therefrom what in their wisdoms shall seem meet, that so the whole work being perfected to the best of their skill, it may be presented to the General Court for confirmation or

---

Sele and others in England to join the colony, if hereditary rank and privileges were conceded. Hutchinson (History, i. 501) copies a letter from Rev. John Cotton to Lord Say, in 1636, wherein he cites this establishment of a council for life, as intended as a concession to him. But the popular feeling was opposed to the plan, and it was dropped informally, though for a year or two some duties were imposed on these three members. — W. H. W.

rejection, as the Court shall adjudge. And it is also ordered, that the said persons shall survey all the orders already made, and reduce them into as few heads as they may, and present them unto the General Court for approbation or refusal as aforesaid."

The next step is shown by the order passed by the General Court, Nov. 5, 1639 (Records, i. 279), viz.: —

"It is ordered that the Governor [J. Winthrop], Deputy Governor [Thomas Dudley], Treasurer and Mr. Stoughton or any three of them, with two or more of the deputies of Boston, Charlestown or Roxbury, shall peruse all those models which have been or shall be further presented to this Court, or themselves, concerning a form of government and laws to be established, and shall draw them up into one body, (altering, adding or omitting what they shall think fit,) and shall take order, that the same shall be copied out and sent to the several towns, that the elders of the churches and freemen may consider of them against the next General Court, and the charges to be defrayed by the Treasurer."

The full meaning of this order and the cause of the endless delays are explained by Winthrop's memorandum under the date of November, 1639. It is as follows (History, i. 388-389): —

"The people had long desired a body of laws, and thought their condition very unsafe, while so much power rested in the discretion of magistrates. Divers attempts had been made at former courts, and the matter referred to some of the magistrates and some of the elders; but still it came to no effect; for, being committed to the care of many, whatsoever was done by some, was still disliked or neglected by others. At last it was referred to Mr. Cotton and Mr. Nathaniel Warde, &c., and each of them framed a model, which were presented to this General Court, and by them committed to the Governor and Deputy and some others, to consider of, and so prepare it for the Court in the third month next. Two great reasons there were, which caused most of the magistrates and some of the elders not to be very forward in this matter. One was, want of sufficient experience of the nature and disposition of the people, considered with the condition of the country and other circumstances, which made them conceive, that such laws would be fittest for us, which should arise *pro re nata* upon occasions, &c., and so the laws of England and other states grew, and therefore the fundamental laws of England are called customs, *consuetudines*. 2. For that it would professedly transgress the limits of our charter, which provide, we shall make no laws repugnant to the laws of England, and that we were assured we must do. But to raise up laws by practice and custom had been no transgression; as in our church discipline, and in matters of marriage, to make a law that marriages shall not be solemnized by ministers, is repugnant to the laws of England; but to bring it to a custom by practice for the magistrates to perform it, is no law made repugnant, &c. At length (to satisfy the people) it proceeded, and the two models were digested with divers alterations and additions, and abbreviated[6] and sent to every town, (12) to be considered of first by the magistrates and elders, and then to be published by the constables to all the people, that if any man should think fit, that any thing therein ought to be altered, he might acquaint some of the deputies therewith against the next Court."

We have here the evidence of a most competent witness, that the delay in framing a code of laws was intentional on the part of the magistrates and elders. It is also clear that two schemes were framed, one by Rev. John Cotton and the other by Rev. Nathaniel Ward, and, fortunately, both documents are extant. As already stated, Cotton's scheme was rejected; and yet, having been put in print under a false title, it has long enjoyed an undeserved credit. The plan proposed by Ward, possibly amended by the towns or the General Court, was adopted in 1641, was known as the Body of Liberties, and is the foundation of the legislation of Massachusetts.

This fact, herein fully set forth and verified, ought to restore this inestimable document to its proper place, to serve as the basis for all future citations of our laws.

The few remaining entries in regard to Ward's Body of Liberties may now be cited. At the General Court, May 13, 1640 (Records, i. 292–293), it was voted: —

"Whereas a Breviate of Laws was formerly sent forth to be considered by the elders of the churches and other freemen of the Commonwealth, it is now desired, that they will endeavour to ripen their thoughts and counsels about the same by the general court in the next 8th month."

At the General Court, June 2, 1641 (Records, i. 320): —

"The Governor [Richard Bellingham] is appointed to peruse all the laws, and take notice what may be fit to be repealed, what to be certified, what to stand, and make return to the next General Court."

---

[6] These manuscript copies were made by Thomas Lechford, as appears by his "Note-Book" (Boston, 1885, pp. 237–8). He enters. "I writt 5 copies more of the Lawes for the Country by the direction of our Governor. 11. 8, 1639. Seven of them and the former had 3 lawes added. A Coppie of the Abstract of the Lawes of New England delivered to the Governor, 11. 15. 1639. And 12 coppies of the said Lawes first delivered, vizt., in 10 last. For writing a Coppy of the breviat of the body of Lawes for the Country. 12. 5. 39. The 3 lawes added to the Copie of Lawes for Dorchester, delivered to the Constable, 12. 6. 1639. The 3 lawes added to 4 more of the said Coppies brought by the marshall. 12. 11. 39. Three Copyes of the said breviat delivered to the Governor besides the first, 12. 12. 1639 . . . . . One coppy of the said breviate delivered to Mr. Bellingham, with one coppy of the originall Institution and limitation of the Councell, 12. 17. 1639. Seven coppyes more of the said breviate. — W. H. W.

At the General Court October 7, 1641 (Records, i. 340): —

"The Governor [Bellingham] and Mr. Hawthorne were desired to speak to Mr. Ward for a Copy of the Liberties and of the Capital laws to be transcribed and sent to the several towns."

Subsequently at the same Court, under the date of December 10, 1641, is the following entry (Records, i. 344): —

"Mr. Deputy Endicot, Mr. Downing, and Mr. Hawthorne are authorized to get nineteen Copies of the Laws, Liberties and the forms of oaths transcribed and subscribed by their several hands, and none to be authentic but such as they subscribe, and to be paid for by the Constable of each Town, ten shillings a piece for each copy, and to be prepared within six weeks."

Finally, at the end of this session of December 10, 1641, on the original record is the written attestation of Gov. Winthrop as follows: —

"At this Court, the bodye of laws formerly sent forth among the Freemen, etc., was voted to stand in force, etc."

Winthrop (History, ii. 66) writes in regard to the General Court of December, 1641, as follows: —

"This session continued three weeks, and established one hundred laws, which were called the Body of Liberties. They had been composed by Mr. Nathaniel Ward (some time pastor of the church of Ipswich: he had been a minister in England and formerly a student and a practiser in the course of the common law) and had been revised and altered by the Court and sent forth into every town to be further considered of, and now again in this Court, they were revised, amended and presented, and so established for three years, by that experience to have them fully amended and established to be perpetual."

We have thus, following the exhaustive selections of authorities made by Mr. F. C. Gray, arrived at a few certain conclusions. First, that John Cotton and Nathaniel Ward each prepared a code of laws; secondly, that Mr. Ward's code was adopted in 1641 and was the Body of Liberties; thirdly, that his code consisted of one hundred laws; and, lastly, that the Athenæum manuscript is a true copy, containing 98 numbered sections, which, with the Preamble and concluding paragraph, make out the requisite one hundred.

That a copy of the manuscript Body of Liberties should have survived is one of the fortunate accidents of literature. In the

Boston Athenæum there is preserved a volume which was formerly owned by Elisha Hutchinson, who was the grandfather of Gov. Thomas Hutchinson, and who died, in 1717, at the age of 77. It is evident from this collection that Hutchinson gave a careful attention to the question of the laws. He had the printed edition of 1672, to which he added the Supplements, making the collection so nearly complete that it was used for our recent reproduction. He copied some laws in manuscript, he corrected errors of pagination, and in fact did everything possible to perfect his copy.

Prefixed to the Laws is a collection of manuscripts, as follows: —

1. King Charles' Letter from Hampton Court, June 28, 1662.
   Printed in Hutchinson's Collection, p. 377.
2. Declaration of the General Court, 23 May, 1665.
3. Commissioners' Reply, May 24, 1665.
   Both printed in Hutchinson, Hist., i. 246, &c.
4.* King Charles' Letter, Whitehall, April 23, 1664.
   Printed in 2d Hazard, 634.
5. Colony Charter March 4, 1629.
   Printed in Hutchinson, Coll. 1.
6.* Copy of the Liberties of the Massachusetts.
7. Parallel between the Fundamental Laws of England & Massachusetts. A part only, the whole is printed in Hutchinson, Coll., 196.
8. Answer of a Committee of the General Court to matters proposed touching their Liberties, June 10, 1661.
   Printed in Hutchinson, Hist., i. 529.
9. King Charles' Commission to Col. Nichols.
   Printed in Hutchinson, Hist., i. 535.
10.* Order in Council, Whitehall July 20, 1677.
11. King Charles' Letter, Newmarket, Sept. 30, 1680.
   Printed in Hutchinson, Coll., 522.

All these documents are on uniform paper with a ruled border, but the first nine seem to be in one handwriting, not that of Elisha Hutchinson. Numbers 10 and 11 seem to be written by the collector and transcriber of the Laws. The pagination is 1–47, covering only the articles Nos. 5, 6, and 7, and the book is in its original sheep binding. On the inside of the last cover is the autograph "Elisha Hutchinson," and on the inside of the first cover that of William S. Shaw, Jan., 1816. Mr. Shaw was Librarian of the Boston Athenæum from 1813 to 1822, and this book

* These three articles were not used by Gov. Hutchinson. — W. H. W.

was doubtless acquired through him, although there is no record of the early accessions to this library.

From the fact that eight out of the eleven manuscripts were printed by Gov. Hutchinson, it must be conceded that he probably used this volume. It seems strange that he did not recognize the value of this copy of the Body of Liberties, and that he should have assigned any hand in the compilation to Rev. John Cotton. In his note to his reprint of Cotton's book, Hutchinson writes:—

"It should rather be entitled An Abstract of a Code or System of Laws prepared for the Commonwealth of the Massachusetts Bay; for although when they compiled their laws, they made this abstract their plan in general, yet they departed from it in many instances, and in some which were very material." Again, Hutchinson writes (Hist., i. 442), "In the first draught of the laws by Mr. Cotton, which I have seen corrected with Mr. Winthrop's hand, divers other offences were made capital, viz.—" (Here he cites Nos. X., XIII., XVIII., XIX., XX., XXI., of Chapter VII. of Cotton's book) —"The punishment by death is erased from all these offences by Mr. Winthrop, and they are left to the discretion of the court to inflict other punishment short of death."

This statement occurs in the fifth chapter of Hutchinson's History, wherein he is explaining "The System or Body of Laws established in the Colony." He adds (Hist., i. 437):—

"In the year 1634 the plantation was greatly increased, settlements were extended more than 30 miles from the capital town, and it was thought high time to have known established laws, that the inhabitants might no longer be subject to the varying uncertain judgments which otherwise would be made concerning their actions. The ministers, and some of the principal laymen, were consulted with, about a body of laws suited to the circumstances of the colony civil and religious. Committees, consisting of magistrates and elders, were appointed almost every year, for 12 or 14 years together, and whilst they were thus fitting a code, particular laws, which were of greatest necessity, from time to time were enacted; and in the year 1648 the whole collected together were ratified by the court and then first printed. Mr. Bellingham of the magistrates, and Mr. Cotton of the clergy had the greatest share in this work."

In reply to these general remarks by Hutchinson, I would urge the fact that he seems never to have used, even if he possessed, a copy of the printed laws of 1660 or of 1649. As will be noted he says the laws were first printed in 1648; but the title of the edition of 1660 says that they were published in the General Court held in May, 1649, and this seems to be the true date. Now, the volume owned by Elisha Hutchinson not only contains merely the edition of 1672, but the manuscript references made in his copy of the Body of Liberties refer entirely to this later edition. It is reasonable to suppose that if Elisha Hutchinson had possessed a copy of the earlier editions, the text of which more nearly conformed to the Liberties, he would have cited one of them.

It does not seem necessary to reprint John Cotton's book, as it has been so often republished. It is to be noted that its first publication, in 1641, was anonymously, in London. The title is, "An Abstract of the Lawes of New England, as they are now established. London, Printed for F. Coules and W. Ley at Paules Chain, 1641." Pp. 1–15 and two pages of the Table. Any one sending this book to the press from Boston, would have known that there was no colony named New England. These laws at most could only relate to the colony of Massachusetts Bay. It was doubtless the work of some English friend of Cotton's, who had a copy of his manuscript, and who, hearing that a code of laws had been established, jumped to the conclusion that this was the one.

But in 1655 William Aspinwall, who had lived here and in Rhode Island, reprinted Cotton's book in London, increasing the bulk by printing at length the citations from the Bible and even adding some that were lacking. A full comparison of the two editions is given in the reprint of Hutchinson's Collection of Papers by the Prince Society of Boston, 1865, i. 181–205.

In his preface, Aspinwall makes the following plain disclaimers of any idea that Cotton's work ever became law. He says these laws were

"Acommodated to the Colonie of the Massachusets in New England, and commended to the General Court there, which had they then had the heart to have received, it might have been better both with them there, and us here, than it now is. . . . . These are not properly Laws, but prudentiall[7] Rules, which he recommended to that Colonie,

[7] This word "prudential" is one which has had a great significance in our legislation. Liberty 66 says: "The freemen of every township shall have power to make such by-laws and constitutions as may concern the welfare of their town, provided that they be not of a criminal, but only of a *prudential* nature, and that their penalties exceed not twenty shillings for one offence; and that they be not repugnant to the public laws and orders of the country. And if any inhabitant shall neglect or refuse to observe them, they shall have power to levy the appointed penalties by distress."

The foundation of the law, but not the term, is in a vote of the General Court, March 3, 1635–6 (Records, i. 172), where it is ordered that "the freemen of every town, or the major part of them, shall only have power to dispose of their own lands and woods, with all the privileges and appurtenances of the said towns, to grant lots, and make such orders as may concern the well ordering of their own towns, not repugnant to the laws and orders here established by

to be ratified with the common assent of the freemen in each Towne, or by their Representatives in the General Court, as publique Contracts. Which being once made and assented to for their owne convenience, do binde as Covenants do, untill by like publique consent they be abrogated and made voyd. For though the Author attribute the word [Law] unto some of them; yet that it was not his meaning that they should be enacted as Lawes (if you take the word *Law* in a proper sense), appears by his conclusion taken out of *Isa.* 33:22. Hee knew full well that it would be an intrenchment upon the Royall power of Jesus Christ, for them or any other of the sonnes of Adam to ordain Lawes."

"It is not my purpose to perswade this or any other nation (were they willing to heare) to enact or ratifie these by any power of their own (in a solemn convention of their Representatives) as Laws: Neither do I believe it was the Authors intention so to do, when he drew up this modell. For alas, what energie or vertue can such an act of poore sinfull creatures adde unto the most perfect and wholesome lawes of God? It is enough for us, and indeed it is all that can be done by any people upon earth: 1. To declare by their Representatives, their voluntary subjection unto them, as unto the lawes of the Lord their God. 2. After such professed subjection to fall unto the practice thereof, in the name and strength of Christ their King and Law-giver."

"This Abstract may serve for this use principally (which I conceive was the main scope of that good man, who was the author of it) to shew the com-

---

the General Court; as also to lay mulcts and penalties for the breach of these orders, and to levy and distrain the same, not exceeding the sum of twenty shillings; also to choose their own particular officers, as constables, surveyors for the highways, and the like."

June 14, 1642, the General Court (Records, ii. 6) passed a law for the proper training and employment of children, and state "that in every town the chosen men appointed for managing the *prudential affairs* of the same shall henceforth stand charged with the care of the redress of this evil."

Again, Oct. 7, 1646 (Records, ii. 162–163) the Court passed this order: "Whereas there is no order made appointing who shall end causes in towns under the value of 20 shillings, where one only magistrate dwells, and the cause concerns himself, it is therefore hereby ordered, that in such cases the 5 or 7 or more men in every such town, which are selected for *prudential affairs*, shall have power to hear and determine such cases," etc., etc.

Nov. 4, 1646, the General Court (Records, ii. 180) passed certain orders entitled Prudentiall Laws, though it is not clear that more than the first section was so designated. That one reads: "Every township, or such as are deputed to order the *prudentialls* thereof, shall have power to present to the Quarter Court all idle and unprofitable persons, and all children who are not diligently employed by their parents, which Court shall have power to dispose of them, for their own welfare and improvement of the common good."

So again an order of the General Court, May 26, 1647 (Records, ii. 19), declares that "henceforth it shall and may be lawful for the freemen within any of the said towns to make choice of such inhabitants, though non-freemen, who have taken or shall take the oath of fidelity to this government, to be jury men, and to have their vote in the choice of selectmen for town affairs, assessment of rates, *and other prudentials*, proper to the selectment of the several towns."

May 26, 1658 (Records, iv. part 1, pp. 335–336) the Court speaks of two laws in the printed book, title Township, about the right of all Englishmen who have taken the oath of fidelity to be chosen jury men or constables, and to have their vote in the choice of the selectmen for the town affairs, assessments of rates, and other *prudentials* proper to the selectmen of the several towns. These laws are all repeated in the edition of 1660, pp. 75–76.

plete sufficiency of the word of God alone, to direct his people in judgment of all causes, both civil and criminal, as we are wonted to distinguish them. Which being by him done, and with all sweetness and amiableness of spirit tendered, but not accepted, he surceased to press it any further at that season, knowing full well that the Lord's people shall be a willing people in the day of his power. But the truth is, both they and we, and the other Gentile nations, are loth to be persuaded to dwell in the tents of Shem, and to lay aside our old earthly forms of government, to submit to the government of Christ."

It seems, therefore, to be certain that any claim that Cotton prepared the Body of Liberties, rests upon an unauthorized title-page and the vague and unsupported opinions of Gov. Hutchinson. The evidence to the contrary is found in Aspinwall's positive statements above cited, and in the very nature of Cotton's book. It is a treatise in ten chapters, stating powers, duties, rights, and penalties, fortified throughout by references to the Old Testament. The sections are not framed as laws are, and the only wonder is that any one could suppose for a moment that any legislature ever enacted them.

The same words are again used in the edition of Laws in 1672, pp. 147. 149.

Under the new Charter, in the session of 1692-3, chap. 28 (Province Laws, Goodell's edition, i. 66) the freeholders and inhabitants in a town meeting could pass "necessary rules, orders and by-laws for the directing, managing and ordering the *prudential affairs* of such town," with penalties not exceeding twenty shillings, etc., to be approved by the justices in Quarter Sessions. In 1696 (Ibid., i. 218) the clause requiring the consent of the justices was repealed, and an appeal to them was granted to any one punished under such by-laws.

Again, after the establishment of the State, chap. 75 of Acts of 1785 repeated the powers of towns to make "rules, orders and by-laws for the directing, managing and ordering the *prudential affairs* of the town," with penalties not exceeding thirty shillings, and provided the laws are approved by the Court of General Sessions of the Peace in the same county.

The Revised Statutes of 1836, chap. 15, § 13, continues the same words, with twenty dollars penalty, and the approval of the Court of Common Pleas.

The General Statutes of 1860, chap. 18, § 11, retains the phrase, "directing and managing the *prudential affairs*" of the town; as does the Public Statutes of 1882, chap. 27, § 15, which, in defining the powers of towns to pass by-laws, allows them "for directing and managing the *prudential affairs*, preserving the peace and good order, and maintaining the internal police thereof."

I have thus briefly traced this phrase, "prudential affairs," from the Body of Liberties in 1641 to the present time, and can only say that the earliest definition is the clearest and best. All matters, not reserved for state jurisdiction, but affecting the welfare of the town in its corporate capacity, and evidently susceptible of proper regulation under the penalty of a moderate fine, have been, and still are, suitable subjects for control in towns by by-laws, and in cities by ordinance. The origin of the term is obscure. One would expect to find it in the contemporary theological literature, but it was certainly not in common use. Perhaps Ward invented it, as his "Cobler" is full of strange words. In 1653 (Records, Vol. iv., part i., p. 145) a matter is said to be "safe and prudential," and there the word is equivalent to "prudent." A similar use of a word is "economy" and "economical." A man is economical, but we speak of political economy, and towns regulate their domestic or internal economy. — W. H. W.

But equally strong evidence remains to show what the Body of Liberties actually contained. The Laws of 1660 as well as those of 1672 contain numerous citations of laws under the date of 1641. These laws, with very few exceptions, are not entered on the Records of the General Court, as passed in that year. Hence these must have been comprehended in some general enactment, to wit, the Body of Liberties. An analysis of these laws is given later on. In the meantime I would cite the following evidence: First, on October 17, 1643 (Records, ii. 48), the General Court declared "that whereas in the Book of Liberties, No. 23, it was ordered none should take above 8£ per cent., — bills of exchange are excepted." This reference is to our No. 23. Secondly, March 7, 1643–4 (Records, ii. 61), the Governor [Winthrop], Mr. Dudley, and Mr. Hibbens, or any two of them, were made "a committee to consider of the Body of Liberties against the next General Court." Third, the General Court voted May 26, 1647 (Records, ii. 194), "for explanation of the order in the Liberties about 6 days warning to be given to the defendant in every action, &c., it is hereby declared that the day of the summons or attachment served and the day of appearance shall be taken inclusively as part of the six days." Here the reference is to Liberty No. 21, as printed herein, amended in Laws of 1660, p. 4, title Attachments, § 2, line 5, by adding the word "inclusively" after the words "six days." Of course our copy of the Liberties is the earlier form, prior to May, 1647.

Lastly and most conclusive of all, the General Court in 1646 had to consider a Remonstrance and Petition from Robert Child and others who were dissatisfied with the government. The Court empowered Governor Winthrop, Deputy Governor Dudley, Richard Bellingham, and the Auditor General (Lieut. Nathaniel Duncan) to draw up a reply to be forwarded to England by Mr. Winslow. This document is printed in Hutchinson's Collection of papers (Prince Soc. edition, i. 223–247). One of their chief arguments, to prove that the laws here are conformable to those of England, is an elaborate parallel of items printed face to face.

"In this they set forth forty-four fundamental propositions, annexing to each the authorities for it. Six times they refer for authority to their Charter; seven times to custom; eight times to laws of specified dates; once to the Bible; and twenty-seven times to the Liberties, citing each by its appropriate number." — *F. C. Gray.*

Not one of these citations of the Liberties conforms to any item in Cotton's book; but every one of them, by specific number, refers to and agrees with a section of the manuscript copy preserved by Elisha Hutchinson. The separate sections (one or two being cited more than once) are Nos. 1, 2, 3, 10, 14, 17, 18, 29, 31, 36, 37, 42, 48, 53, 59, 63, 65, 81, 82, 94, and 95; in all twenty-one out of one hundred, and scattered from number one to number ninety-five. It is impossible to present stronger evidence that this manuscript copy of the Body of Liberties is identical with the one used by the Committee of the General Court in 1646.

As the original book containing these citations is quite rare, and in order that there may be no question of the identification, the following extracts are given of such paragraphs, as they occur in order, which are said to be taken from the Body of Liberties: —

"FUNDAMENTALLS OF THE MASSACHUSETTS.

Compared with Magna Charta.

1. All persons orthodoxe in judgment and not scandalous in life may gather into a church estate according to the rules of the gospell of Jesus Christ. Liberty 1.[8]

Such may choose and ordaine their owne officers, and exercise all the Ordinances of Christ, without any injunction in doctrine, worship or discipline. Liberty 2 & 38.[9]

2. No mans life, honor, liberty, wife, children, goods or estate shall be taken away, punished or endamaged, under colour of lawe, or countenance of authoritie, but by an expresse lawe of the general court, or in defect of such lawe, by the word of God &c. Liberty, 1.

Every person within the jurisdiction &c shall enjoy the same justice and lawe &c without partiality or delay. Liberty 2.

All laws and hereditaments shall be free from all fines, forfeitures &c. Liberty 10.

Every man may remove himselfe and his familie &c if there be no legal impediment. Liberty 17.

6. Difficult cases are finally determinable in the court of assistants or in the generall court by appeale or petition, or by reference from the inferiour court. Liberty 31 & 36.

7. Upon unjust suites the plaintiff shall be fined proportionable to his offence. Liberty 37.

No man's goods shall be taken away but by a due course of justice.

---

[8] This is the clerical error for Item 1 of Liberty 95. — W. H. W.

[9] This is the similar error for Items 2, 3, and 8 of Liberty 95. — W. H. W.

Liberty 1. In criminal causes it shall be at the liberty of the accused partie to be tryed by the bench or by a jury. Liberty 23.[10]

Compared with the Common Laws of England.

7. In our own court of judication all causes civill and criminall are determinable, either by the judges and jury, or by the judges alone &c as in England. This is done both by custome and by divers laws established according to our charter, as Liberty 29, &c.

12. In all criminall offences, where the law hath prescribed no certaine penaltie, the judges have power to inflict penalties, according to the rule of God's word. Liberty 1, and by Charter, &c.

15. All publicke charges are defrayed out of the publicke stocke. Custome and Liberty 63.

19. No mans person shall be restrained or imprisoned &c. before the lawe hath sentenced him thereto, if he can put in sufficient baile, &c. except in crimes capitall, &c. Liberty 18.

20. The full age, for passing lands, giving votes, &c. is twenty one yeares. Liberty 53.

21. Married women cannot dispose of any estate, &c. nor can sue or be sued, without the husband. Custome and Liberty 14.

22–1. The eldest sonne is preferred before the younger in the ancestors inheritance. Liberty 81.

2. Daughters shall inherit as coparceners. Liberty 82.

3. No custome or prescription shall ever prevail &c to maintaine anything morally sinnfull. Liberty 65.

4. Civill authority may deale with any church member or officer, in a way of civill justice. Liberty 59.

5. No man shall be twice sentenced by civill justice for the same offence. Liberty 42.

6. No man shall be urged to take any oath or subscribe any articles, covenant, or remonstrance of a publick and civill nature, but such as the generall court hath considered, allowed and required. Liberty 3.

7. Publick records are open to all inhabitants. Liberty 48.

They also cite under the Common Law.

13. Treason, murther, witchcraft, sodomie and other notorious crimes are punished with death: But theft &c is not so punished, because we read otherwise in the scripture. Capitalls &c.

[10] This is the third clerical error; it should be Liberty 29. A comparison with the fragmentary copy contained in Elisha Hutchinson's book shows that the first citation was Libr. 1; the second was "Libr. 8 & 5 in Eccles." meaning of course Liberty 95 concerning Churches; and the third is plainly Libr. 29. Evidently the errors of the text are simply clerical ones, and not citations from any other arrangement of the Liberties. I have put in an Appendix a facsimile of the manuscript copy of this article, as the larger draft, printed by Gov. Hutchinson, seems to be lost. It is complete as far as it goes. — W. H. W.

14. Adultery is punished according to the canon of the spirituall law, viz. the scripture. Capitalls &c.

These two references are plainly to Liberty 94, which is entitled "Capitall Laws."

The absolute certainty of the identification of our manuscript copy being thus shown, it may be well to say a few words about the author or authors of the drafts. Hutchinson says, as before cited, that Mr. Bellingham of the magistrates and Mr. Cotton of the clergy had the greatest share in this work. We have seen that he was wrong as to Cotton; but Bellingham undoubtedly served on nearly all the committees, as did Winthrop and Dudley. Bellingham was bred a lawyer and was Recorder of Boston in Lincolnshire from 1625 to 1633; hence his connection with the compilation of our code is extremely natural and may well have been of considerable influence. It is to be noted that in the controversies between the Assistants and the Deputies he took sides with the latter, and may thus be claimed as likely to favor popular rights in the establishment of this Magna Charta of New England.

But, after all, the contemporary evidence of Governor Winthrop assigns the main work of compiling the code to one man, namely, Rev. Nathaniel Ward, of Ipswich. From an interesting memoir, prepared by a descendant, John Ward Dean, and published at Albany, 1868, we learn that Ward had special qualifications for this work. He was born about A.D. 1578 at Haverhill, England, and was the son of Rev. John Ward, an eminent minister there. He was graduated at Emmanuel College, Cambridge, A.M., in 1603. He studied and practised law, and Candler says that he was an Utter Barrister. He then travelled on the continent and stayed some time at Heidelberg. He entered the ministry about 1618, and was probably chaplain at Elbing, in Prussia. Returning to England he became rector of Stondon-Massey in Essex, but was suspended by Laud for Puritanism. In 1634 he came to New England, and settled at Ipswich, where he was pastor and Rev. Thomas Parker was teacher. He resigned his charge in about two years, owing to illness. In the winter of 1646–7 he returned to England, leaving his family here; and in June, 1647, he preached before the

House of Commons. In May, 1648, he was appointed minister at Shenfield, about five miles from his former home at Stondon-Massey. Here he ended his days in 1652 or 1653, aged some seventy-five years. He wrote various books,[11] of which the most famous was his "Simple Cobler of Agawam," written here and published in London in January, 1646–7. He was a witty as well as an earnest writer; a conservative, and yet forced by events to stand with the Parliament against the King. There is printed in Mass. Soc. Coll. 4th S. vol. vii, pp. 26–27, a letter from Ward to Governor Winthrop, in 1639, concerning the new laws, wherein he doubts the expediency of "sending the Court business to the common consideration of the freemen." He says, "I see the spirits of the people runne high, and what they gett they hould. They may not be denyed their proper and lawfull liberties; but I question whether it be of God to interest the inferiour sort in that which should be reserved *inter optimates penes quos est sancire leges*. If Mr. Lachford have writ them out, I would be glad to peruse one of his copies, if I may receive them. . . . . There is a necessity that the Covenant, if it be agreed upon, should be considered and celebrated by the several congregations and towns, and happily the tenure, but I dare not determyne concerning the latter. I mean of putting it to the suffrage of the people."

Without overrating the influence of any one man in the preparation of this admirable code, and believing firmly that it embodied the best judgment of Winthrop and other leaders, there seems to be no reason to doubt that the main literary work, at least, was due to Nathaniel Ward, and that his legal abilities and training were at least equal to those of any of his associates. In his "Simple Cobler" (edit. of 1843, p. 68) he writes, "I have read almost all the Common Law of England, and some Statutes." It may well be that the Common Law of England was the source from which these wise provisions were extracted, for in the Reply of the Colony in 1646, already cited, (*ante*, pp. 16, 17,) our laws are compared only with Magna Charta and the Common Laws of England.

We know of one instance in which a change was made in the first draft. Thomas Lechford, of whom we have before spoken as a copyist employed on the work, has recorded the fact that his remonstrance changed one item. In his "Plain Dealing, or News

[11] Among the strange words used by Ward, I note, pudder, exulcerations, colluvies, sedulity, jadish, interturbe, corrive, quidanye, prestigiated, ignotions, mundicidious, dedolent, exadverse, per-peracute, nugiperous, nudinstertian, futilous, perquisquilian, indenominable, precellency, surquedryes, prodromics, digladiations, prosult, bivious, awke; besides many, almost innumerable, oddities of combination. — W. W. H.

from New England," London, 1642 (Trumbull's edition, Boston, 1867, pp. 72–74), he prints a paper delivered by him to the Governor, etc., March 4, 1639–40. We cite as follows: —

Whereas you have been pleased to cause me to transcribe certain Breviats of Propositions delivered to the generall Court, for the establishing a body of Lawes, as is intended, for the glory of God, and the welfare of this People and Country; and published the same, to the intent that any man may acquaint you or the Deputies for the next Court, what he conceives fit to be altered or added, in or unto the said lawes; I conceive it to be my duty to give you timely notice of some things of great moment, about the same Lawes, in discharge of my conscience, which I shall, as *Amicus curiæ*, pray you to present with all faithfulnesse, as is proposed, to the next generall Court, by it, and the reverend Elders, to be further considered of, as followeth: —

1. It is propounded to be one chiefe part of the charge, or office of the Councell intended, to take care that the *conversion* of the *Natives* be endeavoured.

2. It is proposed, as a liberty, that a convenient number of Orthodox Christians, allowed to plant together in this Jurisdiction, may gather themselves into a Church, and elect and ordaine their Officers, men fit for their places, giving notice to seven of the next Churches, one month before thereof, and of their names, and that they may exercise all the ordinances of God according to his Word, and so they proceede according to the rule of God, and shall not be hindered by any Civill power: nor will this Court allow of any Church otherwise gathered.

This clause (*nor will the Court allow of any Church otherwise gathered*) doth as I conceive contradict the first proposition.

He then argues, briefly but clearly, that to convert the Indians they must send evangelists, and that the converts must be gathered into churches. But these churches are not made up, as the law requires, of "a convenient number of orthodox Christians," planting together and gathering themselves into a church; and therefore are prohibited from any recognition under the law. The point seems sound, though very small; and the remonstrance apparently had its effect. The law of March 3, 1635–6 (Records, i, 168), said "it is ordered that all persons are to take notice that this Court doth not, nor will hereafter, approve of any such companies of men as shall henceforth join in any pretended way of church fellowship, without they shall first acquaint the magistrates and the elders of the greater part of the churches in their jurisdiction, with their intentions, and have their approbation herein." Liberty 95, § 1, as enacted, allows that "All the people of God within this jurisdiction who are not in a church way, and be orthodox in judgment, and not scandalous in life, shall have full liberty to gather themselves into a Church estate: provided they do it in a Christian way, with due observance of the rules of Christ revealed in his word."

We see from Lechford's report, the rough draft of a law which was proposed, and in the published Liberty we see the amended statute. How many other cases there were is necessarily unknown. But in this example two things are noteworthy. First, Lechford himself was not a favorite with those in authority. He differed on various topics, he argued with the magistrates and the clergy. He was silenced by order of the rulers, and he was finally starved into returning to England. Yet his comments seem to have been fairly considered, and being found valid, they influenced the form of the law as passed. Secondly, it seems very strange that he, one of the few lawyers in the colony, should have found nothing else to which to object, in view of the great amount of legislation thus put into force, for which the English statutes gave no precedent.

The Body of Liberties as established in 1641 can be traced with only trifling changes in the edition of Laws of 1660. It is not cited in that book by that name, but as nearly all of the sections have the date of their enactment appended, we can easily trace the laws assigned to 1641.

The following table and notes will enable the reader to see that the legislation of 1641, so incorporated into the collected Laws of 1660, is not to be found on the records of the Legislature. It must, therefore, be sought in some other collective body of enactments of that date, and we have already seen that such was the Body of Liberties.

Laws dated 1641.

Acts of 1660.	Acts of 1672.	Title.	Body of Liberties. Number.
P. 1	P. 1	Preamble.	Preamble.
1	1	Ability, Age.	11, 53.
2	3	Actions, § 7, 8.	22, 28, 37.
2	3	Appeal.[12]	36.
3	4	Appearance.	4.

[12] This law is cited as 1642 in both editions of the Laws; but Hutchinson notes that it was founded on Liberty No. 36. — W. H. W.

Laws dated 1641. — Continued.

Acts of 1660.	Acts of 1672.	Title.	Body of Liberties. Number.
P. 4	P. 6	Arrests.	33.
4	8	Attachments, § 1, 2.	39, 21, 25.
5	9	Barratry.	34.
5	9	Benevolences.	See Notes, 1.
5	10	Bond-slavery.	91.
6	10	Bounds of Towns.	See Notes, 2.
8	14, 15	Capital Laws.[13]	94.
10	17	Cask, Cooper.	See Notes, 3.
11	18	Cattle, § 3.[14]	24.
14	22	Charges, Public.	63.
15	25	" § 3.[15]	13.
17	28	Children and Youth, §§ 5 and 6.	83, 84.
18	29	Clerk of the Writs.	See Notes, 4.
19	30	Condemned.	44.

[13] The Capital Laws as printed in 1660 are those contained in Liberty 94, for the first twelve laws, with slight changes in Nos. 3 and 4. The General Court, June 14, 1642 (Records, ii, 22), added three more capital crimes, viz.: criminal connection with a child under ten years of age, ravishing a married woman or betrothed maid, or ravishing a single woman aged over ten years. It was also ordered that all these capital laws be printed. Accordingly, in Major John Child's book, printed in London in 1647, entitled "New England's Jonas cast up at London," etc. (Marvin's edition, Boston, 1869), will be found a reprint of these fifteen Capital Laws, arranged somewhat differently in order. Nos. 3 and 4 are, however, the same as in the Body of Liberties.

But the General Court on November 4, 1646 (Records, ii, 177), passed a preamble and law about Blasphemy, which superseded Law No. 3 of the Liberties, and is the form followed in the Revision of 1660. At the same time (Records, ii, 179) they passed the two capital laws against wicked children, which are Nos. 13 and 14 in the Laws of 1660; and also (Records, ii, 182) the section punishing those accused of capital crimes who did not stand a trial.

The Laws of 1660 contain but one section about Rape, thereby ignoring two of the laws passed, as we have seen, in 1642. These punished fornication with a female child under ten years of age, and ravishing a married woman or a betrothed maid. The citation for this section is 1649, but I fail to find any express legislation on that subject in that year. I am therefore inclined to believe that the change was made in the revision of 1649, under the powers given the revisers.

It is evident that the revision was not satisfactory, for the General Court, Oct. 12, 1669, on a flagrant case, finding that there was then no law, re-enacted (Records, vol. iv, part ii, pp. 437–8) the punishment for abusing a child under ten years, as death. Laws of 1672, p. 15, § 17.

Still there seems to have been no punishment provided for ravishing a married woman. Under the New Charter (Goodell's Province Laws, i, 56), an Act was passed defining capital crimes, including ravishing *any* woman. It was passed in 1693, but disallowed by the Crown. In 1697 (Ibid., i, 296) an Act was passed punishing the rape of *any* woman or the abuse of a woman child under ten years of age. — W. H. W.

[14] Cited as 1646, but referred by Hutchinson to this Liberty. — W. H. W.

[15] This law is dated 1646, 47, 51, 57; but Hutchinson notes that the last paragraph of § 3 is based on Liberty No. 13. — W. H. W.

Laws dated 1641. — Continued.

Acts of 1660.	Acts of 1672.	Title.	Body of Liberties. Number.
P. 20	P. 32	Conveyance, § 3.	40, 15.
21	33	do § 4.	See Notes, 5.
22	35	Courts, § 4.	72, 73.
23	"	do § 6.	69, 71.
"	36	do § 6.	19, 20.
24	38	do § 10.	41.
"	"	do § 12.	See Notes, 6.
24	39	Cruelty.	92.
25	39	Death untimely.	57.
25	41	Deputies, § 2.	62, 68.
26	41	Distress.	35.
26	42	Dowries.	See Notes, 7.
26	43	Drovers.[16]	93.
27	"	Ecclesiastical, § 3–12.	95, §§ 1–10, 58, 59, 60. [§ 2 is new, and the numeration is thereby changed.]
29	48	Elections, § 4.	67.
30	49	Farms.	See Notes, 8.
31	50	Ferries.	See Notes, 9.
40	73	Impresses.	5, 6, 7, 8.
40	74	Imprisonment.	18.
43	77	Indians.	See Notes, 10.
47	86, 87	Jurors, § 1, 2, 3, 5.	50, 61, 31, 76, 49.
48	88	Lands, Free.	10.
50	90, 91	Liberties, Common.	12, 16, 17.
51	101	Marriage, &c.	80.
54	105	Masters & Servants, § 6, 7, 8, 9.	85, 86, 87, 88.

[16] It is worth while to note that in Liberty 93, the word "lambe" is used, and in the Laws of 1660, the word is "lame." — W. H. W.

Laws dated 1641. — Concluded.

Acts of 1660.	Acts of 1672.	Title.	Body of Liberties. Number.
P. 61	P. 116	Mines.	See Notes, 11.
62	119	Monopolies.	9.
62	119	Oaths.[17]	3.
66	126	Prescriptions.	65.
67	128, 129	Protests.	75.
67	129	Punishment, Torture.[18]	42, 43, 45, 46.
68	129–131	Records, &c., § 1, 3.	64, 38, 48.
69	132	Replevin.	32.
72	139	Ships, § 1.	See Notes, 12.
73	143	Strangers.	2, 89.
75	147, 148	Township.[19]	56, 66, 74.
76	150	Treasurer.[20]	78.
77	152	Trials.	29, 30, 52.
78	153	Usury.	23.
78	153	Votes.[21]	54, 70, 77.
81	158	Wills.	81, 82.
81	158	Witnesses.	47.
83	161	Wrecks.	90.

[17] By Hutchinson wrongly marked as p. 219. — W. H. W.

[18] This chapter is undated in the Laws, but Hutchinson refers it to Liberties 42, 43, 45 and 46. — W. H. W.

[19] This chapter is dated 1630, 1642, 47, 53, 58; yet there are three sections taken from the Body of Liberties. The omission of 1641 is clearly a clerical error. — W. H. W.

[20] This chapter has no citation in the Laws under date of 1641, but Hutchinson rightly assigns part of it to Liberty 78. — W. H. W.

[21] This is erroneously dated 1651, yet Hutchinson properly refers it to Liberties nos. 54, 70, and 77. — W. H. W.

The following explanatory notes will, perhaps, make the matter plainer: —

First. Laws of 1660, p. 5, Title "Benevolence." This law is dated 1641, but is not in the Body of Liberties. It was passed June 2, 1641 (Records, i, 327), and therefore probably after the Body of Liberties had been compiled.

Second. Edition of 1660, p. 6, Title "Bounds of Towns." Citation 1641, though in the edition of 1672 cited as 1651. A short law was passed June 2, 1641 (Records, i, 319), but the main part of this act was passed Nov. 11, 1647 (Records, ii, 210).

Third. Laws of 1660, p. 9–10, Title "Cask & Cooper." The laws are dated 1641, 1647, 1651, 1652. I find no law on the subject in 1641, but there was one passed Sept. 27, 1642 (Records, ii, 29), the terms of which are incorporated in the Laws of 1660. Evidently the date is a misprint, by no means the only one.

Fourth. Laws of 1660, p. 18, Title "Clerk of the Writs." This law was passed Dec. 10, 1641 (Records, i, 345), and, of course, after the Body of Liberties was already in form.

Fifth. Laws of 1660, p. 20–21, Title "Conveyances," &c. § 4 is assigned to 1641 and 1642. This law was passed October 7, 1640, and this date is incorporated into the law as printed. Evidently 1641 is a misprint for 1640.

Sixth. Laws of 1660, p. 24, Title "Courts," § 12. This is a law that "every Court in this jurisdiction where two magistrates are present, may admit any church members that are fit, to be freemen; giving them the oath: and the Clerk of each Court shall certify their names to the Secretary at the next General Court." 1641.

This date of 1641 is clearly a misprint. May 20, 1642 (Rec. vol. ii, pp. 2–6 *of the second edition only*) the following order was passed: "There is power given to every Court within our jurisdiction, that hath two magistrates, to admit any church members that are fit to be free, and to give them the freeman's oath, and to certify their names to the Secretary at the next General Court." May 10, 1643 (Records, ii, 38), it was ordered "concerning members that refuse to take their freedom, the churches should be writ unto, to deal with them." In the list of Freemen (Records, ii, 291) all seem to have been made free in May of the respective years, except a few at Salem in Dec., 1642, and February, 1642–3, and some at Springfield, in April, 1648. As to these last, it was ordered Nov. 11, 1647 (Records, ii, 224) that "Mr. Pinchin is authorised to make freemen in the town of Springfeild, of those that are in covenant and live according to their profession."

Again, Nov. 11, 1647 (Records, ii, 208), it was voted that "there being in this jurisdiction many members of churches, who to exempt themselves from all public service in the commonwealth, will not come in to be made freemen," . . . . it is ordered that they be not exempt from serving in town offices, if elected.

June 19, 1650 (Records, iv, pt. 1, p. 19), Robert Clements, at the request of the town of Haverhill, was empowered to give the oath of fidelity. In 1653 (Ibid., p. 127, 129) special commissioners were sent to establish jurisdiction at Kittery and at Saco, and they admitted freemen there. Other special cases may be found on the records.

May 31, 1660 (Records, iv, pt. 1, p. 420) the General Court declared "that no man whatsoever shall be admitted to the freedom of this body politic, but such as are members of some church of Christ, and in full communion; which they declare to be the true intent of the ancient law, page the 8th of the second book, anno g^r 1631."

June 28, 1662, Charles II. sent a letter to the Colony ordering the redress of grievances. It is printed in Hutchinson's Collections, Prince Soc. edit. ii, 100–104. He especially ordered a change in the law concerning freemen. Accordingly on Aug. 3, 1664 (Records, iv, part ii, p. 117), the General Court declared, "that the law prohibiting all persons except members of churches, *and also that for allowance of them in any County Courts*, are hereby repealed."

See my preface for an explanation of the differences between the two editions of the printed Records.

Seventh. In the edition of 1672, p. 42, Title "Dowries," the date is given as 1641. But in the laws of 1660 it is dated 1647, which is somewhat confusing. The reference to 1641 may refer to Liberty No. 79; but it looks more like a misprint. The records do not contain any law of 1647, but May 2, 1649 (Records, ii, 281), reference is made to "the printed law concerning dowries," and amends it by striking out the clause giving the widow "a third part of her husband's money, goods, and chattels, real and personal;" and also by ordering in the 14th line of said order the insertion of the words "then by act or consent of such wife."

Both these changes are incorporated in the text in 1660, and the proviso is made that the law shall not affect houses, lands, etc., sold before the last of November, 1647. Hence, it would seem that there was a law passed and printed in that year, though not entered in the legislative records.

Eighth. Laws of 1660, p. 30, Title "Farms." The order that all farms in a town shall belong therein, except Medford, is dated 1641, and is not in the Liberties. It was passed June 2, 1641 (Records, i, 331), and may have been too late for insertion, or, more probably, was not of a nature to be placed there.

Ninth. Laws of 1660, p. 31, Title "Ferries." Reference is made to law of 1641. Much of § 1 will be found in orders passed

Oct. 7, 1641 (Records, i, 338, 341), explaining this reference. But the law is not in the Body of Liberties for the reasons given in the preceding example.

Tenth. Laws of 1660, p. 43, Title "Indians." At the end of section 10, the citation is 1633, 37, 40, 41, etc. I find nothing passed in 1641 relating to this section; but § 7, cited as passed in 1640, 48, in the last clause does contain a law passed June 2, 1641 (Records, i, 329), that if harm be done by the Indians to the English in their cattle any three magistrates may order satisfaction. Hence I infer the general citations under section 10 cover all the preceding sections, and this is the law of 1641, which is not in the Body of Liberties.

Eleventh. Laws of 1660, p. 61, Title "Mines." Citation of law of 1641, which is not in Body of Liberties. The law was passed June 2, 1641 (Records, i, 327).

Twelfth. Laws of 1660, Title "Ships," p. 72, citation of 1641. The law was passed Oct. 7, 1641 (Records, i, 337–338).

It will be noted that of these twelve laws dated in 1641, and not in the Body of Liberties, Numbers 1, 2, 8, 10 and 11 were passed in June, 1641, Nos. 9 and 12 in October, 1641, and No. 4 in December, 1641. These were all passed too late to be placed in that document. Nos. 3, 5, 6, and 7 are wrongly dated.

The result, however, is to show that nearly all of the acts ascribed to the year 1641 in the late revisions are simply sections of the Body of Liberties.

One other point remains to be considered. A few of the Liberties were not incorporated into the Statutes in 1660, and are not checked by E. Hutchinson on the margin of his manuscript. These are numbered 14, 26, 27, 51, 55, 79, and 95, § 11.

No. 14 is to the effect that a conveyance made by a married woman, a child, an idiot, or distracted person shall be good, if ratified by the General Court.

This may have been dropped on consideration as contrary to English law at that time.

No. 26 empowered any man unable to plead his own case to have any unpaid attorney. The prohibition to employ a paid lawyer was in force in 1641, as Winthrop records (History, ii, p. 43). May 2, 1649 (Records ii, 279), it is ordered that appeals shall be made by the party, or his attorney, in writing. Also, it was ordered that after one month's publication hereof, no one should ask council or advice of any magistrate in regard to a case to be tried. We may infer from these two citations that the necessity of paid attorneys had become so evident that this Liberty was quietly dropped.

No. 27 relates to the defendant's right to answer in writing if the plaintiff put in his case in that form.

No. 51 provides that associates to aid the assistants in the Inferior Courts shall be chosen by the towns.

No. 55 provides and gives the widest liberty to both plaintiffs and defendants in making claims and pleas.

These details in regard to the courts were naturally modified from time to time, between 1641 and 1660, as the records show. There seems to have been a great amount of experimenting in arranging the inferior courts, and hence we cannot find the exact equivalents of these Liberties, though they were preserved in spirit.

No. 79 provides that if a man did not provide for his widow out of his estate, the General Court should relieve her. This idea is carried out in the law of Dowries, as printed in 1660, to which reference has already been made. See also Wills, § 3.

It is evident, therefore, that the Body of Liberties was virtually incorporated into the earliest system of laws, and that no part of it was found to be superfluous. Both in regard to its extent and its phraseology it is a noble monument to the compilers, and to the community which so promptly accepted it. In its present form it will be easily examined, and the most thorough study will confirm the impression of its importance in any investigation of the growth of the Commonwealth, through original processes worked out on the spot, from a trading company to a free state, the parent and exemplar of so many later communities. —W. H. W.

THE BODY OF LIBERTIES.

1641.

IN FAC-SIMILE FROM THE HUTCHINSON MANUSCRIPT, WITH A LINE-FOR-LINE PRINTED VERSION.

TABLE OF CONTENTS.[1]

[1] This Table is put in modern form, and the term Legislature is used for the General Court. W. H. W.

27

A Coppie of the Liberties of the Massachusets Collonie in New England

The free fruition of such liberties Immunities and priveledges as humanitie, Civilitie, and Christianitie call for as due to every man in his place and proportion; without impeachment and Infringement hath ever bene and ever will be the tranquillitie and Stabilitie of Churches and Commonwealths. And the deniall or deprivall thereof, the disturbance if not the ruine of both.

We hould it therefore our dutie and safetie whilst we are about the further establishing of this Government to collect and expresse all such freedomes as for present we foresee may concerne us, and our posteritie after us, And to ratify them with our sollemne consent.

Wee doe therefore this day religiously and unanimously decree and confirme these following Rites, liberties, and priveledges concerneing our Churches, and Civill State to be respectively impartiallie and inviolably enjoyed and observed throughout our Jurisdiction for ever.

1 No mans life shall be taken away, no mans honour or good name shall be stayned, no mans person shall be arested, restrayned, banished, dismembred, nor any wayes punished, no man shall be deprived of his wife or children, no mans goods or estaite shall be taken away from him, nor any way indammaged under coulor of law, or Countenance of Authoritie, unlesse it be by vertue or equitie of some expresse law of the Country warranting the same, established by a generall Court and sufficiently published, or in case of the defect of a law in any parteculer case by the word of god. And in Capitall cases, or in cases concerning dismembring or banishment, according to that word to be judged by the Generall Court. pag. ..

2 Every person within this Jurisdiction, whether Inhabitant or forreiner shall enjoy the same justice and law, that is generall for the plantation, which we constitute and execute one towards another, without partialitie or delay. pag. 143

3 No man shall be urged to take any oath or subscribe any articles, covenants, or remonstrance, of a publique and Civill nature, but such as the Generall Court hath considered, allowed, and required. pag. 119

4 No man shall be punished for not appearing at or before any Civill Assembly, Court, Councell, Magistrate, or Officer, nor for the omission of any office or service, if he shall be necessarily hindred, by any apparent Act or providence of god, which he could neither foresee nor avoid, Provided that this law shall not prejudice any person of his just cost or damage, in any civill action. pag. 4

5 No man shall be compelled to any publique worke or service unlesse the presse be grounded upon some act of the generall Court, and have reasonable allowance therefore. pag. 71. ffol..

6. No man

A COPPIE OF THE LIBERTIES OF THE MASSACHUSETS COLONIE IN NEW ENGLAND.

The free fruition of such liberties Immunities and priveledges as humanitie, Civilitie, and Christianitie call for as due to every man in his place and proportion without impeachment and Infringement hath ever bene and ever will be the tranquillitie and Stabilitie of Churches and Commonwealths. And the deniall or deprivall thereof, the disturbance if not the ruine of both.

We hould it therefore our dutie and safetie whilst we are about the further establishing of this Government to collect and expresse all such freedomes as for present we foresee may concerne us, and our posteritie after us, And to ratify them with our sollemne consent.

We doe therefore this day religiously and unanimously decree and confirme these following Rites, liberties and priveledges concerneing our Churches, and Civill State to be respectively impartiallie and inviolably enjoyed and observed throughout our Jurisdiction for ever.

---

1 No mans life shall be taken away, no mans honour or good name shall be stayned, no mans person shall be arested, restrayned, banished, dismembred, nor any wayes punished, no man shall be deprived of his wife or children, no mans goods or estaite shall be taken away from him, nor any way indammaged under coulor of law or Countenance of Authoritie, unlesse it be by vertue or equitie of some expresse law of the Country waranting the same, established by a generall Court and sufficiently published, or in case of the defect of a law in any parteculer case by the word of god. And in Capitall cases, or in cases concerning dismembring or banishment, according to that word to be judged by the Generall Court. pag. 1.

2 Every person within this Jurisdiction, whether Inhabitant or forreiner shall enjoy the same justice and law, that is generall for the plantation, which we constitute and execute one towards another without partialitie or delay. pag. 143.

3 No man shall be urged to take any oath or subscribe any articles, covenants or remonstrance, of a publique and Civill nature, but such as the Generall Court hath considered, allowed, and required. pag. 219.

4 No man shall be punished for not appearing at or before any Civill Assembly, Court, Councell, Magistrate, or Officer, nor for the omission of any office or service, if he shall be necessarily hindred by any apparent Act or providence of God, which he could neither foresee nor avoid. Provided that this law shall not prejudice any person of his just cost or damage, in any civill action. pag. 4.

5 No man shall be compelled to any publique worke or service unlesse the presse be grounded upon some act of the generall Court, and have reasonable allowance therefore. pag. 73. sect. 2.

6. No man

6 No man shall be pressed in pson to any office, worke, warres, or other publique service, yt is necessarily & sufficiently exempted by any naturall or psonall impediment, as by want of yeares, greatnes of age, defect of minde, fayling of sences, or impotencie of Lymbes. pag 73

7 No man shall be compelled to goe out of ye limits of this plantation upon any offensive warres wch this Comonwealth or any of or freinds or confederats shall volentarily undertake, But onely upon such vindictive & defensive warres in or owne behalfe, or ye behalfe of or freinds, & confederats as shall be enterprized by ye Counsell and consent of a Court generall, or by Authority derived from ye same. pag 73

8 No mans Cattell or goods of what kinde soever shall be pressed or taken for any publique use or service, unlesse it be by warrant grounded upon some act of ye generall Court, nor wthout such reasonable prices & hire as ye ordinarie rates of ye Countrie do afford. And if his Cattle or goods shall perish or suffer damage in such service, ye owner shall be sufficiently recompenced pag 73

9 No monopolies shall be granted or allowed amongst us, but of such new Inventions yt are profitable to ye Countrie, & yt for a short time. pag 119

10 All or lands & heritages shall be free from all fines & licenses upon Alienations, & from all hariotts, wardships, Liveries, Primer-seisins, yeare day & wast, Escheates, & forfeitures, upon ye deaths of parents, or Ancestors, be they naturall, casuall, or Judiciall. pag 8

11 All psons wch are of ye age of 21 yeares, & of right understanding & meamories, whether excomunicate or condemned shall have full power & libertie to make there wills & testaments, & other lawfull alienations of theire lands & estates. pag 1

12 Every man whether Inhabitant or fforreiner, free or not free shall have libertie to come to any publique Court, Councell, or Towne meeting, & either by speech or writeing to move any lawfull, seasonable, & materiall question, or to present any necessary motion, complaint, petition, Bill or information, whereof yt meeting hath proper cognizance, so it be done in convenient time, due order, & respective manner. pag 9

No man shall be rated here for any estaite or revenue he hath in England or in any forreine partes till it be transported hither. pag 115

Any Conveyance or Alienation of land or other estaite what so ever, made by any woman yt is married, any childe under age, Ideott, or distracted pson, shall be good, if it be passed & ratified by ye consent of a generall Court.

15 All Covts

6 No man shall be pressed in person to any office, worke, warres or other publique service, that is necessarily and suffitiently exempted by any naturall or personall impediment, as by want of yeares, greatnes of age, defect of minde, fayling of sences, or impotencie of Lymbes. pag. 73. sect. 2

7 No man shall be compelled to goe out of the limits of this plantation upon any offensive warres which this Commonwealth or any of our freinds or confederats shall volentarily undertake. But onely upon such vindictive and defensive warres in our owne behalfe or the behalfe of our freinds and confederats as shall be enterprized by the Counsell and consent of a Court generall, or by Authority derived from the same. pag. 73.

8 No mans Cattel or goods of what kinde soever shall be pressed or taken for any publique use or service, unlesse it be by warrant grounded upon some act of the generall Court, nor without such reasonable prices and hire as the ordinarie rates of the Countrie do afford. And if his Cattle or goods shall perish or suffer damage in such service, the owner shall be suffitiently recompenced. pag. 73.

9 No monopolies shall be granted or allowed amongst us, but of such new Inventions that are profitable to the Countrie, and that for a short time. pag. 119.

10 All our lands and heritages shall be free from all fines and licences upon Alienations, and from all hariotts, wardships, Liveries, Primerseisins, yeare day and wast, Escheates, and forfeitures, upon the deaths of parents or Ancestors, be they naturall, casuall or Juditiall. pag. 88.

11 All persons which are of the age of 21 yeares, and of right understanding and meamories, whether excommunicate or condemned shall have full power and libertie to make there wills and testaments, and other lawfull alienations of theire lands and estates. pag. 1.

12 Every man whether Inhabitant or fforreiner, free or not free shall have libertie to come to any publique Court, Councel, or Towne meeting, and either by speech or writeing to move any lawfull, seasonable, and materiall question, or to present any necessary motion, complaint, petition, Bill or information, whereof that meeting hath proper cognizance, so it be done in convenient time, due order, and respective manner. pag. 90.

13 No man shall be rated here for any estaite or revenue he hath in England, or in any forreine partes till it be transported hither. pag. 25. sect. 2.

14 Any Conveyance or Alienation of land or other estaite what so ever, made by any woman that is married, any childe under age, Ideott or distracted person, shall be good if it be passed and ratified by the consent of a generall Court.

15. All Coven^ts

15 All Covenous or fraudulent Alienations or Conveyances of Lands, tenem^ts, or any hereditaments, shall be of no validitie to defeate any man from due debts or legacies, or from any just title, clame or possession, of y^t wch is so fraudulently conveyed. pag. 52 sect. 3

16 Every Inhabitant y^t is an howse holder shall have free fishing & fowling in any great ponds & Bayes, Coves & Rivers, so farre as ye sea ebbes & flowes wth in ye precincts of ye towne where they dwell, unlesse ye free men of ye same Towne or ye Generall Court have otherwise appropriated them, provided y^t this shall not be extended to give leave to any man to come upon others proprietie wth out there leave. pag. 90 sec. 2

17 Every man of or wth in this Jurisdiction shall have free libertie, not wth standing any Civill power to remove both himselfe & his familie at their pleasure out of ye same, provided there be no legall impediment to ye contrarie. pag. 91 sec. 3

Rites Rules & Liberties concerning Judiciall proceedings.

18 No mans p^rson shall be restrained or imprisoned by any Authority what so ever, before ye law hath sentenced him thereto, If he can put in sufficient securitie, bayle, or mainprise, for his appearance & good behavio^r in ye meane time, unlesse it be in Crimes Capitall, & Contempts in open Court, & in such cases where some expresse act of Court doth allow it. pag. 79

19 If in a generall Court any miscariage shall be amongst ye Assistants when they are by them selves y^t may deserve an Admonition or fine under 20^s, it shall be examined & sentenced amongst y^m selves, If amongst ye Deputies when they are by themselves, It shall be examined & sentenced amongst themselves, If it be when ye whole Court is togeather, it shall be judged by ye whole Court, & not severallie as before. pag. 16 sec. 6

20 If any wch are to sit as Judges in any other Court shall demeane y^m selves offensively in ye Court, The rest of ye Judges p^rsent shall have power to censure him for it, if ye cause be of a high nature it shall be p^rsented to & censured at ye next superior Court. pag. 16 sec. 6

21 In all cases where ye first sumons are not served six dayes before ye Court, & ye cause breifly specified in ye warrant, where appearance is to be made by ye p^rtie sumoned, it shall be at his libertie whether he will appeare or no, except all cases y^t are to be handled in Courts suddainly called, upon extraordinary occasions, In all cases where there appeares present & urgent cause, any Assistant or officer apointed shal have power to make out attaichments for ye first sumons. pag. 7 sec. 2

22 No man

15 All Covenous or fraudulent Alienations or Conveyances of lands, tenements, or any hereditaments, shall be of no validitie to defeate any man from due debts or legacies, or from any just title, clame or possession, of that which is so fraudulently conveyed. pag. 32. sec. 3.

16 Every Inhabitant that is an howse holder shall have free fishing and fowling in any great ponds and Bayes, Coves and Rivers, so farre as the sea ebbes and flowes within the presincts of the towne where they dwell, unlesse the free men of the same Towne or the Generall Court have otherwise appropriated them, provided that this shall not be extended to give leave to any man to come upon others proprietie without there leave. pag. 90. sec. 2.

17 Every man of or within this Jurisdiction shall have free libertie, notwithstanding any Civill power to remove both himselfe, and his familie at their pleasure out of the same, provided there be no legall impediment to the contrarie. pag. 91. sec. 3.

Rites Rules and Liberties concerning Juditiall proceedings.

18 No mans person shall be restrained or imprisoned by any Authority whatsoever, before the law hath sentenced him thereto, If he can put in sufficient securitie, bayle or mainprise, for his appearance, and good behaviour in the meane time, unlesse it be in Crimes Capital, and Contempts in open Court, and in such cases where some expresse act of Court doth allow it. pag. 74.

19 If in a generall Court any miscariage shall be amongst the Assistants when they are by themselves that may deserve an Admonition or fine under 20 sh. it shall be examined and sentenced among themselves, If amongst the Deputies when they are by themselves, It shall be examined and sentenced amongst themselves, If it be when the whole Court is togeather, it shall be judged by the whole Court, and not severallie as before. pag. 36. sec. 6.

20 If any which are to sit as Judges in any other Court shall demeane themselves offensively in the Court, the rest of the Judges present shall have power to censure him for it, if the cause be of a high nature it shall be presented to and censured at the next superior Court. pag. 36. sec. 6.

21 In all cases where the first summons are not served six dayes before the Court, and the cause breifly specified in the warrant, where appearance is to be made by the partie summoned, it shall be at his libertie whether he will appeare or no, except all cases that are to be handled in Courts suddainly called, upon extraordinary occasions, In all cases where there appeares present and urgent cause Any Assistant or officer apointed shal have power to make out Attaichments for the first summons. pag. 7. sec. 2.

22. No man

22 No man in any suit or action agt an other shall falsely pretend great debts or damages to vex his Adversary. if it shall appeare any doth so. The Court shall have power to set a reasonable fine on his head. pag. 3 sec. 8

23 No man shall be adjudged to pay for detaining any debt from any Crediter above eight pounds in ye hundred for one yeare, And not above yt rate proportionable for all somes what so ever, neither shall this be a coulour or countenance to allow any usurie amongst us contrarie to ye law of god. p. 153

24 In all trespasses or damages done to any man or men; If it can be proved to be done by ye meere default of him or them to whome ye trespasse is done, It shall be judged no trespasse, nor any damage given for it. pag. 18 sec. 3

25 No Summons pleading Judgement, or any kinde of proceeding in Court or course of Justice shall be abated, arested, or reversed, upon any kinde of circumstantiall errors or mistakes, If ye pson & cause be rightly understood & intended by ye Court. pag. 7 sec. 2

26 Every man yt findeth himselfe unfit to plead his owne cause in any Court, shall have Libertie to imploy any man agt whom the Court doth not except, to helpe him, provided he give him noe fee, or reward for his paines. This shall not exempt ye ptie him selfe, from Answering such questions in pson as ye Court shall — thinke meete to demand of him.

27 If any plantife shall give into any Court a declaration of his cause in writeing, The defendant shall also have libertie & time to give in his answer in writeing. And so in all further proceedings betweene ptie & ptie, So it doth not further hinder ye dispach of Justice then ye Court shall be willing unto.

28 The plantife in all Actions brought in any Court shall have libertie to withdraw his Action, or to be non suited before ye Jurie hath given in ye verdict, in wch case he shall alwaies pay full cost & chardges to ye defendt, & may afterwards renew his suite at an other Court if he please. pag. 3 sec. 7

29 In all Actions at law it shall be ye libertie of ye plant & defendt by mutuall consent to choose whether they will be tryed by ye Bench, or by a Jurie, unlesse it be where ye law upon just reason hath otherwise determined. The like libertie shall be granted to all psons in Criminall cases. pag. 15 sec. 1

30 It shall be in ye libertie both of plantife & defendt, & likewise every delinquent (to be judged by a Jurie) to challenge any of ye Jurors. And if his challenge be found just & reasonable by ye Bench, or ye rest of ye Jurie, as ye challenger shall choose it shall be allowed him, & tales de cercumstantibus impanneled in their roome. p. 142 s. 3

31. In all

22 No man in any suit or action against an other shall falsely pretend great debts or damages to vex his Adversary, if it shall appeare any doth so, The Court shall have power to set a reasonable fine on his head. pag. 3. sec. 8.

23 No man shall be adjudged to pay for detaining any debt from any Crediter above eight pounds in the hundred for one yeare, And not above that rate proportionable for all somes what so ever, neither shall this be a coulour or countenance to allow any usurie amongst us contrarie to the law of god. pag. 153.

24 In all Trespasses or damages done to any man or men, If it can be proved to be done by the meere default of him or them to whome the trespasse is done, It shall be judged no trespasse, nor any damage given for it. pag. 18. sec. 3.

25 No Summons pleading Judgement, or any kinde of proceeding in Court or course of Justice shall be abated, arested or reversed upon any kinde of cercumstantiall errors or mistakes, If the person and cause be rightly understood and intended by the Court. pag. 7. sec. 2.

26 Every man that findeth himselfe unfit to plead his owne cause in any Court shall have Libertie to imploy any man against whom the Court doth not except, to helpe him, Provided he give him noe fee or reward for his paines. This shall not exempt the partie him selfe from Answering such Questions in person as the Court shall thinke meete to demand of him.

27 If any plantife shall give into any Court a declaration of his cause in writeing, The defendant shall also have libertie and time to give in his answer in writeing, And so in all further proceedings betwene partie and partie, So it doth not further hinder the dispach of Justice then the Court shall be willing unto.

28 The plantife in all Actions brought in any Court shall have libertie to withdraw his Action, or to be nonsuited before the Jurie hath given in their verdict, in which case he shall alwaies pay full cost and chardges to the defendant, and may afterwards renew his suite at an other Court if he please. pag. 3. sec. 7.

29 In all Actions at law it shall be the libertie of the plantife and defendant by mutual consent to choose whether they will be tryed by the Bench or by a Jurie, unlesse it be where the law upon just reason hath otherwise determined. The like libertie shall be granted to all persons in Criminall cases. pag. 152. sec. 2.

30 It shall be in the libertie both of plantife and defendant, and likewise every delinquent (to be judged by a Jurie) to challenge any of the Jurors. And if his challenge be found just and reasonable by the Bench, or the rest of the Jurie, as the challenger shall choose it shall be allowed him, and tales de cercumstantibus impaneled in their room. pag. 152. S. 3.

31. In all

31 In all cases where evidence is so obscure or defective yt ye Jurie can
not clearely & safely give a positive verdict, whether it be a grand or
petit Jurie, It shall have libertie to give a non Liquit, or a spetiall verdict,
in wch last, yt is in a spetiall verdict, ye Judgement of ye cause shall be left to
the Court, And all Jurors shall have libertie in matters of fact if they p. 87
can not finde ye finde ye maine issue, yet to finde & present in ye verdict s. 7
so much as they can, If ye Bench Jurors shall so differ at any time part of it
about ye verdict yt either of them can not proceede wth peace of con=
science ye case shall be referred to ye Generall Court, who shall take
ye question from both & determine it.

32 Every man shall have libertie to replevy his Cattell, or goods im=
pounded, distreined, seised, or extended, unlesse it be upon execu= p. 132
tion after Judgement, & in paimt of fines. Provided he puts in good
securitie to prosecute his replevin, And to satisfie such demands as
his Adversary shall recover agt him in Law.

33 No mans psn shall be Arrested, or imprisoned upon execution
or judgmt for any debt or fine, If ye law can finde competent meanes
of satisfaction otherwise from his estaite, And if not his psn may pag. 6
be arrested & imprisoned where he shall be kept at his owne
charge, not ye plaintife till satisfaction be made; unlesse ye Court yt
had cognizance of ye cause or some superior Court shall otherwise
provide.

34 If any man shall be proved & Judged a comen Barrator vexing o=
thers wth unjust frequent & endlesse suites, It shall be in ye power p. 9
of Courts both to denie him ye benefit of ye law, & to punish him for
his Barratry.

35 No mans Corne nor hay yt is in ye feild or upon ye Cart, nor his gar=
den stuffe, nor any thing subiect to present decay shall be taken in
any distresse, unles he yt takes it doth presently bestow it where p. 41
it may not be imbesled nor suffer spoile or decay, or give secu=
ritie to satisfie ye worth thereof if it comes to any harme.

36 It shall be in ye libertie of every man cast condemned or sentenced
in any cause in any Inferior Court, to make their Appeale to ye Court of
Assistants, provided they tender their appeale & put in securitie to prosecute
it before ye Court be ended wherein they were condemned, And
within six dayes next ensuing put in good securitie before some p. 3
Assistant to satisfie what his Adversarie shall recover agt him; part of 2
And if ye cause be of a Criminall nature, for his good behaviour, and
appearance, And everie man shall have libertie to complaine
to ye Generall Court of any Injustice done him in any Court of
Assistants or other

37 In all

31 In all cases where evidence is so obscure or defective that the Jurie cannot clearely and safely give a positive verdict, whether it be a grand or petit Jurie, It shall have libertie to give a non Liquit, or a spetiall verdict, in which last, that is in a spetiall verdict, the Judgement of the cause shall be left to the Court, and all Jurors shall have libertie in matters of fact if they cannot finde the maine issue, yet to finde and present in their verdict so much as they can, If the Bench and Jurors shall so differ at any time about their verdict that either of them cannot proceede with peace of conscience the case shall be referred to the Generall Court, who shall take the question from both and determine it. P. 87. S. 3, part of it.

32 Every man shall have libertie to replevy his Cattell or goods impounded, distreined, seised, or extended, unlesse it be upon execution after Judgement, and in paiment of fines. Provided he puts in good securitie to prosecute his replevin, And to satisfie such demands as his Adversary shall recover against him in Law. P. 132.

33 No mans person shall be Arrested, or imprisoned upon execution or judgment for any debt or fine, If the law can finde competent meanes of satisfaction otherwise from his estaite, and if not his person may be arrested and imprisoned where he shall be kept at his owne charge, not the plantife's till satisfaction be made: unlesse the Court that had cognizance of the cause or some superior Court shall otherwise provide. P. 6.

34 If any man shall be proved and Judged a commen Barrator vexing others with unjust frequent and endlesse suites, It shall be in the power of Courts both to denie him the benefit of the law, and to punish him for his Barratry. P. 9.

35 No mans Corne nor hay that is in the feild or upon the Cart, nor his garden stuffe, nor any thing subject to present decay, shall be taken in any distresse, unles he that takes it doth presently bestow it where it may not be imbesled nor suffer spoile or decay, or give securitie to satisfie the worth thereof if it comes to any harme. P. 41.

36 It shall be in the libertie of every man cast condemned or sentenced in any cause in any Inferior Court, to make their Appeale to the Court of Assistants, provided they tender their appeale and put in securitie to prosecute it before the Court be ended wherein they were condemned, And within six dayes next ensuing put in good securitie before some Assistant to satisfie what his Adversarie shall recover against him; And if the cause be of a Criminall nature, for his good behaviour, and appearance, And everie man shall have libertie to complaine to the Generall Court of any Injustice done him in any Court of Assistants or other. P. 3, part of it.

37. In all

37 In all cases where it appeares to ye Court yt ye plant. hath wilingly and witingly done wronge to ye defdt in commenceing & prosecuting any action or complainte agt him, They shall haue power to impose vpon him a proportionable fine to ye vse of ye deft, or accused person, for his false complaint, or clamor. p. 8 S. 8

38 Everie man shall haue libertie to Record in ye publique Rolles of any Court any Testimony given vpon oath in ye same Court, or before two Assistants, or any deede or evidence legally confirmed there to remaine in perpetuam rei memoriam, yt is for perpetuall memoriall or evidence vpon occasion. p. 131

39 In all Actions both reall & personall betweene ptie & ptie, ye Court shall haue power to respite execution for a convenient time, when in their prudence they see just cause so to doe. p. 7 S. 1

40 No Conveyance, Deede, or promise what so ever shall be of validitie, if it be gotten by Illegal violence, imprisonment, threatenings, or any kinde of forcible compulsion called Dures. p. 71 S. 3

41 Everie man yt is to Answere for any Criminall cause, whether he be in prison or vnder bayle, his cause shall be heard & determined at ye next Court yt hath proper Cognizance thereof, And may be done wth out preiudice of Justice. p. 38 S. 10

42 No man shall be twise sentenced by Civill Justice for one & the same Crime, offence, or Trespasse. p. 129

43 No man shall be beaten wth above 40 stripes, nor shall any true gentleman, nor any man equall to a gentleman be punished wth whipping, vnles his crime be very shamefull, & his course of life vitious and profligate. p. 129

44 No man condemned to dye shall be put to death wth in fower dayes next after his condemnation, vnles ye Court see speciall cause to ye contrary, or in case of martiall law, nor shall ye body of any man so put to death be vnburied 12 howers, vnlesse it be in case of Anatomie. p. 30

45 No man shall be forced by Torture to confesse any Crime agt himselfe nor any other vnlesse it be in some Capitall case, where he is first fullie convinced by cleare & suffitient evidence to be guilty, After wch if ye cause be of yt nature, That it is very apparent there be other conspiratours, or confederates wth him, then he may be tortured, yet not wth such Tortures as be Barbarous & inhumane. p. 129

46 For bodilie punishments we allow amongst vs none yt are inhumane Barbarous or cruell. p. 129

47 No man shall be put to death wth out ye testimony of two or three witnesses, or yt wch is equivalent there vnto. p. 15

48 Every Inhabitant

37 In all cases where it appeares to the Court that the plantife hath wilingly and witingly done wronge to the defendant in commenceing and prosecuting any action or complaint against him, They shall have power to impose upon him a proportionable fine to the use of the defendant, or accused person, for his false complaint or clamor. P. 3. S. 8.

38 Everie man shall have libertie to Record in the publique Rolles of any Court any Testimony given upon oath in the same Court, or before two Assistants, or any deede or evidence legally confirmed there to remaine in perpetuam rei memoriam, that is for perpetuall memoriall or evidence upon occasion. P. 131.

39 In all actions both reall and personall betweene partie and partie, the Court shall have power to respite execution for a convenient time, when in their prudence they see just cause so to doe. P. 7. S. 1.

40 No Conveyance, Deede, or promise whatsoever shall be of validitie, If it be gotten by Illegal violence, imprisonment, threatenings, or any kinde of forcible compulsion called Dures. P. 32. S. 3.

41 Everie man that is to Answere for any Criminall cause, whether he be in prison or under bayle, his cause shall be heard and determined at the next Court that hath proper Cognizance thereof, And may be done without prejudice of Justice. P. 38. S. 10

42 No man shall be twise sentenced by Civill Justice for one and the same Crime, offence, or Trespasse. P. 129.

43 No man shall be beaten with above 40 stripes, nor shall any true gentleman, nor any man equall to a gentleman be punished with whipping, unles his crime be very shamefull, and his course of life vitious and profligate. P. 129.

44 No man condemned to dye shall be put to death within fower dayes next after his condemnation, unles the Court see spetiall cause to the contrary, or in case of martiall law, nor shall the body of any man so put to death be unburied 12 howers, unlesse it be in case of Anatomie. P. 30.

45 No man shall be forced by Torture to confesse any Crime against himselfe nor any other unlesse it be in some Capitall case where he is first fullie convicted by cleare and suffitient evidence to be guilty, After which if the cause be of that nature, That it is very apparent there be other conspiratours, or confederates with him, Then he may be tortured, yet not with such Tortures as be Barbarous and inhumane. P. 129.

46 For bodilie punishments we allow amongst us none that are inhumane Barbarous or cruel. P. 129.

47 No man shall be put to death without the testimony of two or three witnesses or that which is equivalent thereunto. P. 158.

48. Every Inhabitant

48 Every Inhabitant of ye Countrie shall have free libertie to search and veewe any Rooles, Records, or Regesters of any Court or office except ye Councell, And to have a transcript or exemplification yrof written examined, & signed by ye hand of ye officer of ye office paying ye appointed fees therefore. p. 151 s. 3

49 No free man shall be compelled to serve upon Juries above two Courts in a yeare, except grand Jurie men, who shall hould two Courts together at ye least. p. 87 s. 5

50 All Jurors shall be chosen continuallie by ye freemen of ye Towne where they dwell. p. 86 s. 1

51 All Associates selected at any time to Assist ye Assistants in Inferior Courts, shall be nominated by ye Townes belonging to yt Court, by orderly agreemt amonge themselves.

52 Children, Idiots, Distracted persons, & all yt are strangers, or new comers to or plantation, shall have such allowances and dispensations in any cause whether Criminall or other as religion & reason require. p. 152 s. 4

53 The age of discretion for passing away of lands or such kinde of herediments, or for giveing of votes, verdicts or Sentence in any Civill Courts or causes, shall be one & twentie yeares. p. 1

54 When so ever any thing is to be put to vote, any sentence to be pronounced, or any other matter to be proposed, or read in any Court or Assembly, If ye president or moderator thereof shall refuse to performe it, ye Major parte of ye members of yt Court or Assembly shall have power to appoint any other meete man of them to do it, And if yr be just cause to punish him yt should & would not. p. 153

55 In all suites or Actions in any Court, the plaintife shall have libertie to make all ye titles & claims to yt he sues for he can. And ye Defendant shall have libertie to plead all ye pleas he can in answere to them, & ye Court shall judge according to ye intire evidence of all.

56 If any man shall behave himselfe offensively at any Towne meeting, ye rest of ye freemen then present, shall have power to sentence him for his offence, So be it ye mulct or penaltie exceede not twentie shilings. p. 147 s. 1

57 When so ever any person shall come to any very suddaine untimely & unnaturall death, Some Assistant, or ye Constables of yt Towne shall forthwith sumon a Jury of twelve free men to inquire of ye cause & manner of their death, & shall present a true verdict thereof to some neere Assistant, or ye next Court to be helde for yt Towne upon their oath. p. 39

Liberties more.

48 Every Inhabitant of the Country shall have free libertie to search and veewe any Rooles, Records, or Regesters of any Court or office except the Councell, And to have a transcript or exemplification thereof written examined. and signed by the hand of the officer of the office paying the appointed fees therefore. P. 131. S. 3.

49 No free man shall be compelled to serve upon Juries above two Courts in a yeare, except grand Jurie men, who shall hould two Courts together at the least. P. 87. S. 5.

50 All Jurors shall be chosen continuallie by the freemen of the Towne where they dwell. P. 86. S. 1.

51 All Associates selected at any time to Assist the Assistants in Inferior Courts shall be nominated by the Townes belonging to that Court, by orderly agreement amonge themselves.

52 Children, Idiots, Distracted persons, and all that are strangers, or new commers to our plantation, shall have such allowances and dispensations in any Cause whether Criminall or other as religion and reason require. P. 152. S. 4.

53 The age of discretion for passing away of lands or such kinde of heredîments, or for giveing of votes, verdicts or Sentence in any Civill Courts or causes, shall be one and twentie yeares. P. 1.

54 Whensoever anything is to be put to vote, any sentence to be pronounced, or any other matter to be proposed, or read in any Court or Assembly, If the president or moderator thereof shall refuse to performe it, the Major parte of the members of that Court or Assembly shall have power to appoint any other meete man of them to do it, And if there be just cause to punish him that should and would not. P. 153.

55 In all suites or Actions in any Court, the plaintife shall have libertie to make all the titles and claims to that he sues for he can. And the Defendant shall have libertie to plead all the pleas he can in answere to them, and the Court shall judge according to the entire evidence of all.

56 If any man shall behave himselfe offensively at any Towne meeting, the rest of the freemen then present, shall have power to sentence him for his offence. So be it the mulct or penaltie exceede not twentie shilings. P. 147. S. 1.

57 Whensoever any person shall come to any very suddaine untimely and unnaturall death, Some assistant, or the Constables of that Towne shall forthwith sumon a Jury of twelve free men to inquire of the cause and manner of their death, and shall present a true verdict thereof to some neere Assistant, or the next Court to be helde for that Towne upon their oath. P. 39.

39. Liberties more

Liberties ~~more pecu~~liarlie concerning the free men.

58 Civill Authoritie hath power and libertie to see the peace, ordinances and Rules of Christ observed in every church according to his word. so it be done in a Civill and not in an Ecclesiasticall way. p. 44 S. 11

59 Civill Authoritie hath power and libertie to deale with any Church member in a way of Civill Justice, notwithstanding any Church relation, office or interest. p. 44 S. 11

60 No church censure shall degrade or depose any man from any Civill dignitie, office, or Authoritie he shall have in the Comonwealth. p. 44 S. 10

61 No Magestrate, Juror, Officer, or other man shall be bound to informe present or reveale any private crim or offence, wherein there is no perill or danger to this plantation or any member thereof, when any necessarie tye of conscience binds him to secresie grounded upon the word of god, unlesse it be in case of testimony lawfully required. p. 86 S. 2

62 Any Shire or Towne shall have libertie to choose their Deputies whom and where they please for the Generall Court. So be it they be freemen, and have taken there oath of fealtie, and Inhabiting in this Jurisdiction. p. 40 S. 2

63 No Governour, Deputie Governour, Assistant, Associate, or grand Jury man at any Court, nor any Deputie for the Generall Court, shall at any time beare his owne chardges at any Court, but their necessary expences shall be defrayed either by the Towne, or Shire on whose service they are, or by the Country in generall. p. 22 S. 1

64 Everie Action betweene partie and partie, and proceedings against delinquents in Criminall causes shall be briefly and destinctly entered on the Rolles of every Court by the Recorder thereof. That such actions be not afterwards brought againe to the vexation of any man. p. 229 S. 1

65 No custome or prescription shall ever prevaile amongst us in any morall cause, our meaneing is maintaine any thinge that can be proved to bee morallie sinfull by the word of god. p. 126

66 The Freemen of every Township shall have power to make such by laws and constitutions as may concerne the wellfare of their Towne, provided they be not of a Criminall, but onely of a prudentiall nature, And that their penalties exceede not 20 sh. for one offence. And that they be not repugnant to the publique laws and orders of the Countrie. And if any Inhabitant shall neglect or refuse to observe them, they shall have power to levy the appointed penalties by distresse. p. 107 S. 1

67 It is the constant libertie of the free men of this plantation to choose yearly at the Court of Election out of the freemen all the Generall officers of this Jurisdiction. If they please to discharge them at the day of Election by way of vote. They may do it without shewing cause. But if at any other Generall Court, we hould it due justice, that the reasons thereof be alleadged and proved. By Generall officers we meane, our Governor, Deputy Governor, Assistants, Treasurer, Generall of our warres. And our Admirall at Sea, and such as are or hereafter may be of the like generall nature. p. 03 S. 9

68. It is the

Liberties more peculiarlie concerning the free men.

58 Civill Authoritie hath power and libertie to see the peace, ordinances and Rules of Christ observed in every church according to his word. so it be done in a Civill and not in an Ecclesiastical way. P. 44. S. 11.

59 Civill Authoritie hath power and libertie to deale with any Church member in a way of Civill Justice, notwithstanding any Church relation, office or interest. P. 44. S. 11.

60 No church censure shall degrad or depose any man from any Civill dignitie, office, or Authoritie he shall have in the Commonwealth. P. 44. S. 10.

61 No Magestrate, Juror, Officer, or other man shall be bound to informe present or reveale any private crim or offence, wherein there is no perill or danger to this plantation or any member thereof, when any necessarie tye of conscience binds him to secresie grounded upon the word of god, unlesse it be in case of testimony lawfully required. P. 86. S. 2.

62 Any Shire or Towne shall have libertie to choose their Deputies whom and where they please for the Generall Court. So be it they be free men, and have taken there oath of fealtie, and Inhabiting in this Jurisdiction. P. 40. S. 2.

63 No Governor, Deputy Governor, Assistant, Associate, or grand Jury man at any Court, nor any Deputie for the Generall Court shall at any time beare his owne chardges at any Court, but their necessary expences shall be defrayed either by the Towne or Shire on whose service they are, or by the Country in generall. P. 22. S. 1.

64 Everie Action betweene partie and partie, and proceedings against delinquents in Criminall causes shall be briefly and destinctly entered on the Rolles of every Court by the Recorder thereof. That such actions be not afterwards brought againe to the vexation of any man. P. 129. S. 1.

65 No custome or prescription shall ever prevaile amongst us in any morall cause, our meaneing is maintaine anythinge that can be proved to bee morrallie sinfull by the word of god. P. 126.

66 The Freemen of every Towneship shall have power to make such by laws and constitutions as may concerne the wellfare of their Towne, provided they be not of a Criminall, but onely of a prudentiall nature, And that their penalties exceede not 20 sh. for one offence. And that they be not repugnant to the publique laws and orders of the Countrie. And if any Inhabitant shall neglect or refuse to observe them, they shall have power to levy the appointed penalties by distresse. P. 147. S. 1.

67 It is the constant libertie of the free men of this plantation to choose yearly at the Court of Election out of the freemen all the General officers of this Jurisdiction. If they please to dischardge them at the day of Election by way of vote. They may do it without shewing cause. But if at any other generall Court, we hould it due justice, that the reasons thereof be alleadged and proved. By Generall officers we meane, our Governor, Deputy Governor, Assistants, Treasurer, Generall of our warres. And our Admirall at Sea, and such as are or hereafter may be of the like generall nature. P. 48. S. 4.

68. It is the

68 It is ye libertie of ye freemen to choose such deputies for ye Generall Court out of themselves, either in ye owne Townes or elsewhere as they judge fitest, And because we cannot foresee what varietie & weight of occasions may fall into future consideration, And what counsells we may stand in neede of, we decree. That ye Deputies (to attend ye Generall Court in ye behalfe of ye Countrie) shall not any time be stated or inacted, but from Court to Court, or at ye most but for one yeare, yt ye Countrie may have an Annuall libertie to do in yt case what is most behoofefull for ye best welfaire thereof. p. 40 S. 2

69 No Generall Court shall be desolved or adjourned without ye consent of ye Major parte thereof. p. 35 S. 5

70 All ffreemen called to give any advise, vote, verdict, or sentence in any Court, Counsell, or Civill Assembly, shall have full freedome to doe it according to their true Judgements & Consciences, So it be done orderly & inoffensively for ye manner. p. 153.

71 The Govr shall have a casting voice whensoever an Equi vote shall fall out in ye Court of Assistants, or generall assembly, So shall ye presedent or moderator have in all Civill Courts or Assemblies. p. 35. S. 6

72 The Govr & Dept Govr Joyntly consenting or any three Assistants concurring in consent shall have power out of Court to reprive a condemned malefactour, till ye next quarter or generall Court. The generall Court only shall have power to pardon a condemned malefactor. p. 38 S. 4

73 The Generall Court hath libertie & Authoritie to send out any member of this Comanwealth of what qualitie, condition or office whatsoever into forreine parts about any publique message or Negotiation. Provided ye partie sent be acquainted wth ye affaire he goeth about, and be willing to undertake ye service. p. 38 S. 4

74 The freemen of every Towne or Towneship, shall have full power to choose yearly or for lesse time out of themselves a convenient number of fitt men to order ye planting or prudentiall occasions of yt Towne, according to Instructions given them in writeing, Provided nothing be done by them contrary to ye publique lawes & orders of ye Countrie. Provided also ye number of such select persons be not above nine. p. 148 S. 2

75 It is & shall be ye libertie of any member or members of any Court Councell or Civill Assembly in cases of makeing or executing any order or law, yt properlie concerne religion, or any cause capitall, or warres, or Subscription to any publique Articles or Remonstrance, in case they cannot in Judgement & conscience consent to yt way the Major vote or suffrage goes, to make their contra Remonstrance or protestation in speech or writeing, & upon request to have their dissent recorded in ye Rolles of that Court. So it be done Christianlie & respectively for ye manner. And their dissent onely be entered without ye reasons thereof, for ye avoiding of tediousness. p. 128

76 Whensoever

68 It is the libertie of the freemen to choose such deputies for the Generall Court out of themselves, either in their owne Townes or elsewhere as they judge fitest. And because we cannot foresee what varietie and weight of occasions may fall into future consideration, And what counsells we may stand in neede of, we decree. That the Deputies (to attend the Generall Court in the behalfe of the Countrie) shall not any time be stated or inacted, but from Court to Court, or at the most but for one yeare, that the Countrie may have an Annuall libertie to do in that case what is most behoofefull for the best welfaire thereof. P. 40. S. 2.

69 No Generall Court shall be desolved or adjourned without the consent of the Major parte thereof. P. 35. S. 5.

70 All Freemen called to give any advise, vote, verdict, or sentence in any Court, Counsell, or Civill Assembly, shall have full freedome to doe it according to their true Judgements and Consciences, So it be done orderly and inofensively for the manner. P. 153.

71 The Governor shall have a casting voice whensoever an Equi vote shall fall out in the Court of Assistants, or generall assembly, So shall the presedent or moderator have in all Civill Courts or Assemblies. P. 35. S. 6.

72 The Governor and Deputy Governor Joyntly consenting or any three Assistants concurring in consent shall have power out of Court to reprive a condemned malefactour, till the next quarter or generall Court. The generall Court onely shall have power to pardon a condemned malefactor. P. 35. S. 4.

73 The Generall Court hath libertie and Authoritie to send out any member of this Comanwealth of what qualitie, condition or office whatsoever into forreine parts about any publique message or Negotiation. Provided the partie sent be acquainted with the affaire he goeth about, and be willing to undertake the service. P. 35. S. 4.

74 The freemen of every Towne or Township, shall have full power to choose yearly or for lesse time out of themselves a convenient number of fitt men to order the planting or prudentiall occasions of that Town, according to Instructions given them in writeing, Provided nothing be done by them contrary to the publique laws and orders of the Countrie, provided also the number of such select persons be not above nine. P. 148. S. 2.

75 It is and shall be the libertie of any member or members of any Court, Councell or Civill Assembly in cases of makeing or executing any order or law, that properlie concerne religion, or any cause capitall, or warres, or Subscription to any publique Articles or Remonstrance, in case they cannot in Judgement and conscience consent to that way the Major vote or suffrage goes, to make their contra Remonstrance or protestation in speech or writeing, and upon request to have their dissent recorded in the Rolles of that Court. So it be done Christianlie and respectively for the manner. And their dissent onely be entered without the reasons thereof, for the avoiding of tediousness. P. 128

76. Whensoever

76 When so ever any Jurie of trialls or Jurours are not cleare in their
Judgmts or consciences conserneing any cause where in they are to give p. 89
ye verdict, they shall have libertie in open Court to advise wth any man S P
they thinke fitt to resolve or direct them, before they give in ye verdict.

77 In all cases where in any freeman is to give his vote, be it in point of
Election, making constitutions & orders, or passing sentence in any case p. 183
of Judicature or ye like, if he can not see reason to give it positively
one way or an other, he shall have libertie to be silent, & not pressed
to a determined vote.

78 The Generall or publique Treasure or any parte thereof shall never be ex=
spended but by ye appointmt of a Generall Court, nor any Shire Treasure, p. 150
but by ye appointmt of ye freemen there of, nor any Towne Treasurie S. 1. 2
but by ye freemen of ye Towneship.

Liberties of Woemen

79 If any man at his death shall not leave his wife a competent portion
of his estaite, upon iust complaint made to ye Genll Court she shall be
relieved.

80 Everie marryed woeman shall be free from bodilie correction or
stripes by her husband, unlesse it be in his owne defence upon her
assalt. If there be any just cause of correction complaint shall be made p. 101
to Authoritie assembled in some Court, from wch onely she shall receive it. S. 2

Liberties of Children

81 When parents dye intestate, ye Elder sonne shall have a doble portion p. 158
of his whole estate reall & personall, unlesse ye Genll Court upon S. 3
iust cause alleadged shall judge otherwise.

82 When parents dye intestate, haveing noe heires males of their bodies
their Daughters shall Inherit as Copartners, unles ye Genll Court p. 153
upon iust reason shall iudge otherwise. S. 3

83 If any parents shall wilfullie & unreasonably deny any childe time
ly or convenient mariage, or shall exercise any unnaturall seve= p. 28
ritie towards them, such childeren shall have free libertie to S. 5
complaine to Authoritie for redresse.

84 No Orphan dureing their minoritie wch was not committed to tu
ition or service by the parents in their life time, shall afterwards
be absolutely disposed of by any kindred, freind, Executor, Towne= p. 28
ship or Church, nor by them selves without ye consent of some Court S. 6
where in two Assistants at least shall be present.

Liberties of Servants

85 If any servants shall flee from ye Tiranny & crueltie of their masters
to ye howse of any freeman of ye same Towne, they shall be there protected & p. 105
susteyned till due order be taken for their relife. Provided due notice thereof be S. 6
speedily given to their maisters from whom they fled. And ye next Assistant or
Constable where ye partie flying is harboured.

86 No servant

76 Whensoever any Jurie of trialls or Jurours are not cleare in their Judgements or consciences conserneing any cause wherein they are to give their verdict, They shall have libertie in open Court to advise with any man they thinke fitt to resolve or direct them, before they give in their verdict. P. 87. S. 5.

77 In all cases wherein any freeman is to give his vote, be it in point of Election, makeing constitutions and orders, or passing sentence in any case of Judicature or the like, if he cannot see reason to give it positively one way or an other, he shall have libertie to be silent, and not pressed to a determined vote. P. 153.

78 The Generall or publique Treasure or any parte thereof shall never be exspended but by the appointment of a Generall Court, nor any Shire Treasure, but by the appointment of the freemen thereof, nor any Towne Treasurie but by the freemen of that Towneship. P. 150. S. 1, 2.

Liberties of Woemen.

79 If any man at his death shall not leave his wife a competent portion of his estaite, upon just complaint made to the Generall Court she shall be relieved.

80 Everie marryed woeman shall be free from bodilie correction or stripes by her husband, unlesse it be in his owne defence upon her assalt. If there be any just cause of correction complaint shall be made to Authoritie assembled in some Court, from which onely she shall receive it. P. 101. S. 1.

Liberties of Children.

81 When parents dye intestate, the Elder sonne shall have a doble portion of his whole estate reall and personall, unlesse the Generall Court upon just cause alleadged shall Judge otherwise. P. 158. S. 3.

82 When parents dye intestate haveing noe heires males of their bodies their Daughters shall inherit as copartners, unles the Generall Court upon just reason shall judge otherwise. P. 158. S. 3.

83 If any parents shall wilfullie and unreasonably deny any childe timely or convenient mariage, or shall exercise any unnaturall severitie towards them, such childeren shall have free libertie to complaine to Authoritie for redresse. P. 28. S. 5.

84 No Orphan dureing their minoritie which was not committed to tuition or service by the parents in their life time shall afterwards be absolutely disposed of by any kindred, freind, Executor, Towneship, or Church, nor by themselves without the consent of some Court, wherein two Assistants at least shall be present. P. 28. S. 6.

Liberties of Servants

85 If any servants shall flee from the Tiranny and crueltie of their masters to the howse of any freeman of the same Towne, they shall be there protected and susteyned till due order be taken for their relife. Provided due notice thereof be speedily given to their maisters from whom they fled. And the next Assistant or Constable where the partie flying is harboured. P. 105. S. 6.

86. No servant

86 No servant shall be put of for above a yeare to any other neither in ye life time of ye maister nor after ye death by ye Executors or Administrators unlesse it be by consent of Authoritie assembled in some Court, or two Assistants. p. 108 S. 7

87 If any man smite out ye eye or tooth of his man servant, or maid servant, or otherwise mayme or much disfigure him, unlesse it be by meere casualtie, he shall let them goe free from his service. And shall have such further recompense as ye Court shall allow him. p. 108 S. 8

88 Servants yt have served deligentlie & faithfully to ye benefitt of their maisters seaven yeares, shall not be sent away emptie. And if any have bene unfaithfull, negligent or unprofitable in their service, notwithstanding ye good usage of their maisters, they shall not be dismissed till they have made satisfaction according to ye Judgement of Authoritie. p. 105 S. 9

Liberties of Forreiners & Strangers

89 If any people of other Nations professing ye true Christian Religion shall flee to us from ye Tiranny or oppression of their persecutors, or from famyne, warres, or ye like necessary & compulsarie cause they shall be entertayned & succoured amongst us, according to yt power & prudence god shall give us. p. 143

90 If any ships or other vessels, be it freind or enemy, shall suffer shipwrack upon our coast. there shall be no violence or wrong offerred to their persons or goods. But their persons shall be harboured, & relieved, & their goods preserved in safety till Authoritie may be certified thereof, & shall take further order therein. p. 162

91 There shall never be any bond slaverie villinage or Captivitie amongst us, unles it be lawfull Captives taken in iust warres, & such strangers as willingly selle themselves or are sold to us. And these shall have all the liberties & Christian usages wch ye law of god established in Israell concerning such persons doeth morally require. This exempts none from servitude who shall be Judged thereto by Authoritie. p. 10

Off the Bruite Creature

92 No man shall exercise any Tirranny or Crueltie towards any bruite Creature wch are usuallie kept for mans use. p. 39

93 If any man shall have occasion to leade or drive Cattel from place to place that is far of, so yt they be weary, or hungry, or fall sick, or lambe, It shall be lawfull to rest or refresh them, for competent time, in any open place that is not Corne, meadow, or inclosed for some peculiar use. p. 141

Capitall Lawes.

86 No servant shall be put of for above a yeare to any other neither in the life time of their maister nor after their death by their Executors or Administrators unlesse it be by consent of Authoritie assembled in some Court or two Assistants. P. 105. S. 7.

87 If any man smite out the eye or tooth of his man-servant, or maid servant, or otherwise mayme or much disfigure him, unlesse it be by meere casualtie, he shall let them goe free from his service. And shall have such further recompense as the Court shall allow him. P. 105. S. 8.

88 Servants that have served deligentlie and faithfully to the benefitt of their maisters seaven yeares, shall not be sent away emptie. And if any have bene unfaithfull, negligent or unprofitable in their service, notwithstanding the good usage of their maisters, they shall not be dismissed till they have made satisfaction according to the Judgement of Authoritie. P. 105. S. 9.

Liberties of Forreiners and Strangers.

89 If any people of other Nations professing the true Christian Religion shall flee to us from the Tiranny or oppression of their persecutors, or from famyne, warres, or the like necessary and compulsarie cause, They shall be entertayned and succoured amongst us, according to that power and prudence god shall give us. P. 143.

90 If any ships or other vessels, be it freind or enemy, shall suffer shipwrack upon our Coast, there shall be no violence or wrong offerred to their persons or goods. But their persons shall be harboured, and relieved, and their goods preserved in safety till Authoritie may be certified thereof, and shall take further order therein. P. 161.

91 There shall never be any bond slaverie, villinage or Captivitie amongst us unles it be lawfull Captives taken in just warres, and such strangers as willingly selle themselves or are sold to us. And these shall have all the liberties and Christian usages which the law of god established in Israell concerning such persons doeth morally require. This exempts none from servitude who shall be Judged thereto by Authoritie. P. 10.

Off the Bruite Creature.

92 No man shall exercise any Tirranny or Crueltie towards any bruite Creature which are usuallie kept for man's use. P. 39.

93 If any man shall have occasion to leade or drive Cattel from place to place that is far of, so that they be weary, or hungry, or fall sick, or lambe, It shall be lawful to rest or refresh them, for a competent time, in any open place that is not Corne, meadow, or inclosed for some peculiar use. P. 42.

Capitall Laws

Capitall Lawes

94 Deut. 13.6.10 Deut. 17.2.6 Ex. 22.20 — If any man after legall conviction shall have or worship p.4
any other god, but ye lord god, he shall be put to death. S.1

2

Ex. 22.18. Lev. 20.27. Deut. 18.10. — If any man or woman be a witch, (that is hath or consulteth wth a familiar spirit,) they shall be put to death. S.2

3

Lev. 24.15.16 — If any person shall blaspheme ye name of god, the father, sonne or Holie ghost, wth direct, expresse, presumptuous S.3
or high handed blasphemie, or shall curse god in ye like manner, he shall be put to death.

4

Ex. 21.12. Numb. 35.13 14. 30.31. — If any person committ any wilfull murther, wch is manslaughter, committed upon premeditated mallice, hatred, S.4
or crueltie, not in a mans necessarie & iust defence, nor by meere casualtie against his will, he shall be put to death.

5

Num. 25.20 21. Lev. 24.17. — If any person slayeth an other suddainely in his anger
or crueltie of passion, he shall be put to death. S.5

6

Ex. 21.14. — If any person shall slay an other through guile, either by S.6
poysoning or other such divelish practice, he shall be put to death.

7

Lev. 20.15. 16. — If any man or woman shall lye wth any beast or brute S.7
creature by carnall copulation, they shall surely be put to death. And ye beast shall be slaine, & buried & not eaten.

8

Lev. 20.13. — If any man lyeth wth mankinde as he lyeth wth a woeman, both
of them have committed abhomination, they both shall surely be put to death. S.9

9

Lev. 20.19. & 18.20. Deut. 22.23. 24. — If any person committeth Adultery wth a maried or espoused wife, S.9
the Adulterer & Adulteresse shall surely be put to death.

10

Ex. 21.16 — If any man stealeth a man or mankinde, he shall surely be put S.10
to death.

11

Deut. 19.16 18.19. — If any man rise up by false witnes, wittingly & of purpose S.11
to take away any mans life; he shall be put to death.

12

If any man shall conspire & attempt any invasion, insurrection, or publique rebellion agt or comon wealth, or shall in- S.12
deavour to surprize any towne or townes, fort or forts therin, or shall treacherously & perfidiouslie attempt ye alteration & subversion of or frame of politie or Government fundamentallie, he shall be put to death.

A declaration

94. *Capitall Laws.*

1.

Dut. 13. 6, 10. Dut. 17. 2, 6. If any man after legall conviction shall have or worship P. 14.
Ex. 22. 20. any other god, but the lord god, he shall be put to death. S. 1.

2.

Ex. 22. 18. Lev. 20. 27. If any man or woeman be a witch, (that is hath or con- S. 2.
Dut. 18. 10. sulteth with a familiar spirit,) They shall be put to death.

3.

If any man shall Blaspheme the name of god, the father,
Lev. 24. 15, 16. Sonne or Holie ghost, with direct, expresse, presumptuous S. 3.
or high handed blasphemie, or shall curse god in the like
manner, he shall be put to death.

4.

Ex. 21. 12. If any person committ any wilfull murther, which is man- S. 4.
Numb. 35. 13, slaughter, committed upon premeditated mallice, hatred,
14, 30, 31. or Crueltie, not in a mans necessarie and just defence,
nor by meere casualtie against his will, he shall be
put to death.

5.

Numb. 25. 20, 21. If any person slayeth an other suddaienly in his anger S. 5.
Lev. 24. 17. or Crueltie of passion, he shall be put to death.

6.

If any person shall slay an other through guile, either by
Ex. 21. 14. poysoning or other such divelish practice, he shall be put to death. S. 6.

7.

Lev. 20. 15, If any man or woeman shall lye with any beaste or bruite S. 7.
16. creature by Carnall Copulation, They shall surely be put to
death. And the beast shall be slaine and buried and not eaten.

8.

If any man lyeth with mankinde as he lyeth with a woeman, both S. 8.
Lev. 20. 13. of them have committed abbomination, they both shall surely
be put to death.

9.

Lev. 20. 19, and 18, 20. If any person committeth Adultery with a maried or espoused wife, S. 9.
Dut. 22. 23, 24. the Adulterer and Adulteresse shall surely be put to death.

10.

If any man stealeth a man or mankinde, he shall surely be put
Ex. 21. 16. to death. S. 10.

11.

Deut. 19. 16, If any man rise up by false witnes, wittingly and of purpose S. 11.
18, 19. to take away any mans life, he shall be put to death.

12.

If any man shall conspire and attempt any invasion, insurrec- S. 12.
tion, or publique rebellion against our commonwealth, or shall in-
deavour to surprize any Towne or Townes, fort or forts therein,
or shall treacherously and perfediouslie attempt the alteration
and subversion of our frame of politie or Government fundamentallie, he shall be put to death.

A declaration

A Declaration of the Liberties the Lord Jesus hath given to ye Churches.

95. 1 All ye people of god wth in this Jurisdiction who are not
in a church way, & be orthodox in Judgement, & not — p. 49.
scandalous in life, shall have full libertie to gather S. 1.
themselves into a Church Estaite. Provided they doe
it in a Christian way, wth due observation of ye rules
of Christ revealed in his word.

2 Every Church hath full libertie to exercise all ye ordi- S. 3
nances of god, according to ye rules of scripture.

3 Every Church hath free libertie of Election & ordination S. 4.
of all their officers from time to time, provided they
be able, pious & orthodox.

4 Every Church hath free libertie of Admission, Recommendation, Dismission, & Expulsion, or deposall of their S. 5
officers, & members, upon due cause, wth free exercise
of ye Discipline & Censures of Christ according to the
rules of his word.

5 No Injunctions are to be put upon any Church, Church S. 6
Officers or member in point of Doctrine, worship or
Discipline, whether for substance or cercumstance besides
ye Institutions of ye lord.

6 Every Church of Christ hath freedome to celebrate S. 7.
dayes of fasting & prayer, & of thanksgiving according
to ye word of god

7. The Elders of Churches have free libertie to meete
monthly, Quarterly, or otherwise, in convenient — S. 8
numbers & places, for conferences, & consultations
about Christian & Church questions & occasions.

8 All churches have libertie to deale wth any of their S. 9
members in a church way yt are in ye hand of Justice.
So it be not to retard or hinder ye course yrof.

9 Every Church hath libertie to deale wth any magestrate, Deputie of Court or other officer what soe p. 49.
ever yt is a member in a church way in case of appa- S. 10
rent & just offence given in their places. so it be done
wth due observance & respect.

10 Wee allowe private meetings for edification in religion amongst Christians of all sortes of people. So S. 12
it be wthout just offence both for number, time, place
& other cercumstances.

11. for ye preventing

95. *A Declaration of the Liberties the Lord Jesus hath given to the Churches.*

1 All the people of god within this Jurisdiction who are not in a church way, and be orthodox in Judgement, and not scandalous in life, shall have full libertie to gather themselves into a Church Estaite. Provided they doe it in a Christian way, with due observation of the rules of Christ revealed in his word. P. 43 S. 1.

2 Every Church hath full libertie to exercise all the ordinances of god, according to the rules of scripture. S. 3.

3 Every Church hath free libertie of Election and ordination of all their officers from time to time, provided they be able, pious and orthodox. S. 4.

4 Every Church hath free libertie of Admission, Recommendation, Dismission, and Expulsion, or deposall of their officers and members, upon due cause, with free exercise of the Discipline and Censures of Christ according to the rules of his word. S. 5.

5 No Injunctions are to be put upon any Church, Church officers or member in point of Doctrine, worship or Discipline, whether for substance or cercumstance besides the Institutions of the lord. S. 6.

6 Every Church of Christ hath freedome to celebrate dayes of fasting and prayer, and of thanksgiveing according to the word of god. S. 7.

7 The Elders of Churches have free libertie to meete monthly, Quarterly, or otherwise, in convenient numbers and places, for conferences and consultations about Christian and Church questions and occasions. S. 8.

8 All Churches have libertie to deale with any of their members in a church way that are in the hand of Justice. So it be not to retard or hinder the course thereof. S. 9.

9 Every Church hath libertie to deale with any magestrate, Deputie of Court or other officer what soe ever that is a member in a church way in case of apparent and just offence given in their places, so it be done with due observance and respect. P. 44. S. 10.

10 Wee allowe private meetings for edification in religion amongst Christians of all sortes of people. So it be without just offence for number, time, place, and other cercumstances. S. 12.

11. For the preventing

11 for the preventing & removeing of errour & offence
that may grow & spread in any of ye Churches in this
Jurisdiction. And for ye preserveing of trueth & peace in
ye severall churches within themselves, & for the —
maintenance & exercise of brotherly communion, amongst
all ye churches in ye Countrie, It is allowed & ratified,
by ye Authoritie of this Generall Court as a lawfull —
libertie of ye Churches of Christ. That once in every
month of ye yeare (when ye season will beare it)
It shall be lawfull for ye ministers & Elders, of ye
Churches neere adioyneing together, wth any other
of ye bretheren wth ye consent of ye churches to assemble by course in each severall Church one after an other. To ye intent after ye preaching of ye word
by such a minister as shall be requested thereto by ye
Elders of ye church where ye Assembly is held, The rest
of ye day may be spent in publique Christian Conference
about ye discussing & resolveing of any such doubts &
cases of conscience concerning matter of doctrine —
or worship or government of ye church as shall be propounded by any of ye Bretheren of yt church, wth leave also to
any other Brother to propound his objections or answeres
for further satisfaction according to ye word of god.
Provided yt ye whole action be guided & moderated by
ye Elders of ye Church where ye Assemblie is helde, or
by such others as they shall appoint. And yt no thing be
concluded & imposed by way of Authoritie from one or
more Churches upon an other, but onely by way of
Brotherly conference & consultations. That ye trueth
may be searched out to ye satisfying of every mans conscience in ye sight of god according to his worde. And
because such an Assembly & ye worke thereof can not
be duely attended to if other lectures be held in ye
same weeke. It is therefore agreed wth ye consent of ye
Churches. That in yt weeke when such an Assembly is held.
All ye lectures in all ye neighbouring Churches for yt weeke
shall be forborne. That so ye publique service of Christ
in this more sollemne Assembly may be transacted wth
greater deligence & attention.

96 Jlowfo

11 For the preventing and removeing of errour and offence that may grow and spread in any of the Churches in this Jurisdiction, and for the preserveing of trueith and peace in the several churches within themselves, and for the maintenance and exercise of brotherly communion, amongst all the churches in the Countrie, It is allowed and ratified, by the Authoritie of this Generall Court as a lawfull libertie of the Churches of Christ. That once in every month of the yeare (when the season will beare it) It shall be lawfull for the minesters and Elders, of the Churches neere adjoyneing together, with any other of the breetheren with the consent of the churches to assemble by course in each severall Church one after an other. To the intent after the preaching of the word by such a minister as shall be requested thereto by the Elders of the church where the Assembly is held, The rest of the day may be spent in publique Christian Conference about the discussing and resolveing of any such doubts and cases of conscience concerning matter of doctrine or worship or government of the church as shall be propounded by any of the Breetheren of that church, with leave also to any other Brother to propound his objections or answeres for further satisfaction according to the word of god. Provided that the whole action be guided and moderated by the Elders of the Church where the Assemblie is helde, or by such others as they shall appoint. And that no thing be concluded and imposed by way of Authoritie from one or more Churches upon an other, but onely by way of Brotherly conference and consultations. That the trueth may be searched out to the satisfying of every mans conscience in the sight of god according his worde. And because such an Assembly and the worke theirof can not be duely attended to if other lectures be held in the same weeke. It is therefore agreed with the consent of the Churches. That in that weeke when such an Assembly is held, All the lectures in all the neighbouring Churches for that weeke shall be forborne. That so the publique service of Christ in this more solemne Assembly may be transacted with greater deligence and attention.

96. Howso-

96 How so ever these above specified rites, freedomes, Immunities, Authorities & priveledges, both Civill & Ecclesiasticall are expressed onely under ye name & title of Liberties, & not in ye exact forme of Laws, or Statutes, yet we do wth one consent fullie Authorise, & earnestly intreate all yt are & shall be in Authoritie to consider them as laws, & not to faile to inflict condigne & proportionable punishments upon every man impartiallie, yt shall infringe or violate any of them.

97 Wee likewise give full power & libertie to any person yt shall at any time be denyed or deprived of any of them, to commence & prosecute their suite, Complaint, or action agt any man yt shall so doe, in any Court yt hath proper Cognizance or iudicature thereof.

98 Lastly because our dutie & desire is to do nothing suddainlie wch fundamentally concerne us. we decree yt these rites & liberties, shall be Audably read & deliberately weighed at every Generall Court yt shall be held, wth in three yeares next insueing, And such of them as shall not be altered or repealed they shall stand so ratified, that no man shall infringe them wth out due punishment.

And if any Generall Court wth in these next thre yeares shall faile or forget to reade & consider them as abovesaid. The Govr & Deput Govr for ye time being, & every Assistant present at such Courts. shall forfeite 20sh a man. & everie Deputie 10sh a man for each neglect. wch shall be paid out of their proper estate, & not by ye Country or ye townes wch choose them. & whensoever there shall arise any question in any Court among ye Assistants & Associates thereof about ye explanation of these Rites & liberties. The Generall Court onely shall have power to interprett them.

96 Howsoever these above specified rites, freedomes, Immunities, Authorities and priveledges, both Civill and Ecclesiastical are expressed onely under the name and title of Liberties, and not in the exact form of Laws or Statutes, yet we do with one consent fullie Authorise, and earnestly intreate all that are and shall be in Authoritie to consider them as laws, and not to faile to inflict condigne and proportionable punishments upon every man impartiallie, that shall infringe or violate any of them.

97 Wee likewise give full power and libertie to any person that shall at any time be denyed or deprived of any of them, to commence and prosecute their suite, Complaint or action against any man that shall so doe in any Court that hath proper Cognizance or judicature thereof.

98 Lastly because our dutie and desire is to do nothing suddainlie which fundamentally concerne us, we decree that these rites and liberties, shall be Audably read and deliberately weighed at every Generall Court that shall be held, within three yeares next insueing, And such of them as shall not be altered or repealed they shall stand so ratified, That no man shall infringe them without due punishment.

And if any Generall Court within these next thre yeares shall faile or forget to reade and consider them as abovesaid. The Governor and Deputy Governor for the time being, and every Assistant present at such Courts shall forfeite 20sh. a man, and everie Deputie 10sh. a man for each neglect, which shall be paid out of their proper estate, and not by the Country or the Townes which choose them, and whensoever there shall arise any question in any Court amonge the Assistants and Associates thereof about the explanation of these Rites and liberties, The Generall Court onely shall have power to interprett them.

INDEX TO BODY OF LIBERTIES.

REFERENCES ARE TO THE NUMBER OF THE LIBERTY.

APPENDIX.

CONTAINING FAC-SIMILES OF THOSE PAGES OF THE ANSWER OF THE GENERAL COURT IN 1646, WHICH CONTAIN REFERENCES TO THE BODY OF LIBERTIES. (See *ante*, p. 16.)

(From the Elisha Hutchinson MS. in the Boston Athenæum.)

Foundamentall Lawes of ye Massachusetts Collonie in New England
Boston · 4·(9)·1646

Ffoundamentalls of ye Massachusetts

1 All psons orthodoxe in Judgement & not scandalous in life, may gather into a Church estaite, according to ye gospell of Jesus Christ. Libr. 2.
Such may choose & ordaine ye owne officers, & exercise all ye ordinances of Christ wth out Iniunction in doctrine, worship, or discipline. Libr. 3. & 5. in Eccles.

2 No mans life, honour, liberty, wife, children, goods or estaite, shall be taken away, punished or endamaged, under colour of law, or countenance of Authoritie, but by an expresse law of ye Genll Court, or in defect of such law, by ye word of god &c. Lib. 1.
Every pson wth in this Jurisdiction &c shall enjoy ye same justice and law &c wth out partiality or delay &c Lib. 2.
All ye lands & hereditaments shall be free from all fines, forfeitures &c Libr: 10
Every man may remove himselfe & his familie &c if ye be no legall impediment. Libr. 17.

3. The free men of every towne may dispose of ye towne lands &c & may make such orders, as may be for ye well ordering of ye townes &c, & may choose ye Constables & other officers. 1·(month) 1635.

4 One measure is appointed through ye Countrie according to the Kings coṁandard. (3m) 1631. & 1638.

5 Courts of Judicature shall be kept at Boston for Suffolke, at Cambrige for midlesex, at Salem & Ipswich for Essex &c upon certaine dayes yearly. (1m) 1635.

6 Difficult cases are finally determinable in ye Court of Assistants, or in ye Generall Court, by appeale or petition, or by reference from ye Inferiour Courts. Libr. 31. & 36.

7 upon uniust suites ye plt shall be fyned proportionable to his offence. Lib. 37.
No mans goods shall be taken away but by due course of Justice. Lib. 1.
In Criminall causes it shall be at ye libertie of ye accused partie to be tryed by ye Bench or by a Jurie. Lib. 29.
We do not fine or sentence any man but upon sufficient testimony upon oath, or confession. Custome

8 Wager of law is not allowed but according to this law, & according to. Exod. 22·8.

9 Letters testimoniall are granted to merchants, when there is occasion. Custome

Fundamentalls of

ffoundamentalls of the Massachusetts

1 The highest Authoritie here is in our Generall Court, both by or Charter & or owne positive Lawes. (3) 1634 &c.

2 In or Genrll Court ye people are present by their deputies, so as no thing can passe without their allowance. ꝑ Charter. & (1) 1635

3 Our deputies are chosen for all ye people, but not by all ye people, but onely by ye Company of freemen, according to or Charter.

4 The Govr & Assistants being ye Aristocraticall, & ye deputies ye Democraticall part, yet make but one Court though they sitt & act a part, & either of them hath alike Negative power. ꝑ Chartam. & (1) 1635

5 The Acts of this Genrll Court do binde all wth in this Jurisdiction, as well non-freemen, who have no vote in Election of ye members of ye Court, as ye freemen who choose them. ꝑ Chartam

6 This Government in ye subordinate exercise thereof, is either in Courts of Judicature, or out of Court, ꝑ Chartam. & many positive Lawes.

7 In or Courts of Judicature all causes Civill & Criminall are determinable, either by ye Judges & Jury, or by ye Judges alone &c as in England. This is both Custome & by divers speciall lawes established, according to or Charter. as Lib. 29. &c

8 In ye vacancy of ye Genrll Court ye Govr & Assistants are ye standing councell to take order in all such affaires. ꝑ Chartam. & (8) 1644

9 The Govr & Assistants out of Court have power to preserve ye peace &c. ꝑ Chartam, & Custome, & divers speciall lawes.

10 Our ministeriall officers are Marshalls, Constables, Clarkes &c.

11 Our ordinary processe are Summons, Attachments, distresses &c ꝑ Chartam.

12 In all Criminall offences, where ye law hath prescribed no certaine penalty, ye Judges have power to inflict penalties, according to ye rule of gods word. — Lib. 1. & by ye Charter &c

13 Treason, murther, witchcraft, Sodomie, & other such notorious Crimes are punished wth death. but Theft &c is not so punished because we reade otherwise in ye Scripture. Capitalls &c.

14 Adultery is punished according to ye Canon of ye spirituall lawe. viz. ye Scriptures. Capitalls.

15 All publick charges are defrayed out of ye publick Stock. Custome. & Lib. 63.

16 when we have no publick Stock, we supply or necessary publick charges, by Assesment, raised by ye Generall Court

17 The Genrll Court intends an Equall Assesment upon every Towne & pson, & indevors it, by ye best meanes they can invent, (yet in some cases ye falls out inequality) this is levied by distresse of such as are able, & yet refuse to pay. Custome. & orders of Court.

18

ffundamentalls of the massachusetts

18 The Generll Court is not bound to give account of ye expence of the sex- Assesments, yet they doe sometimes, for all mens satisfaction.

19 No mans pson shall be restrained or imprisoned &c (before ye law hath sentenced him thereto) if he can put in sufficient Baile &c. Except in Crimes Capitall. Lib. 18.

20 The full age for passing lands, giving voates &c is 21 years. Lib. 53.

21 Married women can not dispose of any estate &c nor can sue or be sued wth out theire husband. Lib. 14. & Custome.

22 In Civill Actions a man may appeare & defend by his Atturney. Custome

1 The Eldest sonne is preferred before ye yonger in his Ancestors inheritance. Lib. 81.

2 Daughters shall inherit as Copartners. Lib. 82.

3 No Custome or prescription shall ever prevaile &c to maintaine any thing morally sinfull. Lib. 65.

4 Civill Authoritie may deale wth any Church member, or officer, in a way of Civill Justice. Lib. 59.

5 Publick Records are open to all Inhabitants. Lib. 48.

6 No man shall be twise sentenced by Civill Justice for ye same offence. Lib. 42.

7 No man shall be urged to take any oath, or subscribe any Articles, Covenant, or Remonstrance, of a publick & Civill nature, but such as ye Generll Court hath Considered allowed & required. Lib. 3.

By this it may appeare yt or pollitie & foundamentalls are framed according to ye Lawes of England & according to or Charter. &c

PART SECOND:

BEING

THE ACCOUNT OF THE LEGISLATION FROM 1641 TO 1672, INCLUDING THE TWO REVISIONS OF THE LAWS IN 1649 AND 1660.

[While these pages were in the printers' hands, Mr. A. C. Goodell, jr., has kindly called my attention to the following important order which is preserved in Mass. Archives, Vol. 88, page 386. Although it has all the marks of an order duly passed by both branches of the Legislature, it will not be found in the printed journals.

The date must be 1652, since that is the only year giving us the necessary coincidence of Bellingham and Glover as magistrates. Glover served only in 1652 and 1653, but in the latter year Bellingham was deputy-governor, and ever afterwards till 1664, except in 1654 when he was governor. I feel sure that with the care taken in bestowing honorary titles at that date, Bellingham would not have been termed simply a magistrate when he was deputy-governor.

This order probably was acted upon, and the report, as amended by the Deputies, was, I presume, presented to the Court in 1653, which "took care of the transcribing" by passing the order of Sept. 10, 1653, printed by me, *post*, p. 95.

The phrase which occurs in this order of 1652, "records that are not extracted, abbreviated or composed *into the books of the printed laws*," may perhaps be cited as an additional proof that at that date there were *two* printed books of the laws, viz. the Code of 1649 and the supplement of 1650, as discussed by me, *post*, p. 80.

W. H. W.]

"Forasmuch as their are two old bookes of Records belonging to the Generall court wherin are many Things involved which are of great concernment as well as in Rights and bounds of Lands as other material things; which bookes are decaid and very Imethodicall, as Well in finding out any Record, as allso in Severall circumstantiall errors in entreing Some of the orders; for Regulating whereof.

This Court orders that a committe be appointed in the vacancy of the court to overlooke those two books of Records afforsaid, and to correct all such circumstantiall errors in words in them contained, but not to alter anything for substanc and matter; and after the said books be viued and Corrected as before, then the Secretary is to take care that the said bookes bee truly transcribed into new books of Good paper, well bound, and covered with velume or parchment, and marginall abreviats of each order colected, an alphebeticall table affixed for finding out of all orders therein, and all due chardge for transcription of the said bookes be duly paid unto the Secretary by the country.

The Magistrates have past this with reference to the consent of our brethren, the Deputies.

Jo. Endecott, Govr."

"The Deputies thinke meete a Comittee shall examine all the records that are not extracted, abbreviated, or composed into the bookes of the printed lawes, and shall make amendment of all circumstantial errors without altering the substance, and present the same to the next sessions of court which may take care of the transcribing them; and Mr. Hill, Capt. Johnson and the Secretary are desired to Joyne with some of the magistrates as a comittee for that end.

Wm. Torrey, Cleric."

"The Magistrates have voted Mr. Bellingham and Mr. Glover to Joyne with the Comitee of the brethren the Deputies to serve in the courte of election.

Edward Rawson, Secret."

"Consented to by the Deputyes,

Wm. Torrey, Cleric."

We resume the history of the publication of the Laws, at the point mentioned on page 9, *ante*, viz.: immediately after the enactment of the Body of Liberties in October, 1641.

The General Court ordered June 14, 1642 (Records, ii. 21): —

"That the Governor [Winthrop], Mr. Bellingham and the Secretary, [Nowell] with the deputies of Boston, shall examine and survey the orders of this last Court, and perfect the same for the publishing."

Also, (Records, ii. 22) "that such laws as make any offence to be capital shall forthwith be imprinted and published, of which laws the Secretary is to send a copy to the printer, when it hath been examined by Governor or Mr. Bellingham with himself, and the Treasurer to pay for the printing of them."

September 27, 1642 (Records, ii. 28) "it is ordered, that every Court should have a copy of the laws at the public charge."

May 10, 1643 (Records, ii. 39), "the former committee of magistrates and deputies are authorized and appointed to examine and perfect the Laws."

March 7, 1643-4 (Records, ii. 61), the following vote was passed: —

"It is ordered that the Governor, [Winthrop] Mr. Dudley and Mr. Hibbens, these or any two of them, shall be a committee to consider of the Body of Liberties, against the next General Court, what is fit to be repealed or allowed, and present the same to the next Court."

"Also the Magistrates residing at Ipswich, or any two of them, are appointed a Committee for the same purpose, that so the Court conferring both together may more easily determine what to settle about the same."

"It is ordered that Richard Bellingham Esq. should finish that which was formerly committed to him about the perusing of the Book of laws, &c. and to present the same to the next Court."

May 27, 1644, the Legislature adjourned to October 30th, but the Journal of the House of Deputies contains the report of the acts

Here the reference is plainly to Liberty No. 1, and this Liberty is republished, unaltered, in 1660, as the first section of the General Laws.

[22] July 1, 1645 (Records, iii. 26), the Journal of Deputies has the following entry: —

"It is ordered that several persons out of each county shall be chosen to draw up a body of laws and present them to the consideration of the General Court at their next sitting.

"For the county of Suffolk, our honored Governor, [Dudley] Mr. Hibbens, Mr. Cotton, Mr. Mather, Lieut. Duncan and Mr. Prichard are chosen a committee to meet, confer together, and draw up a body of laws and to present them to the next session of this Court.

"For the county of Middlesex, Herbert Pelham, Esq., Mr. Nowell, Mr. Thomas Shepard, Mr. Allen, Capt. Cooke, and Lieut. Johnson," were similarly appointed.

"For Essex, Richard Bellingham, Esq., Mr. Bradstreet, Mr. Nathl. Rogers, Mr. Norton, Mr. Ward, and Mr. Hathorne" were similarly appointed. [This Mr. Ward could not be William, as Sudbury was in Middlesex.]

In each case two magistrates, two ministers, and two deputies seem to have been appointed, except that in Essex, Mr. Nathaniel Ward seems to take the place of one deputy.

[23] October 1, 1645 (Records, ii. 128), it was voted

"Whereas this Court, in a former session, chose and appointed several honored members of this commonwealth as commissioners in their several shires, to meet together in some convenient place within each shire, to consult together, and to return to this Court a result of their thoughts, that this Court may proceed thereupon to satisfy the expectation of the country in establishing a body of laws; this Court thinks it meet to desire the persons in the order mentioned, at or before the 12th of November next, in their several shires to meet together; in Boston for Suffolk, in Cambridge for Middlesex, in Ipswich for Essex: and after their first meeting at the time and places above mentioned, by warrant from the Secretary to each committee of each shire, and then as often as they please, to appoint their own meetings for the accomplishment of the end so desired: and to make their return of what they shall do herein, to the next sitting of the General Court.

"In Captain Cooke's room, at his request, Mr. Joseph Hill of Charlestown; in Mr. Allen's room, Mr. Knowles; and Mr. Glover in Mr. Prichard's room. They being out of the way, or shall be suddenly, — Mr. Symonds is

[22] The corresponding entry in the Journal of the two houses is in Records, ii. 109, under date of May 14, 1645, and it varies only by saying that these three committees are to report to the next General Court. — W. H. W.

[23] The corresponding entry in the Journal of the Deputies is dated October 7, 1645 (Records, iii. 46–47). — W. H. W.

instead of Mr. Bellingham for Ipswich, because Mr. Bellingham now resides at Boston; and Mr. Bellingham to be for Boston, added to the former.

"And the calling of each assembly to each place is in Mr. Bellingham for Boston, Mr. Pelham for Cambridge, and Mr. Symonds for Ipswich."

The next step seems to have been the appointment of a small sub-committee to digest and arrange the work of the three general committees.

May 22, 1646 (Records, ii. 157), the following vote was passed:[24] —

"This Court thankfully accepts of the labors returned by the several committees of the several shires, and being very unwilling such precious labors should fall to the ground without [that] good success as is generally hoped for, have thought it meet to desire Richard Bellingham, Esq., Mr. [Samuel] Symonds, Lieut. [Nathaniel] Duncan, Lieut. [Edward] Johnson, and Mr. [Nathaniel] Ward, to cause each committee's return about a body of laws to be transcribed, so as each committee may have the sight of the other's labors. And that the persons mentioned in this order be pleased to meet together, at or before the 10th of August, at Salem or Ipswich; and on their perusing and examining the whole labors of all the committees, — with the abbreviation of the laws in force which Mr. Bellingham took great store of pains and to good purpose in and upon the whole, — and make return to the next session of this Court: at which time the Court intends, by the favor and blessing of God, to proceed to the establishing of so many of them as shall be thought most fit for a body of laws amongst us."

It will be remembered that this year was an anxious period for the colonists. Doctor Child and others had raised questions about the powers of the Legislature, and the answer of the General Court had been prepared for transmission to England. Although Winthrop says nothing about this matter of the publication of the laws, his journal shows that the community was excited and uneasy on the point. The above-named committee of six evidently did not work with sufficient promptness, and a change was desired.

Accordingly,[25] November 4, 1646 (Records, ii. 168), the following order was passed: —

---

[24] The Journal of the Deputies of May 20, 1646 (Records, iii. 74, 75), has the corresponding entry. It makes the revising committee to consist of Bellingham and Duncan, Nowell and Johnson, Symonds and Ward, thus adding Secretary Nowell to it. — W. H. W.

[25] The Journal of Deputies of the same date (Records, iii. 84, 85) has this same order, somewhat abbreviated. — W. H. W.

"The Court being deeply sensible to the earnest expectation of the Country in general for this Court's completing of a body of Laws for the better and more orderly wielding all the affairs of this Commonwealth; willing also to their utmost to answer their honest and hearty desires therein, unexpectedly prevented by multitude of other pressing occasions, think fit and necessary that this Court make choice of two or three of our honored Magistrates, with as many of the Deputies, to peruse and examine, compare, transcribe, and compose in good order, all the liberties, laws and orders extant with us; and further to peruse and perfect all such others as are drawn up, and to present such of them as they find necessary for us, as also to suggest what they deem needful to be added, as also to consider and contrive some good method and order, with titles and tables for compiling the whole; so as we may have ready recourse to any of them, upon all occasions, whereby we may manifest our utter disaffection to arbitrary Government and so all relations be safely and sweetly directed and protected in all their just rights and privileges; desiring thereby to make way for printing our Laws for more public and profitable use of us and our successors. Our honored Governor, [Winthrop] Mr. Bellingham, Mr. Hibbens, Mr. Hill and Mr. Duncan as a Committee for the business above mentioned, or any three of them meeting, the others having notice thereof, shall be sufficient to carry on the work."

It will be noticed that only Bellingham and Duncan were retained of the former committee of six. Their powers probably expired with the term of the Legislature. At all events the next General Court revived and continued their powers by the following order, dated May 26, 1647 (Records, ii. 196): —

"The Court understanding that the Committee for perfecting the laws appointed by the last General Court, through streights of time and other things intervening have not attained what they expected, and on all hands so much desired, touching a body of laws, think meet and necessary that our honored Governor, [Winthrop] Mr. Bellingham, Mr. Hibbens, the Auditor General [Duncan], Lieut. Johnson,[26] and Mr. Hills be chosen as a Committee of this Court to do the same, according to the aforesaid order, against the next sessions in the 8th month or the next General Court."

[26] In copying this entry Mr. F. C. Gray omitted the name of Johnson, doubtless not recognizing therein the author of "Wonder-Working Providence." In the admirable reprint of that book, issued at Andover in 1867, under the care of William F. Poole, the editor has attempted to show that Edward Johnson was one of the most active and important members of the committee. The main argument is, that Johnson was on the committee appointed May 22, 1646, and on that of May 26, 1647, but was omitted on that of November 4, 1646; that the first and last committees were active and the second inactive: that hence this activity was owing to the presence of Johnson. But I fail to see that the first committee did anything, and Bellingham was undoubtedly the controlling spirit throughout. We shall see later that Joseph Hills of Malden was employed about the printed laws, and did all the clerical part of the revision. — W. H. W.

November 11, 1647 (Records, ii. 209), the following vote was passed: —

"The laws being to be put in print, it is meet that they should be conveniently penned: therefore it is desired that the committee for drawing up the laws will be careful therein; and to that purpose they have liberty to make some change of form, to put in apt words as occasion shall require, provided the sense and meaning in any law or part thereof be not changed."[27]

November 11, 1647 (Records, ii. 212), the following vote was passed: —

"It is agreed by the Court, to the end that we may have better light for making and proceeding about laws, that there shall be these books following procured for the use of the Court from time to time: —

Two of Sir Edward Cooke upon Littleton;
two of the Book of Entries;
two of Sir Edward Cooke upon Magna Charta;
two of The New Terms of the Law;
two Dalton's Justice of the Peace;
two of Sir Edward Cook's Reports."

The next entry, at the same session of November, 1647 (Records, ii. 217-8), is as follows: —

"The laws now being in a manner agreed upon, and the Court drawing to an end, it is time to take order: 1. How all alteration of former laws may be without mistaking compared and fair written: 2d. That all old laws not altered be also written in the same copy: 3dly. That there be a Committee chosen for this business, to be made ready against the first day of the first month next, so as the Court of Assistants, if they see cause may advise for a General Court to prepare them for the press: 4thly. That there be large margins left at both sides of the leaf, and the heads of each law written on the two outsides thereof, and upon the other margent any references and scriptures or the like, and that these be written copywise. The Governor [Winthrop], Mr. Bellingham, Mr. Hill, Mr. Auditor [Duncan] and Mr. Ting are joined in this Committee to act according as in this paper is expressed."

Here, again, the committee seems to be reconstructed, Johnson being dropped and Tyng substituted for Hibbens. The other four,

[27] This very important vote must be remembered in comparing the Laws of 1660 with the original records. This Revision of 1649, being approved by the General Court, took the place of former laws, and was undoubtedly taken over without change into the text of the Revision of 1660. It may even be that some law, or part of a law, was enacted for the first time in this Revision, if found to be necessary and acceptable. — W. H. W.

Winthrop, Bellingham, Duncan and Hills seem to have continued the work. The following order of the Court in March, 1647–8 (Records, ii. 227), shows that they had assistance in the clerical portion, and that two standard copies were prepared: —

"The Court doth conceive it meete that John Wayte of Charlestown Village, shall be allowed, out of the next country rate, for his writing, one book of the laws and for finding paper for both books, £4 ,, 18 shillings."

Also (Records, ii. 230), "The Court doth desire that Mr. Rawson and Mr. Hill compare the amendments of the books of laws passed, and make them as one; and one of them to remain in the hands of the Committee for the speedy committing of them to the press, and the other to remain in the hands of the Secretary, sealed up, till the next Court."

Two months later, under date of May 10, 1648 (Records, ii. 239):[28] —

"It is ordered, the copy of the Laws in the two rolls, — which were (by order of the Court) sealed up, with intent that if hereafter any questions should arise about the copy now at the press, it might be examined by this, whereby the faithfulness of the committee might be tried; — and that the other copy (now remaining with Mr. Hill), — should forthwith be sent for, for the use of the Court." [29]

Later, at the same session, May 10, 1648 (Records, ii. 246), it was voted as follows: —

"Mr. Auditor [Duncan] and Mr. Hill to examine the laws now at press, and to see if any material law be not put in or mentioned in the table as being of force, and to make supply of them."

In the Journal of the Deputies for [30] May 13, 1648 (Records, ii. 263), is the following item: —

"Ordered, that in the book of Laws, title Appeals, in the last line save one, (*just*) to be entered next before *charges*; and the Auditor General to see it entered in every book."

---

[28] Compare Journal of the Deputies of May 13, 1648 (Records, iii. 125). — W. H. W.

[29] Mr. F. C. Gray notes that something seems to be omitted in this sentence. I think, however, by inserting two dashes as above, the sense is plain and the sentence grammatical. I apprehend that the phrase "and that the other copy" is in accordance with the custom of the times and "that" is a pronoun. Or it may be that the word "that" is merely superfluous. It seems evident that both copies were to be sent for to be used by the Court. — W. H. W.

[30] This same entry is in the Journal of the Deputies (Records, iii. 130). On the same page is a mention of certain propositions to be made to the United Colonies, and the entry is, "Proposition 3, page 24. This consisting of many branches and the Court not having time to consider their own laws and practice in the case have deferred it to a committee to examine and to certify the next Court." See the same entries in Records, ii. 263–4. — W. H. W.

In October, 1648, provision was made for transcribing in an alphabetical or methodical way, all laws, orders and acts of Court, contained in the old books, which were in force but not included in the printed revision.[31]

---

[31] October 18, 1648 (Records, ii. 259, and iii. 141), the following important order was passed: —

"For the better carrying on the occasions of the General Court, and to the end that the records of the same, together with what shall be presented by way of petition &c, or passes by way of vote, either amongst the magistrates or deputies, may hereafter be more exactly recorded and kept for public use: —

It is hereby ordered, that as there is a Secretary amongst the Magistrates (who is the general officer of the Commonwealth, for the keeping of the public records of the same) so there shall be a Clerk amongst the Deputies to be chosen by them from time to time;

That, (by the Court of Elections and then the officers to begin their entries and their recompense accordingly) there be provided by the Auditor, four large paper books in folio, bound up with vellum and pasteboard, two whereof to be delivered to the Secretary and two to the Clerk of the House of Deputies, one to be a journal to each of them, the other for the fair entry of all laws, acts and orders &c, which shall pass the magistrates and deputies; that of the Secretary to be the public record of the country, that of the Clerk's to be a book only of copies.

That the Secretary and Clerk for the Deputies shall briefly enter into their journals, respectively, the title of all bills, orders, laws, petitions &c, which shall be presented and read amongst them, what are referred to committees, and what are voted negatively or affirmatively, and so for any addition or alteration.

That all bills, laws, petitions, &c., which shall be last concluded amongst the Magistrates, shall remain with the Governor till the latter end of that session; and such as are last assented to by the Deputies shall remain with the Speaker till the said time; when the whole Court shall meet together, or a committee of Magistrates and Deputies, to consider what has passed that session, where the Secretary and Clerk shall be present, and by their journals call for such bills &c, as hath passed either house:

and such as shall appear to have passed the magistrates and Deputies shall be delivered to the Secretary to record, who shall record the same within one month after every sessions; which being done, the Clerk of the Deputies shall have liberty, for one month after, to transcribe the same into his book.

And such bills, orders &c., that hath only passed the Magistrates, shall be delivered to the Secretary to keep upon file; and such as have only passed the Deputies shall be delivered to their Clerk to be kept upon file in like manner, or otherwise disposed of as the whole Court shall appoint.

That all laws, orders and acts of Court, contained in the old books, that are of force and not ordered to be printed, be transcribed in some alphabetical or methodical way, by direction of some committee that this Court shall please to appoint, and delivered to the Secretary to record in the first place in the said book of records, and then the acts of the other sessions in order accordingly, and a copy of all to be transcribed by the Clerk of the Deputies as aforesaid.

That the Secretary be allowed for his pains twenty marks per annum, and the Clerk of the Deputies ten pounds per annum, to be paid out of the treasury, till the Court shall appoint their recompense by fees or otherwise."

Under date of Oct. 18, 1650 (Records, iv. part 1, p. 33), there is an entry showing that William Torrey had not then written up the Deputies' book. See also the references (Records, iv. part 1, p. 324) May 19, 1658, to various books of records, when the laws about Constables were collected and codified.

I am sorry to add that none of these various records and compilations of laws are now extant at our State House. The continuous record to 1686 exists and one volume (1644–1657) of the Journal of the Deputies. These are well known, having been printed by the State. Many of the original orders, papers, and minutes are in the files; but the ill-timed zeal of a former Secretary caused the dispersion of these papers into a new classified arrangement, and the continuity of the record is lost. I am informed that, in some cases, books of orders were cut apart and the items scattered into the various new receptacles. Possibly some of these books ordered in 1648 lasted intact for two centuries, to be improved out of existence in our days. — W. H. W.

of that branch during June. It appears (Records, iii. 6) that on June 7, 1644: —

"It is ordered that Lieut. Sprague, Francis Chickering, Stephen Kingsley, Thomas Mekins, William Hilton, Joseph Batchelor, Mr. Steevens, William Ward, Lieut. Howard, William Eastowe, Thomas Brooke, Lieut. Johnson and Joseph Meadcalfe, are chosen a committee to examine the book delivered in by Mr. Bellingham, and compare it with the book of records, and return their objections and thoughts thereof to this house in writing."

[William Ward was a deputy from Sudbury in 1644, but not later.]

May 29, 1644 (Records, ii. 69), it was ordered: —

"That for the better building of shipping within this jurisdiction, and for the avoiding of many inconveniences which now both owners and builders are subject unto, there be a company of that trade, according to the manner of other places, with power to regulate building of ships, and to make such orders and laws among themselves as may conduce to the public good, if any shall appear the next Court and present laws for consideration."

May 29, 1644 (Records, ii. 76-78). The Court established the commission of the Sergeant-major-general, Thomas Dudley. By it provision was made that

"Yourself, together with the Council of War, shall have power to make such wholesome laws, agreeable to the word of God, as you shall conceive to be necessary for the well-ordering of your army, until the General Court shall provide for the same: which being sufficiently published, you, with the said Council, have power to put in execution, be it to the taking away of life or otherwise."

November 13, 1644 (Records, ii. 89), "it is ordered that all the several orders of general concernment agreed on this whole Court, shall be forthwith published to the several towns within this jurisdiction, and that the several towns shall procure a copy of them within three months, under the Secretary his hand."

At the same Court (Records, ii. 91), there were presented the Answers of the Elders to certain Questions submitted to them. One question was, whether the magistrates were, in cases where no express law was provided, to be guided by the word of God. The answer was: —

"We do not find that by the patent they are expressly directed to proceed according to the word of God; but we understand that by *a law or liberty of the country*, they may act in cases wherein as yet there is no express law, so that in such acts they proceed according to the word of God."

[32] October 27, 1648 (Records, ii. 262): —

"It is ordered by the full Court, that the books of laws, now at the press, may be sold in quires, at three shillings the book; provided that every member of this Court shall have one without price, and the Auditor-general and Mr. Joseph Hill; for which there shall be fifty in all taken up, to be disposed of by the appointment of this Court."

May 2, 1649 (Records, ii. 273, and iii. 162), the following vote was passed: —

"Mr. Joseph Hill is granted, as a gratuity, ten pounds, to be paid him out of the treasury, for his pains about the printed laws."

Having thus completed the entries respecting the first Revision of the Laws, I would renew the statement made *ante*, on p. 11. This edition is often called that of 1648. We have seen, however, that at as late date as October, 1648, it was at the press when the General Court adjourned, and that the title of the edition of 1660 says, "published by the same authority in the General Court holden at Boston in May, 1649." We may fairly conclude that the revision is most correctly entitled that of 1649, although no special entry is found of the publication at the May session in that year. It is understood that a small edition only was printed, not only because no copies have survived, but because the preface to the edition of 1660 states that "the Book of Lawes, of the first Impression, not being to be had for the supply of the Country put us upon the thought of a second." But see *post*, p. 95, note 57.

In the meantime, October 17, 1649 (Records, ii. 286, and iii. 173), the following vote was passed: —

"The Court, finding by experience the great benefit that doth redound to the country by putting of the law in print, do conceive it very requisite that those laws that have passed the consent of the General Court since the Book of Laws were in printing or printed, should be forthwith committed to the press; and for that end appoint Richard Bellingham, esq., Mr. Nowell, Mr. Auditor-general [Duncan], Capt. Keayne, and Mr. Hill, or any three of them, a committee to prepare them against the Court of Election; that upon approbation of the return of the committee, they also may be printed; as also therewith to prepare those laws referred to in the end of the printed laws, with a suitable table, to be printed."

---

[32] The last clause of this order is printed in the form given in Records, iii. 141, it being rather more explicit. — W. H. W.

October 18, 1650 (Records, iv. part 1, p. 35): —

"It is ordered that Richard Bellingham, esq., the Secretary [Rawson] and Mr. Hills, or any two of them, are appointed a committee to take order for the printing the laws agreed upon to be printed, to determine of all things in reference thereunto, agreeing with the president for the printing of them with all expedition, and to allow the title if there be cause."

These last two entries supply us with a fact which has probably not been noticed for the last century, viz., that not only was there an edition of 1649, but a Supplement thereto in 1650. It will also be possible to form a fair idea of the shape and contents of both of these. As to the existence of the Supplement of 1650, citations given later (pp. 89, 90,) show that the General Court in 1654 referred to and amended laws in the "first printed book" and in the "second printed book." Moreover the Code of 1660 is full of marginal citations from L. 1 and L. 2, the former being quoted up to p. 53 (title "Wills,") and the latter to p. 16 (under the same title). And in one case, the law cited by the General Court as being on page 8 of the second book, (referring to Freemen), is in 1660 marked as L. 2, p. 8.

See also a possible citation in 1652, recorded *ante*, p. 70.

Two other facts are significant: First, the annexed Table of the marginal references in the Code of 1660 to Liber 2 shows that the laws copied were all passed prior to 1651. Secondly, that the marginal citations are from Anno 1651 onward, and never backward. That is to say, no year previous to 1651 stands in the margin, though much of the text was enacted in 1648, 1649, and 1650.[33] There are some laws cited as from Liber 2 which were passed earlier than 1648; these are evidently the laws which were omitted in the Code of 1649, but found on examination to be worthy of a place in the General Laws, and therefore put first into the Supplement, and then into the Code of 1660.

The title "Ecclesiastical" (p. 28 of 1660) seems to give us a good proof that the Supplement contained amended or omitted laws. Section 14 contains two long sub-sections or paragraphs. Both were passed November 4, 1646 (Records, ii. p. 178, 179); but

---

[33] I find but two apparent exceptions. In 1660, p. 2, title "Appeals, § 3, the citation is "A. 43, p. 19." This is a typographical error, as the law was passed August 30, 1653 (Records, iv. part 1, p. 152).

The other case is on p. 82 of Code of 1660, title "Wolves," cited as 1648. This law was passed Oct. 18, 1648 (Records, ii. 252), and was to last only four years. It was therefore not in the General Laws of 1649. But it was revived by a law passed August 30, 1653 (Records, iv. part 1, p. 153), and therefore is printed in 1660. The law and the citation are both exceptions. — W. H. W.

the first paragraph is on p. 179, and the second on p. 178. Now the Connecticut Code prints the first paragraph complete, but not the second. Hence I infer this first paragraph alone stood in the Code of 1649; but that in the Supplement (the citation being L. 2, p. 5), the previous section, which had been overlooked, was restored.

Note, also, that in the law of 1646 the culprit was to wear a paper inscribed "A Wanton Gospeller"; but in 1660, and by the Connecticut Code, it was changed to "An Open and Obstinate Contemner of God's Holy Ordinances." This seems to show that the compilers in 1649 altered the text on that point, and Connecticut copied it.

The title "Attachments," in the Laws of 1660, helps to fix the date of the second book. It cites "L. 2, p. 12," for a law passed May 22, 1650 (Records, iv. part 1, p. 5), and farther down it cites "Anno 1651, p. 1," for a law passed May 7, 1651 (Records, iv. part 1, p. 39).

Finally we have the distinct evidence of Joseph Hills, as set forth below, that the Second Book was prepared by him, and put through the press under his supervision. Hills was a member of the House for Charlestown in 1647, and Speaker in that year. He represented Malden 1650-1656; removed to Newbury soon after, and represented that town in 1667; he died in 1688, aged 86 years. His petition will be found in Mass. Archives, vol. 47, p. 19. It is as follows: —

"In as much as it hath pleased the General Court to engage me in sundry great and weighty services in refference to all the generall laws here established, now in print ffor publique good: In consideration whereof as I conceive, a Gratuity of Ten pounds was Appointed me by the Treasurer, which as it holds forth the good acceptance of the Honored Court, I thankfully acknowledge, as duty binds me.

"Yet apprehending that my Great care, paynes and studies in these difficult Imployments was not truly Informed or understood, I desire briefly to tender you an account thereof as follows.

1. "First it pleased the General Court to employ me in a shire Committee to draw up a Body of Laws in which I took unwearied pains, perusing all the Stat. Laws of England in [Pulton?] at Large, out of which I took all such as I conceived sutable to the condition of this Commonwealth: which with such others as, in my observation, experiences and serious studies I thought needful, all which I drew up in a Book, close written, Consisting of 24 pages of paper, in folio, which upon the Committee's perusal, — viz. Mr. Noel, Mr. Pelham, Mr. Thomas Sheppard and myself, — I was Appointed to draw upp for the use of the Generall Court, which Book was by some means

lost and could not be found. For further Improvement by another Committee of the Generall Court, viz. Mr. Bellingham, Mr. Nat. Ward, &c., whereupon Mr. Bellingham spake to me to help them to another coppie of the aforesaid Book, which in tender Respect to publique good, to the Honored Court and Committee, I did forthwith again Transcribe out of my First coppie, although it was in harvest time.

2. "After that, it pleased the Generall Court again to Ingage me in the perusing all the laws in the Books of Records, to Consider, Compare, Compose, and Transcribe all laws of publique Concernment, coppie-wise; all which I did draw upp together, and Drew upp in five Books or Rowls, which done were Examined by the Committee and presented to the Gen^{ll}. Court.

3. "Thereuppon I was Ordered by the Court to Transcribe the five Books afforesaid with some other new laws, all which (save onely a few the Auditor did), I, with Great care and vigilancie, performed, and frequented the press, and otherwise took care to Examine them during the Imprinting the same.

4. "Since which it pleased the Gen^{ll} Court to Appoint me with some others to Compose and Transcribe the Second Booke of Laws, coppie-wise, which I allso did; which affter Examination by the Committee was allso presented to the Gen^{ll} Court, which were pleased further to Imploy another Committee, whereof I was one, to fitt them for the press.

"In all which services in reference to publique good, I putt forth my selfe to the uttermost to the Great neglect of my personall and particular occasions, devoting my selfe thereunto for the most part of two years tyme (as neer as I can remember) the benefit whereof doth I hope verie manifestly Redound both to Court and Country, who doubtless uppon a right understanding will not be unwilling to afford such Due encouragement and Recompense as services of such Importance and Advantage to the Countrie doth Require.

"Your Humble Servant,

"JOS. HILLS."

"The Magistrates Referr the consideration of the Petition to theire brethren the Deputies 27 May, 1653.

"EDWARD RAWSON, Secre^{t}."

"The Deputies think meete to allow Mr. Hills ten pounds out of the next County rate in reference to what is herein exprest, if the honored Magistrates please to Consent thereto.

"WILLIAM TORREY, Cleric."

"Consented to by the Magistrates hereto.

"EDWARD RAWSON, Secre^{t}."

It will be seen, from the following table, that this Supplement was arranged under titles in an alphabetical order. The apparent exceptions are doubtless due to the fact that these titles were changed in 1660; and very possibly the order was not strictly observed. But the main fact remains that Liber 2, or the second printed book, contained all the laws passed after the completion of the printed Code of 1649 (or the first printed book), through the sessions of 1650.

Marginal Citations in the Laws of 1660.

1660.	Title.	LIBER 2.	Date of Original Act.
P. 1	Actions	4	Oct. 15, 1650; Rec. iv, *27.
2	Appeals	1	May 2, 1649; " ii, 279.
4	Attachments	12	May 22, 1650; " iv, 5.
6	Bridges	3	March, 1647–8; " ii, 229.
11	Cattle	8	May 22, 1650; " iv, 4.
13	Criminal Causes	4	May 2, 1649; " ii, 279.
17	Chirurgeons	3	do ; " ii, 278.
18	Clerk of the Writs	13	See Footnote *.
21	Counsel	4	do ; " ii, 279.
"	Courts	10	; " ii, 7, 9.
"	do	13	; " ii, 95.
22	do	24	See Footnote *.
23	do (Lib. 3)	5	Oct. 17, 1648; " ii, 286.
24	do	7	Nov. 13, 1644; " ii, 80.
"	do	15	June 31, 1650; " iv, 20.
"	do	4	See Footnote *.
26	Dowries	5	
27	Ecclesiastical	7	

* References to Records, iv, mean Part 1 of that volume.

Marginal Citations in the Laws of 1660. — Continued.

1660.	Title.	LIBER 2.	Date of Original Act.		
28	Ecclesiastical	5	Nov. 4, 1646;	Rec.	ii, 178.
29	Elections	10	Oct. 17, 1649;	"	ii, 286.
30	Fairs	7	Oct. 18, 1648;	"	ii, 257.
"	Ferries	7	Oct. 27, 1648;	"	ii, 262.
31	Fines	7	May 22, 1646;	"	ii, 153.
33	Freemen	8	May 18, 1631;	"	i, 87.
37	Hides	8	Nov. 4, 1646;	"	ii, 168.
38	Horses	11	May 2, 1649;	"	ii, 280.
39	Imposts	9	Oct. 1, 1645;		ii, 131.
41	Indians	15	June 21, 1650;		iv, 21.
44	Innkeepers	3	Oct. 17, 1649;	"	ii, 286.
	do	6	Oct. 18, 1648;	"	ii, 257.
46	do	31	See Footnote [a].		
47	Jurors	5	Oct. 17, 1649;	"	ii, 285.
	do	8	May 22, 1650;	"	iv, 3.
51	Married Persons	17	Oct. 15, 1650;	"	iv, 26.
53	Marshall	7	May 26, 1647;	"	ii, 194.
56	Military	12	Mch. 1647–8;	"	ii, 226.
60	do [Ammunition]	1	May 2, 1649;	"	ii, 282.
61	Mines	11	May 10, 1648;	"	ii, 242.
63	Petitions	13	Oct. 27, 1648;	"	ii, 261.
68	Records	15	See Footnote [a].		
	do	7	Nov. 11, 1647	"	ii, 215.
70	Sailors	14	May 22, 1650;	"	iv, 2.

Marginal Citations in the Laws of 1660. — Concluded.

1660.	Title.	LIBER 2.	Date of Original Act.		
71	Sheep	14	Oct. 18, 1648;	Rec.	ii, 252.
73	Strangers	32	See Footnote [a].		
74	Swearing	14	June 19, 1650;	"	iv, 19.
75	Townships	10	Mch. 3, 1635–6;	"	i, 172.
78	Wampumpeag	12	Oct. 27, 1648; May 2, 1649;	" "	ii, 261. ii, 279.
80	Wills	16	Oct. 17, 1649;	"	ii, 287.
81	do	6	May 2, 1649;	"	ii, 281.

[a] On p. 13, title "Criminal Causes," the reference is L. p. 2. Probably this means Lib. 2.

On p. 18 the reference is in regard to the "Clerk of the Writs." I have already (*ante*, p. 25) noted part of this law as passed in 1641, but I have not found the law establishing their fees. Yet May 31, 1660 (Records, iv. part 1, p. 421), a law was passed which refers to a "former law" on the subject.

On p. 22, title "Courts," the reference is L. 2, p. 24. This is doubtless a printer's error for p. 14, as the preceding reference is to L. 2, p. 13; or to Lib. 1, p. 24, as that is the bottom reference on the same page, § 4. I prefer the latter solution.

On p. 23, § 7, the reference is to L. 3, p. 5, and as this is the *only* reference to Liber 3, I feel sure that it is an error for Liber 2.

On pp. 24 and 26, titles respectively "Courts and Dowries," I cannot find the laws cited. Both matters are fully discussed *ante*, p. 25 and 26.

As to the reference on p. 27 to title "Ecclesiastical," being a law, that "the Treasurer shall defray the expenses of church elders when employed by special order of the General Court, 1642." — This order was passed May 18, 1642. It is on p. 2 of vol. ii, *second edition only*, and is not indexed in either edition.

On p. 46, title "Innkeepers," § 12, the reference is to L. 2, p. 31; evidently an error for Liber 1, as on the previous page § 8 is referred to L. 1, p. 30.

On p. 68, title "Records," the reference is L. p. 15. Undoubtedly Liber 1 is meant, and I imagine that it therein stood under title "Courts."

On p. 73, title "Strangers," the citation is L. 2, p. 32. This must be an error for L. 1, p. 23, as just above it the citation is L. 1, p. 23. The text is dated 1641, and both paragraphs are in the Body of Liberties.

On p. 81, title "Wills," § 3, the reference is to L. 2, p. 6. I suspect an error for L. 2, p. 16, as that is the citation for § 1 on the previous page.

It is, of course, undesirable to explain difficulties by presuming typographical errors. But the fact remains that the edition of 1650 contains many such about which there can be no dispute. The first three instances noted above are all the references to any page in Liber 2 above 16; and it seems impossible that there could have been 24 or 32 pages in the book, and yet that none of those intervening pages were used in preparing the Code of 1660. — W. H. W.

We may now resume with more confidence the consideration of the probable shape and contents of the Code of 1649. If the "second printed book" was the Supplement, we may safely assume that the "first printed book" was the Code of 1649, and proceed to use the citations from Liber 1, in the edition of 1660, in the same manner. We know in fact that the preface and arrangement of the edition of 1660 was copied from that of 1649, and we may safely believe that all of the sections from the Body of Liberties which occur in the later edition stood in the earlier one. Other evidence in regard to the Code will also be found available.

The neighboring colonies of Connecticut and New Haven promptly availed of our Code of 1649 in preparing their respective laws. Connecticut established a Code by vote of May, 1650, and many sections are exactly the same as those in our Body of Liberties and our Revision of 1660. This Code is printed in the Records of Connecticut, Vol. 1, p. 509–563, edited by J. H. Trumbull, Hartford, 1850.

New Haven published her code at London in 1656, and it is reprinted in the second volume of the Records of New Haven Colony, edited by Charles J. Hoadley, printed at Hartford in 1858. The Code states (p. 571) that in preparing these Laws, Liberties and Orders "they have made use of the Laws published by the Honourable Colony of the Massachusetts." Herein, again, we find literal transcripts from our Body of Liberties and our Laws.

Moreover, between 1649 and 1650 our own Legislature, in enacting laws, on several occasions altered or repealed certain existing laws, and specifically referred to them as part of the printed laws. The following examples of such references give us certain data, viz., that the title "Military Affairs" was on page 42, and that titles "Swine," "Townships," "Weights and Measures," and "Women," occurred, and were, of course, subsequent to that. The evidence of the marginal citation of 1660, which will be given hereafter, makes it morally certain that the title "Watching" was on p. 52, and that of "Wills" was on p. 53.

We may therefore safely assume that our Code of 1649 consisted of about fifty-six pages, or seven octavo sheets.

List of References.

1. May 2, 1649 (Records, ii. 281), "Forasmuch as the printed law concerning Dowries . . . . . appears not so convenient as was formerly conceived" . . . . it is ordered "that these words in the 14 line of that order" . . . . be amended.[34]

1.* October 17, 1649 (Records, ii. 287), "the printed law for Elections in page 51, bearing date 1647, is hereby repealed."

2. May 22, 1650 (Records, iv. part 1, p. 4), "whereas the law concerning fencing against great cattle, folio 7. — Harms done by Great Cattle in Fenced Ground shall be viewed and judged. — for explanation whereof this court declareth and ordereth," etc., etc.

2.* May 22, 1650 (Records, iv. part 1, p. 5), "for explanation of that part of the printed law entitled Military Affairs, s. 10," etc.[35]

3. June 19, 1650 (Records, iv. part 1, p. 19), "for explanation and addition of the law, title Profane Swearing," a new law was passed punishing any one for multiplying profane oaths.[36]

4. It appears by a reference, 21 June, 1650 (Records, iv. part 1, p. 20) that the "law, title Gaming, 1646, 1647," is amended by prohibiting bowling or any other play or game in public houses under the same penalties as are "provided for in the aforesaid game of shovel-board."[37]

---

[34] The New Haven Code (p. 587) has the title Dowry just like ours of 1660, omitting the clause (lines 17 and 18), "signified by writing under her hand and acknowledged before some magistrate or others authorized thereunto, which shall bar her from any right or interest in such estate." The New Haven law says that this law shall not apply to any transaction "before this law was published;" and our Code of 1660 says, "before the last of November, 1647." Hence I imagine the New Haven law is substantially ours of 1649. — W. H. W.

[35] This section will be found Records, ii. 222, and reads: "The Surveyor-general hath power to sell any of the common arms where he sees occasion." As it was repealed in 1650, it is not in the Code of 1660. It is the tenth section of the law of November 11, 1647, which was to stand together with two laws of 1645, and all others were repealed. Of course these last-named laws formed the title in our Code of 1649; but Connecticut and New Haven had very different laws. — W. H. W.

[36] The original law was passed November 4, 1646 (Records, ii. 178), and it is copied exactly in the Connecticut code. But in the revision of 1660, the two laws of 1646 and 1650 are printed, and their place is changed to "Swearing and Cursing," or under letter S instead of letter P. No doubt the Connecticut example shows the law of 1649. — W. H. W.

[37] The law against playing shovel-board was passed May 26, 1647 (Records, ii. 195), and is copied almost word for word in the Connecticut code.

But in the revision of 1660 reference is made to laws passed in 1646, 1647, and 1651, and we find that the new title, Gaming, includes "Shovel-board, Bowling, or any other play or game;" also a section against gaming for money, passed November 4, 1646 (Records, ii. 180), and one in regard to dancing in public houses, passed May 7, 1651 (Records, iv. part 1, p. 40).

Now the Connecticut law adds at the end the clause, "The like penalty shall be for playing in any place at any unlawful game," — which clearly was not in the Massachusetts Laws of 1649, as if there, the addition made in 1650, above noted, would have been unnecessary. But I suspect that the law of 1646, against gaming for money, was not in the revision of 1649, as it is most unlikely that the Connecticut law-makers would have stricken it out. Hence I conclude that in 1649 the title Gaming stood just as in the Connecticut code, except the last line. — W. H. W.

5. June 22, 1650 (Records, iv. part 1, p. 22), it was ordered that recording a sale, mortgage, etc., of houses or lands with the records of the shire shall be sufficient "without any further certifying unto the recorder or secretary for the General Court, and that clause in the close of the printed laws, title Conveyances Fraudulent, page 14, requiring the same, is hereby repealed." [38]

6. June 22, 1650 (Records, iv. part 1, p. 23), the Court answered a question "whether by that clause of the law entitled Innkeepers" a certain person was liable to a fine.[39]

7. Records, iv. part 1, p. 26, October 15, 1650, "the former law, title Women, is hereby repealed." [40]

8. May 7, 1651 (Records, iv. part 1, p. 40), "the former law provides, title Cask and Cooper, page the sixth," etc., and is now amended by adding a penalty for defective casks, and a penalty also on any town neglecting to appoint a gauger.[41]

---

[38] The Connecticut code throws no light on this, as under this title it merely prints the two sections about covenous alienation and papers signed under duress.

Section 4 under this title in Laws of 1660 is referred to laws in 1641 and 1642. I fail to find either, but October 7, 1640 (Records, i. 306), the law was passed which is incorporated, partly literally, in this section. At that time there were to be three recorders, and apparently all entries were to be certified every six months to the recorder at Boston. See also Rec. i, 276, where the Recorder has a fee for "receiving the books of men's houses and lands from the towns" — W. H. W.

[39] I feel very sure that the Connecticut code gives our law of 1649, except the section obliging towns to provide one ordinary in each, which was a local law. All the other provisions are to be found in our law of 1660, though in the latter edition are many later sections. But those copied in the Connecticut code are substantially the ones passed here May 14, 1645 (Records, ii. 100) and November 4, 1646 (Records, ii. 172), and they are mostly marked in the margin L. 1, p. 20. — W. H. W.

[40] The new section refers to a man striking his wife, or a woman her husband. The new form is in our Code of 1660, under title "Marriages," p. 51. I do not find the original section in Conn. or N. Haven code, but it was doubtless the same as Liberty No. 80, which E. Hutchinson considers as covered by the title "Marriages." — W. H. W.

[41] The law as it stands in 1660 refers to acts of 1641, 1647, 1651, and 1652. I have already (*ante*, p. 25) shown that no law of 1641 is found, but Sept. 27, 1642 (Records, ii. 29), a law was passed as follows: "That all vessels of cask used for any liquor, fish or other commodities to be put to sale shall be of London assize and that fit persons shall be appointed from time to time, in places needful, to gage all such vessels or casks; and such as shall be found of due size shall be marked with the gauger's mark and no other; and he shall have for his pains four pence for every tun and so proportionably; and it is ordered that Mr. Will Aspenwall, Mr. Venner and Thomas Boarman shall be gaugers of cask for this year, and till others be chosen in their room. The gauger's mark shall be 'G.'"

Now the Connecticut code agrees entirely with the first order, word for word, except that it begins "that all cask used for Tar or other commodities to be put to sale shall be assized as follows: viz: every cask commonly called barrels or half hogsheads shall contain twenty-eight gallons wine measure and other vessels proportionable." These words seem to define the term "London assize." It also adds "that every cooper shall have a district brand-mark on his own cask, upon pain of forfeiture of twenty shillings in either case and so proportionably for lesser vessels."

The substance of this last order is in our revision of 1660, but I fail to find it in our Records, either in 1647 or any other year.

I infer, therefore, that 1647 is a misprint for 1649, and that the Connecticut code gives exactly the form in which our law stood in that edition; as it is evident that in 1649 this law was codified and received verbal changes. Compare the New Haven Code, which keeps the term "London assize," and adds also the penalty if the cooper omits to brand. — W. H. W.

9. May 7, 1651 (Records, iv. part 1, pp. 41–42), "for explanation of some words in the printed law, entitled Leather, viz. in that section in the margent entitled Searchers sworn their Duty, by the words (line the fourth) to make search and view within the precincts of their limits," etc., etc. Also "concerning those words in the section on the margin entitled Well tanned and dried, penalty, line the fifth," etc., etc. Also "concerning the last words entitled Triers of Leathers seized," etc., etc.[42]

10. May 26, 1652 (Records, iv. part 1, p. 79) an addition is made to the law "as is directed for bread, by order of Court, page 3, title Bakers."[43]

11. May 26, 1652 (Records, iv. part 1, p. 82), "whereas there is a manifest and inconvenient mistake in the penning of the order, title General Court, page the 8th of the last printed book," etc., etc.[44]

12. May 26, 1652 (Records, iv. part 1, p. 84), ordered, "that the printed order about money shall be in force until the first of September next, and no longer."[45]

13. May 26, 1652 (Records, iv. pt. 1, p. 88), "as enjoined by law, title Military, p. 39."

14. Oct. 19, 1652 (Records, iv. pt. 1, p. 106). "Whereas by the law, title Military, page 42, section 6, every captain," etc.[46]

---

[42] Here the Connecticut and New Haven codes are very brief. But the full references above show that our law of 1649 must have been much like that of 1660. — W. H. W.

[43] This means of course the Printed Laws, as in 1660 we find on p. 4 this title, and at the end of it this section as passed in 1652. The New Haven law is almost identical with our law of 1660 (omitting the last section), except that ours has a little clause (p. 5, lines 10 and 11) applying also to butter. I do not find the law authorizing this, and I doubt if it would have been dropped by the New Haven men. Hence I infer it was not in the law of 1649, but was added in 1660. — W. H. W.

[44] This error evidently refers to a law passed October 18, 1650 (Records, iv. part 1, p. 35). This law refers back to law 283, which is the marginal number for a law passed March 3, 1635–6 (Records, i. 169, 170). This primitive law regulated a disagreement between the two houses, where the greater part of each house held its own opinion. In 1650, as above noted, this was declared to mean the greater part of those present and voting. In 1652 this last law was repealed, and it was declared that when there was a difference it should be "determined by the major part of the whole court." Palfrey, iii. 42, says that this means the whole court sitting together, and not action by concurrent votes.

The meaning of the phrase "the last printed book" has been already discussed. — W. H. W.

[45] Here follows a long order establishing the Mint at Boston and making its coin, together with English money, the only legal tender. I presume that the title "Money," in the Code of 1649, was a copy of the law passed Sept. 27, 1642 (Records, ii. 29), which is as follows: —

"Ordered that the Holland ducatour, worth three gilders, shall be current at six shillings in all payments within our jurisdiction; and the rix-dollar, being two and a half gilders, shall be likewise current at five shillings: and the ryall of eight shall be also current at five shillings."

Connecticut had a similar act, but not in its Code. Wampum or Peage was also at times a legal tender, but our law is to be found under those titles. — W. H. W.

[46] These two references to the title Military show that it covered at least pp. 39–42 in the Code of 1649; and I have already shown that there was a section 10 (see *ante*, p. 87,) in this printed law. — W. H. W.

15. Same date (Records, iv. pt. 1, p. 105), "as is provided in the printed law, page first,"—in regard to actions triable in any court, etc.[47]

16. Same date (Records, iv. pt. 1, p. 107), "The late order about swine is repealed and the printed law is in force in that respect."[48]

17. May 18, 1653 (Records, iv. pt. 1, p. 134), the question was decided as to what was meant "by the law, title Weights and Measures."

18. June 2, 1653 (Records, iv. part 1, p. 150), reference is made to "the law, title Masters and Servants," etc., etc.

19. August 30, 1653 (Records, iv. pt. 1, p. 151), a committee was appointed to examine the Treasurer's accounts, etc., "according to the law, page 26, in the second book."[49]

20. August 30, 1653 (Records, iv. part 1, p. 152), reference is made to "the law, title Impost, page 27."

21. May 3, 1654 (Records, iv. part 1, p. 184), "whereas experience hath manifested some inconvenience in the interpretation of the law, title Appeals, the second printed book, page 1, "wherein it is expressed that all appeals shall be accounted in the nature of a writ of error."[50]

22. November 24, 1654 (Records, iv. part 1, p. 218), "whereas this Court hath laid an impost on wines imported into any part of this jurisdiction, as in title Impost, in the first printed book,[51] appears," etc., etc.

23. May 14, 1656 (Records, iv. part 1, p. 259), "the Treasurer cannot send forth his warrants to them, as is provided by the law, Charges Public. page the 9th," etc., etc.

---

[47] This would be under title "Actions," and naturally stand on page 1.—W. H. W.

[48] The title Swine is found in 1660, and evidently, by the citation, it was in the Code of 1649.—W. H. W.

[49] The title "Treasurer," in the Code of 1660, cites laws of 1648, 54, 57, 58. I suppose the printed law here above cited was that passed May 10, 1648 (Records, ii. 244). The citation p. *26* of the second book, as it stands printed in Shurtleff's edition, would be exceptional, if that book, as we have already concluded, did not exceed 16 pages. An examination made by Mr. C. B. Tillinghast, State Librarian, shows that the original is doubtless 16, the corresponding figures where they occur as 1653 having the same peculiar "1" easily to be confounded with a "2." —W. H. W.

[50] This law was passed May 2, 1649 (Records, ii. 279), "to be published forthwith but not to be of force till after the end of the next Quarter Court." It was evidently not in the Code of 1649, but stood on page 1 of the Supplement, or second printed book. I would here note that it is section 2 of title Appeals in the Laws of 1660; and also that section 3 is wrongly cited in the margin as passed in 1643. That section is the law of August 30, *1653* (Records, iv. part 1, p. 152), and at the end of this title in 1660 the citation is 1642, 47, 49, 50, 53, and 54.—W. H. W.

[51] The meaning of the first and second printed books has been already discussed.—W. H. W.

24. May 6, 1657 (Records, iv. part 1, p. 291), "whereas the clause in the law, page thirty-two, mentioning evidence, is obscure, — the jury may bring in a *non liequet*, — which words hath occasioned much trouble and delay in civil proceedings, this Court doth hereby repeal that clause," etc.[52]

25. May 26, 1658 (Records, iv. part 1, pp. 335 and 336), "that the freemen within their several towns have liberty and power according to the last law or order entitled Townships."

"For explanation and emendation of two laws in the printed book, title Townships," etc., etc.

26. October 19, 1658 (Records, iv. part 1, p. 347), in regard to electing magistrates annually, "and that clause of the printed law enjoining the nomination of twenty persons is hereby repealed," etc., etc.

27. May 11, 1659 (Records, iv. part 1, p. 366), in regard to persons aiding the Quakers, etc., "the Court, on perusal of the law, title Arrests, resolve, that the Treasurers of the several counties are and shall hereby be empowered to sell the said persons to any of the English nation at Virginia or Barbadoes."

---

[52] This is a most interesting matter, but I will first explain the text. In the Code of 1660, under title "Jurors," § 2, we find a marginal citation, L. 1. p. 47, and the text establishes Grand Jurors according to the law of March 4, 1634–5 (Records, i. 143). Then follows the clause about jurors not being bound to reveal secrets which do not affect the state, which is Liberty No. 61. Both of these probably were in the Code of 1649, and next to them doubtless stood Liberty No. 31, (the subject of the above amendment in 1657), which allowed the jury in case of doubt to give a *non-liquit*, or a special verdict which left the judgment to the Court.

I do not see why the reference is to Liber 1, p. 47, as the text above is p. 32. But there are so many misprints in our Codes that I suspect this to be one, especially as the page on which it stands in 1660 is numbered 47.

Moreover the marginal references in 1660 are to Lib. 1, p. 32 and p. 31 against the sections preceding and following this very entry of L. 1, p. 47. We have already seen that in the printed laws of 1649 the title "Military" covers pp. 39–42, and the title "Jurors" must have come earlier.

But the whole order in 1657 is worth printing as showing the belief, even then, in the right of juries to judge of the law as well as the facts. It reads: —

"Whereas, in all civil cases depending in suit, the plaintiff affirmeth that the defendant hath done him wrong, and accordingly presents his case for judgment and satisfaction, it behooveth both Court and jury to see that the affirmation be proved by sufficient evidence, else the case must be found for the defendant: and so it is also in a criminal case; for, in the eye of the law, every man is honest and innocent unless it be proved legally to the contrary. All evidence ariseth partly from matter of fact and partly from law or argument. The matter of fact is always feasible to be judged of as well by the jury as by the Court; and concerning the law, or the point of law, in reference to the case in question, it is either more easy and generally known, or more difficult to be discerned. The duty of the jury is, if they do understand the law to the satisfaction of their consciences, not to put it off from themselves, but to find accordingly; but if any of the jury doth rest unsatisfied what is law in the case, then the whole jury have liberty to present a special verdict, viz.: if the law be so or so in such a point, we find for the plaintiff, — but if the law be otherwise, we find for the defendant: — in which case the determination is left to the Court."

Then follows the repeal of the old law and the Court "directeth according to what is above expressed for the future." — W. H. W.

28. May 31, 1660 (Records, iv. part 1, p. 420), the Court declares "that no man whosoever shall be admitted to the freedom of this body politic but such as are members of some church of Christ, and in full communion, which they declare to be the true intent of that ancient law, page the 8th of the 2d month, anno gr. 1631."[53]

The following table gives the marginal citations in the edition of 1660 which are credited to Liber 1. The variations from a strictly alphabetical arrangement may be explained by a change in the title according to the views of the editor in 1649 and the later issue. It seems probable that we must resort to the idea of misprints to account for pages 57 and 58 under the title "Marshal," as "Watching" and "Wills" were on pp. 52 and 53:—

Citations in the Edition of Laws in 1660, from Liber 1.

1660.	Title.	Liber 1.	1660.	Title.	Liber 1.
P. 2,	Actions,	do. p. 16.	P. 41,	Indians,	do. p. 28.
	do.	do. p. 49.	42,	do.	do. p. 28.
4,	Attachments, Summons,	do. p. 49.	44,	Innkeepers,	do. p. 30.
11,	Cattle, Trespass,	do. p. 51.	45,	do.	do. p. 30.
12,	Criminal Cases,	do. p. 46.	47,	Jurors,	do. p. 32.
16,	Constable,	do. p. 46.		do.	do. p. 47. [?]
20,	Conveyances,	do p. 16.	48,	do.	do. p. 31.
22,	Courts,	do. p. 16.	52,	Marshal,	do. p. 38.
	do.	do. p. 36.		do.	do. p. 57. [?]
	do.	do. p. 24.	53,	do.	do. p. 58. [?]
23,	do.	do. p. 14.		do.	do. p. 10.
	do.	do. p. 15.		do.	do. p. 45.
	do.	do. p. 36.	66,	Powder,	do. p. 45.
24,	do.	do. p. 15.	67,	Punishment,	do. p. 50.
	do.	do. p. 36.	68,	Records,	do. p. 47.
31,	Fines,	do. p. 38.	73,	Strangers,	do. p. 23.
	do.	do. p. 22.	74,	Sureties (Courts),	do. p. 15.
33,	Freemen,	do p. 23.	79,	Watching,	do. p. 52.
34,	Heresy,	do. p. 2.	81,	Wills,	do. p. 53.
40,	Impress,	do. p. 9.			

[53] In the Code of 1660 this section has a marginal citation of L. 2, p. 8. It precedes a clause declaring that church-members are not exempt from public service as officers, which is cited as L. 1, p. 23. — W. H. W.

The preceding pages complete the citations from the Records respecting the Code of 1649 and the Supplement of 1650; there remains only to copy the entries in regard to the Laws between 1650 and 1660, when the Code was printed, and the later votes preceding and following the Revision of 1672.

May 23, 1650, the following order[54] was passed (Records, iii. 193): —

"Whereas this Commonwealth is much defective for want of laws for maritime affairs, and forasmuch as there are already many good laws made and published by our own land, and the French nation, and other Kingdoms and commonwealths; this Court doth therefore order that the said laws, printed and published in a book called *Lex Mercatoria*, shall be perused and duly considered, and such of them as are approved by this Court shall be declared and published to be in force within this jurisdiction after such time as this Court shall appoint.

"And it is further ordered that Mr. Bellingham, Mr. Nowell, Mr. Willoughby, Capt. Hathorne, the Auditor-general [Duncan], and Mr. John Allen, shall be a committee to ripen the work, and to make return of that which they shall conclude upon, unto the General Court; and the time of their meeting to be the first third day of the sixth month next."

June 22, 1650 (Records, iv. pt. 1, p. 23, and iii. 204), the following vote was passed:[55] —

"It is ordered by this Court and the authority thereof, that henceforth the Secretary for the General Court, shall, within two months after the end of every session, send unto the clerk of every shire court, as also unto the present or late deputies of each town, or to the constable where no deputy is, a copy of all general orders made in each Court, for which he shall receive of the Treasurer for every such copy after the rate of eight pence per page, which the Treasurer shall charge upon each town together with their country rate from time to time, viz, for the copies sent unto the particular towns.

"And it is farther ordered by the authority aforesaid, that the deputies,

[54] This is from the House Journal, and is more in detail than the regular joint record in Records, iv. part 1, p. 10. — W. H. W.

[55] Records, iv. part 1, p. 63, mention that the Secretary, for this service of transcribing orders and for other services, is to receive forty pounds annually.

August 30, 1653 (Records, iii. 317, and iv. part 1, p. 152), it was ordered "that the several gross sums of all the incomes, viz.: upon the annual rate upon imposts, vintners, entering of actions, fines, forfeitures &c. as also of all expenses, viz. of all Courts, commissioners, gratuities, allowances, payments, debts &c. be exactly by the Auditor certified to the General Court annually, and expressed in all the copies of the laws sent unto the several towns, made in the first session of the Court of Election, whereby the true state of things in that respect may be obvious to all that are concerned therein." — W. H. W.

or constable of each town where no deputy is, shall cause the same to be audibly read, in a public town meeting, warned by the constable of each town, within ten days after their receipt thereof, on penalty of five pounds upon any deputy or constable for neglect of their respective duties.

"And it is farther ordered by the authority aforesaid, that such reading thereof in any shire or market town in each shire, shall be a sufficient publication thereof from time to time; provided also that the Treasurer shall have a copy without payment from time to time."

May 13, 1651 (Records, iv. part 1, p. 50) voted as follows: —

"In answer to the petition of Mr. Richard Russell for his allowance in the late law books, which was occasioned by the Court's alteration of some things therein etc., it is ordered, that in consideration of those losses mentioned in the petition and other that he hath lately sustained, he shall have allowed him twenty pounds out of the next rate."

October 23, 1651 (Records, iv. part 1, p. 69, and iii. 252): —

"Whereas, in the year 1650, there was a committee chosen to peruse a book called *Lex Mercatoria*, to extract such laws from thence as might be suitable for our use in this commonwealth, which said committee have not yet met according as was then concluded: that the said order may be further prosecuted, it is ordered by this Court, that the accomplishing of that work shall be referred to Mr. Nowell and the auditor-general [Duncan], who are hereby chosen a committee and desired to peruse the said book, and to collect from thence such laws as they shall judge meet for our use, according as that order doth direct, and to make return to the next General Court."

[An important order about the Records, passed in 1652, will be found *ante*, p. 70.]

October 26, 1652 (Records, iv. part 1, p. 119): —

"It is ordered that Richard Bellingham, Esq., and William Hibbens, Mr. John Glover and the Secretary [Rawson,] or any three of them, shall be a committee to peruse the laws that have passed this Court, and to determine which of them shall go to the towns."

May 18, 1653 (Records, iv. part 1, p. 138, and iii. 308): —

[56] "In answer to the petition of Mr. Joseph Hills, desiring due recompense for his service done the country about the laws, the Court judgeth it meet to allow him ten pounds out of the next country rate."

June 2, 1653 (Records, iv. part 1, p. 149), voted as follows: —

---

[56] See this petition in full, *ante*, p. 81. — W. H. W.

"Mr. Bellingham, Mr. Glover and Mr. Hill are appointed with the Secretary [Rawson] to peruse the laws that is passed this Court, comparing them with the original copies."

Sept. 10, 1653 (Records, iv. part 1, p. 180): —

"It is ordered that the Deputy Governor [Bellingham], Mr. Hibbens, Mr. Glover, and the Secretary [Rawson], Mr. Hills, or any two of them with the Secretary, shall be a committee to examine the laws that passed this Court.

"It is ordered that the Secretary shall take care that the old book of records shall be fairly written out, for which he shall have satisfaction by the page, as the Court allows."

May 3, 1654 (Records, iv. part 1, p. 182): —

"It is ordered by this Court, that henceforth the Secretary, shall, within ten days after this present sessions and so from time to time, deliver a copy of all laws that are published unto the president,[57] or printer, who shall forthwith

[57] This reference, like the earlier one on p. 80, is to Henry Dunster, President of Harvard College, who had an interest in the only press in the colony. This press was given by Josse Glover, aided by some gentleman of Amsterdam. From an interesting essay by A. M. Davis, in the Proceedings of the American Antiquarian Society for April, 1888, I learn some new facts about this press. Glover died on his passage hither, and his widow married Dunster. Glover's heirs sued Dunster, and thus we learn something of the books printed. It seems that Glover had a claim against the press for some twenty pounds for expenses, and Dunster also improved it. The actual work was done first by Steven Day, and then by Samuel Green. Dunster sold the press, or rather his claim, to the college when he removed, which was in April, 1655. He was president from 1640 to his dismissal, for doctrinal errors, Oct. 24, 1654.

In the papers connected with the lawsuit are notes about some of the books he printed, and of these the following concern our subject: —

The Freeman's Oath.

The Capital Laws.

The Law Book, 17 sheets, 600 copies, using 21 reams of paper. Sold at 17 pence a book, £42.. 10.. 00. The printing cost £15.. 16.. 03, and the paper £5.. 05.. 00.

This, of course, was printed by Day late in 1648, and was the edition cited as the Laws of 1649. The items correspond very well with the similar entries about the Psalm Book, viz., 33 sheets, 1,700 copies, sold at 20 pence each, amounting to £141.. 13.. 04. Printing, £33.. 00.. 00, paper, 116 reams, £29.. 00.. 00.

It will be seen that the Laws, 17 sheets and 600 copies, would take 10,200 sheets; and the Psalms, 33 sheets and 1,700 copies, would require 56,100 sheets. The ratio is exactly that of the paper specified, viz., 21 reams and 116 reams. I believe a printer's ream was then 21½ quires, and 21 reams would be 10,836 sheets.

The Psalm Book, from remaining examples, we know was printed eight pages to a sheet, size of page 6¼ by 3⅜ inches. There are 37 sheets, including two of preface. The Laws of 1660 are eight pages to a sheet, each 9 by 5¼ inches. It seems impossible that the Laws of 1649 could have been printed on as small pages as the Psalms, and, as we have to take either four or eight pages to the sheet, I infer the Laws were four large pages. In this case the 17 sheets would give 68 pages, which would agree very well with our previous estimate of 56 pages for the text, and allow some pages for title, preface, and table or index. As before argued, it seems impossible that there were twice as many pages in the book, and yet no citations can be found above page 58 as the extreme.

There is also an entry for Laws, printed after Green took the press, 5 sheets, cost of paper, £1.. 05.. 00; of printing, £5.. 00.. 00. This may have been some of the special laws.

It seems, indeed, surprising, if we have interpreted these entries correctly, that 600 copies

make an impression thereof, to the number of five, six, or seven hundred, as the Court shall order: all which copies the Treasurer shall take of and pay for in wheat or otherwise, to content, for the number of five hundred after the rate of one penny a sheet, or eight shillings a hundred for five hundred sheets of a sort, for so many sheets as the books shall contain.

"And the Treasurer shall distribute the books to every magistrate one, to every Court one, to the Secretary one, to each town where no magistrate dwells one, and the rest among the towns that bear public charge within the jurisdiction, according to the number of freemen in each town.

"And the order that engageth the Secretary to transcribe copies for the towns and others, is in that respect repeated, the Court allowing him ten pounds this year only, in respect of what benefit hereby is withdrawn from him."

"And it is further ordered, that Mr. Samuel Symonds, Major Dennison, and Mr. Joseph Hills shall examine, compare, reconcile, and place together, in good order, all former laws both printed and written, and make fit titles and tables for ready recourse to any particular contained in them, and to present the same unto the next Court of Election, to be considered of, that so order may be taken for the printing of them together in one book, whereby they be more useful than now they are or can be."

May 14, 1654 (Records, iv. part 1, p. 195): —

"It is ordered, that the honored Governor [Endicott], the Secretary [Rawson], Capt. [Thomas] Clarke, and Mr. [Joseph] Hill, or any three of them, shall be a committee to peruse and view the laws passed this session, according to former order."

June 9, 1654 (Records, iv. part 1, p. 196): —

"Upon conference with Mr. Dunster and the printer, in reference to the imprinting of the Acts of the General Court, whereby we understand some inconveniences may accrue to the printer, by printing that law which recites the agreement for printing, it is therefore ordered that the said law be not put forth in print, but kept amongst the written records of this Court."

October 14, 1656 (Records, iv. part 1, p. 281): —

"It is ordered that the Deputy Governor [Bellingham], Capt. Clarke, Mr. Secretary [Rawson], and Capt. Savage, shall examine the laws of the General Court for two years past, and cause such laws as are of public concern-

should have been printed of the Laws of 1649, and all have disappeared. But if 1,700 copies of the Psalms were printed the extreme rarity of extant copies is perhaps equally remarkable, especially as more persons would keep the psalm-book than would care for the code. The facts collected, however, may renew the attention of collectors, and perhaps lead to the identification of some portion, at least, of one of these volumes. — W. H. W.

ment to be written out, whereby they may forthwith be committed to the press and sent to the several Courts."

May 6, 1657 (Records, iv. part 1, p. 292), the following vote was passed: —

"Whereas it is found by experience that the passing and enacting of divers grants, orders and laws upon the first proposal, hath occasioned many inconveniencies which might have been prevented by mature deliberation, and that it is the laudable custom of the Parliament of England to pass no bills which have not been there read and debated, it is therefore ordered and enacted by this Court, that no grant of land, law or order (except transient acts) shall henceforth be of force but such as, after reading and mature consideration on three several days, shall be approved and consented to by the major part of Magistrates and Deputies."

May 6, 1657 (Records, iv. part 1, p. 299): —

"It is ordered by this Court, that all laws of public concernment, not yet printed, be forthwith transcribed by the Secretary, and sent to the press to be printed at the public charge; the printer to be paid by the Treasurer."

May 26, 1658 (Records, iv. part 1, p. 337): —

"It is ordered, that Major General Daniel Denison diligently peruse, examine and weigh every law and compare them with others of like nature, and such as are clear, plain and good, free from any just exception, to stand without any animadversion, as approved; such as are repealed or fit to be repealed, to be so marked and the reasons given; such as are obscure, contradictory, or seeming so, to be rectified and the emendations prepared; where there is two or more laws about one and the same thing, to prepare a draught of one law that may comprehend the same; to make a plain and easy table; and to prepare what else may present in the perusing of them to be necessary and useful: and make return to the next sessions of this Court."

October 19, 1658 (Records, iv. part 1, p. 350): —

"It is ordered by this Court and the authority thereof that the Book of Laws, as they have been revised and corrected and put in form by order of this Court, together with the alterations and additions here under expressed, shall forthwith be printed, and be of force in one month after the same; and that there shall be a perfect table made there unto what remains yet to be done, to be prepared for the press by our honored major-general; and that in the meantime the laws stand in force as now they be."

Then follow seven amendments to the laws, two being in the negative, and the following vote: —

"It is ordered, that when the present copy of the Laws is finished by the Major-General [Denison], that they be sent to the Treasurer, who shall take care that they be printed as speedily as may be: also, that the preface to the old law book, with such alterations as shall be judged meet by the Governor [Endecott] and Major General, be added thereunto, and presented to the General Court to be approved of: and Mr. Danforth is appointed to oversee the impression."

May 28, 1659 (Records, iv. part 1, p. 381): —

"It is ordered, that the Treasurer dispose of Mr. Norton's books now at the press, delivering every member of this Court one, and to the several towns in proportion to their rates, and twenty or thirty to Mr. Norton, presenting this Court's acknowledgment to him for his pains at present; and giving every minister one: the like order about the laws."

May 31, 1660 (Records, iv. part 1, p. 422): —

"For the more equal distribution of the law books, when they shall be printed, it is ordered by this Court and the authority thereof, that the printer shall deliver the said books to the country Treasurer as soon as they are past the press, who, immediately upon receiving of them, shall deliver or cause to be delivered to every magistrate one; to every deputy of this General Court one; to the Secretary and Clerk of the Deputies one apiece for themselves; to the Recorder or Clerk of every County Court three apiece to be kept for the use of the several Courts:

"And the remainder of the said books, the Treasurer shall send to every county treasurer such a proportion as is due to each county according to what charge they bear in the country rates.

"And the county Treasurers are hereby enjoined to send unto every town in the respective countries their town's proportion, according to the rule above mentioned, and deliver the same to some meet person employed by each town to receive them, engaging to satisfy the Treasurer for them according to his disbursements, that so no charge be put upon the country for the same, as Capt. Gooking, the Treasurer of the country, and Treasurer of each county shall determine, both for price and quality of pay.

"And that provision be made for the eastern parts, it is ordered, that before the division there be fifty books laid apart for their supply, they making like payment to the country Treasurer for the same; and that Portsmouth and Dover have twenty books laid aside for them on the same terms.

"And it is further ordered, that Mr. Thomas Danforth, who was to have the oversight of the impression, make an index to the said book with all convenient speed, that so the work may be no longer delayed."

October 16, 1660 (Records, iv. part 1, p. 432): —

"It being a matter of some concernment to the country rightly to understand when this last impression of the laws are to be in force and begin to take place, this Court doth therefore order and declare, willing and requiring all persons concerned to take notice, that the said impression of laws shall be of force after the expiration of thirty days from the date of these presents, and that in the meantime the old books to stand good and to be attended to as before."

We have thus completed the record up to the issue of the edition of 1660, which is hereinafter presented in a fac-simile reprint. The evidence thus collected seems to show that Nathaniel Ward was the principal compiler of the Body of Liberties; that Bellingham was probably the chief inciter of the edition of 1649; that Joseph Hills prepared the Supplement of 1650; and that Secretary Rawson, Capt. Thomas Clark of Boston, and especially Major General Daniel Denison[58] were chiefly concerned in collecting, condensing, and arranging the code of 1660.

In the nature of things, no finality is ever to be reached in law-making. The code of 1660 was immediately subjected to amendments and additions, and various yearly supplements were considered necessary. The copy preserved in the library of the American Antiquarian Society at Worcester, being the one formerly owned by Secretary Rawson, contains probably all these supplementary sheets. By the kindness of that Society, *fac-similes* of these pages are printed in our edition. In the meantime the following extracts from the Records will show what steps were taken by the Legislature: —

May 22, 1661 (Records, iv. part 2, p. 4): —

"It is ordered and by this Court declared, that the order made in the third month, 1654, appointing the printing of the general orders of Court of

---

[58] Daniel Denison was born in England, in 1612, and came here with his father, William D., in 1631. He settled in Ipswich in 1635, and was a deputy from that town for several years, being Speaker in 1649, 1651, and 1652. He was an Assistant from 1653, till his death in 1682, and Commissioner of the United Colonies for seven years. He was very prominent in military affairs and major-general much of the time from 1653 to 1680. He was town-clerk of Ipswich, and in 1653 was chosen Secretary in the absence of Edward Rawson. He married a daughter of Gov. Thomas Dudley, and was essentially one of the ruling caste in the colony. He must have received a good education in England as his letters and state papers show. He left a treatise in manuscript entitled, "Irenicon, or Salve for New England's Sore," which was published after his death by his pastor, Rev. Wm. Hubbard. A good memoir of him is in the N.E. Historical and Genealogical Register for July, 1869. — W. H. W.

each session within ten days, be again revived, and be in force so far as it refers to the annual printing of laws, any law to the contrary notwithstanding."

October 19, 1664 (Records, iv. part 2, p. 136): —

"Mr. Thomas Danforth, Capt. Thomas Clark, Mr. Wm. Parkes are appointed a committee to join with the Secretary [Rawson], if he be well, to peruse the laws of public concernment, made this year or formerly, not published, and to take care that they be speedily printed and sent to the several towns of this jurisdiction; and, in case of the secretary's sickness, to proceed without him, and that Mr. Danforth supply his place in all other cases."

At the May session in 1665 the General Court was greatly disturbed by the demands of the Royal Commissioners, Nicolls, Carr, Cartwright, and Maverick, who presented twenty-six changes which they desired to have made in the Book of the General Laws and Liberties of 1660. Their principal objects were to substitute for all expressions of the supremacy of the Commonwealth, an acknowledgment of the Royal authority; to procure a recognition of the Church of England, and to destroy the long-standing limitation of citizenship to church-members.

An examination of the edition of 1672 shows that only one or two points were conceded by the Court, either then or prior to that issue, and that the recognition of his majesty's supremacy was allowed in one clause whilst the power of the local authority was asserted in a score. The right of strangers to become citizens was nominally conceded, but on conditions which afforded the minimum of relief to all but church-members. See Code of 1672, p. 56.

October 11, 1665 (Records, iv. part 2, p. 282): —

"This Court doth appoint Mr. Thomas Danforth, the Secretary [Rawson], and Mr. [Anthony] Stoddard, to survey the laws that have been made this year, of public concernment, and cause them forthwith, with such other not yet printed, to be printed."

October 19, 1666 (Records, iv. part 2, p. 330): —

"Mr. Thomas Danforth, the Secretary [Rawson], and Capt. [Francis] Norton, are appointed a committee to peruse the laws of this year, and determine which of them shall be printed."

May 31, 1670 (Records, iv. part 2, p. 453): —

"Whereas there is a great want of law books for the use of several Courts and inhabitants of this jurisdiction at present, and very few of them that are extant are complete, containing all laws now in force amongst us, it is therefore ordered by this Court, that Major Eliazer Lusher, Capt. Thomas Clarke, Capt. Edward Johnson, Capt. Hopestill Foster, Capt. George Corwin, and Capt. Joshua Hubbard, or any four of them whereof Maj. Lusher to be one, shall, and hereby are appointed to be a committee to, peruse all our laws now in force, to collect and draw up any literal errors, or misplacing of words or sentences therein, or any liberties infringed, and to make a convenient table for the ready finding of all things therein, that so they may be fitted for the press; and the same to present to the next session of this Court, to be further considered of and approved by the Court."

This committee seems to have attended to its duty, for at the next session, October 12, 1670, "the Court having perused and considered of the return of committee to whom the review of the laws was referred, etc., by the General Court in May last," proceeded to make a number of verbal changes, all of which will be found in the Records, iv. part 2, pp. 467–9. The following vote may be noted: —

"To some queries, whether, if at any time there appear contradictions betwixt laws or parts of laws, some being made formerly, some latter, shall the late law be accounted of force in all parts, and all laws or parts of laws formerly made be accounted null wherein they are contradicted by any latter law, though they be not repealed or not, — as instance in troopers fined by a former law 5 shillings, by a latter 10 shillings —. It is ordered by the Court that the latter stand."

May 31, 1671 (Records, iv. part 2, p. 488): —

"Mr. Richard Russell, Mr. Thomas Danforth, and Mr. William Stoughton, or any two of them, are appointed with Capt. Thomas Clarke and Capt. [William] Davis, to be a committee, and are empowered to cause the book of laws to be printed, and an exact table to be made thereto with a marginal note of the word 'Repealed' unto all laws that stand repealed; and the Treasurer is required to pay for the impression and dispose of the books, as to him shall seem expedient for the public good and advantage."

May 15, 1672 (Records, iv. part 2, p. 514): —

"It is ordered that the former committee, with the Secretary, formerly appointed to send out the laws to the press, be hereby ordered to peruse the laws now this Court has made, and to make a preface and table and what else is requisite, and send all out to be printed presently."

These extracts bring the matter up to the issue of the edition of 1672, already reprinted in *fac-simile* by the city of Boston. To complete the record I transcribe all the later references to be found in the Records, up to the overthrow of the First Charter in 1686, and the beginning of the Inter-Charter period under Andros.

May 7, 1673 (Records, iv. part 2, p. 559): —

"Mr. John Usher having been at the sole charge of the impression of the book of laws, and presented the Governor, magistrates, secretary, as also every deputy, [*and*] the clerk of the deputies one, and Capt. Davis one, the Court judgeth it meet to order, that for at least this seven years, unless he shall have sold them all before that time, there shall be no other or further impression made by any person thereof, in this jurisdiction, under the penalty this Court shall see cause to lay on any that shall adventure in that kind, beside making full satisfaction to the said Mr. John Usher or his assigns, for his charge and damage therein. Voted by the whole Court met together."

October 15, 1673 (Records, iv. part 2, p. 562): —

"It is ordered by this Court and the authority thereof, that all laws and orders of this Court which are thought fit to be published at the end of every sessions, shall be forthwith sent to the press and also read in the market-place at Boston upon the fifth day, being a lecture day, within ten days after the end of such sessions, which being performed, is and shall be accounted sufficient publication; and further, that printed copies shall be disposed at the discretion of the Treasurer, and care taken for the same by the secretary and marshal-general, as the law directs, folio 231."

It has been already shown, by the reprint of the Revision of 1672, that the Secretary continued to issue consecutive pages annually of a Supplement. After the lapse of some six years, however, the ever-attractive subject of a new codification was again mooted. October 15, 1679 (Records, v. 244), the following vote was passed: —

"Upon perusal of the result of the late Synod, wherein they seem to intimate, at least, as if there were some doubt concerning some of our laws, whether they were sufficiently warranted by the word of God, and other laws not so well worded as may be effectual to the end intended, or honorable to this Court; as also some may be wanting to the ends therein contained; it is therefore ordered, that the honored Thomas Danforth, esq., Deputy Governor, Joseph Dudley, esq., Capt. John Richards, Mr. Anthony Stoddard, and Capt. Daniel Fisher, be a committee to consider our laws already made, that may need emendation or may not so clearly be warranted from the word of God, and to draw up such laws and orders as, being presented by them at the next Court of Election, may then be considered, and upon mature deliberation be confirmed: which this present Court cannot have time to do."

May 19, 1680 (Records, v. 268), it was voted as follows: —

"On a motion made to this Court, for the reprinting of the laws, etc., the Court approves of the motion, and do order that William Stoughton, esq., Joseph Dudley, esq., Peter Bulkeley, esq., or any two of them, with Capt. Daniel Fisher, Mr. Anthony Stoddard, Capt. John Waite, Lieut. William Johnson and Capt. Elisha Hutchinson, or any three of them, be a committee to consider our laws already made, and that need emendation, and what else is necessary referring thereunto, together with his Majesty's letter, now under consideration, as it relates to this matter."

October 13, 1680 (Records, v. p. 294): —

"This Court having in May last appointed a committee for the revisal of our laws, and nothing of that nature being yet done, it is ordered by this Court, that the Committee formerly appointed for that work do effectually apply themselves to the same, and make return of what they do therein to the next Court of Election, and that the charges of this work be defrayed by the country Treasurer."

Under the same date (Records, v. p. 301): —

"Humphrey Davy, esq., John Richards, esq., Capt. Elisha Hutchinson appointed, with Edward Rawson, Secretary, a committee to peruse the acts of this Court and the Laws, and determine what to send out to the press."

January 4, 1680–81 (Records, v. 303): —

"Whereas, notwithstanding what hath already passed this Court, concerning the revisal and amendment of our laws, respecting such things as are objected against them from England, &c. yet nothing is effected, the effectual proceedings therein being no small part of the work of this Court respecting our agents to be sent to England, it is therefore ordered, that the remaining part of that committee, viz. Joseph Dudley and Peter Bulkley, esquires, Mr. Stoddard and Capt. Hutchinson, together with John Richards, esq. Mr. Joseph Cooke and Mr. Joseph Lynde, the senior magistrate appointing time and place, as a committee apply themselves to that work, and make return to the next adjournment of this session, any former order notwithstanding."

October 18, 1681 (Records, v. p. 331): —

"The Court agree to proceed to the consideration of what is necessary to be done touching such laws as are objected against, and others of like nature, and to do therein what shall be incumbent on them and most conducible to their peace and safety."

At this time a serious attempt was made to conciliate the king, by making alterations in the more objectionable laws of the colony. In May, 1681 (Records, v. 321–2), the Legislature amended some laws. At a session held February 16, 1681–2, the court passed a long and humble address to the king, and ordered that the Acts of Trade and Navigation should be published and observed. They established naval officers for Boston and Salem, and passed the following votes, March 17, 1681–2 (Records, v. 339): —

"It is ordered by this Court and the authority thereof, that the 12th section of the capital laws, title *Conspiracy, Rebellion*, and the 18th section of said laws, title *Rebellious Son*, be and are hereby repealed: also the law referring to *Christmas*, page 57, 58, and the word *Commonwealth*, where it imports jurisdiction, is hereby repealed, and the word *Jurisdiction* is hereby inserted."

"If any man conspire and attempt any invasion, insurrection or public rebellion against the King's majesty his government here established, or shall endeavor to surprise any town or towns, fort or forts therein, or shall treacherously and perfidiously attempt the alteration and subversion of our frame of polity or government fundamentally, he shall be put to death."

October 24, 1684 (Records, v. p. 464): —

"It is ordered that Elisha Cook, Esq., Mr. Saffyn, and Mr. Fairweather with the Secretary, be a committee to peruse and fit the laws for the press, and to peruse the Address and the Court's letter to Mr. Humphreys."

(Mass. Archives, Vol. 47, No. 66.) "This Court considering that there is great need for to reprint the Laws in which there is a necessity for the Emendation of severall things: Do therefore think it meet that a Committee be chosen out of both Houses to consider of some expedient for the easing of what may be or hath been gravaminous for many yeares, and to make a report thereof to this Court upon Tuesday next att Eight o clock in the morning; and the Court to be adjourned in the meane while.

Voted by the Deputys the Honored Magistrates Consenting.

John Saffin per Order.

Not consented to

Edward Rawson Secret."

8 May, 85.

May 6, 1685 (Records, v. 473): —

"It is ordered, that John Richards, Samuel Nowell and Elisha Cooke, Esquires, with Mr. Oliver Purchase, Mr. John Saffin, Capt. John Smith, Capt. Richard Sprague, and Mr. Henry Bartholomew, shall and hereby are appointed a committee to revise the laws, and especially such as have been made since the last committee had the perusal and revisal of the body of them, and to make a return to the next Court of Election."[59]

May 27, 1685 (Records, v. p. 476): —

"It is ordered that the committee appointed at the last sessions of General Court, so called upon to make their report to the Court of their revising the laws, especially those more lately made, in order to their consideration at this Court, and that the work of revising the whole book of laws, passing, [*perusing?*] and preparing them for the press, be forthwith attended and set about."

"In obedience to the order of the honored General Court, dated 6th instant, empowering us a committee to revise the laws, especially those lately made, etc., — we accordingly have met and perused the said laws, and transferred them to their proper heads in the former transcript, where they will be found, sometimes wholly in their own words, sometimes in such necessary parts as were intended for alteration or explanation; which are either printed in said transcript in sheets, printed or written as there was occasion; to which we refer, reserving only the liberty of inserting the prefaces where reason may require.

JOHN RICHARDS, SAMUEL NOWELL,
ELISHA COOKE, JOHN SAFFYN, RICHARD SPRAGUE."

Same date (Records, v. p. 479): —

"The Court went on, day by day, to revise and peruse the transcript of the laws."

"For greater expedition in the present revisal of the laws, this Court doth order that they shall be sent to the press sheet by sheet; and that the Treasurer make payment to the printer for the same, paper and work, June 10th, 1685: and that Elisha Cook and Samuel Sewall, Esquires, be desired to oversee the press about that work."[60]

---

[59] Sewall notes in his Diary (i. 71) that the committee was chosen "at the earnest suit of the deputies, which would have had them make a report of next Tuesday, but agreed to be next Election Court." As the Court met on Wednesday, May 6th, and dissolved on May 8th, the order to report even on Election Day, May 27th, did not afford much time. The report, however, according to the record, was called for as soon as the deputies had organized. — W. H. W.

[60] This entry is duplicated exactly under date of June 4, 1685 (Records, v. p. 484). — W. H. W.

It is somewhat surprising to find the foregoing references to a new revision of the Laws as being contemplated by the Legislature in 1681 and again in 1685, since there can be no doubt that the scheme utterly failed. The relations of the Colony to the English Government may, however, explain the mystery. The enemies of the Colony, especially Randolph, were exceedingly busy in their attacks upon the Charter. December 17, 1681, Randolph arrived with a letter from King Charles II., dated October 21, 1681, concluding as follows: "In default whereof, we are fully resolved in Trinity Term next ensuing, to direct our Attorney-General to bring a *quo warranto* in our Court of King's Bench, whereby our Charter granted unto you, with all the powers thereof, may be legally evicted and made void." (Palfrey, iii. 351.)

The General Court promptly assembled, altered some laws, prepared an address to the king, and notified him that the Colony had already sent Joseph Dudley and John Richards as agents to him. These agents arrived in London, August 20, 1682, but, hampered as they were by secret instructions, they were unable to accomplish anything. Randolph hastened home during the winter, and June 27, 1683, the writ of *quo warranto* was issued. He arrived in Boston with a copy of the writ, October 23, 1683, having been preceded by the agents by three days. The Legislature was convened on November 7, 1683, and the documents were presented to them. (Records, v. 421.) Their only action was to empower Mr. Robert Humphreys, of London, a barrister, to appear for them before the court.

Early in 1684, however, the Crown lawyers changed their plans and abandoned the *quo warranto*. Instead of this a *scire facias* against the Governor and Company of Massachusetts Bay was issued from the Court of Chancery, April 16, directed to the Sheriff of Middlesex, who made his return that he could not find the defendants, or anything belonging to them, within his bailiwick. May 12, a second writ was issued and the same return made. June 21, the Lord Keeper (North, Lord Guilford) made a decree vacating the Charter, suspending it, however, till the autumn term, to give time to the defendants to plead to issue.

Of course the Legislature of Massachusetts could not do this within the time, even had it been so inclined; and on October 23, 1684, the final judgment was entered, despite the motion for a stay of proceedings made by Mr. Humphreys. Palfrey (iii. 392–3) gives these facts and discusses the probable reasons why the Crown took this particular mode of cancelling the Charter.

Soon after this judgment, Charles II. died, and James II. succeeded to the throne, February 6, 1685. From the time that the news of both events reached Boston, the colonial government was of necessity known to be only provisional. Bradstreet and Danforth were chosen as Governor and Deputy-Governor, but the General Court transacted little important business. May 14, 1686, Randolph arrived with an exemplification of the judgment and commissions for a new government. There were to be a President, Deputy-President, and sixteen Councillors, and their authority extended over Massachusetts, New Hampshire, Maine, and the King's Province. Joseph Dudley was made President and William Stoughton, Deputy. On May 20, 1686, the General Court dissolved.

Finally, on December 20, 1686, Sir Edmund Andros arrived at Boston with a commission to govern all New England, and the Colonial period of Massachusetts was at an end.

In view of the political troubles in 1685, as hereinbefore recited, it seems impossible that any progress can have been made in printing a revisal of the whole code of laws. Samuel Sewall was one of the committee appointed in May, 1685, to oversee the printing; but his Diary says nothing about any work done. He makes certain entries, however, which may throw light on the abandonment of the scheme. Thus he writes, June 20, 1685, (Diary i., 83) that the Court adjourned till July 7, on a dispute between the branches as to the proviso to the title "Courts", section 2, of the Laws of 1672. Later on, he records very decided disputes between the branches as to what course should be pursued, now that the Charter was cancelled, in case Col. Kirke or any one else should arrive with a commission to be Governor.

Although the formal record of the Legislature as printed gives no light upon the matter of a new edition of the Laws in 1685, the Archives fortunately contain certain votes which failed between the branches and which fully explain it. They are preserved in Volume 47, title Laws.

As we have seen, the out-going Legislature on May 16 appointed a committee to revise the laws, and the new Legislature meeting May 17 promptly called for and received a report.

The following vote does not appear on the record, although it is of much interest as showing what was contemplated: —

(Mass. Archives, Vol. 47, No. 73.) "The Magistrates have voted that there be eight hundred copies of the Lawes printed for the Country's use (and that no more be printed under the penalty of 5s for each book) the said eight hundred to be delivered to the Treasurer. The Magistrates have past this, their brethren the deputys hereto consenting.

13 June 1685 — EDWARD RAWSON Secret.

Consented unto by the Deputys

JNO. SAFFIN per Order."

The temper of the branches was evidently very irritable. The next two votes failed to meet their joint approval, though the matter of the Preface was only the pretext, as will appear later.

(Mass. Archives, Vol. 47, No. 75.) "The Deputyes Consent that a suitable preface be drawn up and agreed upon to be Printed together with the lawes when the whole body of them are fully Revised and Considered of, and such as this Court doe not see meet to Repeale be transcribed and fitted for the press, as is understood to be the Intent and Agreement of this Court.

Voted by the Deputys the honored Magistrates Consenting

June 18, 1685 — JNO. SAFFIN per Order

not consented to by the Magistrates

EDWARD RAWSON, Secret."

(Mass. Archives, Vol. 47, No. 76.) "The Magistrates consent not hereto, and do therefore desire that a suteable preface may be drawn up for the printing of those wherein wee have agreed, and that all further agitation concerning those wherein wee can't agree be forborn at present.

The Magistrates have past this, their brethren the deputys thereto consenting.

18th of June, 1685 — EDWARD RAWSON Secret.

The Deputys Consent not

18 June 1685 — JNO. SAFFIN, per Order"

(Mass. Archives, Vol. 47, No. 77.) "The Deputys Consent not to the repealing of the proviso in the Latter end of the second section of the Law title Courts, nor any part of that section unless our honnoured Magistrates please to Consent with them in passing of this bill annexed, and then the said Proviso to bee repealed.

The Deputys have past this, our honnoured Magistrats heerto consenting.

June the 19th, 1685 — Richard Sprague per Order

8 July 1685 — not consented to by the Magistrates

EDWD. RAWSON, Secret."

Sewall, who was deeply interested and in a position to know, records as follows, in his Diary, i. 83: —

> "Satterday, June 20th, 1685. The Court not agreeing about the Proviso in the end of the 2d Section of the Law, title '*Courts*,' adjourns till Tuesday, July 7th, except Occasions be, and then the Governour is to call them sooner. The final difference between the Magistrates and Deputies is: The Governour and several with him would Repeal the Proviso, letting the rest of the Law stand as it does; the Deputies have voted the Repeal of the Proviso, and withall that the Remainder of the Law have this alteration, viz.: instead of 'greater part of the Magistrates' — 'greater number of the Magistrates present' —: so to make the law new, as it might be construed contrary to the Charter. The Governour, Mr. Stoughton, Dudley and several others would not consent."

The Legislature met on July 7 and adjourned on the 10th. It met again July 21 and adjourned on the 24th; re-assembled August 12 and adjourned the same day to September 16, when it was ordered that the session be ended and a second session be called for October 14. After a short session it adjourned October 22 (Sewall, i. 101) to November 17, sat one day then, and adjourned to February 16, 1685–6.

This matter of the Proviso to the Law about Courts had long been in dispute between the branches. I have already (*ante*, p. 89, foot-note 44) mentioned it, but a fuller account may be needed. The papers preserved in Vol. 48 of Mass. Archives show what was done in 1672. Without going into small details of errors and corrections in old laws, it seems that in 1652 (Rec. iv. part 1, p. 82) it was decided that when the branches differed in any case of judicature, whether civil or criminal, such case should be determined by the major part of the whole court. This was reënacted as a proviso in the code of 1660, and again in that of 1672, the verbal change being, "shall be determined by the major vote of the whole Court met together."

But this method of forcing an agreement was very disagreeable to the magistrates who fought against it in 1672 and 1673, reluctantly yielding the point at last, though their powers were thereby greatly curtailed.

From the numerous messages between the branches I make the following citation from one drawn by the Magistrates, as it seems to state their views most thoroughly. It is in Vol. 48, No. 114: —

"The present question—which is not concerning the power and authority of the General Court, consisting of Magistrates and Deputies, or whether that Court hath not the ultimate determination of all cases and causes proper to their cognizance. But whether the freemen or their delegates (which we acknowledge) may by their greater number over-rule the conclusion and finally determine any and every case without the consent and against the judgment of any of the magistrates, or whether the consent of some of the magistrates with the deputies be not absolutely necessary to make any valid act in the General Court. The magistrates affirme this latter to be the plaine literal sense and true meaning of the patent, the foundation of our Government, consonant to right reason and the best security of the people's, especially the freemen's, liberties."

"That branch of the law made in [16]52, if it may be called a regulation or irregulation or direction of the manner and way of issuing causes of judicature in cases, which did (doubtless through inadvertency) repeale the order of 44 which concludes another manner of determining all causes in the General Court, and is in the first printed book of lawes. But the General Court nor their manner of proceeding is constituted by the order of [16]52 upon which the deputies insist, there being General Courts in act for 20 yeares before." &c &c

May 7, 1673. (Rec. iv. part 2, p. 559), a committee, consisting of Samuel Symonds, Simon Bradstreet, William Stoughton, John Oxenbridge, Uriah Oakes, Joshua Hobart, John Richards, Henry Bartholomew, John Hull, and Samuel Torrey was appointed to consider whether by the Charter there was a negative in any part of the General Court. This seems to be three magistrates, two clergymen, and five deputies, including their clerk. The report dated Sept. 1, 1673, is in the Archives, Vol. 48, No. 125. It seems that eight members were present, and three did not vote. The report against there being such a negative power in either branch is signed by Symonds, Oxenbridge, Bartholomew, Hobart, and Richards. It does not appear to have been accepted, but the papers are voluminous, and quite worthy of being put in print.

The question involved is, of course, the same as we are considering, viz., whether the Charter allowed a convention of the whole court, wherein all of the magistrates might be of one opinion and yet be overpowered by the numerical superiority of the deputies.

This matter was evidently revived by the magistrates in 1685, when the project of revising and altering the Code of 1672 came up.

On account of the bibliographical information[61] contained therein, I copy the following sentence from the Report: —

See Laws in 48 49 fol. 8 of 2d print 52 fol 11 3d print &c.

"It is the sense already given by the General Court, see the Result of s[d] question in 44 the old printed b. fol. 13, where the Governor hath onely a casting voice in case there bee an equall number on different sides."

---

[61] This citation throws light on various points. It seems that the law of 1644 about the Governor's casting vote was on folio 13 of the "old printed book." This must be the Code of 1649, because the law (which is § 6 of title Courts) is on page 23 of the Code of 1660, and page 35 of the edition of 1672. Hence neither of those editions was the "old" printed book.

MARGINAL CITATIONS, CODE OF 1660.

1600	1660	1660
Page 1 A 52, p. 7. (A).	Page 35, A. 56, p. 13	Page 60 A. 56, p 12
2 A. 51, p. 1.	" A 57, p. 26	" A 56, p 12
" A 43, p. 19	" A. 58	" A 54, p 1
" A 54, p. 2	36, A 53, p. 19	" A 56, p. 12
3 A 51, p. 5	" A 58	61 A 53
4 A 51, p. 1	39, A. 53, p. 19	" A 52, p 12
5 A 52, p. 8	40, A 52, p. 16	62 A 54. p. 5
6 A 51, p. 4	41, A 57, p. 22.	" A 52, p. 9
6 A 55	" A 57, p. 23.	63 A 54, p. 5
7 A 58	42 A. 56, p. 18	" A 54, p 1
7 A 52, p. 10.	43 A. 58	65 A 58, p 22 (H).
9 A 51, p. 2	" A 52, p. 10	" A 56, p 10 (E).
" A 52, p. 17	" A 58	" A 57, p 24
11 A 53, p. 20	44 A 51, p. 4	66 A 52, p. 3 (B).
13 A 51, p. 6	" A 53, p. 19	" A 55, p. 10
" A 54, p. 2	45 A 54. p. 2	67 A. 57, p 25
14 A 51, p. 1.	" A. 58	68 A 52, p 13
" A 57, p. 23	46 A 57, p. 21	" A 57, p. 21
16 A 56, p 11. (F).	47 A 54.	" A. 54, p. 24 (D).
" A 54, p. 6	" A 51, p. 5	69 A 52, p 9
17 A 51, p. 4	" A 53, p. 19	" A 53, p. 18
19 A 54, p. 2	" A 57, p. 25	70 A 52
" A 57, p. 26	" A 56, p. 14	71 A 54, p 1
20 A 52, p. 15	49 A 51, p. 3	" A 56, p 12
" A 51, p. 2	53 A. 53, p. 20	" A 53, p 18
22 A 52, p. 11	55 A 52, p. 12	72 A 55 p 11
24 A 54, p. 2	" A 55	73 A 51, p 7
25 A 53.	56 A 56, p. 12	74 A 1658.
" A 54, p. 3	" A 53, p. 13 (C).	75 A 51, p 4
27 A 58.	57 A 52, p. 13	76 A. 58
28 A 54, p. 6	" A 56, p. 12	" A 53, p 18
29 A 52, p. 15	58 A 53	" A 54, p 2
" A 58.	" A 52, p. 14	77 A 58
32 A 52, p. 11	" A 53	78 A. 52, p 12
" A 52, p. 9, 10.	59 A 53	" A. 57, p 25
33 A 51, p. 3	" A 56, p. 12	80 A 55
34 A 57, p. 7, 8. (G).	" A 54, p. 3	81 A 52, p 15
35 A 54, p. 7	" A 55.	82 A. 48.

This extract has a marginal reference to the "third printed book, fol. 11," as affecting a part of title "Courts," which is § 2 in the Code of 1660. It refers to a law passed in 1652. I have discussed in the foot-note this matter of the "third printed book," but other considerations compel a digression here to investigate another important section of this same title of "Courts."

Section 7 (Code of 1660, p. 23) is a very important one. It reads thus: —

"*For the better administration of justice and easing of the Country of unnecessary charges and travaile.*" It is ordered by this Court and the

---

Then the margin says "see Laws in [16]48 and [16]49, fol. 8 of 2d print" — *i.e.* "second printed book." Our printed records, before cited, under date of 1652 (Rec., Vol. iv. part 1, p. 82) refers to an error on "page the 8th of the last printed book;" and the Codes of 1660 and 1672 have marginal citations against "Courts" of Liber 2, pp. 4, 7, 10, 13, and 14. These seem to be additional proofs that Liber 2 was the second *printed* book.

But this reference to the laws of 1652 as being on folio 11 of the *third* printed book is curious, because in the edition of 1660 the marginal citation on p. 22, title "Courts," § 2, is A[nno] [16]52, p. 11. The irresistible inference is that the laws of 1652 were printed in another Supplement, and cited from that book.

The following table gives all of the marginal citations which are by year-dates, according to the pages of the Code of 1660. They are all repeated in the margins of the edition of 1672, without correction even of obvious errors, and with a few additional blunders.

Thus, in 1672, there were *omitted* the following citations of 1660, viz., p. 10, A. 51, p. 4; p. 12, A. 55; p. 16, A. 52, p. 17, and the following errors were added: —

In 1660, p. 19, A. 57, p. 26; In 1672, p. 3, A. 55, p. 26.
" " p. 41, A. 57, p. 23; " " p. 75, A. 52, p. 23.
" " p. 47, A. 53, p. 19; " " p. 86, A. 55, p. 19.
" " p. 63, A. 54, p. 5; " " p. 120, A. 54, p. 4.
" " p. 65, A. 58, p. 22; " " p. 123, A. 58, p. 28.

By rearranging these eighty-four citations we find that they fall into two consecutive series.

The acts of 1651 are cited as pp. 1, 2, 3, 4, 5, 6.
" " 1652 " " 7, 8, 9, 10, 11, 12, 13, 14, 15, 16, and 17.
" " 1653 " " 18, 19, 20, and five times unpaged.
" " 1654 " " 1, 2, 3, 4, 5, 6, and 7.
" " 1655 " " 10 and 11, and four times unpaged.
" " 1656 " " 10, 11, 12, 13, 14, and 18.
" " 1657 " " 21, 22, 23, 24, 25, and 26.
" " 1658 " eleven times, always without a page.

There are a few discrepancies which I will note, and which seem to be mainly owing to printers' errors. They are as follows: —

In the first series (1651, 1652, and 1653) we find on (A.) p. 1, A. 52, p. 7, and on p. 73, A. 51, p. 7, and on p. 34, A. 57, p. 7 and 8. This last citation is clearly wrong, as the law was the well-known law against Heresy, passed in 1652. By a double error the date at the end of the section is 1651 instead of 1652. The law cited on p. 2 was also passed in 1652. Hence, as three out of four citations of this p. 7 refer to 1652, I conclude that the fourth citation, of 1651 as p. 7, is a clerical error for some other page, from 1 to 6.

(B.) On p. 66 we find A. 52, p. 3, but the act was passed in 1651, and is cited at the end as 1651. Clearly this is a printers' error, and should be A. 51, p. 3, agreeing with the series.

(C.) On p. 56 we find A. 53, p. 13, but the law was passed in 1652, and is so cited on p. 57. This is also a printers' error, and should be 1652, p. 13.

In other words the serial arrangement is harmonious for about forty times, and the three apparent exceptions are explained above as obvious errors of the press.

Authority thereof, That there be two Courts of Assistants, yearely kept at *Boston*, by the Governour, Deputie Governour and the rest of the Magistrates, on the first Tuesday of the first month, and of the first Tuesday of the seventh month, to heare and determine all and onely actions of appeals from inferior Courts: all Causes of divorce, all Capital and Criminal causes, extending to life, member or banishment. And that justice be not deferred nor the Country needlessly charged, It shall be Lawfull for the Governour, or in his absence the Deputie Governour (as they should judge necessary) to call a Court of Assistants for the tryal of any malefactour in Capital Causes."

The marginal references are L. 1, p. 14, and L. 3, p. 5.

We are, therefore, to suppose that part of this law was in the Code of 1649, and part was passed later, whether the reference be properly to L. *3*, p. 5, or L. *2*, p. 5.

By this law the Assistants, at their two yearly Courts at Boston, could pass on appeals only from inferior courts; could try divorce cases, and could try all capital cases and criminal cases

---

As to the second series we find that the year 1654 covers pages 1, 2, 3, 4, 5, 6, 7. But we find also (D.) on p. 68, A. 54, p. 24. But the law was passed in 1657, and here again the printers' error, if corrected, makes the series right, as p. 24 comes under the year 1657.

In 1655 the citations are four times by the year alone; on p. 66 as A. 55, p. 10; on p. 72 as A. 55, p. 11.

In 1656 the citations are pp. 10, 11, 12, 13, 14, and 18. Here pp. 10 and 11 are assigned to both years, 1655 and 1656. (E.) But the citation p. 65 of A. 56, p. 10, is an error, for the law was passed in 1655, and is so noted at the end of the section.

(F.) The reference on p. 16 to A. 56, p. 11, is wrong, as the act was passed in 1655. It should be A. 55, p. 11. But very curiously the reference on p. 72 to A. 55, p. 11, is also wrong, as the law about spinning was passed in 1656. The reference must be to *Anno* 1656, some page between 12 and 18.

But, with the balance of errors, I presume that pages 10 and 11 both belong to the year 1655.

In 1657 the citations are, 21, 22, 23, 24, 25, and 26, but we note one exception.

(G.) On p. 34 we find A. 57, pp. 7 and 8. This has already been explained (see item A.) as an error for 1652.

Lastly, we find

(H.) On p. 65, A 58, p. 22, but the law was passed in 1657, and is so cited at the end of the section. Evidently a printers' error, especially as this is the only case where *Anno* 1658 is followed by a page-number.

We may, therefore, say that the second series is also regular and continuous.

Having thus apparently identified the "second printed book" with a Supplement covering the omissions and laws through 1650, I now consider the "third printed book" to have been a second Supplement, of some 19 pages, covering the laws of 1651, 1652, and 1653, printed in accordance with the order of May 3, 1654, already cited (*ante*, pp. 95, 96). Then I doubt not in 1657 a third Supplement, or "fourth printed book" of some 26 pages, was issued, covering the laws of 1654, 1655, 1656, and 1657, according to the orders cited, *ante*, pp. 96, 97. After this the issuing of Supplements was probably stopped while the Revision of 1660 was in hand.

In other words, it is almost absolutely certain that the Code of 1649 was followed by Supplements until the next revision, as we have proof that the Code of 1660 and every subsequent revision down to the present time has been so supplemented.

I cannot explain why the revisers in 1660 quoted the laws in these Supplements by the year-date; but they evidently did, since there is only one marginal citation to Liber 3. I suggest that these little pamphlets were perhaps hardly considered worthy of the title of a book. I hope some of these early fragments may yet appear, and that such facts as I have here brought together may help their identification. — W. H. W.

extending to life, member, or banishment. Very strangely we cannot find the separate acts of the General Court granting these powers. Undoubtedly the Court of Assistants did try criminal cases involving life, member, or banishment. Their records as a Court up to 1640 are printed with the other records in Vol. 1 of Shurtleff's edition. Hon. Charles Cowley, in his pamphlet entitled "Our Divorce Courts," etc. (Lowell, 1880), points out that, though the records of the Assistants' Court from 1640 to 1673 are lost, a volume is preserved by our Supreme Court giving the record from 1673 to 1692.

September 9, 1639 (Records, i. 276), the General Court voted that any five, four, or three of the Assistants residing near Boston, the Governor or Deputy Governor being one, should hold four courts a year to try civil cases not exceeding £20, and all criminal cases *not* extending to life, or member, or banishment, and to summon juries. But on October 18, 1649, according to the record of the Deputies (Record, iii. p. 175), the law was expressly altered, and only two courts were to be held, viz., in the first and the seventh month, and the Governor or Deputy Governor was allowed to call a special court for capital cases.

This act of 1649, owing to its date, could not have been in the Code of 1649. As it is incorporated in the Code of 1660, undoubtedly the citation of L. 3, p. 5, refers to it. It has already been shown that Liber 2 covered the acts of 1649 and 1650, and Liber 3 those of 1651, 1652, and 1653. It is most reasonable to infer that this is a misprint for Liber 2; especially as the citation of the "third printed book, folio 11" refers to Section 2 of this title, and Section 7 would hardly be on p. 5 of the same *liber*.

But this section also gives to the Court of Assistants the power to try divorce cases, and this important power seems to be mentioned explicitly in the revision of 1660, for the first time.

If I am right in the conclusion that no special act can be found of date prior to 1660, it is an indication of the important powers exercised by the committee which prepared that revision, and also a further proof of the presumed fact that this revision marks the limitation of many previous acts. It may well interest lawyers, therefore, to consider how far the "Ancient Charters and Laws" of 1814 can be relied upon as an authoritative statement of the General Laws in force.

As, however, in 1685, the dispute between the branches was limited to Section 2 of title "Courts," we will return to the narrative of the votes in regard to the proposed revision of the laws, which we left in the printers' hands at the date of the adjournment.

We have seen that the matter was unsettled at the adjournment in June, 1685, and the fight was at once renewed in July. On the 8th of that month the magistrates rejected the order then pending. The next two papers show the result of the four days' session, July 7, 10: —

(Mass. Archives, Vol. 47, No. 79.) "As a fynall Conclusion and determination of the question that hath bene soe long in debate, It is hereby ordered and inacted that the second section of the law tytle Courts be and is hereby repealed soe farr as it relates to the way and manner of yssueing and determining all things in the generall Court as the makeing of lawes and decrees &c, and that hereafter all things of that or the like nature shallbe yssued and determined as the Pattent directs.

The Magistrates have past this their brethren the Deputys hereto consenting

8 July 1685 EDWARD RAWSON Secret.

And if our Brethren the Deputyes do not see cause hereto to consent wee desire a speedy end may be putt to this Court."

(Mass. Archives, Vol. 47, No. 80.) "Boston July 9, 1685. The Magistrates doe order that there be a present stopp to the printing of the Lawes till farther order; our brethren the Deputies hereunto consenting.

JA. RUSSELL pr Order."

"The Deputys Consent not hereto; but since so much time and payns hath been already Expended in Reviseing of the lawes and proceeding so farr in the press with them, Desire that all such lawes as are not agreed upon by the vote of this Court to be Repealed, with those which have been amended or altered by Consent of both houses, be carried on to a full impression

July 9, 1685 JOHN SAFFIN per order

Not consented to by the Magistrates

EDWARD RAWSON, Secret."

We have thus arrived to one certain fact. The magistrates had ordered the printing of the laws to be stopped, and the printer doubtless obeyed. When the Court reassembled, Sept. 16, 1685, the following ineffectual order was introduced: —

(Mass. Archives, Vol. 47, No. 81.) "The Deputies beinge informed that there is a present stop in the presse about the Lawes, having bin ordered thither by this Court, and of the expectation of this house and generallytie of the Freemen being that they would ere this time have bin finished, Doe judge meete to order, that, that worke be forthwith proceeded in, to the perfecting of that Impression. And those Gentlemen appoynted and desired to oversee the press be ordered to take all due care thereof, desiring the consent of our honored magistrates herein

17 Sept. 1685 WILLIAM TORREY, Cleric.

Not consented to by the Magistrates

EDWARD RAWSON, Secret."

On October 14, 1685, the Legislature met again, and the deputies renewed their attack, as follows: —

(Mass. Archives, Vol. 47, No. 84.) "The Deputys having once and again pressed the prosecution of the printing of the Lawes, and understanding there is a stopp in the progresse of that work, they haveing bin sent to the press by order of the whole Court, there being great expectation of the Freemen and others throughout the Jurisdiction of a new Impression thereof to come forth, — doe again manifest their desires that they may be proceeded in to a full Issue, according to our former Votes, sent up the 9th of July last; desiring our honored Magistrates' consent hereto.

16th. 8th. 1685 William Torrey, Cleric.

Not consented to by the Magistrates

Edward Rawson, Secret."

Finally, Sewall writes under date of Saturday, October 17: "Court adjourned till Tuesday morning next, partly because of the designed Training. Before adjournment, the Deputies sent down a smart Bill alleging that they were no blamable cause of the Laws not being printed."

This "smart bill" was not entered on the full record, of course, and therefore is not to be found in the printed volume. Fortunately the document is preserved in the State Archives, Vol. 47, No. 82, subject, "Laws." It is as follows: —

"The Deputys, understanding that it is imputed to them that there is a stop in the going forwards with the impression of the Lawes through theire default in denying to Consent to the determining of maters according to our Charter, hold themselves bound for theire owne vindication to Signifie they ar wholy ignorant that ever they have soe declared themselves by any vote or otherwise; but as they alwais have, soe still doe, Manifest theire redyness to Attend the same, soe far forth as they have understood, and as was judged and practised by theire Judicious predecessors, many of them the first patentees, and still desire the procedure to the full impression of the Lawes according to former vote of Ye whole Court.

17th October 1685

the deputies have past this with reference to the consent of our honored Magestrats for a prosecedur.

Samuell Tompson per order

Not consented to by ye Magists.

Edw. Rawson Secrt."

I have found nothing more in regard to the matter, and it is impossible to explain the reason why the magistrates so persistently refused to concede the substitution of the words "greater number of the magistrates present," for the words "the greater part of the magistrates" in Section 2 of the title "Courts." (Edition of 1660, p. 22.) It is true that the corresponding change in the law which required the concurrence of the greater number of the deputies was not proposed. But in this, as in most other political disputes, the points of disagreement were probably trifling, and to us inexplicable, while at the time they seemed to be of transcendent importance.

However, our interest at present is confined to the effect which this dispute had upon the projected issue of a new code of laws.

It may be safely concluded that very little progress had been made towards printing the new revision up to the adjournment in October, 1685, that the two branches were at a stand, with considerable personal feeling evinced; and that, with the well-known disinclination of the magistrates to take any responsibility in the unsettled state of the government, the disagreement between the branches afforded a sufficient pretext for abandoning the project.

We may, therefore, probably conclude that the various Supplements to the Code of 1672, as already reprinted from the Hutchinson copy, contain all the official publications of the Colonial Laws of a general nature, except Tax and Excise Acts, prior to the dissolution of the First Charter government.

In conclusion, I have to ask the reader of this Introduction to pardon its length, urging the apparent necessity of bringing into one collection all available facts in regard to the method adopted by our ancestors in preparing and publishing those general laws which are still, in part, in force in this Commonwealth.

As to the whole book, I hope I may apply the words of Judge Sewall, when sending to a friend a copy of the Statutes at Large for 1684, "You will find much pleasant and profitable Reading in it."

WILLIAM H. WHITMORE.

CITY HALL, BOSTON, October, 1888.

THE BOOK OF THE GENERAL LAVVES AND LIBERTYES

CONCERNING THE INHABITANTS OF THE MASSACHUSETS, COLLECTED OUT OF THE *RECORDS OF THE GENERAL COURT, FOR THE SEVERAL YEARS WHERIN THEY WERE MADE AND ESTABLISHED.*

And
Now Revised by the same Court, and disposed into an Alphabetical order, and published by the same Authority in the General Court holden at *Boston*, in *May* 1649.

VVhosoever therefore resisteth the Power, resisteth the Ordinance of God, and they that resist, receive to themselves damnation. Rom: 13. 2.

CAMBRIDGE,
Printed according to Order of the *GENERAL COURT.*
1660.

TO OUR BELOVED BRETHREN AND NEIGHBOURS

The Inhabitants of the Massachusets, the Governour, Assistants and Deputies Assembled in the Generall Court of that Jurisdiction Wish Grace and Peace in our Lord Jesus Christ.

THE Books of Lawes, of the first Impression, not being to be had for the supply of the Country, put us upon thoughts of a second; and conceiving the Charge would not be considerable, in respect of the benefit, if all our Lawes were (upon this occasion) Revised, Composed and Reduced unto the first method, we have through the blessing of God upon our endeavours, effected the same.

The former Epistle tells you there would be need of alterations and additions, and experience doth witness the same, for while men either through ignorance or enmity, deny or oppose principles and actions of Righteousness, the preservation of humane Society will necessitate the enacting of new Lawes, or alteration of old, to fit the remedy to the disease; So it hath been in former ages, ex malis moribus bonæ legis, *There is the less need of an Apologie for this work, not that we conceive it perfect, some few alterations are made, such Lawes as have been repealed are left out, and such Lawes of a general nature, as have been made since the first Impression, till this present, and are yet in force, are placed under the former heads, in* an Alphabetical order, *which method being at first taken up (though perhaps not the most exact) hath this conveniency and ease, that all Lawes referring to such an head, are presented to view at once whereby the Reader may with more facility comprehend the scope & meaning of the Law.*

If any shall complain of incongruous expressions or obscurity in some passages, let them be sure it be so, before they affirm it; Considering the Supreme Court (which ought to be honoured) hath perused them, and hath judged meet to publish them as they stand: Neither would the time or their Honour permit them, as Criticks, *to call every word to the Tryall before a Jury of Grammarians. Let it suffice that the meaning is intelligible, though the dress be not the most polished; nor is it necessary, seeing* mens Legis est Lex.

They, to whom these Laws are commended as Rules to which they ought to conform, may find better exercise for themselves by endeavoring to make them live by executing of them, which will add a greater lustre to them, then elegancy of expression: When Laws may be read in mens lives, they appear more beautifull than in the fairest Print, and promise a longer duration, than engraven in Marble. Weaker fences will secure against gentle Creatures, though walls of Brass be insufficient against forcible Obtruders. If breach of order doth argue violence of men, more than weakness of the Law, it will be every mans prudence to defend the Authority of the Laws, to avoid the censure of Impetuous, and to cover rather then make gaps, whereat the most innocent may enter, and destroy that provision which was made for their preservation.

Laws are the peoples Birth-right, and Law makers the Parents of the Country: Undutifull unthrifts may despise the one and other, but many obligations command reverence to both. The light of Nature taught the Heathen to account them Sacrosancto, *inviolable: Religion and civil Order should make as deep Impressions in Christians, especially where Benefit and Damage are constant attendants. By this Hedge their All is secured against the Injuries of men, and whosoever breaketh this hedge,* a Serpent shall bite him: *They that rush against it, will find the* thornes will prick them; *they that fly to it for shelter, may find the* leaves to shade them: *To such as you, we need no other inducements but the authority of the Apostle,* 1 Pet. 2. 13. & 17. Submit your selves to every Ordinance of man for the Lords sake: Fear God; Honour the King.

By Order of the Generall Court,

Edward Rawson *Secret:*

THE GENERAL LAWES OF THE MASSACHUSETS COLONY, REVISED AND PUBLISHED BY ORDER OF THE GENERAL COURT in October 1658.

Forasmuch as the free fruition of such liberties, immunities, priviledges as humanity, civility & Christianity, call for as due to every man in his place, & proportion, without impeachment and infringement, hath ever been, and ever will be, the tranquillity & stability of Churches, and Common-wealth, and the denyal or deprival thereof, the disturbance, if not ruine of both. It is therefore Ordered by this Court & the Authority thereof. That no mans life shall be taken away, no mans honour or good name shal be stained; no mans person shall be arrested, restrained, banished dismembred, nor any wayes punished no man shall be deprived of his wife, or children no man's goods or estate shall be taken away from him, nor any wayes indamaged, under colour of Law, or countenance of Authority, unles it be by virtue or equity, of some express Law of the Country warranting the same, established by a General Court, and sufficiently published; or in Case of the defect of a Law, in any particular Case, by the word of God. And in Capital Cases, or in cases concerning dismembring or banishment, according to that word, to be judged by the General Court. [1641]

Ability. Age.

IT is Ordered by this Court & the Authority thereof. That the age for passing away lands, or such kind of hereditaments, or for giving of votes verdicts, or sentences in any civil Courts or causes, shall be one & twenty yeares, but in choosing guardians, fourteen yeares. And all persons of the age of one & twenty yeares, as aforesaid and of understanding & memorie, whether excommunicate, condemned, or other, shall have full power & liberty, to make their Wills & Testamẽts, & other Lawfull Alienations of their lands and estates. [1641. 47] Age of discretion. Liberty to dispose estate

Actions.

IT is Ordered by this Court & the Authority therof. That all actions of debt, accounts, slaunder, & actions of the case concerning debts and accounts, shall henceforth be tryed, where the Plantiff pleaseth so it be in the jurisdiction of that Court, where the Plaintiff or defendant dwelleth unles by consent, under both their hands it appeare, they would have the case tryed in any Court. All other actions shall be tryed, within that jurisdiction, where the cause of the action doth arise. Actiõs whe triable. L. 2 p: 4.

2 In all actions of trespasse where damage shall be pretended, above fourty shillings, and yet on the hearing thereof, it shall appeare to the Court to come under that value, in all such cases, the plaintiff shall lose his action, & pay the defẽdant cost. Actiõs of trespas ũder 40 s.

3 Every person impleading another, in any Court of assistants or County Court, shall pay the summ of ten shillings, before his case be entred; and for every actiõ of above forty shillings value, triable before the Commissioners of Boston; ten shillings, & for all actions under forty shillings, triable before the said Commissioners, one Magistrate, or the three Commissioners for ending smal causes, ten groates, unles the Court see cause to admit any to sue in *forma pauperis*. [1642. 52] Fees for entry of actiõs. A: 52: p: 7:

4 And where the debt or damage recovered shall amount to ten pounds, in every such case to pay five shillings more, & where it shall amount to twenty poũds or upward, there to pay ten shillings more then the first ten shillings, which said additions, together with the charge of the entry of the action, shall be putt to the judgment and execution, to be leavyed by the Marshall, and accounted to the respective Treasurers to whom it appertaineth. [1647] Addition of fees of actiõ

5 *Whereas the Country is put to great charge, by this Court's attending Suites com-*

minced or renewed by petion or review. It is Ordered that in all such cases; if it appear to the Court, that the Plaintiff had no just cause, of any such proceeding, the sayd Plaintiff shall beare the whole charges of the Court, both for time and expences, which they shall Judg to have been expended by his occasion; and may further impose a fine upon him, as the merrit of the cause shall require, but if they find the defendant in fault, they shall impose the just charges upon such defendant.

Actions brought to ẏ General court to beare th charge of ẏ Court.

Plaitiff liberty to withdraw his action.

6 And in all actions brought to any Court, the Plaintiff shall have liberty to withdraw his action or to be non-suited, before the Jury have given in their verdict, in which case, he shall alwayes pay full costs & charges to the defendant, and may afterward renew his suite at another Court. [1641]

L:1:p:16: 49.

Vexation suites to pay 3 fold damag & be fine 40 s.

7 And it is Ordered, that no man in any suite or action against another, shall falsely pretend great damages or debts, to vex his adversary; & in all cases where it appears to the Court that the Plaint.ff hath willingly & wittingly done wrong to the defendant in cōmencing & prosecuting any action, suite, complaint or inditement, in his own name, or in the name of others he shall pay treble damages to the party greived & be fined forty shillings to the common Treasury [1641. 46.]

Appeal.

It is ordered by this Court & the Authority thereof. That it shall be in liberty of every man cast cōdemned or sentenced in any inferiour court to make his appeal to the court of Assistants: as also to appeal from the sentence of one magistrate for other persons deputed to hear & determine small causes, unto the shire court of each Iurisdiction, where the cause was determined. Provided they tender there appeal, & put in security before the Judges of the court, to prosecute it to effect, & also to satisfy all damages, before execution granted; which shall not be till twelve houres after Judgment, except by special order of the Court. And if the cause be of a criminal nature; then also to putt in security for the good behaviour & appearance at the same time and if the point of appeale, be in matter of Law, then to be determined by the Bench, if in matter of fact by the Bench & Jury. And if in the Court of Assistants, two of five, three of seaven, or such a proportion of the Magistrates then present, shall actually dissent from the sentence of the Court in any capital offence, it shall then be in the liberty of the partie sentenced, to appeale to the next Generall Court.

Liberty to appeale.

before execution.

In criminal cases to be bound to ẏ good behaviour.

Appeales to the General Court.

L.2 p.1.

2 It is further Ordered: That all appeales with the security as aforesaid, shal be recorded at the charg of the partie appealing, & certifyed unto the Court, to which they are made. And the partie appealing, shall briefely in writing under his own, or his atturney's hand give in to the Clerke of the Court from which he did appeal, the grounds & reasons of his appeale, six-dayes before the beginning of the Court, to which he did appeale to which Court the said Clerke shall return the sayd writing, & give Copies therof to the defendant if he desire the same. And whosoever shall appeale from the sentence of any Court, and not prosecute the same to effect, according to Law, shall besides his bond to the partie, forfeit to the country the summ of forty shillings for every such neglect.

Appellāt to give his reasons 6 daies before

A:51 p:1

Not prosecuting an appeal forfeit 40 s.

A 43 p: 19.

3 *And for a more cleare & equal hearing & determining all cases of appeals.* It is Ordered. That no person that hath sate as judg, or voted in any inferiour Court, in that case he is appealed from, shall have any vote, in the Superiour Court appealed to, but the case shall be there determined by such, as are no way ingaged in the same, by Judging or voting formerly, Provided there be more Magistrates appealed to, then those that sate in the Court appealed from; And in all cases of appeale, the Court appealed to, shall Iudg the case, according to former evidence, & no other, rectifying what is amiss therein, and where matter of fact is found to agree with the former Court, and the judgment according to Law, not to revoake the sentence or judgment, but to abate or increase damages as shall be judged right, any use or custome to the contrary notwithstanding. [1642. 47. 49. 50. 53 54]

No judg appeal, frō may judg ẏ actiō of appeale.

A:54 p:2

Error may be rectified & reversi g ẏ former judgment.

Appea

Appearance. Non-appearance.

IT is Ordered by this Court, and the Authority thereof, That no man shall bee punished for not Appearing at or before any Civil Assembly, Court, Council, Magistrate or Officer, nor for the Omission of any Office or service; if he shall be necessarily hindred, by any apparent act or Providence of God, which he could neither foresee nor avoid, Provided that this Law shall not prejudice any person of his just cost & damage in Civil action. [1641]

Apparrel.

Although several declarations, and Orders have been made by this Court, against excess in apparrel, both of men & women, which have not taken that effect, as were to to be desired, but on the contrary, we cannot but to our grief, take notice, that intollerable excess, & bravery hath crept in upon us, and especially, amongst people of mean condition, to the dishonour of God, the scandal of our profession, the consumption of estates, and altogether unsuitable to our poverty: And *although we acknowledg it to be a matter of much difficulty, in regard of the blindness of mens minds, and the stubborness of their wills, to set down exact Rules, to confine all sorts of persons, yet we cannot but account it our duty, to commend unto all sorts of persons, the sober and moderate use of those blessings, which beyond expectation, the Lord hath been pleased, to afford unto us in this wilderness, and also to declare our utter detestation & dislike, that men or women of mean condition, should take upon them the garb of Gentlemen by wearing* gold or silvar lace, or buttons, or points at their knees, or to walk in great boots, *or women of the same ranke, to wear* silk or tyffany hoods, or scarfes, *which though allowable to persons of greater estates, or more liberal education, yet wee cannot but judg it intollerable in persons of such like condition.* It is therefore Ordered by this Court and the Authority thereof. That no person within this Jurisdiction, nor any of their relations depending upon them, whose visible estates real & personal, shall not exceed the true & indifferent value of *two hundred pound*; shall weare any gold or silvar lace, or gold & silvar buttons, or any bone lace above two shillings *per yard*, or silk hoods or scarfs, upon the penalty of *ten shillings* for every such offence, and every such delinquent, to be presented by the grand Jury; *And forasmuch as distinct & particular rules, in this case suitable to the estate or quality of each person, cannot easily be given.* It is further Ordered by the Authority aforesaid, that the Selectmen of every Town, or the major part of them, are hereby enabled and required from time to time, to have regard, and take notice of apparrel of any of the Inhabitants, of their several Townes respectively, and whosoever they shall Judg to exceed their rankes & abillities in the costlines, or fashion of their apparrel in any respect, especially in the wearing of Ribbons or great boots, (leather being so scarce a commoditie in this Country.) lace, points &c: silk hoods or scarfes, the Select men aforesaid shall have power to assess such persons, so offending in any of the particulars above mentioned, in the Country rates, *at two hundred pounds* estates according to that proportiom that such men use to pay, to whom such apparrel is suitable & allowed, Provided this Law shall not extend to the restraint of any Magistrate or publicke Officer of this Jurisdiction, their wvies and children, who are left to their discretion in wearing of apparrel, or any setled Millitary Officer or Souldier in the time of Millitary Service, or any other whose education and imployment have been above the ordinary degree, or whose estate have been considerable, though now decayed. [1651]

A. 51. p. 5

Excess in Apparrel prohibited.

Arrests.

IT is Ordered by this Court and Authority thereof: That no mans person shalbe arrested or imprisoned, for any debt or fine, if the Law can find any competent means of satisfaction, otherwise from his estate (except in special contracts, or in the Law of Paiments) And if not, his person may be arrested and imprisoned, where he shall be kept at his own charge, not the plaintifs, till satisfaction be made, unless

None to bee kept in prison for debt that have not to satisfie.

the Court that had cognizance of the cause, or some superiour Court shall otherwise determine; provided neverthelefs, that no mans person shall be kept in prison for debt but when there is an appearance of some estate, which he will not produce, to which end, any Court or Commissionors authorized by the General-Court may administer an oath to the partie, or any other suspected to be privy in concealing his estate, but shall satisfy by service; if the creditor require it, but shall not be sold to any but of the English Nation. [1641. 47.]

Attachments. Summons.

L.2.p.12 IT is Ordered by this Court & Authority thereof. That it shall be the liberty of every Plaintiff, to take out either Summons or Attachment, against any defendant. Provided no Attachment shall be granted in any Civil action, to any forreigner, against a setled inhabitant in this Jurisdiction, before he hath given sufficient security or caution, to prosecute his action, & to answer the defendant such costs, as the Court shall award him.

Plaint liberty to take Sumons or Attachments

Forrain Plai to put in security.

And it is further Ordered that in all Attachments of goods & chattels, or of Lands & hereditaments, legal notice shal be given to the partie, or left in writing at his house, or place of usual abode, otherwise the suite shall not proceed; notwithstanding, if he be out of this Jurisdiction, the cause shall then proceed to tryal, but judgment shall not be entred, before the next Court, & if the defendant do not then appeare; judgment shall be entred, but execution shall not be granted, before the Plaintiff hath given security, to be responsal to the defendant, if he shall reverse the judgment, within one yeare, or such further time as the Court shall Limmitt.

Execution respited.

L.1.p.49 2 And it is hereby declared, that no summons, pleading, judgment, or any kind of proceeding in Courts or course of justice, shall be abated arrested or reversed, upon any kind of circumstantial errours or mistakes, if the person & cause be rightly understood, & intended by the Court And in all cases where the first sumons, are not served six dayes inclusively, before the Court & the case, breifely specifyed in the warrant, where appearance is to be made by the partie Summoned, it shal be at his liberty, whether he will appeare or not, except all cases, that are to be handled in Court, suddainely called on extraordinary occasions.

Circumstantial errours.

Summons to be served 6 dayes before the Court.

A.51.p.1 3 And whereas suites at Law, many times such as doe prosecute the same, in their own name, in procuring the process, intend & doe declare in the name and on the behalfe of others. viz. as Executors, Administrators, Assignes, Atturneyes Guardians, Agents or the like, which is not onely improper, but tendeth also to uncertainty, for prevention whereof. It is Ordered That hencefoorth the Original process, whether summons or attachment, shall express in whose name the Plaintiff sueth, whether in his own name, or as executor of the last will & testament of such a man, or Administrator of the goods & chattels of such a man, or Assigne, Atturney Guardian or Agent of such a man, or the like, or otherwise, if exception be taken, before the parties joyne issue, it shal be good, & the Plaintiff shal be liable to pay Cost. [1641. 44. 47. 51.]

In whose name to take out process.

Bakers.

IT is Ordered by this Court & Authority thereof; That hencefoorth every Baker shall have a distinct mark for his bread, & keep the true assizes, as hereafter is expressed, viz: when wheat is ordinarily sold at these several rates hereafter mentioned the penny white loaf, by averdupois weight, when wheat is by the bushel——

Weight of bread.

at 3s.	od.	The white 11 ouces.	1 qr.	wheate 17 oñc.	1 qr.	houshold 23 oñc.	o.
at 3	6	10	1	15	1	20	2.
at 4	0	09	1	14	0	18	2.
at 4	6	08	1	11	3	16	2.
at 5	0	07	3	11	2	15	2.
at 5	6	07	0	10	2	14	0.
at 6	0	06	2	10	0	13	0.
at 6	6	06	0	09	2	12	2.

and

and so proportionably, under the penaltie of forfeiting all such bread, as shall not be of the several assizes aforementioned, to the use of the poor of the town, where the offence is committed, & otherwise as is hearafter expressed, & for the better executiō of this present order; there shall be in every market town, & all other towns needful one or two able persons annually chosen by each town, who shal be sworn at the next County Court, or by the next Magistrate, unto the faithfull discharge of his or their office; who are hereby authorized, to enter into all houses, either with a Constable or without, where they shall suspect, or be informed of any bread baked for sale and also to weigh the said bread as oft as they see cause, & seize all such as they find defective. As also to weigh all butter, made up for sale, & bringing unto, or being in the town or market to be sold by weight which if found light after notice once given, shall be forfeited in like manner. The like penaltie shall be for not marking all bread made for sale. And the sayd officers shall have one third part of all forfeitures for his paines; the rest to the poor as aforesaid. [1646.]

Clarke of ÿ market.

There power.

Clarks fee.

A: 52: p. 8:

2 Whereas it appeares to this Court, that there is much deceit used by some Bakers, & others, who when the Clarke of the market cometh, to weigh their bread, pretend they have none, but for their owne use, & yet afterward putt their bread to sale, which upon tryal hath been found too light; For prevention of such abuses for time to come. It is ordered That all persons within this Jurisdiction, who shall usually sell bread within dores, or without, shall at all times hereafter, have all their bread, that they either putt to sale or spend in their families, made of the due assizes, marked & yeilded to tryal of the said Clarks as is directed in the order aforesaid under the penaltie therein exprest. [1652.]

To prevent deceit in Bakers

Ballast.

IT is Ordered by this Court & Authority thereof. That no Ballast shall be taken from any town shore, by any person whatsoever, without allowance under the hands of the select men, upon the penaltie of six pence, for every shovel-full so taken, unless such-stones as they had lay there before? It is also Ordered; that no ship, nor other vessel, shall cast out any ballast in the channel, or other place inconvenient, in any harbour within this jurisdiction, upon the penalty of ten pounds. [1646.]

Ballast not to be taken without leav

not cast into ÿ channel.

Barratrie.

IT is Ordered, decreed & by this Court declared; that if any man be proved, and judged a common barrater, vexing others with unjust, frequent & endless suites. it shall be in the power of the Court, both to reject his cause, and to punish him for his Barratry. [1641]

Benevolence.

IT is Ordered, that this Court heerafter will graunt no benevolence, except in forraine occasions, and when there is mony in the treasury sufficient, and our debts first satisfied. [1641]

Bills.

IT is Ordered by the Authority of this Court; That any debt, or debts due upon bill or other specialty assigned to another, shall be as good a debt & estate to the Assignee, as it was to the assigner, at the time of its assignation; And that it shall be Lawful for the sayd Assignee, to sue for, & recover the said debt due upon bill, & so assigned, as fully as the original creditor might have done; provided the sayd assignement be made upon the back-side of the bill or specialtie. [1647]

Bils assigned good debts to the assignee.

Bond-slavery.

IT is Ordered by this Court & Authority thereof; That there shall never be any bond slavery villenage or captivity amongst us, unless it be Lawfull captives, taken in just warrs, as willingly sell themselves, or are sold to us. and such shall have the liberties, & christian usage, which the Law of God established in Israel, concerning such persons, doth morally require, provided this exempts none from servitude who shall be judged thereto by Authority. [1641]

FOrasmuch as the bounds of townes, and of the lands of particular persons, are carefully to be maintained, & not without great danger to be removed by any, which notwithstanding by deficiency & decay of marks, may at unawares be done, wherby great jealousies of persons, trouble in townes, & incumbrances in Courts doe often arise, which by due care & meanes might be prevented. It is therefore Ordered by this Court & Authority thereof; That every towne shall sett out their bounds, within twelve months after their bounds are graunted. And that when their bounds are once sett out; once in three yeares three or more persons of a towne, appointed by the Select men, shall appoint with the adjacent townes, to goe the bounds, betwixt their said townes, & renew their marks; which marks shall be a great heape of stone, or a trench of six foot long & two-foot broad, the most ancient towne to give notice, of the time & place of meeting for this perambulation; Which time shall be in the the first or second month, upon paine of five pound for every towne that shall neglect the same; provided that the three men appointed for perambulation shall goe in their several quarters, by order of the select men, and at the charge of the several townes.

Town bouds to be laid out within one yeare.

To be survayed once in 3 yeare

Particular persõs boũd to be servayed õce a year

2 And it is further Ordered, that if any perticular proprietor of lands, lying in common with others, shall refuse to goe the bounds, betwixt his land and other mens, once a year in the first or second month, being requested thereunto, upon one weeks warning, he shall forfeit for every day so neglecting, ten shillings, half to the partie moving thereto the other halfe to the towne. [1641]

Brewers.

A:51:p.4

TO the end, no other, but good & wholsom beere be brewed at any time, in this jurisdiction, to be sold for the supply of ship or other vessels at sea: and that no oppression or wrong be done to any in this mistery. It is Ordered by this Court & Authority therof. That no person whatsoever, shall henceforth undertake the calling or worke of brewing beere for sale, but onely such as are known, to have sufficient skill and knowledge in the art or mystery of a brewer. And it is further Ordered that if any undertaker for victualling of ships, or other vessels, or Master or owner of any such vessel, or any other person, shall make it appeare, that any beere bought of any person, within this Jurisdiction, doth prove unfitt, unwholesome & uselesse for their supply, either through the insufficiency of the mault, or brewing, or unwholsome cask, the person wronged thereby, shall be, & is hereby enabled, to recover equal & sufficient damage, by action, against the person that putt that beere to sale.

Brewers to make satisfaction for bad beere.

Bridges.

A: 55

THis Court considering that Bridges, in Country highways are for the benefit of the Country in general, & that it may be unequal, to lay the charge thereof, on particular Townes: Doth order, that from time to time, upon information or complaint to each County Court, of the necessity or defect of any bridge or bridges as aforesaid, the Court shall appoint a Committie to view & determine the same, and the charges shall be proportioned by the Magistrates in each County Court, to be levayed upon the several townes in each County according to the direction of the Law for Country rates.

Bridges to be made and repaired by ẏ county.

L.2:p.3

2 *The Court considering the great danger that persones, horses, teames, are exposed to by reason of defective bridges, & Country highways in this jurisdiction.* Doth Order & declare: That if any person, at any time loose his life, in passing any such bridge or high-way, after due warning given unto of any of the Select men of the towne in which such defect is, in writing under the hand of two witnesses or upon presentment to the Shire Court, of such defective wayes or bridges, that then the County or towne which ought to secure such wayes or bridges, shall pay a fine of one hundred pounds, to the parents, husband, wife or children or next of kin, to the partie deceased. And if any person loose a Limb, breake a bone or receive any other bruise or breach in any part of his body, through such defect as aforesaid

Penaltie for damage received by ẏ insufficiency of bridges

aforesaid. The County or towne, through whose neglect, such hurt is done shall pay to the partie so hurt, double damages, the like satisfaction shall be made for any teame, Cart or Cartage, horse, other beast or loadinge, proportionable to the damage sustained as aforesaid.

A. 58.

Power to press workmē to repair Bridges.

3 *And for the prevention of danger, which may come by the insufficiency of bridges and passages, which lye upon town highwayes, the care whereof doth belong either to the towne or particular persons to repaire, who many times cannot procure workmen to doe the same?* It is therefore Ordered by this Court. That upon the complaint of any such town or person, to any one Magistrate, he shall hereby be impowred, to issue out warrants to the Constable, to impress such workmen in their town-ship, as shall be needfull to secure and repair the same, who shall be paid for their work, either by the Town or Persons, to whom such Bridges or passages do belong. [1648. 51, 59]

Burglary and Theft.

Robing in house high-ways penalty.

F*Orasmuch as many persons, of late yeares have been & are apt to be injurious to the goods & lives of others, notwithstanding all care and meanes to prevent and punish the same.* It is therefore Ordered by this Court and Authority thereof, that if any person shall commit Burglary: by breaking up any dwelling house, or shall rob any person in the field or highwayes, such person so offending, shall for the first offence, be branded on the forehead, with the letter (*B*) And if he shal offend in the same kind, the second time, he shall be branded as before & also be severely whipped; and if he shall fall into the like offence, the third time, he shall be put to death as being incorrigible. And if any person shal commit such burglary or rob in the fields or houses on the Lords day; besides the former punishment of branding, he shal for the first offence, have one of his eares cut off. And for the second offence in the same kind, he shal lose his other eare in the same manner. And for the third offence he shal be put to death. [1642. 47]

ō ȳ Lordsday

Rob orchard or garden or steal goods.

2. *For the prevention of pilfring & theft* It is ordered by this Court & the authority thereof That if any person be taken or known to rob any orchard or garden; that shal hurt or steal away any grafts, or fruit-trees, fruites, linnen, woollen, or any other goods left out in orchards, gardens, back-sides, or in any other place in house or fields or shall steal any wood or other goods from the water-side, from mens doores or yards: he shall forfeit treble damage, to the owners thereof.

pay 3 ble damage.

or be whipt

And if they be children, or servants, that shall trespass herein, if their parents or masters will not pay the penallty before exprest, they shall bee openly whipped. *And forasmuch as many times it so falls out that small thefts & other offences of a criminall nature are committed both by English & Indians in towns remote from any prison or other fit place to which such malefactors may bee committed untill the next court.* It is therefore Ordered that any magistrate, upon Complaint made to him may hear, and upon due proof determine, any such small offences of the aforesaid nature according to the lawes here established & give warrant to the constable of that town, where the offender lives, to leavy the same: provided the damage or fine exceed not forty shillings: provided also it shall bee lawfull for either partie to appeal to the next court to be holden in that Jurisdiction, giving sufficient caution to prosecute the same to effect, at the said court. And every Magistrate shall make a return yearly to the County Court where he liveth, of what cases hee hath so ended. And also the Constables of all such fines as they have received.

One Magistrate may determine such cases.

Magistrate & Constable to return to the cuūty court.

And where the offender hath nothing to satisfy, such magistrate may punish by stocks or whipping, as the cause shall deserve, not exceeding ten stripes; It is also ordered that all servants and workmen imbeazling the goods of their masters, or such as set them on work, shall make restitution, & be lyable to all laws & penalties as other men. [1646]

Servants and workmen.

A. 52. p. 10.

3. It is further ordered by this Court. That what person shall steal from any person, any Coyn, goods or Chattels, to the vallue of ten shillings, or up ward

Stealing above 10 s

wards, shall be whipp, or pay such a summ or summs of money, as the Court or Magistrate, that hath proper Cognizance thereof, shall adjudg to be sufficient to satisfie all costs and charges of the Court and Country, in prosecuting & trying the sayd offender; to the use of the common treasury, and for smaller thefts, it is left to the discretion of the judg or judges that shal have cognizance of the crime, to appoint smaller mulcts or punishments, or onely legal admonition as they shall find cause.

Constable to make search for goods stolen.

And further it is declared & Ordered, that when any goods are stolen from any person, the constable of the town, by warrant from Authority, shall search for the same, in any suspected places or houses, & upon search or otherwise, if he shal find the same or any part thereof, or any ground of suspition, appearing to the Officer, he shall bring the delinquent or suspected party to a Magistrate to be proceeded with according to the Law.

Concealing of theft and receiving satisfaction privately penalty.

And if any person having goods stolen from him, shall privately receive his sayd stolen goods (except the fact be private, or committed by some member of his own family) & so smother the theft, and shall not legally prosecute the offender, he shall forfeit to the common treasury, the goods or chattels so received or the true value thereof. [1652]

CAPITAL LAVVES.

Idolatrie.

If any man after legal conviction shall HAVE OR WORSHIP any other God, but the LORD GOD he shall be put to death. *Exod.* 22.20. *Deut.* 13.6 & 10 *Deut.* 17.2,6.

Witch-craft

2 If any man or woman be a WITCH, that is, hath or consulteth with a familiar Spirit they shall be put to death. *Exod.* 22.18. *Levit.* 20.27. *Deut.* 18,10,11.

Blasphemy.

3 If any person within this Jurisdiction, whether Christian or Pagan, shall wittingly & willingly presume to BLASPHEME the holy name of God, FATHER, SON, or HOLY GHOST, with direct, expresse, presumptuous, or high-handed blasphemy, either by wilfull or obstinate denying the true God, or his Creation, or Government of the world, or shall curse God in like manner, or reproach the holy Religion of God, as if it were but a politick device; to keep ignorant men in awe; or shall utter any other kind of Blasphemy, of the like nature and degree, they shall be put to death. *Levit.* 24. 15,16.

Murder.

4 If any person shall commit any wilfull MURTHER upon premeditate mallice, hatred or cruelty, not in a mans necessary and just defence, nor by meer casualty against his will, he shall be putt to death. *Exod.* 21 12,13. *Numb.* 35. 31.

5 If any person slayeth another suddenly, in his ANGER or CRUELTY of passion, he shall be put to death. *Levit.* 24. 17. *Numb.* 35. 20,21.

Poysoning

6 If any person shall slay another through guile, either by POYSONING, or other such divelish practise, he shall be put to death. *Exod* 21. 14.

Bestiality

7 If any man or woman shall LYE WITH ANY BEAST, or bruit creature, by carnal copulation, they shal surely be putt to death, and the beast shall be slayn and buried, and not eaten. *Levit.* 20. 15,16.

Sodomie

8 If any man LYETH WITH MAN-KINDE as he lieth with a woman both of them have committed abomination, they both shall surely be put to death, unles the one partie were forced, or be under fourteen yeares of age in which case he shall be severely punished. *Levit.* 20.13.

Adulterie

9 If any person commit ADULTERY with a married or espoused wife, the Adulterer and Adulteresse shall surely be putt to death. *Levit.* 20. 19. & 18. 20. *Deut.* 22. 23.27.

Man stealing

10 If any man STEALETH A MAN or mankind, he shall surely be put to death. *Exodus.* 21. 16.

False witnes

11 If any man rise up by FALSE-WITNES wittingly, & of purpose, to take away any mans life, he shall be put to death. *Deu.* 19. 16. 18. 16.

Conspiracy

12 If any man CONSPIRE, and attempt any INVASION, INSURRECTION, or publick Rebellion against our Common-Wealth: or shall endeavour to surprize

surprise any Town, or Townes, Fort, or Forts therin; or shall treacherously, and perfidiously attempt the Alteration & subversion of our frame of Politie, or Government fundamentally, he shall be put to death, *Numb*: 16. 2 *Sam*: 3. 2 *Sam*: 18. 2 *Sam*. 20. Rebellion.

13. If any Child, or Children, above sixteen years old, and of sufficient understanding, shall CURSE, or SMITE their natural FATHER, or MOTHER, he or they shall be putt to death, unles it can be sufficiently testifyed, that the Parents have been very unChristianly negligent in the education of such Children: or so provoked them by extream & cruel correction, that they have been forced therunto, to preserve themselves from death or maiming.: *Exod* 21 17, *Lev* 20, 9, *Exod* 21 15. Child to curse or smite parents.

14: If a man have a STUBBORNE or REBELLIOUS SON of sufficient yeares and understanding (*viz*) sixteen yeares of age, which will not obey the voice of his Father, or the voyce of his Mother, and that when they have chastned him, will not hearken unto them, then shall his Father and Mother, being his natural Parents lay hold on him, and bring him to the Magistrates assembled in Court, and testifie unto them, that their Son is stubborn and rebellious, and will not obey their voyce and chastisement, but lives in sundry notorious crimes: Such a Son shall be put to death. *Deut*: 22. 20, 21. Rebellious Son.

15. If any man shall RAVISH any maid, or single woman, committing carnal copulation with her by force, against her own will; that is above the age of ten years, he shall be punished either with death, or with some other greivous punishment, according to circumstances, as the Judges, or General Court shall determine [1649] Rape.

16. If any person shall be indited for any CAPITAL CRIME, (who is not then in durance) and shall refuse to render his person, to some Magistrate within one month, after three proclamations publickly made, in the Town where he usually abides, there being a month between proclamation and proclamation: his lands and goods shall be seized, to the use of the Common Treasury, till he make his lawfull appearance. And such withdrawing of himself, shall stand in stead of one witness to prove his crime, unless he can make it appear to the Court that he was necessarily hindred. [1646] Not-appearance in a Capital crime.

Cask & Cooper. Gager. Packer.

IT is Ordered by this Court, and Authority therof. That all Cask used for any liquor, fish, beef, pork, or other commodities to be put to sale, shall be of London Assize, and of sound & well seasoned timber. And that fit persons shall be appointed from time to time, in all places needfull, to gage all such vessels or cask and such as shall be found of due assize, shall be marked with the Gagers mark, who shall have for his paines, *four-pence per tun*. And every Cooper shall have a distinct *brand-mark* on his own Cask, upon the penalty of forfeiture of *twenty shillings*. And whosoever shall put to sale, any new cask, being defective, either in workmanship, timber, or assize as aforesaid, upon due proof made before any one Magistrate, he shall forfeit such cask to the informer, and be fined to the use of the Country, *ten shillings per tun*, and so proportionably for greater or lesser cask. And because there may be no neglect in the choise of a Gager or Packer, It is Ordered, that every Town within this Jurisdiction, wherein any cask are made, shall yearly make choise of a fit man for that imployment, who being presented by the Constable within one month after the choise made, before any one Magistrate, shall there take his Oath belonging to his place, which if he shall refuse, he shall pay the summ of *forty-shillings*, and another shall be chosen in his room. Also the Town or Constable shall either of them, suffer the like penalty for their neglect of this order. And every Gager or Packer, shall see that all cask be packs, beef, porke, mackeril, fish or other goods in cōmitted to his care, be of true & full assize, & that he packs the same, in no other cask whatsoever, on penalty of *ten shillings* for every cask by him

Cask their assize & quality. Gagers fee. Coopers mark. A. 51. p. 2. Defective cask forfeit. Choise of Gager and Packer. A. 51. p. 17. Packer must pack no good but in cask of full assize.

him packed, that is or shall be defective in that respect, one half to the informer, and the other half to the Country.

2. *And for the preventing deceit of any person in the packing of fish, beef, and porke to be put to sale, in this & other Jurisdictions.* It is Ordered, That in every Town where any such goods are packed up for sale, the Gager or Packer of that Town, or of the Town wherein it is put to sale or shipped, shall see that it be well and orderly performed: that is to say: beef and porke, the whole, halfe or quarter, & so proportionably that the best be not left out, and for fish, that they be packed all of one kind, and that all Casks so packed be full and sound and well seasoned setting his seal on all cask so packed, and he shall receive of the owners for so packing & sealing four shillings per tun, but if the Gager do onely view them, and finde them good & sufficient, he shall set his seal upon them, and have one shilling per tun for so doing, and if such goods so packed shall be put to sale without the Gagers mark he shall forfeit the said goods, that so puts them to sale, the one halfe to the Informer the other halfe to the countrey. [1641: 47, 51, 52.]

To prevent deceit in packing beef porke &c: Packers fees 4 s. per tun. Cask not marked forfeit

Cattle, Corn-field. Fences.

IT is Ordered by this Court and the Authority thereof. That, in all Corn fields, which are inclosed in common: every party interested therin, shall from time to time make good his part of the fence, and shall not put in any cattle, so long as any corn shall be upon any part of it, upon payn to answer all the damage that shall come thereby. [1647]

Owner make good his fence. No cattle to be put in till corn be out

2. *Whereas it is found by experience, that there hath been much trouble & difference in several Townes, about the fencing, planting, sowing, feeding, & ordering of common fields.* It is therefore Ordered by this Court, and Authority therof: That where the occupiers of the land, or the greatest part thereof, cannot agree about the fencing or improvement of such their said fields, that then the Select men in the several Towns shall order the same, or in case where no such are, then the major part of the freemen (with what convenient speed they may, shall determine any such difference as may arise upon any information, given them by the sayd occupiers, excepting, such Occupiers land shall be sufficiently fenced in by it self, which any Occupier of land may Lawfully do. [1643. 47]

Occupiers of land may order common field. Liberty to fence in several.

3 *Whereas this Court hath long since provided, that all men shall fence their Corn meadow ground and such like, against great cattle, to the end the increase of cattle especially of Cowes, & their breed should not be hindred; there being then but few horses in the Country, which since are much increased, many whereof run in a sort wild, doing much damage in corn & other things, notwithstanding fence made up according to the true intent of the Order, in that case established, many whereof are unknown, most so unruly that they can by no meanes be caught, or get into onsway, whereby their owners might answer damages, and if sometimes with much difficulty and charge they be, they are in danger of perishing, before the owner appears, or can be found out, all which to prevent.* It is therfore Ordered by this Court and the Authority thereof. That every Town & peculiar in this Jurisdiction, shall hence forth give some distinct Brand-mark, appointed by this Court (a copy of which marks, each Clerk of the writs in every Town, shall keep a Record) upon the horne, or left buttock or shoulder of all their cattle, which feed in open Commons without constant keepers, whereby it may be known to what Town they do belong. And if any trespass, not so marked, they shall pay double damages: nor shall any person knowing, or after due notice given, of any beast of his, to be unruly in respect of fences, suffer such beast, to go common, or against Cornfields, or other in propriate inclosed grounds, fenced as aforesaid without such shackles or fetters, as may restrain and prevent trespass therein, by them from time to time. And if any horse or other beast, trespass in any Corn or other inclosure, being fenced in such sort as secures against Cowes, oxen & such like orderly cattle: the partie or parties trespassed; shall procure two sufficient Inhabitants of that town, of good repute & credit, to veiw and adiudge the damages, which the owner of the beast shall satisfie, when known, upon reasonable demand; whether the beast were impounded or not.

Every town to have a distinct mark for cattle. Cattle not marked trespassing pay double damage. Unruly cattel to go in fetters. Harmes to be veiwed by sufficient mē

But if the owner be known, and near residing, as in the same Town or the like? he shall forthwith have notice of the trespass, and damage charged upon him, that if he approve not thereof he may nominate one such man, who with one other chosen by the partie damnified as aforesaid shall reveiw & adjudge the harmes; Provided they agree of damage within one day after due notice given, & that no after harms intervene to hinder it, which being forthwith discharged, together with the charge of the notice, former view, & determination of damage, the first judgment to be voyd, or else to stand good in Law. Provided notwithstanding the party trespassed shall not be barred of his action, albeit the harms be not veiwed & judged according to the direction aforesayd And if any cattle be found damage faisant, the party damnifyed, may impound, or keep them in his own private close or yard, till he may give notice to the owner, and if they cannot agree, the owner may replevie them, or the other partie may return them to the owner, & take his remedy according to Law, yet in case of involuntary trespasses, where such trespasser shall pay, or legally render full recompence for all the damage done by him, before any suite commenced, the Plaintiff shall recover no cost of his suite. And in all trespasses or damages done, to any man, if it can be proved to be done by the meer default of him, to whom the damage is done it shall be judged no trespas, nor any damage given for it. [1646]

Notice to be given to the owner of the beast.

L:2: p.8.

L:2 p 8.

Involuntary trespas pay no cost

L:1 p:51:

4 For all harms done by goates there shall be double damages allowed, and when any goates are taken in Corne or gardens, the owner of such Corn or garden, may keep & use the sayd goates till full satisfaction be made by the owners. 1646

Goates pay double dam.

5 *Forasmuch as Complaints have been made, of a very evil practise of some disordered persons in the Country, who use to take other mens horses, sometimes upon the Commons and sometimes out of their owne grounds & inclosures, and ride them at their pleasure without any leave or privity of the owners?* It is therfore Ordered and enacted by the Authority of this Court. That whosoever shall take any other mans horse, mare, asse, or drawing beast, either out of his inclosure, or upon any Common or elswhere, (except such be taken damage faisant & disposed of according to Law) without leave of the owner and shall ride or use the same he shall pay to the party wronged treble damages, or if the Complainant shall desire it, then to pay onely ten shillings, & such as have not to make satisfaction, shall be punished by whipping imprisonment, or otherwise as by Law shall be adjudged, and any one Magistrate or County Court may heare and determine the same. [1647]

Riding or working other mens horses or Cattle without leave

Penalty 3ble damage or whip.

6 *For the better preserving of Corne from damage, by all kind of Cattle, and that all fences of Corn-feilds, may from time to time, be sufficiently upheld & maintained.* It is Ordered by this Court, that the Select men of all Townes, shall make wholsom orders, for the repairing of all fences both general & particular, within their several Townships, excepting fences belonging to farms of one hundred acres or above, and have power to impose fines upon all delinquents not exceeding twenty shillings for one offence, and if any Select men shall neglect to make orders as aforesayd they shall forfeit five pounds to the use of the Town, & so for every months default from time to time; And the said Select men of every Town shall appoint, from yeare to yeare, two or more (if need require) of the inhabitants therof to veiw the common fences, of all their corn-feilds, to the end, to take due notice of the real defects & insufficiency thereof, who shall forthwith acquaint the owners thereof with the same: and if the sayd owners, doe not within six dayes time, or otherwise as the Select men shall appoint, sufficiently repaire their sayd defective fences; then the sayd two or more inhabitants appointed as aforesayd, shall forthwith repaire or renew them, and shall have double recompence for all their labour, care, cost & trouble, to be payd by the owners of the sayd insufficient fence or fences & shall have warrant from the sayd Select men, directed to the Constable to leavy the same either upon the Corne or other estate of the delinquent. Provided the defect of the fence or fences be sufficiently proved by two or three witnesses. [1647]

A:53 pen.

Select men to order ye repair of fences.

to appoint veiwers of comon fences

To give notice of defects to ye owners

Owners to repaire in 6 dayes.

Else ye veiwers to mend them & have double recompence.

Partitiō fēce betwe en neighbours born by both

7 Where lands lye in Common unfenced, if one man shall improve his land, by fencing in several, & another shall not, he who shall so improve, shall secure his Land against other mens cattle, and shall not compel such as joyn upon him, to make any fence with him, except he shall also improve in several as the other doth. And where one man shall improve before his neighbour, & so make the whole fence, if after his sayd neighbour shall improve also, he shall then satisfy for half the others fence against him, according to the present value & shall maintain the same: and if the first man shall after lay open his sayd feild, then the sayd neighbour shall enjoy his sayd half fence so purchased to his owne use, and shall also have liberty to buy the other half fence, paying according to present valuation, to be sett by two men chosen by either party one: the like order shall be where any man shall improve land against any Town Common. Provided this order shall not extend to house lotts, not exceeding ten acres, but if in such, one shall improve, his neighbour shall be compellable to make and maintaine one half of the fence between them, whether he improve or not. Provided also no man shall be liable to satisfy for damage done in any ground not sufficiently fenced, except it shall be for damage done by Swine or Calves under a year old, or unruly cattle which will not be restrained by ordinary fences, or where any man shall put his cattle, or otherwise voluntarily trespas upon his neighbours ground, and if the party damnifyed find the cattle damage faisant he may impound or otherwise dispose of them. [1642]

House Lotts Fences.

Insufficient fence no damage except by Swine & Calves.

Causes smal Causes.

FOR easing the charge and incumbrance of Courts by smal Causes: It is Ordered by this Court and Authority thereof. That any Magistrate, in the Town where he dwels, may hear and determine by his discretion (not by Jury) according to the Laws here established, all causes arising in that County, wherein the debt trespas, or damage doth not exceed forty shillings who may send for parties & witnesses, by summons or attachment directed to the Marshal or Constable who shall faithfully execute the same, & it is further ordered that in such towns where no Magistrate dwels, the Court of assistants or County Court may from time to time upon request of the said towns, signifyed under the hand of the Constable, appoint three of the Freemen, as Commissioners in such cases, any two whereof, shall have like power to hear & determine all such causes, wherein either partie is an inhabitant of that Towne who have hereby power to send for parties & witnesses, by sūmons or Attachment directed to the Constable, as also to administer oaths to witnesses, and to give time to the defendant to answer if they see cause, & if the partie summoned refuse to give his bond for appearance, or sentenced, refuse to give satisfaction where no goods appeare in the same Town, where the partie dwells, they may charge the Constable with the partie to carry him before a Magistrate, or Shire Court (if then sitting) to be further proceeded with according to Law, but the sayd Commissioners may not commit to prison in any case. And where the parties live in Several Townes, the defendant shall be lyable to be sued in either Town at the libertie of the plaintiff.

One Magistrate may end causes under 40 s.

3 Cōmissioners in towns to end small causes.

L:1: p:46

2 *And forasmuch as the Magistrates are under an Oath of God for dispensing equal justice according to Law.* It is Ordered by the Authority aforesayd. That all Associates for County courts when & where there shall be any, & all such Commissioners authorized as aforesayd shall be sworn before each County Court, or some Magistrate in that County, unto the faithfull dischaige of the trust and power cōmitted to them. And it is further Ordered. That in all small causes as aforesayd, where onely one Magistrate dwels in the Town, & the cause concerns himself, as also in such Towns where no Magistrate is, and the cause concerns any of the three Commissioners, that in such cases, the Select men of the Town, shall have power to hear & determine the same, and also to graunt execution for the levying, and gathering up such damages, for the use of the person damnifyed, as one Magistrate

Associates & Cōmissiōers to be sworn.

Select me to try causes.

or

or the three Commissioners may do. And no debt or action proper to the Cognizance of one Magistrate or the three Commissioners as aforesayd, shall be received into any County Court, but by appeal from such Magistrate or Commissioners, except in cases of defamation and battery. [1647. 49]

L. p. 4.

Coũn Court to reject all Act ons under 40 s.

3 *Whereas by reason of the Concourse of people, and increase of trade in the Towne of Boston, suites at Law are growne more frequent, whereby the County Courts are much prolonged, and forasmuch as many crimes are also committed in the sayd town, by strangers and others, which often escape unpunished.* For the prevention whereof it is Ordered by this Court, & the Authoritie thereof, That there be seaven freemen resident in Boston, annually chosen by the freemen of the sayd Town, & presented to the Court of Assistants, who hereby have power to authorize the sayd seaven freemen to be Commissioners of the sayd Town, to act in things committed to their trust, as is hereafter expressed, who shall from time to time be sworn before the said Court, or the Governour. And this Court doth hereby give & graunt Commission and Authority unto the said seven men, or any five of them, or any three of them with one Magistrate, to hear and determine all Civil actions, which shall be brought before them, not exceeding the summ of ten pounds, arising within the neck of land on which the Town is Scituate, as also on Nodles Island, or betwixt any persons where both parties shall be Inhabitants or residents within the said neck or Noddles Island aforesaid or where either partie shall bee an Inhabitant or resident as aforesaid, Provided they keep a book of Records for the entry of all causes, evidences, testimonies, sentences & Judgments as the Law provides in like cases: which said Cõmissioners are Authorized, añually to appoint a Clerk of their Court & to demaũd & receive of every plaintiff in all cases or actions not exceeding forty shillings, the summ of three shillings four-pence, and for all other actions the summ of ten shillings, and for all other things the accustomed fees; And the said Commissioners shall from time to time publish their Court-dayes, as the three Commissioners in Towns are bound to do: *And for the discovery, prevention and punishment of misdemeanours in the Town of Boston,* Power & Authority is hereby given and graunted to the said Commissioners, and every of them, by warrant under their or his hand, to Convent before them, or any of them, all such persons as shall be complained of, for such offences, or otherwise brought to their cognizance, and to hear and determine the same, according to the Lawes here established as any Magistrate may do, Provided the fines imposed by them, do not exceed forty shillings for one offence. *And that the said Commissioners may the better and more diligently endeavour, the suppressing of Sin, & misdemeanours and the breach of the peace in the said Town;* Their Commission shall be from time to time, under the hand of the Secretary of the General Court. And also all Marshals, Constables, and other Inhabitants respectively, are required to be ayding and assisting our Commissioners aforesaid, in this behalf. *And that no person may be discouraged or damnified by this Commission;* It shall be lawfull for any person to appeal from the sentence of all or any of them, to the Court of Assistants. [1651]

A. 51. p. 6

Commissioners of Boston.

Chosen.

Sworn.

Power in Civil Cases to ten pound.

In Criminal cases.

Officers required to assist the Commissioners.

4 *And because the Commissioners in the several Townes have power of Judicature, the excercise whereof is of great concernment, both to townes & country,* It is therefore Ordered, That henceforth there shall be none admitted to be a Cõmissioner for any town in this Jurisdiction but such whose Conversation are inoffensive, & whose fidelity to the Country is sufficiently known & approved of by the County Court of that shire. [1654]

A. 4. p. 2

None to be Cõmissioner but such as are approved

Charges Publicke

IT is Ordered by this Court, and the Authority thereof, That no Governour, Deputy Governour, Assistant, Associate, Grand or petty Jury man, at any court

 nor

None to be imployed in publick service at their own charge.

nor any Deputy for the General Court nor any commissioner for Military discipline at the time of their publick meetings shall at any time beare his owne charges, but their necessary expences, shall be defrayed, either by the Towne, or the Shire on whose service they are, or by the country in General. [1631. 41.]

Every inhab: to pay to all charges in Church and Common weal.

2 *The Court considering the necessity of an equal contribution to all common charges in Townes,* Doth Order, That every Inhabitant, shall contribute to all charges, both in Church and Common wealth whereof he doth or may receive benefit: And every such Inhabitant, who shall not contribute, proportionably to his ability, to all common charges, both Civil and Ecclesiastical, shall be compelled thereunto, by Assessment and distress, to be levyed by the Constable, or other Officer of the Town? and the lands and estates of all men (wherein they dwell) shall be Rated for all Town charges, both civil & Ecclesiastical (as aforesaid) where the lands & estates shall lye. and their persons where they dwel.

Lands & estates (to pay where they ly.

Country rate

Treasurers warrant to ye Constable.

Persons & estates to be valued in ye sixth month.

3 *For a more equal & ready way, of raising means for defraying the publick charges, and for preventing such inconveniences, as have fallen out upon former assessments.* It is Ordered & enacted by the Authority of this Court. That the Treasurer for the time being, shall from yeare to yeare in the fift month, without expecting any other order, send his warrants to the Constable, & Select men of every Town within this Jurisdiction, requiring the Constable to call together the Inhabitants of the Towne, who being so assembled, shall chose some one of their freemen, to be a Commissioner for the Towne, who together with the Select men, for their prudential affaires, shall some time in the sixt month, then next ensuing, make a List of all the male persons in the same Towne, from sixteene yeares old & upwards, and a true estimation of all personal & real estates, being or reputed to be the estate of all & every the persons in the same Town, or otherwise under their custody or managing according to just valuation, and to what persons the same doe belong, whether in their owne Town or elsewhere, so neer as they can by all lawfull meanes, which they may use, viz, of houses, lands of all sorts as wel broken up as other (except such as doth or shall lye common for free feed of cattle, to the use of the inhabitants in general, whether belonging to Townes or particular persons, but not to be kept or hearded upon it, to the damage of the proprietours,) mils, ships & all small vessells, merchantable goods, cranes, wharfs, and all sorts of cattle; and all other known estate whatsoever, either at sea or on shore, all which persons & estates are by the said Commissioners and Select men to be assessed, and rated as here followeth; viz every person aforesayd, (except Magistrates & Elders of Churches) one shilling & eight pence by the head, & all estates, both real & personal, at one penny for every twenty shillings, according to the rates of cattle, hereafter mentioned. The estates of all marchants, shopkeepers and factors, shall be assessed by the Rule of common estimation, according to the will and doom of the assessours, having regard to their stock & estate, be it presented to view or not, in whose hands soever it be, & if any such merchants find themselves over valued, if they can make it appear to the Assessours, they are to be eased by them, if not by the next County Court; And houses and land of all sorts (except as aforesayd) shall be rated at an equal & indifferent value, according to their worth in the Towns & places, where they ly. Also every Bull and Cow of four years old and upward at three pounds, Heifers & steers between three and four years old at fifty shillings, & between two & three years old at forty shilling, and between one & two, at twenty shillings, and every ox of four years old & upward at five pound, every horse & mare of three years old & upwards *ten pounds*, between two & three at *seven pounds*, of one year old and upwards, *at five pounds*, every ewe sheep above one year old, at *five & twenty shillings*, every goat above a year old, at *eight shillings*, every weather sheep above one year old, at *ten shillings*, every swine above one year old, at *twenty shillings*, Every Asse above one year old, at *forty shillings*, And all cattle of all sorts, under a year

Persōs at 1 s 8 d. per head

Estates at 1d per pound.

A.51.p.1

Merchants rated by will and doom.

A.57.p23

Rate of hous. & lands

Rates of Cattle.

a year old, are hereby exempted, as also all hay and corn in the husbandmans hand because all meadow, arable ground, & cattle, are rateable as aforesaid. And for all such persons as by the advantage of their arts and trades are more enabled to help bear the publick charge, then common labourers and workmen, as *Butchers, Bakers Brewers, vitualers, Smiths, Carpenters, Taylers, Shoemakers, joyners, Barbers, Millers and Masons*, with all other manual persons and Artists, such are to be rated for returnes and gaines, proportionable unto other men, for the produce of their estates. Provided that in the rate by the poll, such persons as are disabled by sicknes, lameness or other infirmitie, shall be exempted. And for such servants and children as take not wages, their parents and masters shall pay for them, but such as take wages shall pay for themselves. And it is farther Ordered, that the Commissioners for the several Towns in every shire, shall yearly upon the first fourth day of the week, in the seventh month, assemble at their shire Town: and bring with them fairely written the just number of males, listed as aforesaid, and the assessments of estates made in their several Towns, according to the rules and directions in this present Order expressed, and the said Commissioners being so assembled, shall duely and carefully examine all the said lists and assessments of the several Towns in that shire, and shall correct and perfect the same, according to the true intent of this Order, as they or the major part of them shall determine, and the same so perfected, they shall speedily transmit to the Treasurer under their hands, or the hands of the major part of them; and thereupon the Treasurer shall give warrants to the Constables to collect & leavy the same; so as the whole assessment, both for persons & estates, may be payd in, unto the Treasurer, before the twentieth day of the ninth month yearly; and every one shall pay their rate to the Constable, in the same Town where it shall be assessed, (nor shall any land or estate be rated in any other Town, but where the same shall lye, or was imployed to the owners, reputed owners, or other proprietors use or behoof, if it be within this jurisdiction) And if the Treasurer cannot dispose of it there, the Constable shall send it to such place in Boston, or elswhere, as the Treasurer shall appoint at the charg of the Country, to be allowed the Constable, upon his account with the Treasurer, and for all peculiars, *viz*: Such places as are not yet layd within the bounds of any Town, the same lands, with the persons & estates thereupon, shall be assessed by the rates of the Town next unto it, the measure or estimation shall be by the distance of the meeting houses.

Artificers & handicrafts rated.

Impotent person exempt.

Commissioner meet at the Shire Town.

To perfect ÿ assessments.

Constable to collect in ÿ 9 month.

Peculiars to be rated by ÿ next town.

And if any of the sayd Commissioners, or of the Select men, shall wittingly fail or neglect to perform the trust Committed to them, by this Order, in not making, correcting, perfecting or transmitting any of the sayd lists or assessments according to the intent of this Order, Every such offender shall be fined forty shillings for every such offence or so much as the Country shall be damnified thereby, so it exceed not forty shillings for one offence, provided such offence be complained of & prosecuted within six-months. And it is further Ordered that upon all distresses, to be taken for any of the rates & assessments aforesayd, the Officer shall distreyn goods or cattle, if they may be had, and if no goods then lands or houses, if neither goods nor lands can be had within the Town, where such distress is to be taken, then to attach the body of such person to be carryed to prison there to be kept till the next Court of that shire, except they put in security for their appearance there, or that paiment be made in the mean time. And it is Ordered that the prices of all sorts of corn to be received upon any rate by virtue of this order, shall be such as this Court shall sett from year to year, and in want thereof at the price currant to be judged by the Commissioners of Essex, Middlessex and Suffolk. And it is further Ordered that no estate of land in England, shall be rated in any publick assessment And it is hereby declared that by publick assessment & rates, is intended onely such as are assessed by order of the General Court for the countrys occasions & no other;

Commissioners or select mē failings forfeit 40 s.

Prices of corn to be set by the Court.

Land in England rate free.

A.56.P. 11.

Conſtables to clear their accounts with ye Treaſurer by the 1 of May

L.1.P.46

Cõſtable after ye expiration of his Office hath powr to collect ye rates.

Treaſur. may diſtrayn the Conſtable or any other Inhabitant.

4. It is Ordered, that every Conſtable within this Juriſdiction, ſhall on the penalty of *five pounds*, clear up all their accounts with the Treaſurer, for the Rates of there ſeveral Towns, by the firſt of *May* yearly, and they and every of them are impowred to preſs *boats* or *cartes*, for the better and more ſpeedy ſending in their Rates, according to the time appointed. And if any Conſtable ſhall not have collected the Rates and aſſeſsments, committed to his charge by the Treaſurer, during the time of his Office, that he ſhall, notwithſtanding the expiration of his Office, have power to leavy by diſtreſs, all ſuch rates and leavyes; and if he bring them not into the Treaſurer according to his warrant, the Treaſurer ſhall diſtreyn ſuch Conſtables goods for the ſame. And if the Treaſurer ſhall not ſo diſtreyn the Conſtable, he ſhall be anſwerable to the Country for the ſame And if the Conſtable be not able to make paymēt, it ſhall be lawfull for the Treaſurer to diſtreyn for all arrearages of rates and leavyes, any man or men of that Town, where the Conſtables are unable, and that man or men upon petition to the General Court, ſhall have Order to collect the ſame again, equally of the Town, with his juſt damages for the ſame. [1640 56]

Children & Youth,

Select mens to ſee that all childrē may be taught to read.

Foraſmuch as the good education of children is of ſingular behooſe & benefit to any Common-wealth, & whereas many parents & maſters are too indulgent & negligent of their duty in that kind. It is Ordered that the Select men of every Town, in the ſeveral precincts, and quarters where they dwel, ſhal have a vigilant eye over their brethren and neighbours, to ſee, firſt that none of them ſhall ſuffer ſo much barbariſm in any of their families, as not to endeavour to teach, by themſelves or others, their children & apprentices, ſo much learning, as may enable them perfectly to read the engliſh tongue, & knowledg of the Capital laws: upon penaltie of twenty ſhillings for each neglect therein. Alſo that all maſters of families, do once a week (at the leaſt) catechiſe their children and ſervants in the grounds and principles of Religion, & if any be unable to do ſo much; that then at the leaſt they procure ſuch children and apprentices, to learn ſome ſhort orthodox catachiſm without book, that they may be able to anſwer unto the queſtions, that ſhall be propounded to them, out of ſuch catachiſm by their parents or maſters or any of the Select men, when they ſhall call them to a tryall, of what they have learned in this kind. And further that all parents & maſters do breed & bring up their children & apprentices in ſome honeſt Lawfull calling, labour, or imployment, either in husbandry or ſome other trade, profitable for themſelves and the Common-wealth, if they will not, or cannot train them up in learning to fitt them for higher imployments. And if any of the Select men after admonition by them given to ſuch maſters of families ſhall find then ſtil negligent of their duty in the particulars aforementiōed, whereby children & ſervants become rude, ſtubborn & unruly, the ſayd Select men with the help of two Magiſtrates or the next County Court for that Shire, ſhall take ſuch children or apprentices from them, and place them with ſome maſters for yeares, (boyes till they come to twenty one, & girls eighteen years of age compleat) which will more ſtrictly look unto, & force them to ſubmit unto government, according to the Rules of this order, if by fair meanes & former inſtructions they will not be drawn unto it. [1642.]

And Catechiſed.

Children to be brought up in ſome calling.

Unruly children placed out by the Select men.

A.54.P6

Diſobedient children and ſervants puniſhed by one Magiſtr.

2 *Foraſmuch as it appeareth, by too much experience, that diverſe children and ſervants doe behave themſelves diſobediently & diſorderly, towards their parents, maſters, & Governours, to the diſturbance of families, & diſcouragment of ſuch parents & Governours.* It is Ordered by this Court & Authority thereof. That it ſhall be in the power of any one Magiſtrate, by warrant directed to the Conſtable of that Town, where ſuch offender dwels, upon complaint, to call before him any ſuch offender, & upon conviction of ſuch miſdemeanors, to ſentence him

to endure

to endure such Corporal punishment, by whipping or otherwise, as in his judgment the merit of the fact shall deserve, not exceeding ten stripes for one offence. or bind the offender to make his appearance at the next County Court; And further it is also Ordered, That the Commissioners of *Boston* and the three Commissioners of each towne, where no Magistrate dwels, shall have the like power, provided that the person or persons so sentenced, shall have liberty to make their appeale to the next County Court, in any such cases. Or by the Commissioner

3 *Upon information of diverse loose, vaine and corrupt persons, both such as come from forraine parts, as also some others here inhabiting or residing, which insinuate themselves into the fellowship of the young people of this Country, drawing them both by night, and by day, from their callings, studyes, and honest occupations, & lodging places, to the dishonour of God and greif of their parents, Masters, Teachers, Tutors, Guardians, Overseers &c:* It is Ordered by this Court and the Authority thereof That whosoever shall any wayes cause or suffer any young people or persons whatsoever whether children, servants, apprentices, schollers belonging to the Colledg or any Latine schoole, to spend any of their time or estate, by night or day, in his or their company, ship or other vessel, shop or house, whether Ordinary, Tavern, victualing house, cellar or other place where they have to doe, and shall not from time to time, discharge and hasten all such youths, to their several imployments & places of abode, or lodging aforesayd, if their being in any such place, be known to them, or any other servant or help in the family, or supplying the place of a servant at sea or on land, that then such person, housholder, shop-keeper, ship-master, ordinary-keeper, taverner, victualler, or other shall forfeit the sum of *forty shillings* upon legal conviction before any Magistrate, or the commissioners anthorized to end small causes, one half to the informer, the other half to the Country; and all Constables in their several limits, are required to act herein as is provided in reference to the Law concerning inkeepers. A.51.P.4 Persons under government not to be entertained in comon houses. On penalty of 40 s.

4 *Whereas sundry Gentlemen of quality, and others, oft times send over their children into this Country, to some freinds here, hoping (at least) thereby to prevent their extravagant and riotous courses, who notwithstanding (by meanes of some unadvised or ill affected persons, which give them credit, in expectation their freinds, either in favour to them, or prevention of blemish to themselves, will discharge their debts) they are no less lavish and profuse here, to the great greife of their freinds, dishonour of God, reproach of the Country.* It is therefore Ordered by this Court. That if any person after publication hereof, shall any way give credit to any such youth, or other person under one & twenty yeares of age, without order from their freinds here or elswhere, under their hands in writing, they shall loose their debt whatever it be; And further, if such youth or person, incur any penalty by such means and have not wherewith to pay, such person or persons, as are occasions thereof, shall pay it, as delinquents in the like case should doe [1647] Debts made by persons underage not recoverable.

5 If any person shall wilfully and unreasonably deny any child, timely or convenient marriage, or shall excercise any unatural severity toward them, such children shall have liberty to complaine to Authority for redress in such cases. [1641] Parents denying marriage &c.

6. No Orphan, during their minority, which was not committed to tuition or service by their Parents in their life time, shall afterwards be absolutely disposed of by any, without the consent of some Court, wherin two Assistants (at least) shall be present, except in case of marriage, in which the approbation of the major part of the Select men in that Town, or any one of the next Assistants shall be sufficient, and the minority of women in case of marriage, shall be sixteen yeares. [1646] Orphās not to be disposed on without a Court.

Chirurgions, Midwives, Physitians.

F*Orasmuch as the Law of God allowes no man to impair the life or limbs, of any person, but in a judiciall way* It is therefore Ordered, That no person or persons whatsoever imployed at any time, about the bodyes of men, women or childre L.2.P.3.

for preservation of life or health, as Chirurgeons, Midwives, Physitians or others, presume to excercise or put forth, any act, contrary to the known approved rules of art, in each mistery or occupation, nor excercise any force violence, or cruelty upon, or towards, the body of any, whether young or old, (nor not in the most difficult and desperate cases without the advice and consent of such as are skilfull in the same art (if such may be had) or at least of some of the wisest and gravest then present, and consent of the patient or patients if they be *mentis compotes*, much less contrary to such advice and consent, upon such severe punishment, as the nature of the fact may deserve, which Law nevertheless, is not intended to discourage any from all lawful use of their skill, but rather to incourage & direct them, in the right use thereof, and to inhibit and restreine the presumptuous arrogancy of such as through presidence of their own skil, or any other sinister respects, dare boldly attempt to excercise any violence upon or towards the bodyes of young or old, one or other, to the prejudice or hazard of the life or limb of man, woman or child [1649]

No force or violence to be used in any case without consent &c.

Clerke of the writts.

L:2:p:13:

IT is Ordered by this Court and Authority thereof. That (notwithstanding every Magistrate hath power to grant Warrants, Summons and Attachments) in every towne within this Jurisdiction, there shall henceforth be a Clerke of the writts nominated by each town and allowe'd by each Shire Court, to grant Sumons and Attachments in all civil actions, at the liberty of the Plaintiff, and Summons for witness.s; And the sayd Clerks are allowed to grant replevins, and to take bond with sufficient security of the party to prosecute the suite, whose fees shall be, for every warrant two pence, a replevin or Attachment three pence, and for a bond foure pence. And all Attachments are to be directed to the Constables, in such townes where there is no Marshal dwelling. [1641]

Clerke fees.

Warrats directed to y Constable.

Colledge.

WHeras through the good hand of God upon us, there is a Colledg founded in Cambridge *in the county of Middlesex, called Harvard Colledg, for incouragemet wherof, this* Court *hath given the sum of four hundred pounds & also the revenue of the ferry betwixt* Charlstown & Boston, *and that the well ordering and mannaging of the sayd Colledg is of great concernment:* It is therefore Ordered by this Court and Authority thereof. That the Governour & Deputy Governour for the time being, and all the Magistrates of this Jurisdiction, together with the teaching Elders, of the six next adjoyning townes. *viz: Cambridg: Water-towne, Charlstown, Boston, Roxbury,* and *Dorchester,* and the President of the sayd Colledg for the time being, shall from time to time have full power and Authority to make & establish all such orders, statutes, and constitutions, as they shall see necessary for the instituting guiding and furthering of the sayd Colledg, and several members thereof, from time to time, in piety, morallity and learning, and also to dispose, order & mannage to the use and behoofe of the sayd Colledg and members thereof, all gifts, legacyes, bequeaths, revenues, lands and donations, as either have been, are, or shall be conferred, bestowed, or any wayes shall fall or come to the sayd Colledg. And whereas it may come to pass that many of the Magistrates & said Elders may be absent, or otherwise imployed in other weighty affaires, when the sayd Colledg may need their present help & counsel. It is therfore Ordered that the greater number of Magistrates and Elders, which shall be present with the President, shall have the power of the whole. Provided that if any constitution, order or orders by them made, shall be found hurtfull unto the sayd Colledg, or the members thereof, or to the weale publicke, then upon appeal of the partie or parties greived unto the company of Overseers first mentioned, they shall repeale the sayd Order or Orders (if they see cause) at their next meeting, or stand accountable thereof, to the next Generall Court. [1636. 40. 42]

Comissioners, & feffees of the Colledg.

To make orders.

Dispose of gifts & revenues.

2. Whereas

2. *Whereas wee cannot but acknowledg the great goodneſs of God, towards his people in this wilderneſs, in rayſing up Schooles of Learning and eſpecially the Colledg from whence there hath ſprung many inſtruments, both in Church & Common-wealth both to this and other places: And whereas at preſent, the work of the Colledg hath been ſeveral wayes obſtructed, and ſeems yet alſo at preſent for want of comfortable maintenace, for the incouragement of a Preſident:* This Court *taking the ſame into their ſerious conſideration, and finding that though many propoſitions have been made for a voluntary contribution, yet nothing hath hitherto been obtained, from ſeveral perſons and Townes, although ſome have done very liberally & freely, and fearing leaſt wee ſhould ſhew our ſelves ungratefull to God or unfaithfull to poſterity, if ſo good a ſeminary of knowledg & virtue, ſhould fall to the ground through any neglect of ours.* It is therefore Ordered by this Court and the Authority thereof (That beſides the Proffit of the ferry formerly granted to the Colledge, which ſhall be continued) that there ſhall be yearely leavyed by addition to the Country rate *one hundred pounds*, to be payd by the Treaſurer of the Country to the Colledg Treaſurer, for the behoof & maintenance of the Preſident & Fellows, to be diſtributed between the Preſident & Fellowes according to the determination of the Overſeers of the Colledg, and this to continue, during the pleaſure of the Country. And it is hereby Ordered That no man ſhall ſtand engaged, to pay his voluntary contribution, that he hath under-written by virtue of this Courts propoſitions and that ſuch perſons, as have already done voluntarily, ſhall be conſidered for the ſame in the country rate, ſuch a proportion, as this addition of *one hundred pounds* doth add to the rate, to be allowed by the Conſtable to each perſon, & by the Treaſurer to the Conſtable, [1659]

A:54 :p:2

100 pounds given by the Court to the Preſident & Fellows.

Condemned.

IT is Ordered by this Court. That no man Condemned to dye, ſhall be put to death, within four dayes next after his condemnation unles the Court ſee ſpecial cauſe to the contrary, or in caſe of Martial law; nor ſhall the body of any man ſo put to death, be unburied twelve houres, unles it be in caſe of anatomie, [1641]

None to be execut: in 4 days after condem.

Conſtables.

IT is Ordered by this Court & Authority thereof; That the Conſtable ſhall whip or puniſh any to be puniſhed by Order of Authority (where there is not another Officer appointed to do it) in their own townes, unles they can get another to do it; Alſo every Conſtable is impowred, & hereby enjoyned, faithfully to collect ſuch rates & aſſeſments as ſhall from time to time, be committed unto them, by the ſelect men, of the ſeveral townes, provided it be by warrant under their hand.

Conſtable to whip.

A57:p:26

To collect Towne rates

2 It is further Ordered. That any & every perſon tendred to any Conſtable of this Juriſdiction, by any Conſtable, or other officer of our own, or belonging to any forraine juriſdiction in this country, or by warrant from any ſuch Authority, ſhall be preſently received and conveyed forth with, from Conſtable to Conſtable, till they be brought to the place, to which they are ſent, or before ſome Magiſtrate of this juriſdiction, who ſhall diſpoſe of them, as the juſtice of the cauſe ſhall require And all *Hue-&-cryes* ſhall be duely received & diligently purſued, to full effect; And where no Magiſtrate is neer, every Conſtable ſhall have full power to make, ſigne and put forth purſuites or *Hue & cryes*, after Murderers, manſlayers, peace breakers, Theeves, Robbers, Burglarers & other capital offenders, as alſo to apprehend without warrant ſuch as are overtaken with drink, ſwearing, Sabbath breaking, Lying vagrant perſons, night-walkers, provided they be taken in the manner either by the ſight of the Conſtable, or by preſent information from others. As alſo to make ſearch for al ſuch perſons, either on the Sabbath day, or other, when there ſhall be occaſion, in all houſes licenſed to ſel either beer or wine, or in any other ſuſpected or diſordered places, & thoſe to apprehend, & keep in ſafe cuſtody, til opportunity ſerve to bring them before one of the next Magiſtrates, to further examination.

To convey offenders.

Hue & cryes to be perſued

To be put forth by the Conſtable.

Offenders to be apprehend

Provided when any Constable is imployed by any of the Magistrats, for apprehending of any person, he shall not do it without warrant in writing; and if any person shal refuse to assist any Constable, in the execution of his office, in any of the things aforementioned being by him required thereto, they shall pay for neglect thereof *ten shillings*, to the use of the country, to be leavyed by warrant from any Magistrat, before whom any such offender shall be brought: And if it appear by good tistimony, that any shall wilfully, obstinately or contemptuously refuse or neglect to assist any Constable, as is before expressed, he shall pay to the use of the country *forty shillings*; And that no man may plead ignorance for such neglect or refusal: It is Ordered that every Constable shall have a black staff, of five foot long, tipped at the upper end about five inches with brass, as a badge of his office, which he shall take with him, when he goeth to discharge any part of his office, which staff shall be provided at the charg of the town, and if any Magistrat, Constable, or any other upon urgent occasion, shall refuse to do their best endeavour, in raising & prosecuting *Hue-&-cryes* by foot, and if need be by horse, after such as have committed capital crimes, they shall forfeit for every such offence to the use aforesayd *fourty shillings*. [1646]

All to assist ye Const: on penalty of loss

Wilful neglect 40 s.

Const. staff

Not raising Hue& Cry in Capical cases forfeit

A. 52. p: 15:

Conveyances, Deeds & writings.

FOR *the prevention of Clandestine & uncertaine sales & titles*. It is Ordered and declared by this Court. That henceforth no sale or alienation of houses & lands in this jurisdictiō, shal be holdē good in Law except the same be done by deed in writing, under hand & seal, and delivered & possession given upon part, in the name of the whole, by the seller, or his atturney so authorized under hand & seale, unles the sayd deed be acknowledged & recorded according to Law. [1652]

No sale of Land valid without deed &c.

A: 51: p 2

2 *Whereas through the unskilfulnes of some, that make deeds and conveyances of houses & land, the word Heire is oftentimes omitted, when as an estate of inheritance is intended to be passed by the parties; whereupon questions & suites at Law are apt to arise. For the prevention whereof for time to come.* This Court Ordereth. That all deeds & conveyances of houses and lands in this jurisdiction, wherein an estate of inheritance is to be passed, it shal be expressed in these words, or to the like effect, *viz:* To have & to hold the sayd house or lands respectively to the partie or grantee his heires and Assigns for ever, or if it be an estate entayled then to have & to hold &c. To the partie or grantee & to the heires of his body lawfully begotten or to the Heires male of his body lawfully begotten between him & such an one his wife, or to have & to hold to the grantee for tearm of life, or for so many years. Provided this Law shall not include former deeds & conveyances, but leave them in the same condition, as they were or shall be in before this Law takes effect, which shall be at the last of October one thousand six hundred & fifty one, provided also that this Law shall not extend to houses or lands given by will or testament, or to any land granted or to be granted by the Inhabitants of a town. [1651]

How deeds & conveyāce ought to be made.

L: 1: p: 16

3 It is Ordered. That no conveyance, deed or promise whatsoever, shall be of vallidity, if it be obtained by illegal violence, imprisonment, threatning or any kind of forcible compulsion called Dures. [1641]

Deeds obtained by force invalid.

And all covenous or fraudulent alienations or conveyances of lands, tenements or any hereditaments, shall be of no force or vallidity; to defeate any man from his due debts or legacies, or from any just title, claime or possession, of that which is so fraudulently conveyed.

Fraudulent deeds invalid.

4 *And for the avoyding all fraudulent conveyances, and that every man may know what estate or interest, other men may have in any houses, lands or other hereditaments, they are to deal in.* It is Ordered by the Authority of this Court. That after the end of October one Thousand six hundred & forty, no morgage, bargain, sale or graunt made, of any houses lands, rents or other hereditaments, where the granter remaines in possession, shall be of force against other persons, except the granter, & his heires, unles the same be acknowledged, before some Magistrate, and recorded

Sales to be acknowledg-ed & recorded.

recorded as is heerafter expressed: and that no such bargaine, sale or graunt already made in way of Mortgage, where the granter remaines in possession, shall be of force against other, but the grauntee or his heires except the same shall be entred as is heereafter expressed, within one month after the date beforementioned, if the partie be within this Jurisdiction, or elsewhere, within three months after he shall returne; And if any such Granter, being required by the grantee his heires or Assignes to make an acknowledgment of any grants, sale, bargaine or Mortgage by him made, shall refuse so to doe, it shall be in the power of any Magistrate to send for the party so refusing, & commit him to prison without Baile or Maineprise, untill he shall acknowledg the same, & the grantee is to enter his caution, with the Recorder of the County Court, and this shall save his interest in the mean-time. And if it be doubtfull whether it be the deed & grant of the party, he shall be bound with sureties, to the next Court of Assistants, and the caution shall remaine good as aforesayd. And for the recording of all such grants, sales, Mortgages; It is ordered that the Clerke of every Shire Court shall enter all such grants, sales, bargaines, mortgages of houses, lands, rents & hereditaments as aforesayd, together with the names of the granter & grantee, thing & estate granted, together with the date thereof. [1641 42]

Party refusing to acknowledg his deeds to be imprisoned.

Grantee to enter his caution.

Clerk of the Court to enter deeds.

Council.

THIS *Court considering, how the weighty affaires of this Jurisdiction, whether they concerne this peculiarly, or have reference to the rest of our confederated Colonies, may be duely & speedily transacted, in the vacancy of the General Court, for the satisfaction: of the Commissioners, in respect of the weighty & suddaine occasions, which may be then in hand.* Doth heereby express & declare. That the General Court ought to be called by the Governer, when the importancy of the busines doth require it, & that time & opportunity will safely admitt the same; and that all other necessary matters are to be ordered and dispatched, by the major part of the Council of the Commonwealth, and therefore to that end, letters signifying breifly the busines, & the time & place of meeting for consultation, ought to be sent unto the Assistants. Also it is hereby declared, that seaven of the sayd Assistants meeting, the Governer or Deputie Governer being one, is a sufficient assembly to act, by impressing of souldiers, or otherwise as need shall be, and in case of extream and urgent necessity, when indeavours are reasonably used to call together the Assistants, and the busines will not admit delay, then the acts of so many as do assemble are to be accounted & are accounted vallid, & sufficient: Also it is intended that the general words aforementioned, conteine in them power to impress & send forth souldiers and all manner of victuals, vessels at sea, carriages & all other neccessaries, and to send *warrants* to the Treasurer to pay for the same: [1645]

Council how to be called together.

How many may act.

their power

Counsel: Advice:

L.2: p:4

IT is Ordered by this Court; That it shall not be Lawfull for any person to aske Counsel or advice, of any Magistrate, or Commissioner in townes, in any case wherein afterwards, he shall or may be Plaintiff, before such Magistrate or Commissioner, under penalty of being disinabled to prosecute any such action (that he hath so propounded or taken advice, as aforesayd) at the next Court where the case shall come to triall, being pleaded by way of barr, either by the defendant, or any on his behalf; in which case the Plaintiff shall pay full costs to the defendant, & if the defendant aske counsel, or advice as aforesaid, he shall forfeit *ten shillings* for every such offence, to the Plaintiff:

None to ask Coūsel of Magistrat: or Cōmissi: in civil actions

Courts:

L:1:p.10: 13:

IT is hereby declared, that the General Court, consisting of Magistrates and Deputies is the Chief Civil power of this Cōmonwealth which onely hath power to raise money and taxes upon the whole Country, & dispose of lands, viz: to give and confirme proprieties, appertaining to, & immediately derived from the Country, & may act in all affaires of this Cōmonwealth, according to such power, both

General Court the Cheif power.

in matters of Counsel, making of Lawes, & matters of judicature, by impeaching & sentencing any person, or persons according to Law, & by receiving & hearing any complaints, orderly presented, against any person or Court;

L:2 p 24

And it is agreed, that the Court, will not proceed to Judgment in any cause civil or criminall, before the Deputies have taken this Oath following: [1634 42: 44]

Deputy Oath

I *Doe swear by the most great & dreadfull name, of the everliving God, that in all cases wherein I am to deliver my vote, or sentence, against any criminal offence, or between parties in any civil case, I will deale uprightly & justly, according to my judgment & conscience, And I will according to my skill & ability, assist in all other publick affaires of this* Court, *faithfully & truely, according to the duty of my place, when I shall be present to attend the service:*

L:1 p:16:

2 *Forasmuch as after long experience, diverse inconveniencies are found in the manner of proceeding in this* Court, *by Magistrates & deputies sitting together:*

Magistrates & Deputies to sit apart.

It is therefore Ordered by this Court & Authority thereof. That henceforth the Magistrates sitt apart, & act all busines belonging to this Court by themselves, by drawing up bills, & orders, as they shall see good in their wisdom, which haveing agreed upon, they may present to the Deputies to be considered, & accordingly, to give their consent or dissent: The Deputies in like manner sitting by themselves, & consulting about such orders & Lawes, as they in their discretion & experience, shall find meet for the common good, which agreed on by them, they may present to the Magistrates, who haveing considered, thereof, may manifest their consent or dissent, thereto:

L. 1 :p 36

No act to pass w-out cōsent of ye major part of both.

And no Law, order or sentence shall passe, or be accounted, an act of this Court, without Consent of the greater part of the Magistrates on the one partie, & the greater number of deputies, on the other partie, but all orders & conclusions, that have passed by approbation of Magistrates & Deputies as aforesayd, shall be accounted acts of this Court and accordingly be ingrossed, which on the last day of every session, shall be deliberately read over before the whole Court,

A.52 p11

Provided that if the Magistrates & Deputies, shall happen to differ in any case of Judicature, either civil or criminal, such case shall be determined by the Major Vote of the whole Court met together:

3 *For the Electing of the Governour, Deputy Governour, Assistants, & General Officers, upon the day appointed by our Patent, to hold our yearly* Court *of Election, being the last wednesday of every Easter Tearm;*

Day of election to be attended w-out Summons.

It is solemnly & unanimously decreed & established; That henceforth the Freemen of this Iurisdiction, shall either in person or by proxie, without any Summons attend & Consūmate the Elections on the day aforesayd yearely:

Deputies also to be sēt.

at which time also they shal send their Deputies with full power, to consult of & determaine such matters as concern the welfare of this Cōmon-wealth:

None to depart without leave.

from which General Court, no Magstrate or Deputie shall depart or be discharged, without the consent of the Major part both of Magistrates and Deputies, during the first foure daies of the first session, under the penaltie of one hundred pounds, nor afterwards, under such penaltie, as the Court shall impose, provided that the Deputies of Dover, and of such other Townes, as are not by Law bound, to send deputies are at liberty of attending any after sessions. [1643. 53]

L:1.p.24:

Governer & Dep. Governor; Assistants power to reperive one condem.

4 It is hereby Ordered & declared that the Governour & Deputie Governour joyntly agreeing, or any three Assistants consenting, have power out of Court, to reprieve a condemned Malefactor, till the next Court of Assistants or General Court, And that the General Court onely, hath power to pardon a condemned malefactor.

Gen: Cour may send forth any person.

Also it is declared that the General Court hath Authority to send forth into forraine parts, any member of this commonwealth, of whatsoever quallity, condition, Office or relation, about any publick message or negotiation, provided the party so sent, be acquainted with the affaires he goeth about, & be willing to undertake the service. [1641]

L 1. p:36 24.

4 It is Ordered by this Court, That the Governour, Deputie Governour,

or greater

or greater part of the Assistants, may upon urgent occasion call a General Court, at any time; But no General Court shall be dissolved, or adjourned, without the consent of the Major part thereof. Power to cal a Gen: court Not to be dissolved but by votes &c

6 It is Ordered and declared that the Governour shall have a casting Vote, wheresoever there shall be an *equivote*, in the Court of Assistants or General Court; and the President or Moderator in all Courts or Civil Assemblies. [1641] Governour & President casting vote.

The Court being sensible, of the great necessity of maintaining the Authority of Courts and Magistrates. Doth Order. That whosoever shall openly or willingly, defame any Court of justice, or the sentences & proceedings of the same, or any of the Magistrates, or other Judges of any such Court, in respect of any act or sentence therein passed, and being convicted thereof, shall be punished for the same, by whipping, fine, imprisonment, disfranchisement, or banishment, as the quality and measure of the offence shall deserve. L 1:p:36: Reproach: Courts or Magistrates: penaltie.

And if any Magistrate or other member of any Court, shall use any reproachfull or unbeseeming speeches, or behaviour, towards any Magistrate, judge, or member of that Court, in the face of the Court, he shall be sharpely reproved, by the Governour or President of the sayd Court, and if the quality of the offence; be such, as shall deserve a further censure; or if the person so reproved, shall reply again without leave, the Court may proceed to punish any such offender by fine, or imprisonment, or may bind him over to the next superiour Court. And if in a General Court, any miscarriage shall be amongst the Magistrates, when they are by themselves, it shall be examined and sentenced amongst themselves, if amongst the Deputies when they are by themselves, it shall be examined and sentenced when they are by themselves, if it be when the whole Court is together, it shall be judged by the whole Court. [1637. 41] Offences to members o Court in Court how censured.

7 *FOR the better administration of justice, & easing of the Country of unnecessary charges and travaile.* It is Ordered by this Court & the Authority thereof. That there be two Courts of Assistants, yearely kept at *Boston*, by the Governour, Deputie Governour and the rest of the Magistrates, on the first Tuesday of the first month, and on the first Tuesday of the seventh month, to heare and determine all and onely actions of appeale from inferiour Courts; all Causes of divorce, all Capital and Criminal causes, extending to life, member or banishment. And that justice be not deferred nor the Country needlessly charged, It shall be Lawfull for the Governour, or in his absence the Deputie Governour (as they shall judge necessary) to call a Court of Assistants for the tryal of any Malefactour in Capital Causes. L:1:p 14 a Court of Assistants. their power. L 3: p: 5: Govern: may cal a Court of Assistants.

Also there shall be County Courts held in the several Counties, by the Magistrates living in the respective Counties, or any other Magistrates that can attend the same, or by such Magistrates as the General Court shall appoint from time to time; together with such persons of wroth, where there shall be need, as shall from time to time be appointed by the General Court (at the nomination of the Freemen of the County) to be joyned in Commission with the Magistrates, so that they may be five in all, three whereof may keep a Court, provided there be one Magistrate. Every of which Courts shal have full power to hear & determine all causes Civil & Criminal, not extending to life, mēber or banishment, (which with Causes of divorce are reserved to the Court of Assistants) and to make & constitute Clerks and other needfull Officers, and to Summon juryes of inquest and tryals out of the Towns of the County, provided no Jurors shall be warned from *Salem to Ipswich* nor from *Ipswich to Salem*, & the times & places for holding the coūty Courts shal be as followeth. L 1:p:14 15. Couty Court who keep them. How many judges. their Power

Suffolk. Boston the last tuesday of the (2 / 5 / 8 / 11) month. | *Norfolk* Salisbury / Hampto } 2 tuesday of (2 m. / 8 m. Time and place of the countye courts

Essex. (Salem (Ipswich the last tuesday of ye (4 (9 (1 (7 month. | *Pascataq* (Dover (Portsmouth ye last tuesday of 4 mōth

Middlesex (Charlestown the 3 tuesday (4 (10 of month (Cambridg the 1 tuesday (2 (8 | *Yorkshire.* York ye 1 tuesday of 5 mōth

L:2: p.7. Judgmēt acknowl: before a Magist:

A judgment acknowledged before any two Magistrates & the Secretary or Clerk of any Court, shall be good in Law, and the Clerk's fee for Recording the same, shall be *twelve-pence*, and if the Secretary or Clerk be a Magistrate, he with one Magistrate may do it

L:1: p:15 Special Courts for strangers.

Records of spec Courts to be transmitted to ye Court of assi

8. *For the more speedy dispatch of all Causes, which shall concern Strangers, who cannot without prejudice, stay to attend the ordinary Courts of Justice.* It is Ordered, That the Governour, or deputy Governour, with any two Magistrates, or when the Governour, Deputy Governour cannot attend it, that any three Magistrates, shall have power upon the request of such stranger, to call a speciall Court to hear and determine all causes Civill & criminall (triable in any County court) according to the manner of proceeding in County Courts) which shall arise between such strangers or wherein any such stranger shall be party. And all records of such proceedings, shall be transmitted to the records of the Court of Assistants, to be entred as tryals in other Courts) which shall be at the charge of the partie cast or condemned in the case. 1639.

L:2: p 15 Strāgers liberty to sue at ay Court.

It is further ordered that it shall be lawfull for any stranger, upon legal Sūmons. to to enter any action, in any Court of this Jurisdiction, against any person not residing or Inhabitant amongst us.

L:1:p:36 judges relatedto parties not to give sentence.

9 *FOR preventing all occasions of partial or undue proceedings, in Courts of justice, and avoyding of jealousies,* It is Ordered. That in every Civil Cause, between partie and partie, where there is between any judge of the Court, and any of the parties, the relation of Father and Son either by nature or marriage, Brother and Brother, Unckle & Nephew, Landlord & Tenant in matters of considerable value, Such judge, though he may have liberty to give reasonable advice, in the case, yet shal have no power to vote or give sentence therein, neither shall sitt as a judge, when he shall so plead or give advice therein. [1635]

L:1: p:16 Offender to be judged ye next Court.

10 It is Ordered by this Court; That every person, that is to answer for any criminal cause, whether, in person, or under bayle, his cause shall be heard and determined, at the next Court, that hath proper Cognizance thereof, if it may be done without prejudice of justice. [1641]

A:54 p: 2 In difficult cases Courts may consult ye gen. Court

11 *Forasmuch as the proceedings of this Court, are often hindred by introducing particular cases of a private nature;* It is therefore Ordered. That no Court shall transferr the cases comming before them, and proper to their cognizance, whether civil or criminal, but if there be difficulty in any case, the Court shall state the question, leaving out the parties names, and may present the same to the General Court, where it may be resolved, and according to the sayd resolution of the General Court, the Inferiour Court that presented the question, shall at their next meeting, proceed to judgment or sentence, [1654]

L: 2. p.4. Coūty courts may admit Freemen.

12 Every Court in this Jurisdiction, where two Magistrates are present, may admit any church members, that are fitt, to be Freemen, giving them the Oath. and the Clerke of each Court, shall certify their names to the Secretary at the next General Court. [1641]

Crueltie.

IT is Ordered by this Court. That no man shall exercise any tyranny or cruelty towards any bruite creatures, which are usually kept for the use of man. [1641]

It is

Death untimely.

IT is Ordered by this Court & Authority thereof, That whensoever any Person shall come to any suddain, untimely, or unnaturall death, some Assistant or the Constable of the Town, shall forthwith Summon a Jury of twelve discreet men . to inquire of the cause and manner of their death , who shall present a true verdict thereof, to some neer Assistant, or the next County Court upon their Oath. [1641]

Untimely death to be inquired by a Jury.

Deputies for the Generall Court.

IT is Ordered by this Court & the Authority hereof, That henceforth it shall be Lawfull for the *Freemen* of every Town, to choose (by papers) Deputies for the Generall Court, Who have liberty to meet together, to confer & prepare such publick busines, as by them shall be thought fit to be Considered of at the next Generall Court, who also shall have the full power of all the freemen deputed to them, for the making and establishing of lawes, granting lands, and to deal in all other affaires of the Common wealth, wherein the freemen have to doe, the matter of Election of Magistrates, & other Officers onely excepted: wherin every freeman is to give in his vote; provided that no Towne shall send more then two Deputies & no Town that hath not to the number of *Twenty freemen* shall send more then one Deputy, & such plantations as have not Ten freemen shall send none, but such freemen may vote with the next Towne, in the choice of their Deputies, till this Court take further Order. And all Townes that have not more then *Thirty freemen*, shall be at Liberty of sending or not sending Deputies to the Generall Court. [1636. 38. 53.]

Deputys chosen by paper

Their powr

Number of Deputies to be sent from particular Townes

A: 53.

2. And the freemen of any *shire or Town*, have liberty to choose such Deputies for the Generall Court, either in their own shire Towne, or else where, as they judg fittest, so be it they be freemen, and Inhabiting this Jurisdiction. And when the Deputies, for the severall Townes are met together, at any Generall Court, it shall be lawfull for them, or the Major part of them, to hear & determine any difference that may arise about the Election of any of their members . and to Order, what may concern the well Ordering of their body. *And because wee cannot foresee what variety & weight of occasions may fall into future consideration, and what counsells wee may stand in need of*, It is Ordered that the Deputies of the General Court, shall not at any time be stated & continued but from Court to Court or at most but for a year, that the Country may have an annuall Liberty, to do in that case, what is most behoofull for the wellfare thereof. [1641. 34. 35.]

Liberty to chose Deputies dweling any where in this Jurisdiction. Deputies may order their own house.

No deputies to hold long. then one year

A 54:p:3:

And it is further Ordered. That no man although a freeman, shall be accepted as a Deputy in the Generall Court. that is unsound in judgment, concerning the main points of Christian religion as they have been held forth & acknowledged by the generality of the Protestant Orthodox writers, or that is *Scandalous in his conversation*, or that is *unfaithfull to this Government*. And it is further ordered that it shall not be Lawfull for any freeman to make choice of any such person as aforesaid, that is known to himself to be under such offence or offences specifyed upon paine or penalty of *five pounds* , & the Cases of such persons to be tryed by the whole Generall Court [1654.]

Deputies to be orthodox

And henceforth the Constables of each Towne, shall return the name of the person or persons chosen by the freemen, to be Deputies for the Generall Court, & the time for which they are chosen whether for the first session or for the whole year. And every Constable that shall faile in his duty herein shall forfeit the Summ of *Twenty shillings* , to be payd to the Common Treasury, and all persons so chosen as aforesayd, accepting thereof, which shall be absent from the house during the time of their sitting without just grounds so judged by the house, shall pay *Twenty shillings* a day, for every such defect & the severall returnes of each Constable, shall be kept on file by the Clerke of the Deputys untill the Court be ended. [1654.]

Constable to return who are chosen deputies & for what time.

Distress.

IT is Ordered by this Court & the Authority therof. That no mans Corn or hay that is in the feild, or upon the Cart, nor his Garden stuff, nor any thing subject to present decay shall be taken in distreis, unless he that takes it, doth presently bestow it, where it may not be imbeazled, nor suffer spoile or decay, or give security to satisfy the worth therof, if it comes to any harme. [1641]

Dowries.

Wives to enjoy the third of their husbands Lands &c:

FORasmuch as no provision hath been made, *For any certaine maintenance for wives after the decease of their husbands.* It is Ordered by this Court & the Authority therof. That every *Marryed Women*, (living with her husband in this Jurisdiction, or other where absent from him, with his consent, or through his meer default, or inevitable providence. or in case of divorce, where she is the inocent partie that shall not before Marriage, be estated by way of joynture, in some Houses Lands, Tenements or other Hereditaments for tearm of life, shall immediately after the death of her husband, have right and interest by way of dowry, in, and to, one *third part*, of all such Houses, Lands Tenements and Hereditaments, as her husband was seized of to his own use, either in possession, reversion or remainder, in any estate of inheritance, (or frank-tenement not then determined) at any time during the Marriage, to have and enjoy, for the tearm of her *naturall life*, according to the estate of such husband, free & freely discharged of, & from all titles, debts, rents, charges judgements, executions & other incumbrances whatsoever, had, made or suffered by her husband, during the said Marriage between them: or by any other person claiming by, from or under him, otherwise then by some act or consent of such wife signifyed by writing under her hand, & acknowledged before some Magistrate, or others Authorized therennto wh & shall barr her from any right or interest in such estate. And if the heire of the husband, or other person interested, shall not within one month, after lawfull demand made, assign & set out, to such widdow, her just third part with conveniency, or to her satisfaction, according to the intent of this Law then upon a *writ of dowry*, in the Court of that shire where the said houses, lands, tenements, or other hereditaments shall ly, or in the Court of Assistants, if the same lye in several shires, her third part, or dowry, shall be assigned her, to be set out in severall, by mets & bounds, by such Persons as the same Court shall appoint for that purpose, with all costs and damages sustained, provided alwayes this Law shall not extend to any Houses Lands Tenements or other Hereditaments, sold or conveyed away, by any husband, *bona fide*. for valuable consideration before the last of November *one Thousand Six Hunhred and forty seaven*. Provided also that every such widdow so endowed, as aforesaid, shall not commit or suffer any *strip or wast*, but shall maintaine all such Houses, fences & inclosures as shall be assigned to her, for her Dowrie, and shall leave the same in good and sufficient reparation in all respects [1647]

L. 2 p: 5.

Widdowes third part to be set out.

Not to suffer strip or wast.

Drovers.

IT is ordered by this Court and the Authority therof. That if any man shall have occasion to lead, or drive Cattle from place to place, that is far off, so that they be weary or hungry or fall sick or lame, it shall be lawfull to rest and refresh them for a competent time in any open place, that is not Corne, meddow or inclosed for some particular use. [1641.]

Eclesiasticals.

ALL the *People of God*, *within this Jurisdiction who are not in a Church way. and be orthodox in judgment, and not scandalous in life* shall have full Liberty to gather to gather themselves into a Church estate, provided they doe it in a Christian way, with the observation of the Rules of Christ revealed in his word.

Liberty to gather Churches.

Provided also that the Generall Court doth not, nor will hereafter approve of any such companies of men, as shall joyne in any pretended way of Church-fellowship, unless they shall acquaint the Magistrates, and the Elders of the neighbour Churches, where they intend to joyne, & have their approbation therein.

With approbation of Magistrates and Elders.

2. It is further Ordered, that no person being a member of any Church, which shall be gathered without the approbation of the Magistrates & the said Churches shall be admitted to the freedom of this Cōmon-wealth.

3. Every Church hath free libertie to exercise all the Ordināces of God, according to the rule of the Scripture.

4. Every Church hath free liberty of Election & ordination of all her Officers from time to time, provided they be able, pious & Orthodox.

To choose church-Officers.

5. Every Church hath also free liberty of admission, recommendation, dismission & expulsion or disposall of their Officers & members upon due cause, with free excercise of the discipline & censures of Christ, according to the Rules of the word.

Members.

6. No injunction shall be put upon any Church, Church Officer, or member in poynt of doctrine, worship, or discipline, whether for substance or circumstance besides the Institutions of the Lord.

No humane institutions.

7. Every Church of Christ, hath freedom to celebrate dayes of *fasting & prayer* and of *thanksgiving*, according to the word of God.

8. The Elders of Churches and other brethren and messengers, have liberty to meet *monthly*, *quarterly*, or otherwise, in convenient numbers and places, for conference and consultations about christian and Church questions & occasions, provided that nothing be concluded and imposed by way of Authority from one or more Churches upon another, but onely by way of brotherly conference & consultation.

Elders meeting.

9. All Churches also have liberty to deale with any of their members in a Church-way, that are in the hands of justice, so it be not to retard and hinder the course thereof.

10. Every Church hath liberty to deal with any Magistrate, Deputy of Court or other Officer whatsoever, that is a member of theirs, in a Church-way, in case of apparent and just offence, given in their places, so it be done with due observance and respect. But no Church censure shall degrade or depose any man from any Civill dignity, Office or Authority he shall have in the Common-wealth.

Churches liberty to deal with their members.

11. The Civil Authority here established, hath power and liberty to see the Peace, Ordinances and Rules of Christ be observed in every Church, according to his word, as also to deal with any Church-member, in a way of Civil justice, notwithstanding any Church relation, office or interest.

12. Private meetings for edification in Religion, amongst Christians of all sorts shall be allowed, so it be done without just offence, for number, time, place and other circumstances. [1641]

Private meetings.

13. The Treasurer of the Country, shall defray the Charges of the Elders, of our Churches, when they are imployed by special order of the General Court. 1642. L: 2. p: 7

A. 58.

Whereas it is the duty of the Christian Magistrate, to take care the people be fed with wholesom and sound Doctrine, and in this hour of Temptation, wherein the enemy designeth to sow Corrupt seed. Every company cannot be thought able or fitt to judg, of the Gospel-qualifications required in the publick dispensers of the word and all societyes of Christians are bound to attend Order & Communion of Churches, Considering also the rich blessing of God, flowing from the good agreement of the Civil and Church estate, and the horrible mischiefs and confusions, that follow on the the contrary, It is therefore Ordered, That henceforth, no person shall publickly and constantly preach to any company of people, whether in Church society or not, or be ordained to the Office of a *teaching Elder*, where any two Organick

Constant preachers to be without offence.

ganick Churches, Counsel of state, or Generall Court, shall declare their dissatisfaction thereat, either in reference to doctrine or practise, the said offence being declared to the said company of people, Church, or person, untill the offence be orderly removed, and in case of Ordination of any teaching Elder, timely notice thereof shall be given unto three or four of the neighbouring Organick Churches for their approbation. [1658]

Open opposers of the Word

14. *Forasmuch as the open contempt of Gods word, and messengers thereof, is the desolating sin of Civil states & Churches.* It is Ordered, That if any Christian (so called) within this Jurisdiction; shall contemptuously behave himself, towards the word preached, or the messengers therof, called to dispense the same, in any Congregation, when he doth faithfully execute his service and office therein, according to the will and word of God, either by interrupting him in his preaching, or by charging him falsely with any error, which he hath not taught in the open face of the Church, or like a son of *Korah* cast upon his true doctrine or himselfe any reproach, to the dishonour of the Lord Jesus, who hath sent him, & to the disparragement of his holy Ordinance and making Gods wayes contemptible, & ridiculous: That every such person or persons (whatsoever censure the Church may pass) shall for the first scandal be convented, & reproved opely by the Magistrate at some lecture and bound to their good behaviour. And if a second time they break forth into the like contemptuous carriage, they shall either pay *five pounds* to the publick Treasury, or stand two houres openly upon a block or stool, four foot high, on a lecture day, with a paper fixed on his breast, written in Capital letters, AN OPEN AND OBSTINATE CONTEMNER OF GODS HOLY ORDINANCES, that others may fear & be ashamed of breaking out into the like wickednes. [1646]

L:2 P:5.

Disturbers of order and peace of Churches penalty.

And every Christian as aforesaid that shall goe about to destroy or disturb, the order & peace of the Churches established, in this Jurisdiction, by open renouncing their Church estate or their Ministry, or other Ordinances dispensed in them, either upon pretence that the Churches were not planted by any new Apostle, or that ordinances are for carnal Christians, or for babes in Christ, & not for spiritual or illuminated persons, or upon any other such like groundless conceit, every such person who shall be found Culpable herein, after due meanes of Conviction, shall forfeit to the publick Treasury, forty shillings for every month so long as he shall continue in that his obstinacy. [1640]

Absence from meetings.

15. *Wherever the ministry of the word is established, according to the order of the Gospel throughout this Jurisdiction:* Every Person shall duely resort, and attend thereunto, respectively on the Lords dayes, & upon such publick fast dayes, & dayes of thanksgiving, as are to be generally observed by appointment of Authority. And if any person within this Jurisdiction shall without just & necessary cause, withdraw himselfe from the publick ministry of the word, after due meanes of conviction used he shall forfeit for his absence, from every such publick meeting *five shillings*. And all such offences may be heard & determined from time to time by any one or more Magistrates [1646]

Ministers houses how to be provided for.

26. *To the end there may be convenient habitations for the Ministers of the Word.* It is Ordered, That the Inhabitants of every Town, shall take care to provide the same, either by hiring some convenient house, for the use of the present *Minister*, or by compounding with him, allowing him a competent and reasonable Summ to provide for himself, so long as he shall continue with them, or by building or purchasing an house for the *Minister* and his successors in the ministry, as the major part of the said Inhabitants shall agree. And the particular summs assessed upon each person, by a just rate, shall be collected & levyed as other town rates.

A.54.p.6

17. *That there may be a settled and incouraging maintenance of* Ministers, *in all Towns and Congregations within this Jurisdiction*, It is Ordered, That the County Court in every shire, shall upon information given them, of any defect of any Congregation

gregation or Town within the Shire, order and appoint what maintenance ſhall be allowed to the *Miniſters of the place*, and ſhall iſſue out warrants to the Select men to aſſeſs the Inhabitants, which the Conſtable of the ſaid Town ſhall Collect and levy as other Town rates, And it is hereby declared to be our intention that an honourable allowance be made to the Miniſter, reſpecting the ability of the place, and if any Town ſhall find themſelves burdened by the Aſſeſment of the County Court, they may complain to the Court, which will at all times be ready to give juſt releiſe to all men. [1654]

Proviſo for miniſt maintenance.

Elections.

IT is Ordered by this Court and the Authority thereof, That for the yearly choſing of Aſſiſtants, the freemen ſhall uſe Indian Corn & Beanes, the Indian Corn to maniſeſt Election, the Beanes contrary, and if any freeman ſhall put in more then one Indian Corne or Beane for the Choice or refuſal of any publick Officer, he ſhall forfeit for every ſuch offence, Ten Pounds, and that any man that is not free, or hath not liberty of voting, putting in any vote ſhall forfeit the like Summ of Ten Pounds. [1643]

Election by indian corn & beanes.

None but freemen to put in votes.

2. *For the preventing many inconveniences, that otherwiſe may ariſe upon the yearly day of Election, and that the work of that day, may be the more orderly, eaſily and ſpeedily iſſued.* It is Ordered by this Court and the Authority thereof. That the *Freemen* of this Iuriſdiction, which ſhall not perſonally appear at *Boston*, to give in their votes on the day of *Election*, ſhall and may in their ſeverall Townes, from time to time give in their votes for *Elections*, before their *Deputie*, & the *Conſtable*, who ſhall take thẽ & Seal them up in diſtinct papers, & ſend them to the Court of *Elections*, All the *Aſſiſtants* to be Choſen by *Indian Corn & Beane*, as aboveſaid.

Election by proxies ſent ſealed up.

The Governour, Deputy Governour, Major Generall, Treaſurer, Secretary and Commiſſioners of the United Colonies, by writing the names of the perſon Elected, *in papers* open, or once foulded, not twiſted nor rouled up, that they may be the ſooner peruſed. And ſuch ſmall villages as ſend no Deputies, the cõſtable there of with two or three of the cheif *freemen* ſhal receive the votes of the reſt of the *freemen*, and deliver them together with their own, Sealed up, to the *Deputy* of the next Towne, who ſhall Careſully convey the ſame, unto the ſaid Court of *Election*. [1647.]

Elect: of Governour &c. by papers.

3. *Foraſmuch as the choice of Aſſiſtants or Magiſtrates yearly, is of great concernment & with all care & circumſpection to be attended.* It is Ordered by this Court & the Authority therof. That the Cõſtables of every Town in this Juriſdiction ſhall call together all their freemen ſome day in the *ſecond week* of the *firſt month* yearly, to give in their votes in diſtinct papers for ſuch perſons (being freemen and reſident within this Juriſdiction, as well the Magiſtrates in preſent being as others) whom they deſire to have choſen for *Magiſtrates* or *Aſſiſtants* at the next Court of *Election*, not exceeding the number of *Fourteen*, And no freeman ſhall put in above one vote, for one perſon, under the penalty of *Tenn Pounds* for every offence And the ſaid freemen (ſo met together) or the major part of them, ſhall then and there, appoint one to carry their votes ſealed up, unto their ſhire Townes, upon the laſt *Fourth day of the week* in the *Firſt month* following, at *Twelve* of the Clock from time to time, which Perſons for each Town ſo aſſembled, ſhall appoint one of themſelves as a Cõmiſſioner of each ſhire to carry them to *Boſton* the *Second third day* of the *Second month*, there to be opened and peruſed in the preſence of one or two Magiſtrates (if they be in Town) if otherwiſe by thoſe perſons that brought them, at the Court houſe in Boſton, or ſuch other place as the Cõmiſſioner of *Suffolk* ſhall appoint, and thoſe fourteen that have moſt votes ſhall be the men and they onely) which ſhall be *nominated at the Court of Election* for Magiſtrates or Aſſiſtants as aforeſaid, and the ſaid Commiſſioner of each ſhire, ſhall forthwith ſignify to the cõſtable of the ſeveral towns within their County, in writing under their hands,

L:2.P 10

A.52 p15

Nomination of Magiſtrats in townes.

A.58.

Votes to be ſent to the Shire town.

To Boſtõ to be numbred by ẏ Cõmiſ.

Cõmiſſioner of ẏ ſhire to return the names of the perſõs nominated to the Conſtables.

Old Magist: to be first put to Election.

the names of those *Fourteen persons* aforesaid all which the Constable in each Town, shall timely signify to their *Freemen*. And as any have more votes then other, so shall they be nominated *for Election*, except such of the fourteen, who were Magistrates, the year before, who shall have precedency of all others, in nomination on the day of Election. And if any person be-trusted in this Order, shall fail in the discharge of their trust, they shall forfeit *Ten pounds*. [1649]

Freemen to choose all General Officers.

4. It is declared by this Court, to be the constant liberty of the Freemen of this Jurisdiction, to choose yearly at the Court of *Election* out of the freemen all the *Generall Officers* of this Jurisdiction, & if they please to *discharge them*, at the Court of Election by way of vote they may doe it, without *shewing cause*, But if at any other Generall Court, we hold it due Justice that the reason thereof be alledged & proved By Generall officers we meane our *Governour, Deputy Governour, Assistants, Treasurer, Major General, Admirall at sea, Commissioners for the United Colonies, Secretary* of the General Court, and such others as are, or hereafter may be of like generall nature. [41.]

Escheats.

IT is Ordered by this Court and the Authority thereof. that where no heire or owner of houses, Lands, tenements, goods or chattels can be found, they shall be seized to the publick Treasury, till such heires or owners shall make due claime thereto, unto whom they shall be restored upon just and reasonable tearms. [1646.]

Farms.

IT is Ordered by this Court and the Authority thereof. That all Farmes which are within the bounds of any Towne, shall henceforth be of the same Towne, in which they ly, except Meadford. [1641]

Faires & Markets.

Bosto Salem

IT is Ordered by the Authority of this Court. That there shall henceforth be a Market kept at *Boston* in the County of *Suffolk* upon the fifth day of the week from time to time, and at *Salem* in the County of *Essex* upon the fourth day of the week from time to time. And at *Linn* on the third day of the week from time to time. And at *Charlestown* in the County of *Middlesex* upon the sixth day of the week from time to time. It is also Ordered and hereby Graunted to *Boston* aforesaid to have two Faires in a year, on the first third day of the third month, and on the first third day of the eight month from year to year to continue for two or three dayes together. Allso to *Salem* aforesaid to have two Fayres in a year on the last fourth day of the third month, and the last fourth day of the seaventh month from year to year, Also to *Watertown* in the County of *Middlesex* two Faires in a year, on the first sixt day of the fourth month, and the first sixt day of the seventh month. Also to *Dorchester* in the County of *Suffolk* two Faires in a year, on the third fourth day of the first month and the last fourth day of the eight month, from year to year. [1633. 34. 36. 38. 48.]

Lin. Charlestown.

L.2. P.7.

Watertown.

Ferryes.

FOR settling all common Ferryes in a right course, both for the passengers and owners, It is Ordered by this Court & the Authority thereof. That whosoever hath a ferry graunted upon any passage, shall have the sole liberty, for transporting passengers from the place where such ferry is graunted, to any other ferry place, where ferry boats use to land, and any ferry boat that shall land passengers at any other ferry, may not take Passengers from thence, if the ferry boat of that place be ready, provided this Order, shall not prejudice the liberty of any, that doe use to pass in their own or neighbours *Canoas* or *boates* to their ordinary labour, or business. But no ferryman shall cary over the water any passengers in a *Canoe*, but in case of necessity and upon his own desire, under the pain of forfeiture of the *Canoa*

Men may pass ferryes in their own boats.

L.2. P.7.

Ferrimē not to carry in Canoas.

or the Value thereof to the Treasury. And at *Weimouth* ferry every single person shall pay for his passage *two pence*. And all Ferrymen are allowed to take double pay, at all common ferries after day light is done, & those that make not present pay being required, shall give their names in writing, or a pawn to the ferrymen, or else he may complaine of any such, to a Magistrate for satisfaction, And it is Ordered that all Magistrates, & such as are, or from time to time shall be chosen Deputies of the Generall Court, with their necessary attendance viz: a man & a horse at all times, during the time of their being Magistrates or Deputies (but not their families) shall bee passage-free over all ferries, that pay no rent to the Country.

Magistrates & Deputies to pass free.

2. *And for the preventing of danger in the passing at Common ferries.* It is Ordered. That no person shall press or enter into a ferry boat contrary to the will of the ferryman or of the most of the Passengers first entred upon paine of *Ten shillings* for every such attempt. And that every ferryman that shall permit or allow, any person to come into his *Boat* against the will of any of the Magistrates or Deputies or any of the Elders shipped in such *Boat* or the greater part of the Passengers in the said *Boat* shall forfeit for every person so admitted or received against such their will so declared, the summ of *Twenty shillings*. And it shall be in the power of any of the ferrymen, to keep out, or put out of his boate, any person that shall press, enter into or stay in any such ferry boate, contrary to this Order. And it is further Ordered, That all persons shall be received into such *ferry boats* according to their comming, first or last, onely all publick persons, or such as goe upon publick or urgent occasions, as *Physitians, Chirurgeons* and *Midwives*, and such other as are called to womens labours, such shal be transported with the first. [1641. 44. 46. 47]

None to enter y ferry boat without leave of the ferrimen Magist. Dep. or Elders.

Men pass as they come except publick persons.

Fines.

L. 1: p: 38:

IT is Ordered by this Court and Authority thereof. That every offender fined for the breach of any *penal Law*, shall forthwith pay his or their fine or penaltie, or give security speedily to doe it, or be imprisoned, or kept to worke till it be payd, unles the Court or Judge that imposed the fine see cause to respit the same; And in all Courts where any fine or fines, or other summs of money shall be assessed or received, And also when any Magistrate or Commissioner, shall assess any fines, or receive any summ, for the use of the Country, by vertue of any special Order, *the Secretary* or *Clerke* of each Court, and every such Magistrate and Comissioner, shall within fourteen dayes, send a transcript or note of the sayd fines, & other dues, to the Treasurer of the Country or County to whom it doth belong, who shall forthwith give warrant to the Marshal to collect & leavy the same. And if no goods can be found, to satisfy such fine or other dues, the Marshal shall attach the body of such persons, and imprison them till satisfaction be made. Provided that any Court of Assistants or County Court, may discharge any such person from imprisonment, if they be unable to make satisfaction. [1638. 46]

Fines to be payd presently

L. 2: p: 7:

Clerk to return all fines to y Treas. in 14 dayes:

L. 1: p: 22

Marshal to attach y body where goods are not &c:

Firing & Burning.

IT is Ordered by this Court and Authority thereof, That whosoever shall kindle any *fires in the woods*, or grounds lying in Common, or inclosed, so as the same shall run into corne grounds or inclosures before the *tenth day of the first month*, or after the *last of the second month*, or on the *last day of the week*; or on the *Lords day*, shall pay all damages, and half so much for a fine, or if not able to pay, then to be Corporally punished, by warrant from one Magistrate, or the next County Court, as the offence shall deserve, not exceeding *Twenty stripes* for one offence. Provided that any man may kindle fire in his own ground so as no danger come thereby either to the Country or to any particular person and whosoever shall wittingly and willingly burne or destroy any frame, Timber, hewed sawen or riven, heapes of wood, Charcoal, Corn, Hay, Straw, Hemp or flax, he shall pay double damages.

Firing of ground whē lawfull whē forbidden.

A:52.p21

2 *VVhereas some dwelling houses, and other houses, within this jurisdiction, have been set on fire, and the meanes or occasion thereof not discovered, though some persons have been vehemently suspected, to have been instrumental therein.* The Court *taking into consideration the danger of such a wicked practise, especially in Townes where the houses are neere adjoyning, and there being no Law yet provided for the punishment of so heinous a crime:* Doth therefore hereby Order, and be it enacted by the Authority of this Court, That any person or persons whatsoever, of the age of *sixteen yeares* and upward, that shall after the publication hereof, wittingly and willingly set on fire any Barn, Stable, Mill, out-house, stack of wood, Corne or hay, or any other thing of like nature, shall upon due conviction by testimony or confession, pay double damages to the partie damnifyed, and be severely whipt, And if any person of the age aforesayd, shall after the publication hereof, wittingly & willingly & feloniously set on fire any dwelling house, meeting-house, storehouse, or shall in like manner set on fire any out-house barne, stable, leanto, stacke of hay, corn or wood, or any thing of like nature, whereby any dwelling house, meeting house or storehouse, cometh to be burnt, the party or parties vehemently suspected thereof, shall be apprehēded by warrant from one or more of the Magistrates, &c. committed to prison, there to remaine without baile, til the next Court of Assistants, who upon legal conviction by due proof, or confession of the Crime, shall adjudg such person or persons to be putt to death, and to forfeit so much of his lands, goods or chattels, as shall make full satisfaction, to the party or parties damnifyed. [1652

Burning houses.

Capital

Fish Fishermen.

W*Hereas it hath been a Custome for forreine fishermen, to make use of such harbours and grounds in this Country, as have not been inhabited by Englishmen, & to take timber and wood at their pleasure, for all their occasions, yet in these parts which are now possessed, and the lands disposed in proprieties, unto several townes & persons, by the kings grannt under the great seale of England.* It is declared, That it is not lawfull for any person either fisherman or other, either forreiner or of this Country, to enter upon the lands so appropriate to any town or person or to take wood or timber, in any such place, without the licence of such Town or proprietor, and if any person shall trespass herein, the Town or proprietor so injured, may take their remedy by action at law, or may preserve their goods or other interest, by apposing Lawfull force against such unjust violence, Provided that it shall be Lawfull for such fishermen, as shall be imployed by any Inhabitants of this Jurisdiction, in the severall seasons of the year, to make use of any of our harbours, & such Lands as are neer adjoyning, for the drying of their fish, or other needfull occasions, as also to have such timber & fire-wood, as they shall have necessary use of, for their fishing seasons, where it may be spared, so as they make due satisfaction for the same to such Town or proprietor. [1646]

Fishermē liberty to fish in our harb:

And to take wood for their occasiō

Making satisfaction to y proprietors.

A. 52.p. 9,10.

2 *Wheras much damage hath arisen to merchants trading hence by bad making of fish, & the credit of our trade therein hath much suffered,* It is therefore ordered, That at every fishing place, within this Jurisdiction some discreet and honest person be appointed by the County Court, unto which such fishing place doth belong, and those persons so nominated & appointed, are by this Court impowred, to give Oath unto such persons as shall be chosen by the deliverers and receivers of any fish, who have liberty hereby, either of them, to choose one or more sufficient knowing men, in such cases, to veiw what fish is delivered and received, which veiwers shall be sworn as aforesaid, and what they approove of as Merchantable, the receiver shall accept, and what is refuse fish, shall be cast by, & the said veiwers for their labour & paines aforesaid, shall be allowed *one penny per quintal* for so much Merchantable fish, as he or they shall veiw to be payd one halfe by the deliverer & the other half by the receiver, *and for further direction in the veiwers in tryal of fish* It is hereby Ordered, That all sun burnt, salt-burnt and dry fish, that hath been first pickled shall be judged unmerchantable.

Sworn viewers of fish at all fishing places.

It is

Forgery.

IT is Ordered by this Court and the Authority thereof, That if any person shall *Forge* any Deed or Conveyance, Testament, Bond, Bill, Release, Acquittance, letter of Atturney, or any writing to pervert equity and justice, he shall *stand in the Pillory*, three several Lecture dayes, and render double damages to the party wronged, and also be disabled to give any evidence or verdict, to any Court or Magistrate. [1646]

Fornication.

IT is Ordered by this Court and Authority thereof, That if any man commit *Fornication*, with any single woman, they shall be punished, either by enjoyning marriage, or fine, or corporal punishment, or all or any of these, as the Judges of the Court that hath Cognizance of the cause shall appoint. [1642]

Freemen non-freemen.

TO *the end the body of the freemen may be preserved of honest and good men*, It is Ordered, That henceforth no man shall be admitted to the freedome of this Common-wealth, but such as are members of some of the Churches, within the limits of this Iurisdiction; *And whereas many members of Churches to exempt themselves from Publick service, will not come in to be made freemen*, It is Ordered, That no members of Churches within this Jurisdiction, shall be exempt from any publick service, they shall be chosen to, by the Inhabitants of the severall Townes, as Constables, Iurors, Select men, surveiors of the High-wayes. And if any such person shall refuse to serve in, or take upon him any such Office. being Legally chosen thereunto, he shall pay for every such refusall, such fine, as the Town shall impose not exceeding *Twenty shillings* for one Offence. [1647]

L.2.P.8. None but Church-mebers to bee freemen

L.1.p.23

Gaming & dauncing.

UPON *Complaint of the disorders, by the use of the Games of shuffle-board and Bowling, in and about houses of common entertainment, whereby much precious time is spent unprofitably, & much wast of wine and beer occasioned*; It is Ordered by this Court and the Authority thereof, That no Person shall henceforth, use the said Games of shufle-board, or bowling, or any other play or game, in, or about any such house, nor in any other house used as Common for such purpose, upon paine for every keeper of such house, to forfeit for every such Offence *Twenty Shillings*, & every person Playing at the sayd Games &c: in or about any such house shall forfeit for every such Offence *Five Shillings*. Nor shall any person at any time, play or Game for any mony, or mony worth, upon penalty of forfeiting treble the Value thereof, one halfe to the party informing and the other halfe to the Treasury, nor shall any person be an Abettor to any kind of gaming on the like penaltie. Nor shall there be any dauncing in ordinaries upon any occasion, on the penaltie of *five shillings* for every person that shall offend: and any Magistrate may hear & determine any offence against this Law. [1646, 47, 51.]

L.2.P.8. No gaming in Ordinaries.

No gaming for money

No dancing in Ordinaries

A.51.p 3

For preventing disorders arising in several places within this Jurisdiction; by reason of some still observing such feastivals, as were superstitiously kept in other Countryes, to the Great dishonour of God and Offence of others It is therefore Ordered by this Court and the Authority thereof. That whosoever shall be found observing any such day, as Christmas or the like, either by forbearing labour, feasting, or any other way upon any such account as aforesayd, every such person so offending, shall pay for every such Offence *Five shillings*, as a fine to the County. *And whereas not onely at such times but severall other times also, it is a Custome too frequent in many places to expend time in unlawfull Games, as Cards, Dice &c*: It is therefore further Ordered and by this Court declared. That after publication hereof whosoever shall be found in any place within this Iurisdiction playing either at cards or at dice, Contrary to this Order, shall pay as a fine to the County the sum of *Five Shilings* for every such Offence.

Penalty for keeping christmas

Penalty for playing at Cards & dice

Herefie Error.

Although no humane Power, be Lord over the Faith & Conscienses of men, yet because such as bring in damnable Heresies, tending to the subversion of the Christian Faith & distructions of the soules of men, ought duely to be restrained, from such notorious impieties. It is therefore Ordered and declared by the Court. That if any *Christian* within this Iurisdiction, shall go about to subvert and destroy the *Christian Faith and Religion*, by broaching and maintaining any *Damnable Heresies:* as denying the immortallity of the soule, or resurrection of the body, or any sin to be repented of in the regenerate, or any evil done by the outward man to be accounted sin, or denying that Christ gave himselfe a ransom for our sins, or shall affirm that we are not justifyed by his death and righteousnes, but by the perfections of our own works, or shall deny the morallity of the Fourth Commandement, or shall openly Condemn or oppose the Baptizing of Infants, or shall purposely depart the Congregation at the administration of that Ordinance, or shall deny the ordinance of Magistracy, or their Lawfull Authority to make war, or to punish the outward breaches of the first Table, or shall endeavour to seduce others to any of the errors or heresies above mentioned, every such person continuing obstinate therin, after due meanes of Conviction, shall be sentenced to Banishment. [1646, 44]

Errors

L. 1 P. 2.

Anabaptists

Obstinate to be banished.

A. 57. p. 78.

2 *The holy Scriptures of the Old and New Testament, being written by the Prophets, Apostles, and holy Men of God, inspired by the holy Ghost, containing in them, the infallible & whole will of God, which he Purposed to make known to Mankind, both for his own worship & service & also for the instruction, Obedience, Faith & salvation, of Man, which yet by Heretiieks in former ages, & now of late have been oppugned and denyed so to be, which tends to the overthrow of all true Religion and salvation, for the prevention of so heinous a crime.* It is Ordered by this Court and the Authority thereof. That what person or persons soever professing the Christian religion, above the age of Sixteen yeares, that shall within this Iurisdiction, Wittingly and Willingly, at any time after the publication of this Order, deny either by word or writing, any of the Books of the Old Testament, as *Genesis, Exodus Leviticus, Numbers, Deuteronomy, Joshua, Judges, Ruth, Samuell, Samuell, Kings Kings, Cronicles Cronicles, Ezra, Nehemiah, Esther, Iob, Psalmes, Proverbs, Eclesiastes, Canticles Esaiah Jeremiah, Lamentations, Ezekiel, Daniel, Hosea, Joel, Amos, Obadiah, Jonah, Micah, Nahum, Habbakuk, Zephaniah, Haggy, Zachariah, Malachi.* Or New, as *Mathew, Mark, Luke, John, Acts, Romans Corrinthians, Corrinthians, Galathians, Ephesians, Philippians, Collossions, Thessalonians, Thessalonians, Timothy, Timothy, Titus, Philemon, Hebrewes, James, Peter, Peter, John, Iohn, Iohn, Iude & Revelation.* To be the written & infalible Word of GOD, or if any person as aforesayd, belonging to this Iurisdiction shall Commit the sayd crime upon the Sea, not being or belonging to the Iurisdiction, of any other Commonwealth, shall be forthwith apprehended, by the next Officer or Officers, whether Marshall or Constable or their Deputy, who shall have power so to doe by warrant from any one of the Magistrates, & shall be Committed to the prison at Boston, without Bayle or maine prize, there to be safely kept till the next County Court, where upon sufficient Testemony brought against the said delinquent he shall be adjudged for his offence, after Legal Conviction, to pay such a fine as the Court which shall have Cognizance of the Crime shall judg meet, not exceeding the Sum of *Fifty Pounds*, or shall be *openly & severely whipt*, by the executioner, whether Constable or any other appointed, not exceeding *forty strokes*, unles he shall publickly recant before his sentence (which if he doe) he shall not pay above the fine of *Ten pounds*, to the Treasurer for the use of the Commenwealth, or *be whipt* in case he pay not the fine. And it is further Ordered & enacted, That if the sayd offender after his recantation, sentence or execution, shall the second time publish, & obstinately and pertinaciously maintaine the sayd wicked opinion, he shall be Banished or put to death as the Court shall judg. [1651]

Denying the Scripture to be ye Word of God.

Penalty

3 It is

3. It is Ordered, that all and every of the Inhabitants of this Jurisdiction, that have any of the bookes in their Custody that goe under the names of *John Reeves*, & *Lodowick Muggleton* (who pretend themselves to be the two *last witnesses*, and *Prophets of Jesus Christ*) which are full of blasphemies, and shall not bring or send in all such bookes in their Custody, to the next Magistrate, shall forfeit the Sūm of *ten pounds*, for every such book foūd in his hand the one half to the Informer the other half to the Country. And as many of the sayd bookes as are, or shal be in Custody shall *be burnt* in the Market place at Boston, on the next Lecture-day by the common executioner. A:54 p:7: Muggletons books to be delivered in to some Magistrates To be burnt

4. *VVhereas there is a Cursed sect of hereticks, lately risen up in the world, which are commonly called Quakers, who take upon them to be immediately sent of God, and infallibly assisted by the Spirit, to speake and write blasphemous opinions despising government, and the order of God in Church & commonwealth, speaking evil of dignities, reproaching and reviling Magistrates and Ministers, seeking to turn the people from the faith, and gaine proselites to their pernicious wayes.* The Court *considering the premisses, and to prevent the like mischiefe, as by their meanes is wrought in our native land;* Doth hereby Order, And by the Authority of this Court be it Ordered & Enacted, That no *Master* or *Commander of any Ship, Barke, Pinnace, Catch* or other *Vessel*, shall henceforth bring into any harbour, Creek or Cove, within this Jurisdiction, any known *Quaker* or *Quakers*, or any other blasphemous hereticks as aforesayd, upon the penaltie of the forfeiture of *one hundred pounds*, to be forthwith payd to the Treasurer of the Country, except it appeareth that such Master, wanted true notice or information that they were such, and in that case he may cleare himself by his Oath, when sufficient proofe to the contrary is wanting. And for default of paiment of the sayd fine of *one hundred pounds*, or good security for the same, such Master shall be committed to prison, by warrant from any Magistrate, there to continue till the sayd fine be satisfyed to the Treasurer as aforesayd. And the *Master* or *Commander* of any such ship or vessel, that shall bring them being legally convicted, shall give in sufficient security to the Governour or any one or more of the Magistrates, to carry them backe to the place, whence he brought them, and on his refusall so to doe, the Governour, or the said Magistrate or Magistrates, shall commit such Master or Commander to prison, there to continue till he shall give in sufficient security to the Content of the Governour or sayd Magistrates. And if any person or persons within this Jurisdiction, shall henceforth entertain & conceale any such *Quaker* or *Quakers* or other *Blasphemous hereticks* (knowing them to be such) every such person shall forfeit to the Countrey, *Fourty shillings* for every houres entertainement and concealment of any *Quaker* or *Quakers*, &c: as aforesayd, and shall be Committed to prison as aforesayd, till the fine's be fully satisfyed and payd. A: 56: p: 13. Quakers. Not to bee brought into this Jurisdiction by any Master of Ship. On penalty of 100 pound Masters that bring in quakers must carry them back A.57.p. 26. entertaining Quakers pen. 40 s. a hour

5. And every person or persons, that shall *incourage or defend* any of their pernicious wayes by speaking, writing, or meeting on the Lords day, or at any other time, shall after due meanes of conviction, incurr the penalty ensuing, *viz*: every person so meeting, shall pay to the use of the Country, for every time ten shillings & every one speaking in such meeting, shall forfeit five pounds. A. 58. Incouragers of Quakers their penalt.

6. If any person shall knowingly import into any harbour of this Jurisdiction, any *Quakers Books* or *Writings*, cōcerning their damnable opinions, he shall forfeit for every such book or writing *Five Pounds*, and whosoever shall disperse or conceale any such book or writing, and it be found with him or her, or in his or her house, & shall not immediately deliver the same to the next Magistrate, shall forfeit and pay *Five Pounds* for dispersing or Concealing every such Book or writing. Dispersing Quakers books penalt. 5 li.

Reviling of Magistrates or Ministers.

7 And every person or persons whatsoever, that shall revile the office of person of Magistrates or Ministers, as is usuall with the Quakers, such Person or Persons shall be *Severely Whipt*, or pay the Summ of *Five Pounds*.

A. 53. p. 19. Publishers of Errors.

8. And every person that shall publish and maintaine, any Heterodox or erroneous Doctrine, shall be liable to be questioned and Censured by the County Court where he liveth, according to the merit of his offence.

A. 58.

9. *VVhereas there is a pernicious Sect commonly called Quakers lately arisen, who by word and writing, have published and maintained many dangerous and horrid tenents, and do take upon them to change & alter, the received laudable customes of our nation in giving Civil respect to equals, or reverence to Superiours, whose actions tend to undermine the Authority of Civil Government, as also to destroy the Order of the churches, by denying all established formes of worship, and by withdrawing from the orderly church assemblies, allowed & approoved, by all Orthodox professors of the truth; and instead thereof & opposition thereunto, frequenting private meetings of their own, Insinuating themselves into the minds of the Simpler, or such as are less affected to the Order & Government of the Church and Commonwealth, whereby divers of our Inhabitants have been infected and seduced, notwithstanding all former Lawes made, (upon experience of their arrogant bold obtrusions, to disseminate their principles amongst us) prohibiting their Comming into this Jurisdiction, they have not been deterred from their impetuous attempts, to undermine our peace, and hasten our ruine.* For prevention thereof this Court doth Order and Enact, That every person or persons of the Cursed sect of the *Quakers*, who is not an Inhabitant of, but found within this Iurisdiction, shall be apprehended (without warrant, where no Magistrate is at hand) by any Constable Commissioner or Select Man, and conveyed from Constable to Constable untill they come before the next Magistrate who shall Committ the sayd person or persons to Close Prison, there to remaine without Baile, untill the next Court of Assistants where they shall have a Legall tryall, by a speciall jury, and being Convicted to be of the sect of the *Quakers*, shall be sentenced to banishment upon paine of Death. And that every Inhabitant of this Jurisdiction being Convicted to be of the aforesayd sect, either by taking up, publishing and defending, the horrid opinions of the *Quakers*, or by stirring up *mutinie*, *Sedition* or *Rebellion*, against the Government, or by taking up their absurd & destructive practises, viz. denying Civil respect and reverence to equals and Superiours, withdrawing from our Church assemblies, & instead thereof frequenting private meetings of their own, in opposition to Church Order, or by adhering to, or approving of any known Quakers, that are opposite to the Orthodox received opinions & practises of the godly, & endeavoring to disaffect others to Civil Government, and Church order, and Condemning the practise & proceedings of this Court against the Quakers, manifesting thereby cōplyance with those, whose design is to overthrow the Order established in Church and Common wealth, every such person upon examination and legall conviction before the Court of Assistants in manner as aforesayd shall be committed to close prison, for one Month, and then unless they choose voluntarily to depart the Jurisdiction, shall give bond for their good abbearance and appearance at the next Court of Assistants, where Continuing obstinate, and refusing to retract & reform the aforesaid opinions & practises shall be sentenced to Banishment, upon paine of Death, and in case of the aforesaid voluntary departure not to remaine; or againe to returne into this Iurisdiction without the allowance of the major part of the Councell first had and published, on penalty of being Banished upon paine of Death, and any one Magistrate, upon information given him, of any such person, shall cause them to be apprehended, and if upon examination of the case he shall according to his best discretion find just ground for such complaint, he shall commit such person to prison, untill he comes to his tryall as is above expressed. [1646]

Quakers to be Apprehended. Imprisoned. Banished on paine of death. Qualification of Quakers. Quakers voluntarily depart may not return without licence. One Magistrate may commit to prison.

Hides and Skins.

WHereas some persons, more seeking their own private advantage, then the good of the Publick, do transport raw hydes & pelts, It is Ordered that henceforth no person shall deliver aboard any ship or other vessel, directly or indirectly, any raw hide, skin, pelt or leather unwrought, with intent to have the same transported out of this Iurisdiction, upon pain to forfeit the same, or the value therof. And that no Master of any Ship or Vessel shall receive any raw hide, skin, pelt or leather unwrought, directly or indirectly aboard his Ship or Vessel to be so transported upon the like penalty. Provided that any person, stranger or other, may transport any hides or skins, brought hither from beyond the Seas by way of Merchandise, or the skins of Beaver, Moose, Beare, & Otter. [1646] Raw hides not to be transported

L. 2. p. 8.

2. *Upon information of the neglect of many persons, in not saving such Hides or skins, as either by casualty or Slaughter come to hand, whereby dammage redounds to the Country.* It is Ordered, that every hide or Skin, shall carefully be dryed, before it corrupt, and that such hides or skins, shall be sent where they may be tanned or dressed, and whosoevr shall neglect to do as aforesayd, shall forfeit for every such hide *five shillings*, & for every skin of Calves or small Cattle *twelve pence.* [1640,46.] Hides & skins to be preserved.

High-wayes.

TO the end there may be convenient High-wayes for Travellers. It is Ordered by the Authority of this Court. That all Country High-wayes shall be such as may be most easy and safe for travellers, to which purpose, every Town (where any such high-way is made, or to be made) shall appoint two or three men of the next Town, whose Inhabitants have most occasions thereof, chosen & appointed by their sayd Town, who shall from time to time lay out all Common High-wayes, where they may be most convenient, notwithstanding any mans proprietyes (So as it occasion not the pulling down of any mans house, or laying open any Gardē or Orchard who in common Grounds, or where the soyl is wett, Myrie or very rockey, shall lay out such High-wayes the wider *viz* six, eight, ten, or more rods. Provided that if any man be thereby damaged in his improved ground the town shall make him reasonable satisfaction, by estimation of those that layd out the same: & if such persons deputed cannot agree it shall be referred unto the County Court of the shire, who shall have power to hear and determine the case, and if any Person find himselfe justly greived, with any act or thing, done by the persons deputed aforesaid he may appeal to the County Court aforesayd, but if he be found to complaine without cause, he shall surely pay all charges of the parties and Court, during that action, and also be fined to the Country, as the Court shall adjudg. [1639] By whom to be laid. Satisfaction to be given proprietor

2. It is Ordered and declared by this Court, that the Select Townes-men of every town, have power to lay out (by themselves or others) Particular & private wayes concerning their own town, only so as no damage be done to any man, without due Recompence, to be given by the judgment of the sayd Select men, and one or two chosen by the sayd Select men, and one or two chosen by the party, and if any person shall find himselfe justly greived, he may appeal to the next County Court of that shire, who shall do justice therein as in other Cases [1642] Private ways in Towns

3. *Upon information that divers High-wayes are much annoyed and incumbred by gates and railes erected upon them,* It is Ordered by the Authority of this Court. That upon any information or Complaint made to any County Court, or to any Magistrate of any such gates or railes, erected or to be erected, upon any Cōmon highway, the said Court or Magistrate shall appoint a Cōmittee of discreet & indifferent men to veiw such incumbrance, and to Order the reformation thereof. And if the parties whom it shall concern, shall not submitt to such Orders, they shall require them to appear at the next Court of that shire, and also shall certify the incumbrance found, and Order by them made, under their hands unto the sayd Court or appear in person to prosecute the cause where it shall be heard and determined for Incumbrāce in high ways to be removed

ease and conveniency of travellers, with due respect to the proprietors cost & damage, but no person shall stand charged with the repaire of common high-wayes through his own ground. [1647]

Horses Mares

L.2.p:11. Horses to be trans ported are to be entred in a book.

IT is Ordered by this Court and Authority thereof. That no Master or Commander of any Ship or Bark, shall receive on board his Ship or Vessel, any Horse Gelding or Mare, but such as shall be entred into a book, with the Colour, particular marks and age, (as neer as may be known) and person of whom such Horse was last bought; and proof by witnes or Oath, that he was the true owner thereof, to be kept by the Clerks of the writs in all their Townes, who are hereby authorized to veiw all such as shall be Shipped, and for every Horse so entred there shall be payd to the sayd Officers, by the owner or Merchant of such Horse, six pence a peice, And every Cômander or Master of any Vessel, who shall take on board, any other Horse or Mare, except such as he shall receive a note under the hand of the said Clerke & be entred as aforesayd, shall for every such Offence forfeit the Summ of Forty Shillings to the informer, and Forty Shillings to the Treasury. [1649]

Penaltie:

No horses to be sold to Indians.

It is Ordered that no person, shall under any pretence sell or any way dispose any Horse. Mare or Colt, to any Indian, upon the Penalty of one Hundred Pounds. [1655.]

Idleness.

Constable to take notice of Idle persons:

IT is Ordered that no person, Housholder or other, shall spend his time, idlely or unprofitably, under paine of such punishment, as the County Court shall think meet to inflict. And the Constables of every Towne are required to use speciall care to take notice of offenders in this kind, especially of common Coasters, unprofitable Foulers, and Tobacco takers, and Present the same to the next Magistrate, who is hereby impowred to Hear and Determine the Cause, or transfer it to the next Court [1633.]

Jesuites.

Forbidden to enter our Jurisdiction

THIS Court taking into Consideration the great warrs, Combustions and divisions which are this Day in Europe, and that the same are Observed to be raised and fomented cheifly by the Secret underminings, and sollicitations, of those of the Jesuiticall Order, men brought up & devoted to the religion and Court of Room, which hath occasioned divers States to expell them their Territoryes, for prevention whereof among our selves. It is Ordered and enacted by Authority of this Court, That no *Jesuit* or spiritual or Eclesiastical person (as they are tearmed) ordained by the Authority of the *Pope*, or *See of Room*, shall henceforth at any time repaire to, or come within this Jurisdiction: And if any person shall give just cause of suspition, that he is one of such society or Order, he shall be brought befo e some of the Magistrates, and if he cannot free himselfe of such suspition, he shall be Committed to prison or bound over to the next Court of Assistants, to be tryed and proceeded with, by Banishment or otherwise, as the Court shall see cause, and if any person so Banished, be taken the Second time within this Jurisdiction, upon Lawfull tryall & Conviction, he shall be put to death. Provided this Law shall not extend to any such Jesuit, Spiritual or Eclesiastical person, as shall be cast upô our shores by ship-wrack or other accident, so as he continue no longer then till he may have opportunity of passage for his departure, not to any such as shall come in Company with any Messenger hither upon publick occasions, or Merchant or Master of any Ship belonging to any place not in enmity with the State of England, or our selves, so as they depart againe with the same Messenger, Master or Merchant, & behave themselves inoffensively during their abode here [1647]

To be banished:

Imposts.

F*OR the support of the Government and Maintenance of fortification, for the protecting and safe guarding our Harbours, for our selves and others, that come to trade with us.*

with us. It is Ordered by this Court and the Authority thereof. That every person, Merchant, Seaman or other, that bring wines or strong waters into any of our Harbours, in any ships or vessels whatsoever (except they come directly from England as their first port) before they land any of the said wines or strongwaters more or less, shall first make entry of as many Butts Pipes or other Vessels, as they or any of them shall put on shore, by a note under their hands, delivered to the officer that is to receive the Customes, at his house, upon paine of forfeiture & confiscation of all such wines, and strong waters as are landed, before such entry made, wheresoever found, the one halfe to the Country the other halfe to the Officer, & the Merchant or owner of such wines, of any kind, or strong waters, as soon as he lands them, shall deliver and pay unto the sayd Officer, what is due for Custom of them according to this Order, in wine or strongwater according to the proportion of the goodness of the parcel that is brought in, as the Officer and owner can agree, to the contentment and satisfaction, of the sayd Officer, but if they cannot agree, the Treasurer, for the time being shall determine the price thereof. And it is further Ordered that the cheife Officer or Customer shall have under him a deputie or deputies, who shall be as searchers or waiters in severall places, to take up such wines or strong waters by Order of the sayd cheif Officer, and to take notice of what is landed in any place, of this Jurisdiction, that the Country be not defrauded, who shall have due recompence, as the cheife Officer shall agree with them, and all wines shall pay Custome according to the rates following. Every Butt or Pipe of Fyall wines or any other wines of the Western Ilands *Five shillings*, Every Pipe of Madera wine *Six shillings eight pence*, Every Butt or Pipe of Sherry Sack, Malaga or Canary wines *Ten shillings*, Muscadels, Malmsies and other wines from the streights, *Ten shillings*, Bastards, Tents, and Aligants, *Ten shillings*, and proportionably for greater or lesser Vessels of each kind, every hogshead of french wines *Two shillings Six pence*, And every hogshed of strong waters, *Ten shillings*, and proportionably for greater or lesser quantities

A. 53. P. 19.

Wines to be entred befor landed

Custom to be paid upon the landing

Customers Deputy

Rates of the Custom of wine

2 *And for the better recovering any such Customes of wines and strong waters or forfeitures, for not entering according to this Order.* It is Ordered, that the said Officer or his Deputy, hath hereby power, and is required to go into all houses or cellars, where he knoweth, or suspecteth any wine or strong-waters to be, and shall seize all such wines and strong-waters, as are not entered, according to this Order, and also seize and take possession of, so much wines & strong-waters, as shall make paiment for what custom is due, according to entryes made, and is refused or neglected to be paid in due maner according to this Order. And all Cōstables & other officers are hereby required to assist & ayd the officer, in the discharge of his duty, and helping to breake open such houses or Cellars, if the owners of such wines or strong waters shall refuse to open their doores, or deliver their keyes in a peacable manner, And any Smith, Carter, owner of boate, Porter or other, that shall be required by the officer to help and assist, in taking, loading and transporting such wines for the use of the Country, and shall refuse or neglect such service, for due hire, shall forfeit to the common Treasury, *ten shillings* for such default, to be levied by the Constable, by warrant from any one Magistrate. And all debts due unto the Country for custom of wines or strong-waters, where wines or strong-waters are not to be found, they shall be recoverable in a way of Action, according to the course of Law in other cases.

Customers power and duty

Constables to assist the Officer

Constables & others to assist ẏ Customer

On penalty of 10 s.

3 And it is further Ordered, That besides the customs of wines or strong waters aforesaid, all Merchants, or Masters of strangers Ships, which shall arrive with Merchandize, in any of our harbours of Boston or Charlestown, and shall make sale thereof, or of the greater part of the same, shall pay by way of Custom or Imposition, after the Rate of *six pence per Tun*, for every Ship, to be paid out of the said Merchandize, And the Master of every such Ship, shall also pay *ten shillings* towards

L. 2. P. 9

Six pēce per Tunn to be paid by every Ship.

towards the maintenance of our Fortificatiōs, for the defence of our sayd Harbours Provided no English ship, or other ship or Vessel, fraught in England, by any English man arriving in our sayd Harbours, nor any Vessel of our confederates, or any other parts where our ships are free of Customes, imposts & taxes, shall pay the sayd Custome of *Six pence per tun*, but only towards the maintenance of the sayd fortifications, *Ten shillings* for every ship above the burden of two Hundred tun, & *Six shillings eight pence*, for all other Vessels and ships under that burden. [1645]

For a ship of 200 tun 10 s For lesse: ships 6 s 8 d

Impresses.

L. 1. P. 9.

Labourers pressed for any publick work

IT is Ordered by this Court and the Authority thereof, That in all publick works of this Common wealth, one magistrate, and the overseer of the work, shall have power to send their warrants, to the Constables of the next Townes, to send so many labourers, and artificers, as the warrant shall direct, which the Constable and two other or more of the freemen, which he shall chose, shall forthwith execute, for which service, such Magistrate & overseer aforesaid, shall have power to give such wages, as they shall jung the work to deserve. Provided that for any ordinary work, no man shall be compelled to work from home, above one week together.

Persons free for defects

2. It is also Ordered, That no man shall be compelled, to any publick work or service, unles the press be grounded upon some act of the Generall Court, and have reasonable allowance for the same, nor shall any man be compelled in Person, to any Office, work, warrs, or other publick service, that is necessarily & sufficiently exempted, by any naturall or personal impediment, as by want of yeares, greatnes of yeares, defect of mind, failing of sences, or impotency of limbs nor shall any mā be compelled to goe out of this jurisdiction upon any Offensive warrs, which this Cōmon wealth, or any of our friends or Confederates, shall voluntarily ūdertake, but onely upon such vindictive & defensive wars, in our own behalf, or the behalf of our friends and Confederates, as shall be enterprized by the Counsell and consent of a Generall Court, or by Authority derived from the same. Nor shall any mans cattle, or goods of what kind soever, be pressed, or taken for any publick use or service, unless it be by warrant, grounded upon some Act of the General Court, nor without such reasonable prises and hire, as the ordinary Rates of the Cōtry do afford, and if his cattle or goods shall perish, or suffer damage in such service the owner shall be sufficiently recompenced. [1641]

Cattle and other goods demnified in ÿ Country service to be made good

Imprisonment.

Who Bayleable.

IT is Ordered, and by this Court declared, That no mans person shall be restrained or imprisoned, by any Authority whatsoever, before the Law hath sentenced him thereto if he can put in sufficient security, Baile or mainprize, for his appearance and good behaviour in the mean time, unles it be in Crimes Capital, and Contempt in Open Court, and in such Cases where such express Act of Court doth allow it. [1641[

Indians.

A. 52. P 16.

Indiās title to land

FOR settleing the Indians title to Lands, in this Jurisdiction. It is declared & Ordered by this Court and Authority thereof. That what Lands any of the Indians in this Jurisdiction, have Possessed and improoved by subduing the same, they have just right unto, according to that in Genesis, 1.28. and Chap: 9.1 and Psal, 115. 16. *And for the further incouragement of the hopeful work amongst them, for the Civilizing, and helping them forward to Christianity, If any of the Indians shall be brought to Civility, and shall come among the English to Inhabit in any of their plantations and shall there live Civilly and Orderly*, that such Indians shall have allotments amongst the English, according to the Custom of the English in like case, Further it is Ordered that if upon good experience, there shall be a Competent number of the Indians brought on to Civility, so as to be Capable of a Township, upon their request to the Generall Court, they shall have grant of Lands undisposed

Civil Indians to have plantations amōg them

indisposed of, for a plantation,as the English have ; And further it is Ordered by this Court that if any plantation or person of the English, shall offer injuriously to put any of the Indians from their planting grounds or fishing places, upon their Complaint and proof thereof, they shall have releife, in any of the Courts of justice amongst the English as the English have ; And further it is Ordered by this Court, and the Authority thereof,and be it hereby Enacted that all the tract of Land within this Jurisdiction, whether already graunted to any English plantations or persons,, or to be graunted by this Court,(not being under the quallification of right to the Indians, is and shall be accounted the just right of such english as already have or hereafter shall have graunt of lands from this Court, & the Authority thereof from that of *Genesis*. 1.28. and the Invitation of the Indians. Indians not to be dispossessed.

2 And it is Ordered, That no person whatsoever, shall henceforth buy Land of any Indian without License first had and obtained of the Generall Court; and if any offend herein , such Land, so bought shall be forfeited to the Country. Nor shall any person, sell,give or barter, directly or indirectly, any Gun or Guns, Powder, Bullits, shott, Lead, to any Indian whatsoever , or to any person Inhabiting out of this Jurisdiction, nor shall amend or repaire any Gun, belonging to any Indian , nor shall sell any Armour or Weapons , upon penalty of *ten pounds;* for every Gun, Armour or Weapons so sold, given or bartered, *five pound* for every pound of powder, forty shillings for every pound of shot or lead, and portionably for any greater or lesser quantity. [1633. 37.] L.1.p.28 None to buy land of Indi: No armes or amunition to be traded to the Indians.

3. *Whereas the French and Dutch and other Forreine nations do ordinarily trade Guns,powder, shott &c: with Indians, to our great prejudice, & strengthning and animating the Indians against us ; And the aforesaid French, Dutch &c: doe prohibit all trade with the Indians, within their respective Jurisdictions under penalty of confiscation &c:* It is therefore Ordered. That it shall not be Lawfull, for any Frenchman, Dutchman,or any person of any other Forreine nation whatsoever,or any English dwelling amongst them, or under them, or any of them;to trade with any Indian or Indians, within the limits of our Jurisdiction , directly or indirectly by themselves or others under penalty of confiscation of all such goods & Vessels as shall be found so trading, or the due value thereof, upon just proof, of any goods or Vessels so trading or traded ; And it shall be lawfull for any person or persons Inhabiting within this Jurisdiction, to make seizure of any such goods or Vessels trading with the Indians, one half whereof, shall be for the proper use & benefit of the party seizing, and the other halfe to the Country L.2.p.25 Forraigners prohibited trade w the Indians.

4. *And because the trade of furrs with the Indians, in this Jurisdiction, doth properly belong to this Common--wealth, and not unto particular persons ;* It is therefore Ordered that henceforth no person or persons, directly or indirectly, shall trade with the Indians for any sort of peltry,excepting onely such as are Authorized by this Court or by such Committee as this Court shall appoint from time to time, under the penalty of *one hundred pounds fine* for every offence, *ten pound* whereof shall be to the informer, the rest to the Country. A.57.p. 22. None to trad furrs w Ind: without License under penal 100 li

5. *Whereas severall Orders, for the preventing of Drunkenes amongst the Indians have been made, yet notwithstanding there is little or no reformation. For the prevention thereof, and the frequent effects thereof. Murder and other outrages amongst them .* This Court doth Order, That no person of what quallity or condition soever shall henceforth sell, truck, barter, or give any strong liquors to any Indian directly or indirectly. whether known by the name of Rumm , Strong-Waters. Wine,Strong-Beer, Brandy, Cider, Perry, or any other Strong Liquors. going under any other name whatsoever under the penalty of *forty shillings* for one pint, and so proportionably for greater or lesser quantityes so sold,Bartered or given directly or indirectly as abovesaid. *And for the better execution of this Order*, all trucking houses erected (not allowed by this Court) shall be forthwith demolished: A.57.p. 23. Strong liqu. prohib. to be sold or given to Indian on penalty of 40 s. per pint

And for the better effecting of this Order. It is declared that one third part of the penalty, shall be graunted to the informer; It is also Ordered, that speciall care shall be had by the Grand-Jury of every Shire Court, to inquire and present to the Court, what they find, to discover matter tending to such apractise, aganst the true intent of this Law; And all other Orders giveing liberty to sell strong Liquors, to the Indians, are hereby repealed, and all Licences formerly granted, are hereby disabled and called in, Provided alwayes, that it is not intended that this Law shall extend to restraine any person, from any charitable act in releiving any Indian (*Bona fide*) in case of suddaine extremity, by sicknes or fainting, which calls for such help, not exceeding one dram, nor when any Physitian shall prescribe in way of Phisick, any of the particulars before mentioned, so as upon sight of his direction in writing there be allowance had, under the hand of one Magistrate or where no Magistrates in the Towne residing, being under the hands of the town Comissioners or two of them. [1657]

Except in case of sicknes &c.

A:56p:18

6. *The Court Considering the necessity of Restraining the Indians, from whatever may be a meanes to disturb our peace, and quiet.* Doth Order. That henceforth no person or persons Inhabiting within this Jurisdiction, shall directly or indirectly, any wayes give, sell, Barter, or otherwise dispose of any Boat, Skift, or any greater Vessel unto any Indian or Indians whatsoever, under the penalty of *fifty pounds* to be paid to the Country Treasurer for every such Vessel so sold or disposed as aforesaid. [1656)

No boats to be sold to Indians

L:1:p.28

7. It is Ordered by this Court. That in all places within this Jurisdiction, the English shall keep their Cattle, from destroying the Indians Corne, in any ground where they have right to plant, and if any of their Corne be destroyed for want of fencing or herdning; the Town shall make satisfaction, & shall have power among themselves, to lay the charge, where the occasion of the dammage did arise. Provided that the Indians shal make proof, that the Cattle of such a town, Farme, or person did the damage; *And for incouragement of the Indians, towards the fencing in of their Corne fields*; Such Towns, Farmes, or Persons, whose Cattle may annoy them that way, shall direct, assist, and help them, in felling of Trees, ryving & sharpning railes, and holing of posts; Allowing one Englishman to three or more Indians; And shall also draw the fencing into place for them, and allow one man a day or two, towards the setting up the same, and either lend or sell them tooles to finish it; Provided that such Indians to whom the Country, or any Towne have given, or shall give ground to plant upon, or shall purchase ground of the English, shall fence such their Corn feilds, or ground at their own charge as the English doe, or should do; And if any Indian refuse to fence their Corn ground (being tendred help as aforesayd,) in the presence and hearing of sufficient witnesses, they shall keep off all Cattle, or loose their damages. And it is also Ordered that if any harm be done at any time by the Indians, unto the English in their Cattle, the Governour or Deputy Governour with two of the Assistants, or any three Magistrates, or any County Court, may Order satisfaction, according to law and justice. [1640 48.]

Damag done to Indians in there corn to be satisfied.

help Indians fence their ground.

Indians to pay for hurt done to cattle.

Lawes to be published to the Indians.

8. *Whereas one end in planting these parts was to propagate the true Religion unto the Indians, and that divers of them are become subject to the English & have engaged themselves to be willing and ready to understand the Law of God.* It is therefore Ordered. That such necessary and wholsome Lawes which are in force and may be made from time to time, to Reduce them to Civility of life, shall be once a year (if the times be safe) made known to them, by such fitt persons as the Generall Court shall appoint.

For

9 *For the better Ordering and Governing the Indians subject to us, especially those of Natick and Punquepaog.* It is Ordered that *Major Atherton* doe take care that all such *Indians* doe live according to our Lawes, as far as they are capable, & to that end the said *Major* is hereby Authorized to constitute & appoint *Indian Commissioners* in their severall Plantations, to hear and determine all such matters, that do arise amongst themselves as one Magistrate may doe, amongst the English, with Officers to execute all Commands and warrants, as Marshall & Constables, And further that the sayd Major with the said Commissioners shall have the power of a County Court to hear and determine all causes arising among them, the said Major appointing the time & place of the Court, and consenting to the determination or judgment, and all other matters beyond their Cognizance shall be issued & determined by the Court of Assistants A. 58.

Courts to be kept among § Indians:

10. And it is Ordered that no Indian shall at any time *Powaw* or performe outward worship to their *False Gods*, or to the *Devil*, in any part of our Jurisdiction, whether they be such as shall dwel here, or shall come hither, and if any shall transgress this law the *Powawer* shall pay *five pounds*, the procurer *five pounds*, & every other countenancing by his presence or otherwise (being of age of discretion) *twenty shillings*, & every Town shall have power to restraine all Indians that shall come into their townes, from Prophaning the Lords day. [1633. 37, 40, 41, 42, 46, 48, 56, 57, 58.]

Powaws forbidden.

Townes to restrain Indians from prophaning the Sabboth.

Inditements.

IT is Ordered by this Court. That no Person shall be Indited, presented, informed against or Complained of, to any Court or Magistrate within this jurisdiction, for the breach of any penall law, or any other misdemeanor, the forfeiture whereof belongs to the Country, unles the said Inditement or Complaint be made and exhibited within one year after the Offence be Committed, and if any such Inditement, presentment, information or Complaint, be not made within the time limited, then the same shall be void and of none effect. Provided alwayes, this law shall not extend to any Capitall Offences, nor any Crimes that may concerne loss of member or Banishment, or to any Treasonable Plotts or Conspiracies against the Common wealth, nor to any fellonies above *ten shillings*, nor shall it hinder any person greived or any wrong done to him or his wife, children or servants, or estate real or personal but that every such person shall have such remedies as formerly he might or ought to have. [1652] A. 52, P. 10.

Complaints and presentments to be made within a year.

Inkeepers, Ordinaries, Tipling, Drunkennes.

FOR as much as there is a necessary use of houses of Common-entertainment, in every Common wealth and of such as retaile wine, beer, and victuals, yet because there are so many abuses, both by persons entertaining, and by persons entertained, It is therefore Ordered by this Court and Authority thereof, That no person or persons shall at any time, under any pretence or Colour whatsoever, undertake to be a Common victualer, keeper of a Cooks shop, or house for Common entertainment Taverner or publick seller of wine, Ale, beer or strong-waters, by retaile, (nor shall any sell wine privately in his house, or out of doores, by a less quantity then a quarter caske) without approbation of the Selected Townsmen, and License of the County Court, where they dwell, upon pain of forfeiture of *five pounds*, for every such offence; or imprisonment at the pleasure of the Court. Provided it shall be Lawfull for any whole-sale Merchant of wines, or the present Stillers of strong waters, being Masters of families, or such as receive the same from Forraine parts. in cases &c: or makers of Cyder, to sell by retaile; Provided the quantity of wine and cyder, be not less then three gallons at a time, to one person, nor strong waters less then a quart; and that it be only to masters of families of good and honest report, or persons going to Sea, and they suffer not any person to drink the same in their houses, cellars or yards. A. 58.

None to keep Ordinaries without Licence.

Liberty to sel wine & strong waters by retaile.

Ordinarys to have Signes.

And every Person so Licensed, for common entertainment, shall have some inoffensive Sign, obvious, for direction of Strangers, and such as have no such sign, after three months so Licensed, shall loose their licenie, and others be allowed in their stead.

L. 2. p. 3.
A. 51. p. 4
A. 53. P. 19.
To be alway provided of strong beere 2 d. per quart

2. And every person Licensed to keep an Ordinary, shall allwayes be provided of strong wholesome Beer, of four bushels of Mault (at the least) to a hogshead, which he shall not sell at above two-pence the Ale-quart, upon penalty of *Fourty shillings* for the first offence, and for the second offence to loose his License.

And it is permitted to any that will, to sell beer out of dores, at one penny the ale-quart, or under.

L. 1. p. 30
Not to permit any to be drunke &c:

3. And no Licensed person as aforesaid, shall suffer any to be drunke, or to drinke excessively, viz: above halfe a pint of wine for one person, at a time, or to continue Tipling, above the space of halfe an hour, or at unseasonable times, or after nine of the Clock at night, in, or about any of their houses, on penalty of *five shillings* for every such Offence.

L. 2. p. 6.
Not to conceal drũkard

And if any person Licenced to sell wine or Beer as aforesayd, shall Conceale in his house any person that shall be found Drunken, and shall not forthwith procure a Constable to carry such Drunken person, before some Magistrate or Cõmissioner; and in the interim, the said Vintner or drawer of beer, shall make stay of such persons, till the Constable shall come, under the penalty of *Five Pounds*, for every default.

L. 1. p. 30
Drunkennes tipling the penalty.

4. And every person found Drunken. viz. so as he be thereby bereaved or disabled in the use of his understanding, appearing in his speech or gesture, in any of the said houses or elsewhere, shall forfeit, *ten shillings*, and for excessive Drinking *three shillings foure pence*, and for continueing above halfe an houre tipling, *two shillings six pence*, and for tipling at unseasonable times, or after nine of the clock at night, *five shillings* for every Offence in those particulars, being Lawfully convict thereof, and for want of paiment they shall be imprisoned til they pay, or be set in the Stocks one hour or more, (in some open place) as the weather will permit not exceeding three houres.

L. 2. p. 6.
Drunkards abusing the Constable to be cõmitted

5. And if any person be found drunken, by night or by day, or shall in his drunkenness offer any abuse to the Constable or others, either by striking, or reviling him or them, or using any endeavours, by himselfe or others, to make an escape, it shall be in the power of the Constable, to commit such person or persons, to safe keeping or imprisonment, or take bond for his appearance, as he shall see cause; and the keepers of each prison, upon Warrant from any Magistrate, or Cõmissioner or Select men, shall receive all such as shall be so cõmitted, and take but *twelve-pence* for his fee in such cases: And the Constable shall inform the next Magistrate thereof, but if no Magistrate be in Town, he shall Convent such person or persons,

Convented before some Magistrate Cõmiss. or Select men:

before one or more of the Commissioners for ending small causes, and where no Commissioners are, before any one or more of the Select men of the Town, who have hereby power given them, to do as any one Magistrate may do in like case; Provided neverthelels, if any such delinquent, shall confess his fault, and pay his fine, & other charges, the Constable shall receive it, and dismiss the offender, and every person hereby Authorized to receive the fines aforesaid, shall forthwith make return to the Treasurer of the County, where such offence is committed, of what he hath done and received in such cases.

L. 1. p. 30
Travellers entertained by night

6. It shall be Lawfull notwithstanding, for all licensed persons to entertain land-travellors, or sea-faring men, in the night season, when they come on shore, or from their journey, for their necessary refreshment, or when they prepare for their voyage or journey the next day early, so there be no disorder among them; and also strangers, lodgers, or other persons, in an orderly way, may continue in such houses of common entertainment during meale times, or upon lawfull busines, what time

each

their occasions shall require.

7. Nor shall any Merchant, Cooper, owner or keeper of wines, or other persons that have them in their custody, suffer any person to drinke to excess or drunkennes, in any of their wine-cellars, ships or other vessels, or places where wines doly, on pain to forfeit for each person so doing, *ten shillings*. Nor shall any person licensed to sell strong waters, or any private house-keeper, permit any person or persons to sit drinking or tipling strong-waters wine or strong beer in their houses: And if any such seller of strong-waters or private housekeeper, shall be Legally convicted before any County Court, any one Magistrate or Commissioners Court, such persons shall for the first Offence be fined *twenty shillings*, and if the party so convicted be not able to pay his fine, he shall be *set in the stocks*, where he shall continue one whole houre, and if any such seller of strong-waters shall be convicted as aforesayd of a second Offence, of the same nature, he shall forfeit his Licence and shall also pay twenty shillings as a fine to the Country, and if any private house-keeper shall be convicted as aforesaid, of a second Offence, against this law, he shall pay a fine of *five pound*, & for a third Offence, such person or persons. being so Convicted, shall be *bound to their good behaviour in twenty pound bond*, with two sufficient sureties, or be Committed to prison.

Wine Merchants, Coop: &c. not to permit any to be drunke

A. 54. p 2

Privat house keepers not to permit any to tipple in their houses

First offence 20 s.

Second offence 5 li.

Third offence good behav:

8. And if any person offend in drunkennes, excessive or long drinking, the second time, they shall pay double fines. And if they fall into the same offence the third time, they shall pay treble the fines; & if the parties be not able to pay the fines, then he that is found drunke, shall be punished by whipping, to the number of *ten stripes*, and he that offends in excessive or long drinking, shall be put into the stocks, for three houres, when the weather may not hazzard his life or limbs. And if they offend the fourth time, they shall be imprisoned, untill they put in two sufficient suretyes for their good behaviour.

L. 1. p. 30

Drunke the 2 time doubl fine

3 treble

4 time imprisonment

9. And it is further Ordered, That if any person that keepeth, or hereafter shall keep a comon house of entertainment, shal be lawfully convicted the third time for any offence against this Law; he shall (for the space of three yeares next ensuing the said conviction) be disabled to keep any such house of entertainment, or sel beer, or the like, unles the Court aforesaid shall see cause to continue him.

Inkeepers convict. of 3 offence:

Forfeit their licence

10. It is further Ordered, that every Inkeeper or victualler, shall provide for the entertainment of strangers horses, *viz* one or more inclosures, for summer, hay and Provender for winter, with convenient stable-roome and attendance, under the penalty of *two shillings six pence* for every dayes default, & double damage to the party thereby wronged, except it be by inevitable accident.

Provisions for horses

11. And it is further Ordered by the Authority aforesayd. That no Taverner seller of wine by retaile, Licensed as aforesayd, shall take above *nine pound profit*, by the Butt or Pipe of wine, (and proportionably for all other Vessels) towards his wast in drawing, and otherwise, out of which allowance, every such Taverner or Vintner, shall pay *fifty shillings* by the Butt or Pipe, and proportionably for all other Vessels to the Country, for which they shall account with the Treasurer or his Deputy every six monthes, and discharge the same, all which they may do by selling *six-pence a quart* in retaile (which they shall no time exceed) more then it cost by the Butt. Besides the benefit of their art and mistery which they know how to make use of. And every Taverner or Vintner shall give a true account & notice, unto the Treasurer or his Deputy, of every Vessell of wine he buyes from time to time, within three dayes, upon paine of forfeiting the same, or the value thereof, the one halfe to the Country, the other halfe to the Treasurer and informer. And it is Ordered, That the said Impost, shall from time to time be paid in wines at merchantable price, or other equivalēt merchātable good pay, to the contēt of the Treasurer, and that the Treasurer shall take special care in collecting the same, who is hereby Impowered to substitute, such deputies under him, as he shall see meet, in the several

Vintners to pay 50 s per Butt.

To give notice to the Treasurer what wine they buy

A. 58.

Treasurer to have 2 s. per pound of this Impost

verall Townes, for his help and furtherance herein. for all whith paines and care he shall be allowed two shillings in the pound of all such imposts, as he shall bring into his anual account, with the Country. Provided allwayes that if any Vintner Taverner or retailer of wines, shall give an account to the Treasurer of any part of any wine entred as abovesayd that he hath sold away againe by whole sale, being no less in quantity then a quarter Cask, to one person at one time, and shall Timely certify the Person who had it, and the time when, such person or persons shall be abated of their impost, in proportion, to what they have so sold. And all such as Retaile strong-waters, shall in like manner pay *two-pence* upon every quart, to the use of the Country who shall also give notice to the Marshall-Generall, of every Case & bottle, or other quantity they buy, within three dayes, upon paine of forfeiture as before.

Sellers of strong water to give notice to ye Marshall within 3 days

L.2.P.31

Ordinarykeepers to clear their houses in meeting time.

12. And it is Ordered. That in all places where week day Lectures are kept, All Taverners, Victuallers and Ordinaries, that are within one Mile of the Meeting-house to which they belong, shall from time to time, Cleer their houses of all persons able to go to meeting, during the time of the exercise, (except upon extraordinary cause, for the necessary refreshing of strangers unexpectedly repairing to them) upon paine of *five shillings* for every such Offence over and besides the penalties incurred by this Law for any other Disorder.

One Magistr to hear & determine all offences against this Law.

13. It is also Ordered that all Offences against this Law, may be heard & Determined by any one Magistrate, who shall hereby have power by warrant to send for, & examine parties and witnesses, Concerning any of these Offences: And upon due conviction either by Veiw of the said Magistrate, or affirmation of the Constable and one sufficient witnes with Circumstances concurring, or two witnesses, or Confession of the party; to Leavie the said severall fines by warrant to the Constable for that end. And if any person shall voluntarily confess his offence against this Law in any the particulars thereof, his oath shall be taken in evidence and stand good against any other offending at the same time.

Delinquents Testimony

Constable to search in Ordinaryes

14. It is further Ordered by the Authority aforesayd. That all Constables may, and shall from time to time, duely make search, throughout the limits of their Townes upon Lords Dayes and Lecture dayes in times of excercise, and also at all other times so oft as they shall see cause for all Offences and Offenders against this Law, in any the particulars thereof. And if upon due information, or Complaint of any of their inhabitants or other credible persons, whether Taverner, victualer, Tabler or other, they shall refuse or neglect to make search as aforesayd, or shall not to their power performe, all other things belonging to their place and Office of Constable, then upon Complaint and due proof before any one Magistrate within three months of such refusall or neglect, they shall be fined for every such Offence *ten shillings*, to be levyed by the Marshall as in other cases by warrant from such Magistrate, before whom they are Convicted or warrant from the Treasurer, upon notice from such Magistrate.

Constables neglect

Fined 10 ss:

A.57.P.21.

Ordinaries to renew their Licenses Yearly.

15. *And because it is difficult to Order and keep the houses for publick entertainment in conformity to the wholsome Lawes established, as is necessary for preventing Drunkenes, excessive Drinking, vaine expences of mony, time, & the abuse of the good Creatures of God.* It is therefore Ordered by this Court and the Authority thereof. That no person or persons hereafter shall be licensed. to keep a house of Common-entertainment, for any longer then one year at one time, and that such as keep houses of publick-entertainment, (the present vintners during their contract excepted) shall and hereby are enjoyned, once every year, to repaire to the severall County Courts for renewing their several licences (for which they shall pay *two shillings six-pence* to the Clerke of the Court,) or else they shall forfeit *five pounds* as unlicenced Ale house keepers. |1645, 46, 47, 48, 51, 53, 57, 58.

Whereas

Judgments & Executions.

WHERE *as there is a great abuse in selling of Judgments and executions, and so altering the property of them, before they be satisfyed, or goods seized, whereby great inconvenience may arise as experience hath Prooved,* This Court doth therefore Order That after the end of this Session, no person shall Sell, Alienate, or Assigne, any judgment or execution whatsoever, & if any shall presume to act contrary to this Order, his sale, assignment, or Alienation shall be voyd in Law. And in case the party dy after the Iudgment, before he hath taken out an execution, or before satisfactiō be received, his executor or his administrator shall take out or renew the execution, as the Testator himselfe might have done. A: 54: Judgments & Executions not to be sold.

Jurors Juries.

IT is Ordered by this Court and the Authority thereof, That the Secretary or Clerk of every Court, shall in convenient time, before the sitting of the Court send warrants to the Constables of the severall Townes, of the Iurisdiction of that Court for jury-men proportionable to the Inhabitants of each Towne, And the Constable upon the receipt of such warrant, shall give timely notice to the freemen of their respective Townes, to chose so many able discreet men, as the warrant shall require, which men so chosen he shall warne to attend the Court, whereto they are appointed, and shall make returne, of the warrant, unto the Clerk aforesayd; L. 1: p 5. Clerk to grant warrāts for Jurors. Chosen by ŷ freemen, Constable to return ŷ warrant A: 51: p. 5

The like Order shall be observed, in the choice and Sūmoning juries to attend special Courts; At which Courts every jury-man shall be allowed *four shillings per diem* for their charges, to be payd by him, upon whose motion the Court was graunted. L 2 p. 8. Jurys at special courts allowed 4 s per diem.

And all juries serving at the Court of Assistants at Boston, shall be Summoned respectively, out of the Counties of Suffolk and Middlesex; And all jurors so chosen, shall be impanneled and sworne, truely to try betwen party and party, and shall find the matter of fact, with the damages and costs, according to their evidence. & the judges shall declare the Sentence, or direct the jury to find according to Law, and if there be matter of apparent equity, as the forfeiture of an obligation, breach of Covenant without damage, or the like, the Bench shall determine such matters of equity And no tryal shall pass upon any man for life or banishment in any inferiour Court; but by a special jury Sūmoned for that purpose. L 1: p: 32: Jury to find according to evidence. Bench to determine matter of equity

2. It is also Ordered, That there shall be Grand-juryes Summoned in like manner, every year unto the severall Courts in each Iurisdiction, to present al misdemeanours they shall know, or hear to be Committed by any person within the jurisdiction, and to do any other service of the Common wealth, they shall be required by the sayd Court. Provided no Iuror, nor any person whatsoever, shall be bound to informe, present or reveal any private Crime, or Offence wherein there is no peril or danger to this Colony, or any Member thereof, when any necessary tye of Conscience binds him to secresie, unless it be in Testimonies Lawfully required. Grand Jurys L: 1. p 47: Jurors not bound to reveal secrets A: 53 p 19

And every Grand Iuror shall be allowed *three shillings per diem* for his charges, out of the fees & other profits arising in each Court, where they do service, or by the County if those in-comes fall short. Jurors allowance.

3. In all cases wherein the Law is obscure, so as the jury cannot be satisfied therein, whether it be Grand or Petty jury, they have liberty to present a special Verdict: *viz:* If the Law be so in such a point, we find for the Plantiff, but if the Law be otherwise, we find for the defendant, in which Case, the determination doth properly belong to the Court, And all Iurors shall have liberty in matter of fact, if they cannot find the maine issue, yet to find & present in their Verdict so much as they can. A 57. p 29 Juryes liberty to give a special verdict.

4. And if the Court and jury shall so differ at any time about their verdict that either of them cannot proceed, with peace of conscience, the case shall be Issued, and determined at the next Court of Assistants, in manner following, (*i.e.*) the attachment with the security for appearance at the County Court, shall be continued Court & jury not agreed case comes to ŷ General Court A 56. p 14

to the

to the Court of Affistants: and if the Plaintiff, shall see cause further to prosecute his action, he shall give Sumons to the Deffendant, as the Law provideth, and shall also take out of the Record of the County Court the Records of the said case with the Evidences presented by both parties, and bring the same to the Court of Assistants, where after the Case is presented, as it was at the County Court, both Parties shall have liberty to make any new pleas, or evidence before the Bench & jury, and in case the Plaintiff shall not further Prosecute his action, in manner as is hereby provided, the Defendant shall then have judgment graunted him, for his costs at the next Court of that County.

L. 1. p. 31

Juryes liberty to take advice in open Court.

Jurors to serve but a year except

5. It is further Ordered, That whensoever any jury or jurors, are not clear in their Judgments or conscience concerning any case wherein they are to give their verdict, they shall have liberty in open Court, (but not otherwise) to advise with any man they shall think fitt to resolve or direct them, before they give in their verdict. And no Juror shall be compelled to serve, above one ordinary Court in a year, except Grand Jurors, who shall hold two Courts together at the least; and such as shall be sumoned to serve, in cases of life & death or banishment. [1634. 41, 42, 49, 50, 51, 53, 56, 57.]

Plaintiff and defend. Penalty for not answ at their call

6. *VVhereas in Suits and Actions, brought into Courts, between party & party sometimes the Plantiff & sometimes the Defendant, & sometimes neither of them, do attend to Answer when they are called, to prosecute or Answer, which hath been too long connived at, by the Magistrates; And much time lost in sending to seek them out, or waite their comming in, whereby the Country charge is encreased, and the Magistrats jurors, witnesses & others abused, contrary to the Laudable, reasonable practise and Custome of all Courts, in our native Country, and other Countryes known unto us.*

It is therefore hereby Ordered & Enacted, that if any Plantiff, he or shee have entred any Action to be tryed in any court, or which comes Orderly into any Court, by Replevin, appeal, or by the disagreement between the Magistrates and Jury, in an inferiour Court: And do not by him or her self or by their Attourneis make their appearace & prosecute their action Imediately after they have been three times called in the Court by name, after the first forenoon of the Court: that then they shall be non-suited, and if Plantiff or defendant appear upon such call, they shall have their Costs graunted by the Court against him or her that doth not appear, and if afterwards both parties do agree to try their case at the same Court, they shall be allowed so to do the plaintiff paying half so much for a new entry as he did before, And if any person Presented by the Grand-jury for any offence, or Sumoned by a Magistrate to answer any Crime, do not upon sumons appear at the time appointed, upon the third call as aforesaid, he or shee shall be proceeded against for contempt, except he or shee be restrained or prevented by the hand of God.

Plaintiffs liberty to make new entry in case.

Delinquents penalty for not answer at their call

Lands free Lands.

IT is also Ordered & by this Court declared; That all our lands and heritages shall be free from all fines and licenses, upon alienations and from all hariots, wardships, Liveries. Primerseizins, year, day and wast, Escheates & forfeitures, upon the death of Parents or Ancestors, naturall, unnaturall, casuall or judiciall and that for ever. [1641.]

Leather.

T*HIS Court Considering the severall deceits and abuses, which in other places have been, and are Commonly practised by the Tanners, Curriers and workers of Leather, as also the abuses and inconveniences, which acrue to the severall members of this Commonwealth, by Leather not sufficiently Tanned and wrought, which is occasioned, by the negligence and unskilfulnes of those severall Tradesmen, which before, and after it is in the hand of the Tanner may be much bettered or impoved, for prevention whereof* It is Ordered by this Court and the Authority thereof.

Butchers. Curriers shal not tan h

That no person using, or ocupying the feat and mistery of a Butcher, Currier or Shoe maker *make* by himselfe or any other, shall use or exercise the feat or mystery of a *tanner*, on paine of the forfeiture of *six shillings eigh-pence* for every Hide or skin by him or them so Tanned, whilst he or they shall use or occupy any of the Mysteries aforesayd. Nor shall any *Tanner* during his using the sayd trade of Tanning, use or occupy, the feat or Mystery of either *Butcher, Currier, or shoemaker*, by himselfe or any other upon paine of the like forfeiture. Nor shall any *Butcher* by himselfe or any other person, gash or cut any hide of Ox, Bull, steer, or Cow, in fleaing thereof, or otherwise whereby the same shall be impaired or hurt on pain of forfeiting *twelvepence* for any such gash or cut in any hide or skin. Nor shall any person or persons henceforth bargaine, buy, make any contract, or bespeak any rough hide of ox, bull, steer, or cow in the haire, but only such persons as have & doe use & exercise the art of Tanning.

Gashing of Hides forfeit twelve pence.

onely Tanners may buy raw hides.

2. Nor shall any person or persons using or which shall use the Mystery or faculty of Tanning at any time or times hereafter, offer to put to Sale, any kind of leather, which shall be insufficiently or not throughly tanned, or which hath bee over Limed, or burnt in the limes, or which shall not have been, after the tanning thereof well & throughly dryed, upon pain of forfeiting that whole Hide, halfe hide, or other peece of Leather wherein one sixteenth part shall be found, by the searcher or Sealer of Leather (Lawfully appointed) to be either over Limed or insufficiently Tanned or not throughly dryed as aforesaid. Nor shall any person using the mistery of tanning as aforesaid, set any of their fatts in tan-hills or other places where the woozes or leather put to tann in the same, shall or may take any unkind heates, nor shall put any leather into any hot or warme woozes whatsoever on pain of *twenty pound* for every such Offence.

Leather not to be overlimed or insufficiently Tanned.

penalty.

3. Nor shall any person or persons, using or occupying the Mystery or faculty of Currying Curry any kind of Leather, except it be well & throughly tanned, nor shall Curry any hide being not throughly dryed after his wet season, in which wet season, he shall not use any stale, urine or any other deceitfull or subtil mixture, thing, way or meanes to Corrupt or hurt the same, nor shall Curry any leather meet for outer sole Leather, with any other then good hard tallow, nor with any less of that, then the Leather will receive, nor shall Curry any kind of Leather, meet for upper Leather & inner soles, but with good and sufficient stuff being fresh and not salt, and throughly liquored, till it will receive no more, nor shall burn or scald any hide, or Leather in the Currying, but shall work the same sufficiently in all points and respects on pain of forfeiture for every such Offence or act done Contrary to the true meaning of this Order, the full Value of every such Hide, Marred by his evill Workmanship or Handling, which shall be Judged, by two or more sufficient and honest skilfull persons, Curriers or others on their Oath given to them for that end by any Magistrate.

Curriers duty.

Penaltie.

4. And every Town where need is, or shall be, shall chuse one or two persons of the most honest and skilfull, within their severall townships, & present them unto the County Court, or one Magistrate, who shall appoint and swear the sayd persons, by their discretion to make search and Veiw within the precincts of their Limits, In any House, Shop, or Warehouse, where they conceive such Leather may be, whether wrought into shoes, Bootes or otherwise, as oft as they shall think meet and need shall bee, who shall have a mark or Seal prepared by each Town, for that purpose and the sayd searchers or one of them, shall keep the same, and therewith shall Seal such Leather as they shall find sufficient in all respects and no other, And if the sayd searchers or any of them, shall find any Leather sold or offered to be sold, brought or Offered to be searched or sealed, which shall be Tanned, wrought, converted or used, contrary to the true intent and meaning of this Order. It shall be lawfull for the sayd searchers or any of them to seize all such Leather & to retaine the same, in their Custody, and if the owner shall not submit to the judgmet

Serchers of leather to be sworne.

A. 51 p. 3.

To seize all defective leather.

of the Officer or Officers, the sayd Officer so seizing the same, shall within three dayes, call to him four or six men, honest and skilfull in such ware, to veiw the same in the presence of the partie (or without him having notice thereof) who shall certify upon their oathes unto the next County Court of that shire, or unto one of the Magistrates the defect of the said Leather.

The like power shall the said searchers have, to search all Leather, wrought into shoes or boots, as allso to seize all such as they find to be made of insufficient Leather, or not well and sufficiently wrought up; And if any searcher or sealer of Leather shall refuse with Convenient speed to Seale any Leather sufficiently Tanned, wrought and used according to the true meaning of this Order, or shall seale that which shall be insufficient, then every such searcher and Sealer of Leather shall forfeit for every such Offence the full Value of so much as shall be insufficiently Tanned. And the fees for Searching and Sealing of leather, shall be one penny a Hide, for any parcel less then five, and for all other parcels, after the rate of *six pence a Dicker*, which the Tanner shall pay, upon the Sealing of the sayd leather from time to time.

Searching leather made into shoes or boots,

Searchers default

Penalty.

Fees.

5. Lastly It is Ordered by the Authority aforesayd, That the several fines and forfeitures in this Order mentioned, shall be equally divided into three parts, and distributed as, *viz*: One third part to the Common Treasury of the Shire wherin the offence is committed, another third part to the comon Treasury of the Township where the offender inhabiteth, and the other third part to the Seizer or Seizers of such leather, shoes or boots, as is insufficiently tanned, curried or wrought from time to time. [1642, 51]

Liberties Common.

Liberty at publick assemblies,

IT is Ordered by this Court, Decreed and Declared; That every man whether Inhabitant or forreigner, free or not free, shall have liberty to come to any publick Court, Council or town meeting, and either by speech or writing, to move any lawful, seasonable or materiall question, or to present any necessary motion, Complaint, Petition, Bill, or Information, whereof that Meeting hath proper Cognizance, so it be done in convenient time, due Order and respective manner. [1641.]

Fishing and fowling

2. Every Inhabitant who is an housholder shall have free fishing and fowling in any great ponds, bayes Coves and Rivers, so farr as the Sea ebbs and flowes, within the precincts of the towne where they dwell, unles the freemen of the same Town or the General Court have otherwise appropriated them. Provided that no Town shall appropriate to any particular person or persons, any great Pond containing more then ten acres of land, and that no man shall come upon anothers propriety without their leave otherwise then as hereafter expressed. The which clearly to determine, It is Declared, That in all *Creeks*, *Coves* and other places, about and upon *Salt-water*, where the Sea ebbs and flowes, the proprietor of the land adjoyning, shall have propriety to the low-water-mark, where the Sea doth not ebb above a hundred Rods, and not more wheresoever it ebbs further. Provided that such proprietor shall not by this liberty, have power to stop or hinder the passage of boates or other vessels, in or through any Sea, Creeks or Coves, to other mens houses or lands. And for great Ponds lying in common, though within the bounds of some Town, it shall be free for any man to fish and fowle there, and may pass and repass on foot through any mans propriety for that end, so they trespass not upon any mans Corn or Meddow. [1641, 47]

Water passage free

Liberty to pass through propriety to fish & fowle

Liberty to remove out of ye Jurisd:

2. Every man of, or within this Jurisdiction, shall have free liberty (notwithstanding any Civil Power) to remove both himselfe and his family, at their pleasure out of the same. Provided there be no Legal impediment to the contrary. [1641]

Lying.

WHEREAS Trueth in Words, as well as in actions, is required of all men, Especially of Christians, who are the professed Servants of the God of Trueth; And whereas all Lying is contrary to truth, and some sort of lyes are not onely sinfull (as all lyes are) but also pernicious to the Publick weal, and injurious to particular persons; It is therefore Ordered by this Court and Authority thereof, That every person of the age of discretion (which is accounted fourteen yeares) who shall wittingly and willingly make, or publish any lye, which may be pernicious to the publick weal, or tending to the damage or injury of any particular persõ, or with intent to deceive and abuse the people, with false newes and reports, and the same duely prooved in any Court or before any one Magistrate (who hath hereby power granted to hear and determine all Offences against this law) such person shall be fined for the first Offence *ten shillings*, or if the party be unable to pay the same, then to be *set in the stocks*, so long as the said Court or Magistrate shall appoint, in some open place not exceeding two houres. For the second Offence in that kind, wherof any shall be Legally convicted, the sum of *twenty shillings* or be *whipped* upon the naked body not exceeding ten stripes. And for the third Offence *forty shillings*, or if the party be unable to pay, then to be whipped with more stripes, not exceeding fifteen. And if yet any shall offend in like kind and be Legally convicted thereof, such person, male or female, shall be fined *ten shillings* a time more then formerly, or if the party so offending be unable to pay, then to be whipt with five or six more stripes then formerly, not exceeding fourty at any time. The aforesaid fines shall be levyed or stripes inflicted either by the Marshall of that Jurisdiction, or Constable of the town, where the Offence is Committed according as the Court or Magistrate shall direct. And such fines so levyed shall be payd to the Treasury of the shire where the cause is tryed. Age of discretion 14 years. First offence 10 s. or stocs. Second offēc 20 s. or whipt. 3d & 4 offēc

And if any person shall find himselfe greived with the sentence of any such Magistrate out of Court, he may appeale to the next Court of the same Shire, giving sufficient security to prosecute his appeale, and abide the Order of the Court, and if the said Court shall judg his appeal causless he shall be double fined, and pay the charges of the Court, during his action, or Corrected by whipping as aforesayd, not exceeding *forty stripes*, & pay the costs of the Court, and party complaining or informing and of the witnesses in the case. And for all such as being under age of discretion that shall offend in *Lying* contrary to this Order, their parents or masters shall give them due Correction & that in the presence of some Officer if any Magistrate shall so appoint, Provided allwaies, that no person shall be barred of his just action of slaunder, or otherwise, by any proceeding upon this Order. [1645] Liberty to appeale. If Causles doubly fined. Under age to be corrected by parents.

Manslaughter.

IT is Ordered by this Court and the Authority thereof, That if any person in the just and necessary defence of his life, or the life of any other shall kill any person attempting to Rob, or Murder in the field or High-way, or to break into any dwelling house, if he conceive he cannot with safety of his own person, otherwise take the Fellon or Assailant or bring him to tryall, he shall be holden blameles. [1647.]

Marriages & Married persons.

IT is Ordered by this Court and Authority thereof; That no man shall strike his wife, nor any woman her husband, on penalty of such fine, not exceeding Ten Pounds for one Offence, or such Corporall punnishment as the County Court shall determine. L:2.p: 17

2. *For prevention of all unlawfull Marriages,* It is ordered that henceforth no person shall be joyned in Marriage, before the intention of the parties proceeding therein, hath been three times published at some time of publick Lecture, or town meeting in both the townes, where the parties or either of them doe ordinarily re- 3 times published or posted 14 dayes

or be set up in writing upon some post of their Meeting-house door in publick veiw, there to stand, so as it may easily be read, by the space of fourteen dayes [1639.]

3. *And whereas God hath committed the care and power, into the hands of parents for the disposing their Children in Marriage, so that it is against rule, to seek to draw away the affections of young Maidens under pretence of purpose of Marriage, before their parents have given way and allowance in that respect; And whereas it is a Common practise in divers places for young men irregularly & disorderly to watch all advantages for their evill purposes, to insinuate into the affections of young Maidens, by coming to them in places, & seasons unknown to their parents, for such ends, whereby much evil hath grown amongst us, to the dishonour of God & damage of parties; For prevention whereof for time to come.* It is further Ordered.

No motion of marriage to be made to any maid without consent of parents. Ten: 5 pounds

That whatsoever person, from hencefoorth shall endeavour directly or indirectly, to draw away the affection of any Mayd in this Jurisdiction, under pretence of Marriage, before he hath obtained liberty & allowance from her parents or Governours (or in absence of such) of the neerest Magistrate, he shall forfeit for the first offence five pounds, for the second towards the partie ten pounds, and be bound to forbare any further attempt and proceedings in that unlawfull designe, without or against the allowance aforesayd. And for the third offence upon information or complaint by such Parents. or Governours to any Magistrate, giving bond to prosecute the party, he shall be committed to prison, and upon hearing and conviction by the next Court shal be adjudged to continue in prison, untill the Court of Assistants shall see Cause to release him. [1647]

4 *VVhereas divers persons both men & women, living within this Jurisdiction, whose Wives, and Husbands are in England, or elsewhere, by means whereof, they live under great temptations here, and some of them committing lewdnes & filthines here among us, others make love to women & attempt marriage, and some have attained it, & some of them live under suspition of uncleanes, and all to the great dishonour of God, reproach of Religion, Commonwealth and Churches.* It is therefore

Married persons to go to their relatiō on paine of 20 pound.

Constable to present such to ÿ Court.

Ordered by this Court and Authority thereof, *for the prevention of all such future evils.* That all such marryed persons as aforesayd, shall repaire to their sayd relatiōs by the first opportunity of shipping, upon the paine or penalty of *twenty pounds*, except they can shew just cause to the contrary to the next County Court or Court of Assistants, after they are summoned by the Constable thereto to appear, who are hereby required so to doe, upon paine of *twenty shillings* for every such default wittingly made. Provided this Order doe not extend to such as are come over to make way for their families, or are in a transient way, onely for traffick or merchādize for some smal time, [1647]

5 *As the Ordinance of Marriage is honourable amongst all, so should it be accordingly solemnized.* It is therefore Ordered by this Court and Authority

Who may solemnize marriage.

thereof. That no person whatsoever in this Jurisdiction, shall joyne any persons together in Marriage, but the Magistrate, or such other as the General Court, or Court of Assistants shal Authorize in such place, where no Magistrate is neer. Nor shal any joyne themselves in Marriage, but before some Magistrate or person authorized as aforesaid. Nor shal any Magistrate, or other person authorized as

Not before publication.

aforesaid, joyne any persons together in Marriage, or suffer them to joyne together in Marriage in their presence, before the parties to be marryed have been published according to Law. [1646]

L:1 p:38:

Marshal.

57 Marshal to levy all fines

IT is Ordered by this Court and Authority thereof. That every Marshal shall diligently and faithfully Collect, and levy all such fines, and sums of money of every person, for which he shall have Warrant from the respective Treasurers, or other Authority, which he shall returne to the said Treasurer, with all convenient

speed,

speed, upon penalty of forfeiting *two shillings* out of his owne estate, for every pound not collected or returned as aforesaid or such fine as any Court shall impose on him for his neglect:

And every Marshal, shall with all speed and faithfulnes levy the goods of every person for which he shall have *Warrant*, by vertue of any execution granted & signed by the Secretary or other Clerk authorized thereunto, and the said goods so levyed, shall with all convenient speed, deliver to the party or atturney, that obtained the judgment and execution, or be liable to make full satisfaction to the party, for all damage susteined by his neglect; And the said Marshal shal within two months, after the receipt of any such execution make return of the said execution, with what he hath done by vertue thereof, under his hand to the Clerke that granted the same, to be by him kept and recorded, and if the execution be not fully satisfyed, the sayd Clerke shall at the request of the partie, grant execution for the remainder; And every Marshal neglecting to make return of executions as aforesaid, shall forfeit double to the damage, any person concerned therein may sustaine by such neglect. L 1 p, 58.

To serve all execution.

To returne execution to the Clerke

Further the said Marshals shall with like care and faithfulnes, serve all Attachments directed to them, and return the same to the Courts, to which they are returnable at the times of the returns thereof, and henceforth no Marshal shall be Clerke or Recorder of any Court.

Marshal not to be Clerke

And it is heereby Ordered that the Marshals fees shall be *twelve pence* in the pound, to be payd by the respective Treasurers, for all fines levyed by the said Marshals, and returned to the sayd Treasurers, and for serving attachments within one mile *one shilling three pence* to be payd by the party that imployes them, & for serving executions *twelve pence* in the pound for all sums not exceeding *ten pounds*, and for all sums above *ten pounds* and not exceeding *forty pounds*, *six pence* in the *pound* more, and for all sums above *forty pounds* and not exceeding *one hundred pounds*, *three pence* in the *pound* more, and *one penny* in the *pound* more, for all sums above *one hundred pounds*, out of the estate of the person the execution is served upon, over and above for the execution. And in all Cases; where the aforesaid fees for levying executions or fines, will not answer the Marshals traveill, and other necessary charges, the Marshal or other officer imployed shall have power to demaund *six pence per mile*, and upon refusal, to levy the same together with his other fees. L:2 p: 7:

Marshals fees

And it is Ordered, that all Marshals and Constables within this Jurisdiction, shall henceforth from time to time, allow and pay unto the Marshal General *three pence* out of every *fifteene pence*, they receive for serving attachments, also *three pence* out of every shilling, due to them, for levying of fines and executions; And it is further Ordered, that the said Marshal general shall from time to time, have & enjoy to his own use & benefit the custome of *two pence per quart* upon all such as doe or shall retaile strong-waters, and all such as shall sell under one gallon, at a time, shall be accounted retailers) whether Licenced or not, and the one halfe of the fine of *five pounds*: of all such persons, as shall upon his information or complaint be convicted to have sold strong-waters without Licence, as also the sole Benefitt of the Impost of all strong-waters brought into the Country, which this Court doth allow as a meet incouragement and sallary for the service of the said Marshall Generall A: 53 p: 20

Marshal Gen: his fees.

L: 1 p: 10.

Whereas the Marshalls and their Deputies have often need of Assistants in the execution of their Office: It is Ordered that they & every of them have & shall have the same power to enjoyne & charge any person to aide them and Assist them therein as every Constable hath, and whosoever shall refuse, or not yeild Obedience thereto, shall incurr the like penalty, that those doe or should doe, that refuse to ayd the Constable in his Office.

Marshal may require ayd as Constable may.

And in all cases of fines and Assesments to be levyed, & upon execution in civill actions, the Marshall or other Officer shall demand the same of the party at his house or place of L: 1 p 45

Officer may break open doors or chests

or place of usuall abode, & upon refusal or non paiment, he shall have power, caling Assistants if he see cause to break open the door of any house, chest or place where he shall give notice, that any goods liable to such Levie or execution shall be, & if he be to take the person, he may do the like; If upon demand he shall refuse to render himselfe.

Necessary charges to be levyed.

And what ever charges the Officer shall necessarily be put unto, upon any such occasion, he shall have power to levie the same, as he doth the debt, fine or execution and where the Officer shall levie any such goods upon execution as cannot be conveyed to the place, where the partie dwels, for whom such execution shall be levied without Considerable charge; he shall levie the said Charge also with the execution. The like Order shall be observed in levying of fines, provided it shall not be lawfull, for such Officer to levie any mans necessary bedding, apparrel, tooles

Goods exempt from execution.

or armes, neither implements of house-hold, which are for the necessary upholding of his life. but in such cases, he shall levie his land or person according to Law, & in no case shall the Officer be put to seek out any mans estate, further then his place of

Officer doeing wrōg to make satisfaction

abode, but if the partie will not discover his goods or Lands the Officer may take his person. And it is also Ordered, That if any Officer shall doe injury to any by Colour of his Office, in these or any other Cases, he shall bee Liable upon Complaint of the Partie wronged, by action or information to make full restitution. [1647.]

Masters Servants Labourers.

Servants not to give or truck

IT is Ordered by this Court and the Authority thereof. That no servant either Man or Mayd shall either give, Sell, or truck, any Commodity whatsoever, without Licēce from their Masters, during the time of their service under pain of fine or corporal punishment at the discretion of the Court as the Offence shall deserve.

work y͏̄ whole day.

2. And that all Workmen shall worke the whole day, allowing convenient time for food and rest.

Servants run-away to be pursued.

3 It is also Ordered that when any Servants shall run from their Masters or any other Inhabitants shall Privily go away, with suspicion of evill intentions, it shall be lawfull for the next Magistrate or the Constable and two of the cheife inhabitants, where no Magistrate is, to press men, and Boates or Pinnaces at the publick charge, to pursue such Persons by Sea and Land, and bring them back by force of Armes.

Wages to be sett by y͏̄ freemē in towns

4. It is also Ordered by the authority aforesaid. That the freemen of every Town may from time to time as occasion shall require, agree amongst themselves about the prizes and rates of all workmens Labour and servants wages. And every person Inhabiting in any Towne, whether Workmen, Labourer or servant shall be bound to the same rates, which the said freemen, or the greater part shall bind themselves unto, and whosoever shall exceed those rates, so agreed, shall be punished by the discretion of the Court of that shire, according to the quality and measure of the Offence; And if any Town shall have Cause of Complaint against the freemen of any other Town, for allowing greater Rates or wages then themselves, the County Court of that shire, shall from Time to Time set Order therein.

Wages to be paid in corn

to be valued

5. *And for servants and workmens wages,* It is Ordered, that they may be payd in Corne to be valued by two indifferent freemen, chosen, the one by the Master, the other by the Servant or workman, who also are to have respect, to the Value of the work or service, and if they cannot agree, then a third man shall be chosen by the next Magistrate, or if no Magistrate be in the Town, then by the next Constable, unles the parties agree the price themselves. Provided if any servant or workmen agree for any particular paiment, then to be payd in specie or consideration for default therein, And for all other paiments in Corn, if the parties cannot agree, they shall chuse two indifferent men, & if they cannot agree, then a third as before.

6. It is Ordered, and by this Court Declared, That if any Servant shall flee from the tiranny and cruelty, of his or her Master. to the house of any free-man of the same Town, they shall be there protected and susteined till due order be taken for their relief; Provided due notice thereof be speedily given to their master from whom they fled; and to the next Magistrate or Constable where the party so fled is harboured. Servants flying cruelty of masters may be harb:

7. Also that no servant shall be put off for above a year to any other, neither in the life time of their Master, nor after their death by their executors or administrators, unles it be by consent of Authority assembled in some Court, or two Assistants, otherwise all, and every such assignement to be voyd in Law. Servants not put off wout allowance of two Magistr:

8. And if any man smite out the ey or Tooth of his Man-servant or Maydservant, or otherwise Maim or much disfigure them (unles it be by meer casualty) he shall let them go free from his service, and shall allow such further recompence as the Court shall adjudg him. Servants maimed to be discharged

9. And all servants that have served diligently and faithfully to the benefit of their masters, Seven yeares, shall not be sent away empty; and if any have been unfaithfull, negligent or unprofitable in their service, notwithstanding the the good usage of their masters, they shall not be dismissed, till they have made satisfaction according to the judgement of Authority. [1630, 33, 35, 36, 41] Faithful Servants reward. Unfaithful punished

Malt.

IT is Ordered, That no *Maltster*, or *maker of malt*, shall henceforth deliver or pas away any *malt* by him or his procurement made before it be cleansed from the dust and tayle, which ariseth in the malting, drying and ordering it, in his hands on penalty of *twelve pence per bushel*, upon conviction before any Magistrate or Court the one half to the informer, the other half to the Country. A. 52. P. 12. Malt to be cleansed fro dust

This Court *taking into serious Consideration, the great necessity of upholding the Staple commodityes of this Country, for the supply and Support of the Inhabitants thereof, And finding by experience, the bringing in of Malt, wheat, barley, bisket, beife, meal and flower, (which are the principall Comodityes of this Country) from Forreign parts, to be exceeding prejudicial to the subsistance of this place and people here,* Have therefore Ordered, That no person whatsoever, either Inhabitant or stranger, shall directly or indirectly, after the first of March next, import into this Jurisdiction from any part of *Europe*, any of the aforesayd provisions under the penalty of Confiscation of the same, (except it be for the ships provisions) that shall be so imported, landed, set to sale, or otherwise disposed, contrary to the intent of this Order. And it is further Ordered and enacted, that all Marshals and Constables where no Marshal is, in the severall Townes in this Jurisdiction, are hereby required and impowred to make diligent search, within their respective townes, & Harbours where any such provisions are Landed sold or otherwise disposed of, and to make seizure of the same for the use of the Country, for which each & every Marshal and Constable shall have allowed them, one *fourth part* of what shall be so seized, for their care and Paines herein. And all former Lawes concerning Impost, upon any of the Provisions aforesayd are hereby Repealed. [1652. 55.] A. 55. No malt, wheat, bisket beife to be brought in on penal: of confiscation. Marshall or Constable to seis it. The fourth part for the paines

Mills, Millers.

IT is Ordered by this Court and the Authority thereof, that no miller shall take above one *sixteenth part of the Corn* he grinds, and that every Miller shall have alwayes ready in his Mill weights and Scales, provided at his own charge, to weigh Corne to and from Mill if men desire it. [1635. 38.] Millers toll. To have weights

Military.

FORasmuch as the well Ordering of the Militia is a matter of great concernment to the safety & welfare of this Common-wealth, It is Ordered by this Court & the

Militia Commanded by Majors

I,2.p.12

A:56.P.12.

Majors how & by whom chosen.

the Authority thereof, That the Military forces of *Suffolk*, *Middlesex* and *Essex*, shall be under the Command of the *Sergeant Majors* Chosen in each County and that the Militia of *Norfolk* shall be Commanded by the *Major* of the *Regiment* of *Essex*, Provided the said Militia be not drawn out of the sayd County to any Regimentall exercise; and if any of the sayd *Majors* be remooved or discharged their places, the *Major Generall* for the time being shall within one Month at furthest after such change, send forth his *warrants* to each town in the shire, to make choice of a *Major* in manner following viz. : The *freemen Housholders* and such *souldiers* as have taken the *Oath of fidelity* before the *fifteenth of May* [1656.] and no other, being met together in their respective townes (by vertue of such *warrant* from the *Major Generall* or from the *Generall Court* shall give in their votes for such a person as they judg fit, for the Office of *Sergeant Major* of that *Regiment* which votes, shall be sealed up by the cheif *Military Officer* of the place, or by the Constable (as the warrant shall direct (and sent by some *freeman*, chosen by the Town, to carry them to the *Shire town* of that County at such time as the warrant shall direct, where the sayd votes shall be opened and numbred, in the presence of one or two of the nearest *Magistrates* and the sayd *freemen*, and he that shall have the greater number of votes being a *freeman*, shall be presented by one of the sayd *Magistrates* unto the *Major Generall*, within one week after such *Election*, who shall by giving the Oath accustomed & delvering him a *Commission*, install & confirm such *Sergeant Major* in his place.

Regimentall meetings once in 3 yeares.

Meeting of the Officers of y Regim:

2. And every *Sergeant Major* is hereby Ordered and required, once in *three yeares* to draw his *Regiment*, *both horse & foot*, in one Convenient place in the Country, and to instruct and exercise the *Officers and souldiers* in Military discipline according to his best skil and Ability, for which service he shall have *twenty pounds* allowed him, out of the Treasury of the Country for his paines and charges for every such Meeting, also every *Sergeant Major*, may as often as he shall see cause send his warrants to require the cheife Officer of each *Company* in his *Regiment*, to meet at such time and place, as he shall appoint, and there with them to Confer and give in Command, such Orders as shall by them, be Judged meet, for the better Ordering and setling the particular Companies in *Military exercises*, and to impose *fines* and *penalties* upon such *delinquents* as have not given satisfaction to their *Captain or Chief Officer*, for all defects either in their *armes*, *ammunition*, *appearances*, *watches*, *offences &c:* And the *Sergeant Major* shall with the consent of the said *Officers*, give Order to the *Clerks* of the several Companyes, to take *distress* for the same, within one month after such Order,

Nomination of Officers of Companyes.

To be allow. by y County Courts.

3. *And for the setling particular military Officers in every Town of this Jurisdiction*, It is Ordered, That every *freeman*, *housholder*, and *listed Souldier*, having taken the *Oath of fidelity* as abovesaid (and no other) shall have liberty to give his vote for the nomination of *military Officers*, of that Town or Company where he dwells, Provided they be freemen, and all persons so nominated, shall be presented to the Court of that County, to be allowed and confirmed in their respective Offices, unles the said Court shall see cause to the Contrary, & no person shall be acknowledged or accepted as an Officer of any Company without the allowance and approbation of the County Court first had and obtained.

A.53.P.13.

Sixty foure Souldiers to be a Comps.

4. And in every Town where there is *sixty four* Souldiers (liable to attend Constant training) besides the Officers, such number of souldiers shall be accounted a *foot Company*, and have liberty of nomination of all the *Officers* of a *foot Company*, and shall have *two Drums*. And in smaller Townes, where there shall be a

less

less number, then *sixty four* as aforesaid, they shall have liberty of nomination of *Sergeants* and other inferiour Officers only, to teach and instruct them in the exercise of armes. And the *Major* of the *Regiment* shall have power, to order & regulate the smaller Townes, and to joyn them into one compleat Company, (as occasion may require) which shall have liberty of choise of all Officers as aforesaid. And every *Captain, Leivtenant and Ensign*, shall have *Commissions* from the General Court, for the holding of their places, and exercise of their duties. Captain Leiftenant Ensign to have commissions.

5. The sayd Military Officers of every Company shall take care that their Souldiers be wel and Compleatly Armed, and shall appoint what armes every souldier shall serve with, Provided two thirds of each Company be Musquetiers, & those which serve with pikes, have *Corslets and head peeces* and they shall exercise their souldiers eight dayes every year, when the Captaine or Cheife Officer shall appoint by giving publick warning thereof, three or four dayes before the day of exercise, Provided that so many dayes as shall be expended, by Order of the Major of the Regiment in the exercise of the Regiment, and in Marching to and from the place of exercise, shall be accounted as part of the eight dayes. Capt: to appoint ye souldiers armes. To exercise 8 days yearly

6. Also the three Cheife Officers of each Company shall have power to punish such Souldiers as shall Commit any disorder or Contempt upon any day or time of Military exercise, or upon any watch or ward; by *stocks, bilboes* or any other *usuall military punishmēt*, or by *fine* not exceeding *twenty shillings*, or may cōmit such offender to the Constable to be Carried before some Magistrate who may bind him over to the next Court of that shire, if the Cause so require, or Commit him to the prison. 3 Cheif officers to punish disorders of souldiers

7. Every foot souldier shall be compleatly Armed & furnished, the pikemen with a good *Pike* wel headed, *Corslet, head peece, sword, & snapsack*, the Musquetiers with a *good fixed musquet*, not under Bastard Musquet bore, nor under three foot nine inches in length, nor above four foot three inches long, with a *priming wire, worm, scourer and mould*, fitted to the bore of his Musquet, also with a good *sword, rest, Bandaleres, one pound of powder, twenty bullets, and two fathom of match*, upon the the penalty of *ten shillings* for every defect; And all other Inhabitants of this Jurisdiction, except Magistrates & Elders of Churches, the Pressident, Fellowes and Students of Harvard Colledg, shall alwaies be provided of Armes, & furnished as aforesaid under the penalty aforesayd. Souldiers how to be armed. on penal of 10s: And other inhabitants.

8 And if any person cannot procure Armes or ammunition, with such means as he hath, if he shall bring to the Clerke, so much Corne as by apprizement of, the said Clerke and two other indifferent men (whereof one to be chosen by the party) shall be adjudged of greater value, by a fifth part then such armes or Ammunition is of, he shall be excused of the penalty for want of armes untill he be provided: And the Clerke shall endeavour to furnish him so soon as may be, by sale of such goods so deposited, rendering the party the overplus; But if any person shall not be able to Provide himself armes & amunitiō, through meer poverty, if he be single he shall be put to service by some Magistrate, or the Constable shall provide him Armes & ammunition, and shall appoint him when & with whom to earn it out. Wanting arms to carry pay to the Clerk to provide. Poor how to be furnished with arms

9. Every person above the age of *Sixteen yeares*, shall duely attend al Military exercise and service, as *training, watching, warding*, under the penalty of *five shillings* for every fault, except *Magistrates, Deputies, & Officers of Court, Elders, & Deacons, the President, Fellows, Students & Officers of Harvard Colledg, & professed school-masters Physitians & Chirurgeons allowed* by two Magistrates, *Treasurers, Surveyer General, Publick notary, Masters of Ships* and other Vessels above *twenty tuns, fishermen* constantly imployed at all fishing seasons, *constant heardsmen*, and such other, as for *bodily infirmity or other just Cause* shall by any County Court or Court of Assistant (after notice of the parties desire to the Cheife Officer of the Company to which he belongs) be discharged, also one servant of every Magistrate & teaching Elder, and the sons & servants of the Major General for the time being, also such as dwell at remote A52:p13 Persons exempt from training. A56:p12

H farmes

A. 53.

farmes or have a *ferry* to paſs, ſhall be exempt from watching in the town, but ſhall watch and ward, as their Cheife Officer ſhall direct otherwiſe, and all farmes diſtant above four miles, from the place of exerciſing the Company, or have a *ferry to paſs* over, that have above twenty acres of land in tillage, and twenty head of great Cattle upon ſuch farme, ſhall upon Reaſonable allowance to the Company have one man exempted from ordinary trainings.

Clerk of the band.

To call the Rol & attend on training daies

10. And it is Ordered, that in every town or Company there ſhall be choſen (as other military Officers are choſen) a diſcreet able man to be Clerke of the Band & if any ſhall refuſe to accept the place, or to take his Oath, he ſhall pay to the uſe of the company *fortty ſhillings* & the Company ſhall chuſe another; & all that refuſe the place or Oath as aforeſaid, ſhall pay *forty ſhillings* a peice, till one doth accept the place and he that doth hold the place, ſhall have a fourth part of the fines for his labour. And the Clerk ſhall upon every training day, twice, once in the forenoon, as alſo in the afternoon, at ſuch time as the Captain or Cheif Officer then in the field, ſhall appoint, call or cauſe to be called over the liſts of the names of all the Souldiers, & ſhall give attendance in the field all the day (except he have leave from his Captain or Chief Officer) to take notice of any defect, by abſence of Souldiers, or other offences that may fall out in time of exerciſe; And the ſaid clerke ſhall twice every year,

To veiw the Armes

veiw all armes & ammunition of the company, and take notice that every ſouldier be furniſhed according to this Law, to which end by direction of the Cheife Officer, he ſhall give notice to the ſouldiers that upon ſuch a training day appointed, they are required to bring, in the forenoon) all their armes & ammunitiō into the field, where they ſhall be approoved or diſallowed by the judgment of the ſaid Cheif Officer then in the field, & further the ſaid Clerk ſhall once in the year at leaſt ſurvey the armes of of all other Inhabitants, & ſee that all, (except as before excepted) be provided in their houſes with armes & ammunition, and upon every occaſion he is required to uſe all diligence to veiw every mans armes whether they be compleatly furniſhed with all armes & ammunition as the Law requireth. And the ſaid Clerke ſhall within

Give notice to the Capt. of all defects within one week.

one week after any default made, or defect obſerved, preſent a liſt of the names of all that are delinquent, and of their defects to the Captaine or Cheif Officer of the company. And ſhall without partiality demaund and Receive all fines due for ſuch defects according to this Law, which if any ſhall Refuſe to pay, he ſhall make diſtreſs

To diſtreine within ten dayes

upon the goods of ſuch perſons, as ſhall not within *ten dayes* after their default be diſcharged, or have them fines mitigated by the Captain or Cheife *Officer* of the company, unles the ſaid Cheife Officer ſhall ſee cauſe to Refer the judgment & determinatiō of ſuch default to the Major & Cheif Officer of the Regiment at their meeting.

To diſpoſe of fines for ẏ uſe of the Company

And the Clerk ſhall with the advice of the Chief Officers of the Company, ſpeedily lay out all fines received or levied, in *Enſign, Drums, Halberts, Candle,* and *wood for the watch*, or provide *powder & armes for the poorer ſort*, or otherwiſe as in their diſcretion they ſhall judg meet, for the uſe of the Company.

A. 52. P. 14, & 53.

Comitree of Militia in ẏ ſeverall towns

Their power

11. And for the better Ordering the *Militia* in the ſeveral Towns, in caſes of any ſuddain exigent, It is Ordered, That there be a *Committee of Militia* in every Town, and that the *committee of Militia* in *Boſton*, ſhall conſiſt of the Magiſtrates living in the town, the Chief Officer of the horſe if living in town, and the Chief Officer of each Company of foot, or the greateſt part of them, and in ſuddain exigents, any three of them may act, when due meanes being uſed, a greater number cannot be aſſembled, which Cōmittee ſhall have a *Commiſſion* of like tenour *Major Gibbons* had graunted A. D. 1645. Who ſhall alſo have power to appoint a Military watch, when they ſhall ſee cauſe for the ſafety of the Town and Country; And Charleſtown, Salem and Ipſwich, ſhall have the like Committee of Militia, who ſhall have like power by Commiſſion: And for all other Townes, where there is one or more Magiſtrates the ſaid Magiſtrate or Magiſtrates, with ẏ three chief Military Officers, and where no Magiſtrate dwells, ẏ Deputy or Deputies to the General Court, with the three chief Officers of ſuch Town, or any three of them, ſhall be the Committee of Militia for ſuch Town, and have power in all ſuddain exigents, to Order & diſpoſe the Militia of their Town, for their own ſafety and defence, till further Order be taken, and upon Alarme, or any invaſion to ſtrengthen their quarters, and to hinder any approaching or aſſaulting them, in a way of hoſtility, by bearing Armes in Companyes, or refuſing upon ſuch approaches to come under Command, or give an account what they are, and wherefore they are in ſuch poſture.

And

And every such Committee, where any such *alarme* shall be given or received or shall be assaulted as aforesayd, is required with all possible speed to give intelligence to the next Magistrate and the *Major* of the *Regiment* where such *Alarm* is taken or assault made, of the reason thereof, and state of the place so alarmed. And the sayd Major is hereby required to send forth to procure intelligence of the estate of any place so *Alarm'd* or assaulted, and to Order Assistance to them, from any other Company or Companies of his *Regiment*, as the Case shall require, & shall give constant intelligence to the *Governour* or *Councel* of the Country and *Major Generall* of the state of such affaires with all Convenient speed. But no *Major* of any *Regiment* shall march with his *Regiment* out of the County, wherein he hath Cōmand, nor cause any part thereof so to do without Order from the *Generall Court*, *Councell of the Common-wealth* or *Major Generall*, except it be in pursuit of the Enemy upon a rout. And in case of death or absence of the *Major upon any* such occasion of service, the eldest *Captaine* of the *Regimen* shall supply his place, til further Order be taken, and the *seniority* of all *Captaines* & *Cheife Officers* of every Company in the severall *Regiments* shall be accounted according to the *seniority* of the Townes or Companies they Cōmand except the Cōmanders of the four companies of Boston, being of equal standing, the *seniority* of the *Captaines* shall be according to the priority of their *Commissions*.

In case of Alarme.

To give notice to ÿ Major.

Major to Order assistance

To give intel. to ÿ Council & Major Ge.

Major not to lead his Regment out of ÿ County

Seniority of Captains

A. 53.

A. 56. P. 12.

It is Further Ordered, that henceforth all warrants for impressing & raising of souldiers, for any expedition, shall be directed to the *Comitty of militia* of the severall Townes who may execute the same by the Cōstable & the said *Committee* are hereby impowred & required to suppress all raising of souldiers, but such as shall be by the Authority of this government.

Commit: to press Sould:

A. 54. p. 3

And in all Townes where there are *great Artillery*, *forts* or *Batteryes*, the *Committee of Militia* and *Select-men* of the Town, shall mount such *Guns*, and fit them with appertinaces for service, and repaire such *Forts or Batteries*, as they shall see necessary for the security of the Town, the charge whereof, the Select men are hereby impowred and required to Levy on the estate of the Inhabitants, according to the proportion of the Country Rate to be Collected by the Constables of the said town, for the use aforesayd.

A. 55.

To take care of great guns

And repaire Forts

12. It is Ordered that the *Military watches* shall be set by *beat of Drum* half an hour after sun set, by the *Military Officers* in such places as they shall judg most convenient, and shall be Ordered and disposed by their Command and direction, and if any man shall shoot off a gun after the watch is set, (except in case of *Alarme*) he shall forfeit *forty shillings*.

Military watches how set

The sayd *watch* or *Centinels* being set, shall examine all Persons, that shall come within their *Watch* or *Round*, and all they suspect, they shall carry to their guard, there to be kept till morning, & before they be dismissed, they shall Carry them to their *Cheife Officer*, to be examined and proceeded with according to Law, and if the *Centinell* or *Watch* shall meet with such persons, as shall be too strong for them or by their Carriage shall give just cause of suspition or will not submit to their cōmand, or if they shall either draw upon them or offer any such affront in words or actions, as shall put them in fear or hazzard of their lives, they shall discharge upon them and retire with speed to the guard, and raise an *Alarme*, provided alwayes that in time of peace, when the Councel of war, or the cheife Officers of the Company shall not apprehend present danger by the nearness of an enemy, it shall not be in the Liberty of any *Centinell*, to hazzard the killing of any person, except in his own necessary defence, but if the cause require it, he shall retire to the guard, and raise an *Alarme*, by discharging his Musquet and Crying *Arm Arm*; which shall be taken for an *Alarme* by the souldiers of that town, and if there appear danger to the cheife *Officer* he shall either strengthen his guard, or give a generall *Alarme*, which shall be either the distinct dischage of *three Musquets* or the *continued beat of the Drum*

Instructio & duty of Centinels

What shall be taken for an Alarme

 or firing

Not answering ; Alarme pen: 5 poūd

or *firing a beacon* or the discharge of a *peece of Ordinance*, and two Musquets after it, any of which in the night, shall be accounted a *generall Alarme*, which every souldier is immediately to answer, by repairing *Armed to his Colours*, or *Court of guard*, upon the penalty of *five pounds*.

Smiths to repaire armes

Penalty

13. And upon any expedition, upon occasion of any enemy, or any present military service to be done, all *Smiths* and other *needfull workmen*, shall immediatly repaire such armes & other necessaries as shall be brought unto them. for that end, for which they shall not refuse such pay, as the Country affoords, upon the penalty of *five pounds*, for every such default, and for such neglect at any other time, more thē *ten dayes* shall forfeit for every such offence *ten shillings*.

A. 56. P. 12.

14. The *Serveyor Generall* shall yearly give an account of the Cōmon stock of *Powder* and *Amunition* to the Councel, that the *Generall Court*, being by them informed may out of the publick Treasury make a Constant supply, according to the need of the Country.

L. 2. P. 1.

Townes to provide watch-house & stock of powder and amunition.

15. Every Town shall be provided of a sufficient watch-house, under the penalty of *five pound*. and shall also provide at their own charges a safe & convenièt place, to keep all such *Powder and Amunition* in, as the cheife Military Officer by Order of the Generall Court shall appoint under the penalty of *ten pounds* And the Select men of every town, shall provide for every fifty Souldiers, *one barrel of good powder* conteining neer *one hundred pounds*, *one hundred and fifty pounds of musquet bullets*, and *twenty eight pound of good match*, and after that proportion for every Company of souldiers in number more or less, which they shall carefully renew frō time to time as shall be needfull, under the penalty of *five pounds*, for the want of every *Barrel of Powder*, *one hundred and fifty pound* of *Bullets*, & *eight and twenty pound of match*. as before mentioned, and the Select men of every Town as aforesayd, are hereby Authorized to assess their inhabitants for making the Provisions aforesayd, which shall remaine as a town stock, besides all other Provisions of that kind. [1649.]

A. 56. P. 12.

Troop not exceed 70

To be under Majors com:

A 54. p. 1

A. 56. P. 12.

16.. It is Ordered by this Court and the Authority thereof. That no *Troop of horse* within this Jurisdiction, shall exceed the number of *seventy Listed souldiers* besides Officers, And that the troopes Raised in the severall Countyes be under the command of the *Majors*, of the Regiment in the respective Countyes, and all priviledges formerly granted to incourege troopers, shall be continued, except free *ferriage* and free Commonage in divided & appropriate Commons, And every troop Consisting of *forty* shall have Liberty of nomination of *all Officers* to be allowed and Confirmed by the Countie Courts as the *foot Officers*, and the *three cheife Officers* to have *Commission*.

Troopers how to be furnished.

To exercise six dayes yearly

Clerke his fees.

And every *Trooper* shall keep alwayes a *good Horse*, and be wel fitted with *saddle, bridle, holsters, Pistols* or *Carbines* and *Sword* under the penalty of *ten shillings*, for every defect, & having Listed his *Horse*, shall not change or put him off, without Licence from his *Captaine* or *Cheife Officer*, under the like penalty. And every Trooper shall attend six dayes exercise yearly, at such time and place as shall be appointed by the cheif Officer, under the penalty of *five shillings* for every default, to be levyed and distreined by the Clerke of the Troop, who is hereby required to execute the place, as the Clerkes of the foot companies *mutatis mutandis*. And because the Troopers living remote, do often avoyd their penalties, or occasion much travaile and charge to the Clerke to collect the same, It is Ordered that the Clerkes of the troopes for thir charge and travaile in levying all fines, shall be allowed the fees of the Marshall, to be by him Levied and distreined, together with the fines, Provided no such distress be made within one month after the default, that the parties may have Liberty to present their excuses, to the Officers who have power upon just cause, to abate or remit the fines as the Officers of the foot have in like cases.

And

And in case of *Alarme*, every Trooper shall fit himselfe in all respects for service, and shall speedily repair to the guard, in the Town where he dwells, under the penalty of *five pounds*, and shall duely attend such service, as the Committee of *Militia* of that town shall require until he shall otherwise be Commanded by Order from his Captaine or other *superiour Officer*, And no Officer of any foot Company shall be a listed Trooper; And no Troop shall be drawn out of the County upon any pretence, by the Captaine and Officers thereof (except in pursuit of an enemy upon a rout) but by Order of the *Major Generall*. And the *Captaines of Horse and of foot* respectively, the *Majors* of the *Regiments* and the *Major Generall* are required in their respective Charges, to take Care the military Orders respecting foot & horses be duely executed & observed. [1645, 47, 48, 52, 53, 54, 55, 56] A. 53. How Troop are disposed in case of Alarme. No Troop to be drawn out of County.

Also it is Ordered. That no Trooper put off or change his horse, without leave from his Commander, under the penalty of *five pounds*, and that for non-appearance on dayes of exercise, the fine shall be *ten shillings*, and that no Trooper being listed, may at his pleasure disband himself, without leave orderly obteined from his Commander, and returned by certificat to the Commander of the foot, in the Town to which they belong, under the penalty of such a fine, as his cheif Officer shall impose, not exceeding *fifty shillings*. Troopers penalty.

Mines.

FOR *incouragement of such as will adventure for the discovery of Mines*, It is Ordered by this Court, That whosoever will be at the charge, for the *discovery of any Mine*, within this Jurisdiction, shall enjoy the *profits thereof*, with a fit *proportion of Land* to the same, for *twenty one yeares* to their proper use, and also that such persons shall have liberty to purchase the interest of any of the Indians in such lands where such Mines shall be found, provided they shall not enter upon any townes or persons propriety without his leave. [1641.] L. 2. p 11. Discoverers of mines to enjoy ỹ profits for 21 years.

2. And any Inhabitant within this jurisdiction, that shall have or find any kind of *Mine* or *Mines* whatsoever, in any of their own proprietyes, the whole benefit and *profit* of such *Mines* are due & shall belong to such *Proprietor* of land wherin such mine shall be found, to them & to their *heires* for ever, as any part of *their lands minneries, possessions or profits* whatsoever, paying onely the *fifth part of gold & silver Oar*, according to proviso made on that behalfe.

Money.

IT is Ordered by this Court and the Authority thereof, That a *Mint house* be Erected at *Boston* and that the Master of the sayd *Mint* and all the Officers thereof shall be *Sworn and allowed by this Court*, or by such as shall be Authorized by this Court for that purpose. And all persons whatsoever have liberty to bring into the sayd Mint, all *Bullion, plate or spanish Coyn*, there to be melted and brought to alloy of *sterling Money*, by the Master of the said Mint and his *sworne Officers* from time to time, by him or them to be Coyned into *twelve penny, six penny and three penny* peices, which shall be stamped with a double Ring on either side with this inscription *MASSACHUSETS*, & a tree in the cẽter on the one side, *NEWENGLAND* with the year of our Lord, and the figure XII. VI. III. according to the Value of each peice on the other side, together with a privy mark, which shall be appointed every three months by the *Governour*, and known onely to him and the sworn Officers of the mint. And further the master of the mint aforesaid, is hereby required, to coyn all the said money of good silver, of the just alloy of new sterling English money, and for value *two pence* in the *shilling* of lesser value then the present English coyn, and the lesser pieces proportionably: and all such coyn as aforesaid, (and no other, except English) shall be acknowledged to be the currant money of this Common-wealth, and to pass from man to man in all payments accordingly within this jurisdiction, And the *Mint master* for himself and officers, for A. 52. P. 12. Mint-house at Boston. Stamp of the Coyn. Value of the Coyn.

Allowance for Coyning

their paines & Labour in Melting, refining and Coyning is allowed by this Court to take *one shilling* out of every *twenty shillings*, which he shall Stamp as aforesayd, & it shall be in the liberty of any person who brings into the Mint house any *Bullion, plate or Spanish Coyn*, to be present and see the same melted, refined and alloyed, and then to take a receit of the *Master of the Mint* for the weight of that which is good Silver alloyed as aforesayd, for which the *Mint Master* shall deliver him the like weight, in Currant Mony. viz. Every shilling to weigh *three pence troy weight* & lesser peices proportionably, deducting allowance for coynage as before is expressed. And it is further Ordered, that a Comittee be chosen by this Court to appoint a *mint house* in some convenient place in Boston and to approve and swear the *master* of all the Officers, and to order & determine what shall further appear necessary to carry on this Order to effect.

Weight of ẏ Coyn

Mint master & Officers to be sworn

A.54.p.5

2. And it is further Ordered, That no Inhabitant of this Jurisdiction, or stranger, shall from henceforth *send, carry or transport* out of this Jurisdiction, by Sea or by Land, directly or indirectly, any of the *money* that hath been or shall be *Coyned* in this Jurisdiction; except *twenty shillings* for necessary expences, on penalty of *Confiscation*, not only of such *money so coyned*, but also all the visible estate of him that shall any way be found, sending or exporting any of the coyn aforesaid, one third part whereof, shall be to the use of the informer and Officer, the other two thirds to the Country. *And that this Law may be duely Observed*, The County Courts shall from time to time, as there shall be need in *Boston, Charlestown, Salem, Ipswich, Pascataquay, Isles of Shoales, Sudbury*, and *other needfull places*, appoint & authorize meet persons as searchers, to examine & search all persons, vessels, packs, trunks, Chests, boxes or the like, that shall be transporting out of this Jurisdiction, who finding any Money shall seiz the same, and forthwith informe the next Magistrate thereof, who shall issue out his warrant for the present seizure of the whole visible estate of the Party so transporting contrary to this Law, for the use of the Cōmonwealth, & for the parties searching or informing as is above exprest & it is further declared that all such *Masters, Mariners or other Persons*, that shall be found to be privie or Consenting to the exporting of any of the *Coyn* aforesaid out of this Jurisdiction, he or they shall for every such offence forfeit the summ of *twenty pound* a peice to be to the uses aforesaid, and the severall searchers shall take the Oath appointed for searchers, onely in stead of halfe, a *third part to be inserted* and in stead of certifying the *Auditor Generall*, to insert to *Certify the next Magistrate*. [1652. 54]

Exportation of coyn prohibited on penalty of confiscation of estate

Searchers to be appoint:

To take an Oath

Monopolies.

IT is Ordered, Decreed and by this Court Declared, That there shall be no *Monopolies* graunted or allowed amongst us, but of such new inventions that are Profitable to the Country, and that for a short time [1641.]

Oathes Subscriptions

No Oath but what are imposed by the Gen: Court.

IT is Ordered and by this Court declared, that no man shall be urged to take any Oath or subscribe to any *Articles, Covenants or Remonstrances*, of publick and Civil nature, but such as the Generall Court hath Considered, allowed and required, and no Oath of any Magistrate or of any Officer, shall bind him any further or longer, then he is Resident or Reputed an Inhabitant of this Jurisdiction. [1641.]

Officers oath how long binding

A.52.p.9

2. *For as much as divers Inhabitants of this Jurisdiction who have long continued amongst us, receiving Protection from this Government, have as we are informed uttered Offencive speeches, whereby their fidelity to this Government may justly be suspected, and also that divers Strangers of forreign parts do repaire to us of whose fidelity we have not that Assurance which is Commonly required of all Goverments.* It is therefore Ordered by this Court and the Authority thereof. That the County Courts or any one Magistrate out of Court, shall have power and is hereby Authorized to Require the *Oath of fidelity* of all settled Inhabitants amongst us, who have not that

Strangers to swear fidelity to this Government

not already taken the same, as also to Require the Oath under written, of all strangers, who after two months have their abode here; And if any Person shall refuse to take the Respective Oath, he or they shall be bound over to the next County Court or Court of Assistants, where if he shall Refuse, he shall forfeit *five Pound a week* for every week he shall Continue in this Jurisdiction after his sayd Refusall, unles he can give sufficient security to the satisfaction of the Court or Magistrate for his fidelity, during his or their residence amongst us.

You A. B. *Do acknowledg your self Subject to the Lawes of this Jurisdiction during your Residence under this Government, and do here Swear by the Great Name of the Everliving GOD, and ingage your self to be true and faithfull to the same, and not to plot, contrive, or conceal any thing that is to the hurt or detriment thereof.* [1652] *Strangers Oath.*

Oppression.

F*OR avoyding such mischiefs, as may follow by such ill dispoſed persons, as may take liberty to Oppress and wrong their neighbours, by taking excessive wages for their work, or unreasonable prizes, for such merchantizes or other necessary comodities, as shall pass from man to man*, It is Ordered, That if any man shall offend in any of the said cases, he shall be punished by *fine* or *imprisonment*, according to the quality of the offence, as the Court to which he is presented, upon lawfull tryall & conviction, shall adjudg. [1635]

Payments.

IT is by this Court Ordered and Declared, That all *contracts* and *engagements*, for *money, corn, cattle*, or *fish*, shall be satisfied in kind according to Covenant, or in defaulr of the very kind contracted for, in one of the said kinds, Provided that in such cases, where payment in kind is not made according to covenant; all just damage shall be satisfied (together with the debt for not paying in kind, according to bargaine; And in no case shall any Creditor, be forced to take any other commodities for satisfaction of his debt, unles it be according to his Contract, but it shall be lawfull for such Creditor to imprison the partie, till he make satisfaction according to Covenant, or to take upon execution such goods, houses or lands, as shall be to his satisfaction, any Law, Custom or usage to the contrary notwithstanding. [1654] A.54.p.5 Debts to be paid in the kind contract

Petitions.

IT is hereby Ordered, That all *Petitions to the General Court*, which are of a Common and ordinary nature, the petitioner shall pay on the delivery therof to the Secretary or Clerk *two shillings six-pence*, for each petition, and all petitions for abatement of fines, mitigation of penalties &c: shall pay unto the Clerke or Secretary as aforesaid, *ten shillings*, and all petitions for gratuities, or that concern Controversies between partie and partie, Town and Town, shall pay *ten shillings*, and all petitions for debts, or other controversies between partie and partie: brought from inferiour Courts, shall pay *ten shillings*, besides the charges of the Court, during the tryal of such cause. And henceforth no petition whatsoever, shall be received into the General Court, after the first four dayes of the Court of Election, nor after the first week of any other Session. Nevertheless it is hereby Ordered, That all such petitions, that concern any ingagement of the Country to any person, are hereby exempted; And that any Magistrate or Deputie of the Court, may present any petition, wherein his own personal right is concerned, without paiment, and that there shall be a true entry made, by the *Secretary* of the nūber of petitions, that shall be delivered to the Magistrates & the like account shall be kept by the Clerke of the deputies, of all petitions received by the deputies & al such fees, as are produced by such petitions, shall be Received or secured by the *Secretary* or *Clerke*, and discounted in part of their annual allowance [1648. 54.]

L.2.p.13 Paiment for entring petitions in the Gen: Court. A.54.p.1 Time of ent. Petitions exempt from payments Secretary & Clerk to secure ẏ pay

Whereas

Pipestaves.

Searchers of pipestaves

WHereas information hath come to this Court, from forreigne parts, of the insufficiency of our Pipestaves, especially in regard of worm-holes, whereby the Commodity is like to be prohibited in those parts to the great damage of the Country. It is therefore Ordered by this Court and the Authority thereof, that the select men of *Boston, Charlstown, Salem, Dover, Portsmouth, Kitterie*, & all other Townes in this Jurisdiction, where pipestaves use to be shipped, shall forthwith and so from time to time, as need shall Require, nominate two men of each Towne, skilful in the Commodity, and such as can attend the service, to be *veiwers of pipestaves*, who so chosen, shall by the Constable be convented before some Magistrate, to be sworne diligently and faithfully to veiw and search all such Pipestaves as are to be transported to any parts of *Spain, Portugall* or within either of their dominions, or elswhere to be used for making of tight Caske, who shall Cast by all such, as they shall Judg not Merchantable, both in respect of wormeholes, and *due Assize* viz: that are not in Lenght *four foot and halfe*, in bredth *three inches and halfe* without sap. in thicknes *three quarters of an inch* & not more or less then an eight part of an inch, then *three quarters thick*, well and even hewed and sufficient for use. And they or some one of them shall at all times upon request. give attendance, and they shall enter into a book the number of all such Merchantable pipestaves as they shall approve, and for whom. And if any man shall put aboard any ship or other vessel any pipestaves, other then shall be so searched and approved, to the end to be transported to any part of *Spain* or *Portugall*, except they should be shipped for dry Cask: he shall forfeit the same whole parcel or *the Value thereof*, and the sayd veiwers shall be allowed *two shillings* for every thousand of Pipestaves, which they shall so search as well the Refuse as the Merchantable, to be payd by him that sets them on work.

Sworne

Assize of pipestaves

Pipestaves shipt unsearched to be forfeit

Searchers allowed

And if any Master or other Officer of any Ship, or other vessell, shall receive into such ship or vessell, any parcel of Pipestaves, to be transported into any of the sayd dominions, which shall not be searched, and allowed as Merchantable, and so Certifyed by a note under the hand of one of the sayd veiwers, such Master shal forfeit for every thousand of pipestaves so unduely Received *five pounds*, except he can Procure one of the sayd Veiwers to come aboard and search such staves as they shall be delivered into the ship. Provided cast or Refuse staves or other red Oakstaves may be transported into those parts (which may be of good use for dry Cask) so as the same be Carried in distinct Parcels, & not intermixed with Merchantable staves. [1646.]

Masters of ship receivig unsearcht staves forfeit 5 pounds.

Dry Cask staves

Poor.

IT is Ordered by this Court and the Authority thereof. That any shire Court or any two magistrates out of Court, shall have power to determine all differēces about Lawfull setling and providing for *poor persons*: and shall have power to dispose of all unsetled Persons into such townes as they shall Judg to be most fitt for the maintenance & imployment of such persons and famylies, for the ease of this Country. [1639.

And for the avoiding of all future inconveniences referring to the settling of poor People that may need releife from the place where they dwell. It is Ordered by this Court and the Authority thereof. That where any person with his family or in Case he hath no family, shall be Resident in any town or peculiar of this Jurisdiction for more then three months without notice given to such person or persons by the Constable or one of the Select men of the said place, or their Order; That the Town is not willing that they should remain as an Inhabitant amongst them; And in Case after such notice given such person or persōs shall notwithstanding remain in the said place, if the Select men of the sayd place shall not by way of Complaint petition to the next County court of that shire for releife in the sayd Case and the same prosecuted to effect, every such person or persons (as the Case may require

Order ye settle poore.

may require) shall be provided for and Releived in case of necessity, by the Inhabitants of the said place, where he or shee is so found, and it is further Ordered, that each County Court shall from time to time, hear & determine all complaints of this nature and setle all poor persons according to directions of this Law in any town or peculiar within this Colony, and every such person or persons shall accordingly be entertained and Provided for by the Select men or Constable of the sayd place at a Town charge, and in case any Town or Peculiar shall find themselves agreived at such disposure of the County Court, they may appeal to the next Court of Assistants and where any person or persons cannot according to this Law be setled in any Town or Peculiar, they shall then be placed in any town of that County wherein they are found, according as the County Court shall appoint & their charges satisfied unto them by the County *Treasurer*.

Possession.

THE *Court taking into consideration the great neglect of many persons in the Infancy of these Plantations, to observe any due Order, or Legall course for the conformation of such sales and alienation of houses and lands, as have passed from man to man, which thing may severall wayes be of very evil consequence to posterity.* Doth therefore Order and hereby Enact, that any person or persons that hath either himselfe, or by his grantees or Assignes, before the Law made for direction about inheritances, bearing date *October the nineteenth, one Thousand six-hundred & fifty two*, possessed & occupied, as his or their own proper Right, in fee simple, any houses or Lands within this Jurisdiction, & shall so continue, whether in their own persons, their heires or Assignes or by any *other person or persons, from by, or under* them, without disturbance, lett, suit, or denyall Legally made, by having the claime of any person thereto, entred with the Recorder of the County where such houses or lands do ly, with the names of the person so claiming, & the quantity, bounds of the Lands or houses claimed, and such claime prosecuted to effect, within the tearme of *five yeares*, next after the *twentieth of this present May one Thousand six hundred & fifty seven*, every such Proprietor, their Heires and Assignes shall for ever after enjoy the same; without any Lawfull let, suit, disturbance, or denyall, by any after claime of any person or persons whatsoever, any law or Custome to the contrary notwithstanding, and for all bargaines or alienations made, or to be made, after the aforesaid time, that every Person concerned therein, observe the directions given in the above Recited Law, upon perill of suffering *all the damage*, that shall accrue to them, their Heires and Assignes by neglect thereof. [1657]

A.58.P. 22.

Title to Inheritances limited w^in five yeares.

Porters.

THERE *being a very great abuse in the Townes of Boston and Charlestown, by Porters, who many times do require and exact, more then is just and righteous for their Labours,* It is Ordered by this Court, That from henceforth the Select men of the said Townes, from time to time, shall have power to regulate in this case, and to *state their wages*, as in their understanding shall be most just, and equal, as also to determine what persons shall be imployed therin. [1655]

A.56.P. 10.

Porters to be ordered by ye Select men.

Pound, Pound-breach.

FOR *prevention, and due recompence of damages in Corn fields, and other inclosures, done by Swine and Cattle,* It is Ordered by this Court, and Authority thereof, That there shall be one *sufficient pound*, or more, made and maintained in every Town and village within this Jurisdiction, for the impounding of all such Swine and Cattle, as shall be found in any corn-field, or other inclosure. And who soever impounds any Swine or Cattle, shall give present notice to the owner, if he be known, or otherwise, they shall be Cryed at the two next Lectures or markets, and if Swine or cattle *escape out of pound*, the owner if known, shall pay all damages according to Law. And every person or persons, having notice given, or otherwise left in writing at their house, or place of their usuall abode, of any of their

Pound in every Town.

A.57.P. 24.

Catle impounded to be Replevied or damage satisfied

Cattle impounded or otherwise restrained, shall forthwith give satisfaction to the party so wronged, or otherwise Replevy their Cattle, and Prosecute the same according to Law, upon Perill of Suffering all the loss and Damage that shall Come to their Cattle, by standing in the Pound, or other Lawfull place of restraint. [1645. 47, 57.]

Rescues and pound breach fine, or bewhipped.

2 And if any person shall Resist, or Rescue any Cattle going to Pound, or shall by any way or meanes convey them out of Pound, or other Custody of the Law, whereby the party wronged may loose his damages, & the law be deluded, that in case of meer Rescues, the party so Offending, shall forfeit to the Treasury *forty shillings*. And in case of pound breach *five pound* & shall also pay all damages to the party wronged, and if in the Rescues, any bodily harme be done to the person of any man or other Creature they may have Remedy against the Rescuers, and if either be done by any not of Ability to answer the forfeiture and damages aforesayd, they shall be openly Whipped by warrant from any Magistrate, before whom the Offender is Convicted, in the Town or plantation where the Offence was committed, not exceeding *twenty stripes* for the meer Rescue or pound-breach; And for all damages to the party they shall satisfy by service as in case of theft. And if it appear there were any procurement of the owner of the Cattle thereunto, and that they were abetters therein, they shall pay forfeiture and damages, as if themselves had done it. [1647]

Powder.

A. 52. p. 3

Powder imported to be entred with the pub: Notary

WHERAS *by Favour of the Government in England, several quantities of Powder, and other Ammunition, are yearly Imported into this Jurisdiction, for our necessary use and defence. To the end, the favour we receive, may not bee abused, nor our selves deprived of the just and necessary use thereof,* It is hereby Ordered and Enacted, That all Merchants or others, that shall import into this Jurisdiction, either *powder, lead, bullets, shot,* or any *ammunition* whatsoever, shall give particular notice of the quantity thereof, to the *publick Notary,* upon the pain and penalty of *fourty pounds,* within *one month* after the landing of such goods, who is hereby enjoyned to take particular notice of the same, with the mark & number, and faithfully to enter the same in a book, and the names of the persons to whom they are sold, or into whose custody or power they are committed, that he may give account thereof, upon Oath to the *Governour, Deputy Governour,* or any of the *Councill* from time to time, and the said *Notary* is hereby prohibited upon the penalty of *one hundred pounds,* to grant Certificate to any Merchant or other, of any such goods but such as he shall have particular notice of, & entered as aforesaid. *And to the end this Order may be duely observed, and that no person may plead ignorance thereof,* It is hereby Ordered, That the Captain of the Castle, shall upon the arrivall of any ship or vessel, in the *Massachusets Bay* from any forreign parts, give notice of the Contents of this Order, to the Master or Merchant of any such vessels, and the Constables of all other Port townes in this jurisdiction, are hereby required to do the same

1651.

L. 1. p. 45

2. And it is further Ordered, That no Person (except for the defence of themselves and their vessels at Sea) shall transport any *Gunpowder* out of this jurisdiction, without License first obtained, from some two of the Magistrates, upon penalty of forfeiting all such powder, as shall be transporting or transported, or the value thereof;

Searchers for powder exporting

And that there may be no defect for want of an Officer to take care herein. This Court, the Court of Assistants, or any Shire Court, Shall appoint meet Persons, from time to time in all needfull places who have hereby power granted them, to search all persons & vessels, that are or any way shall be suspicious to them, to be breakers of this Order, and what they find in any Vessel or hands without licenses as aforesaid; to seize the same, and to keep the one half to their own use, in Recompence of their paines, and to deliver the other half forthwith unto the Treasurer. [1645, 51]

Prescriptions.

IT is Ordered, Decreed, and by this Court Declared, That no Custom or Prescription, shall ever prevaile amongst us in any moral Case, (our meaning is) to maintain any thing, that can be proved to be morally sinfull by the word of God. [1641]

Prisoners, Prison, House of Correction.

Prisoners caried at their own charge. A. 55. P. 10. House of correction in each County

IT is Ordered, that such Malefactors as are Comitted to any comon Prison, shall be conveyed thither at their own charge, if they be able, otherwise at the charge of the Country. [1646]

2. For *Prevention and Redress of many misdemeanours & evill practises, dayly increasing,* It is Ordered, That there shall be an house of Correction, provided in each County, at the Counties charge, to be setled, ordered and improved as the Magistrates in each County Court or Court of Assistants shall agree & direct. And

3. And it shall be in the Power of every County Court to make use of such *prison*, as is at present Erected in the County, for an *house of Correction*, till houses of *Correction* be provided and finished. Also to provide and Authorize the *keeper* or some *meet person*, to be *Master of such house* as they shall Judg meet and the Select men of the Town, where such house is appointed, shall procure in the most Prudent way, some Competent stock of *Hemp, flax*, or other *Matterials*, and upon account to Commit the same, into the hands of the *Master of the house*, to be imployed at his discretion by the Labour of such delinquents, as shall be Committed to him by Authority, and the stock being in Value or Kind *preserved*, to such as put in the same, all the benefit attained by the Labour of the person Committed, shall be to the use of the *Master*, allowing onely so much as will keep the delinquent, with necessary *bread* and *water*, or other mean food out of the same, or six pence out of the *shilling* earned by his or her Labour; And at the first coming into the House of *Correction*, the *Master* thereof, or any he shall procure, or the *common Correcton*, Residing in the Town, shall *whip* every delinquent not exceeding *ten stripes*, & after shall imploy him or her by duely stint,, and if the party be *stubborn disorderly* or *Idle* & not performe their task & that in good Condition, the Master shall *Correct them* or *abridg them of their food*, as the Cause shall Require, till they are brought to some meet Order; And it shall be in the power of one Magistrate to Commit *Idle persons*, or *stubborn persons* against such as have Authority over them *Runawates, common Drunkards, Pilferers, common night walkers*, & *wanton persons*, as tending to *uncleanes in speches or actions* &c: And it shall not be in the power of the Master to deliver out of the *house of Correction*, unles he hath a discharge or warrant under the hand of a Magistrate, and if the delinquent be Committed by the Court, not to be delivered but by Order of the Court, or under the hand of the greater part of the Members of the Court. [1046. 55. 57.]

A. 57. P. 25.

Co. Court to appoint a Master

Select men to provide materials to work.

Masters fees.

Delinquēt to be Correct. & kept to work

One Magist: may cōmit to ye house of Correction

Protestation. Contra Remonstrance.

IT is Ordered and by this Court Declared, that it is, and shall be, in the liberty of any *Member* or *Members of any Court, Councel or Civill assembly*, in cases of making and executing any Order, or that properly concerneth Religion, or any Cause Capitall, or *warrs*, or *subscriptions to any publick Article* or *Remonstrance*, in Case they cannot in Judgment and Conscience Consent to that way the *Major vote* or suffrage goes, to make their *Contra Remonstrance* or *Protestation in speech or Writing*, & upon their Request, to have their disent Recorded in the Rols of that Court, so it be done *Christianly* & *respectively* for the manner, and the disent onely be entred wihtout the reasons thereof for avoiding tediousnes. [1641.]

Liberty to enter a dissēt in cases in Court.

Punishment, Torture.

IT is Ordered, and by this Court Declared that no man shall be *twice sentenced* by Civil Justice, for one & the same *Crime Offence* or *Trespass, and for bodily punishments*, we allow amongst us none that are inhumane, *barbarous or Cruel*. And no man shall be beaten with above *fourty stripes for one fact at one time*, nor shall any man be punished with *whipping*, except he have not otherwise to answer the Law, unless his Crime be very shamefull, & his course of Life *Vitious and profligate*. And no man shall be forced by *Torture to confess any crime against himselfe or any other*, unless it be in some capitall case, where he is first fully Convicted by clear & sufficient evidence to be guilty, after which if the case be of that nature, that it is very apparent, there be other *conspirators or confederates* with him, then he may be *Tortured*, yet not with such *Tortures* as are *barbarous & inhumane*.

None punished twice for one offence.

L. 1. P. 50

Not above 40 stripes

No torture before conviction.

Records. Recorders Clerks.

VVHERAS *Records of the Evidence, whereupon the Verdict and Judgment in cases doth pass, being duely entred and kept, would be of good use, both for presidents, & to such as shall have Just cause to have their cases reveiwed.* It is therefore Ordered by this Court and the Authority thereof. That every *Judgment* given

A:52p13 L:p.15. Evidence to be given in writing. To be kept on file.

given in any Court, or by one Magistrate, or by Commissioners, shall be *Recorded in .. book* and all the evidences, (which are to be given in, in writing, in fair and large papers,) shall be kept, and the party for whom such evidence is brought, shall pay to the *Recorder* or *Clerke* of the Court for *filing & safe keeping the same, twopence* fore. eh evidence, and the fore-man of every jury, shall faithfully deliver up all such Testimonie, or other Writings Cōmitted to them, unto the *Recorder* or *Clerk* of the Court, when they give in their Verdict in every Case, And the fees of the *Recorder* or *Clerk of every* County Court shall be as followeth, for *Transcribing a coppy* of any evidence for every page consisting of *eight and twenty or thirty lines, eight words* in a Line *twelve-pence*, and proportionable to *eight pence* a page for what it doth exceed, for entry of a *mortgage or sale of houses* or *Lands verbatim*, not exceeding a page as aforesayd *twelve pence*, and proportinable to *eightpence* a page for what it doth exceed, and for attesting the *Record on the Originall deed, six-pence*, and in like manner for *Wils & inventories*, with *sixpence* a peece, for filing up the Originall & safe keeping thereof, and for entring an Order for the determining of an estate of such as dyed intestate, or other, wherein the Court is to give their approbation or determination *twelve pence*, & for entry of the *examination & proceedings of this Court* in any criminal cases or *presentment*, with the Judgment of the Court therein *two shillings & six pence*, and for entry of a Recognizance *twelve pence*, to be payd or secured in Court by the delinquent party, & for entring a *Judgment* acknowledged *twelve-pence*, and for Entry of an Action *One shilling Six Pence*, and a judgment thereupon, *Six Pence*, and for making an Execution *Two Shillings*.

A:57:p21. Recorders fees.

L:2:p:7.

2. It is Ordered, that the Clerk of the Writs in the several Towns, shall Record all *Births & Deaths* of persons in their Towns, and for every *Birth and Death* they so *Record*, they shall be allowed *Three-pence*, and they shall yearly deliver in to the *Recorder of the* Court, of the Jurisdiction where they live: a true *Transcript thereof* together with so many *pence as* there are *Births or Deaths* to be *Recorded*. And all *Parents, Masters of servants, Executors or Administrators* respectively, shall bring into the Clerk *of the Writs* in their Several Townes, the names of such persons belonging to them or any of them, as shall either be borne or dye. And also every new *Married Man*, shall likewise bring a *Certificate* under the hand of the Magistrate which Marryed him, unto the sayd Clerke to be by him Recorded, who shall be allowed *three pence for the same*, and the sayd Clerk shall deliver as aforesayd, unto the Recorder a Certificate with a *penny* a name for Recording the sayd *Marriage*. And if any person shall neglect to bring a note or certificate as aforesaid, together with *three pence a name*, to the said *Clerk of the Writs* to be *Recorded*, more then one month after such *Birth, Death, or Marriage*, he shall pay *twelve pence* to the sayd Clerk, who shall demand the same. and in case any shall Refuse to satisfy him, he shall then Returne the name of such person or persons, to the next Magistrate, or Cōmissioners, of the Town where such person dwels, who shall fine for the partie so Refusing, and in case he shall stil persist therein, shall give Order to the Constable to Levy the same, and if any Clerk *of the writs*, shall neglect his duty hereby enjoyned he shall pay the follwing penalties; *viz*: for neglecting a yearly Return to the County Court, *five Pound*, and for neglect of Returning the name of any person Returnable, by this Order, whether *Borne, Marryed or Dead* more then *thirty dayes* before his Return to the County Court, *five shillings*, and that no neglect may be herein for the *future*, the Clerk of each County Court, is hereby enjoyned from time to time, to certify the County Courts Respectively, the names of all such *Clerkes of the writts* who shall neglect to make their Yearly Returne, according to this law, who upon such notice given, shall send for such clerks and doe in the case as the law Requireth.

Birth, Death Marriages.

Parents Masters, &c. to certify the Clerke.

Penalty of not certifiing

A 54:P: 24.

Clerk to return al births deaths &c. to ye County Court.

L.1.P.47

3. It is Ordered and Declared, that every man shall have liberty to *Record in the publick*

the publick Rolls, of any Court, any Testimony given upon Oath, in the same Court or before two Magistrates, or any deed or evidence Legally Concerned, there to remain *in perpetuam rei memoriam*. And that every Inhabitant of the Country, shall have free liberty to search & veiw any *Rolls, Records, or Registers*, of any Court or Office, except of the Councell, and to have a transcript or Exemplification thereof written, examined and signed by the hand of the Officer, paying the accustomed fees; And if any person or persons repairing to any publick Officer of this Jurisdiction, to veiw any *Record* or *Writings* committed to his Charge, shall Wittingly and Willingly deface or *rent* any such *Record* or *Writing*, upon Complaint of such Officer to any Magistrate, and proof by Oath of the said Officer, or other sufficient Witnes, every person so Offending, shall forfeit by the party concerned therein, *treble the damage* that might have ensued, or accrued to him or them, thereby, & shall also be fined as much to the Country, or suffer *two months imprisonment* without Baile or main-prise, or stand in the Pillory two houres in Boston Market with a paper over his head written in Capitall Letters *A DEFACER OF RECORDS*, the speciall or particular Punishment to be determined by the next County Court where the Offence was Committed, and shall also stand Bound to the *Good behaviour* during the pleasure of the Court. [1639. 42. 43. 44. 47. 52. 57. Liberty to record Testimonies and evidence to veiw publick records. A: 52: p: 9 penalty of defacing records.

Repievin.

IT is Ordered and by this Court Declared, That every man shall have liberty to Replevie his Cattle or goods impounded, distreined, seized or extended, unless it be upon execution after Judgment & in payment of fines. Provided he puts in good security to prosecute the *replevin*, & to satisfy such demand, as his adversary shall recover against him in Law. [1641.]

Sabbath.

UPON *information of sundry Abuses and Misdmeanours Committed by divers Persons on the Lordsday, not onely by Children playing in the streets, and other places, but by Youths, Mayds, and other persons, both strangers and others, uncivilly walking in the streets and fields, travailing from town to town, going on Ship-board, frequenting common houses, and other places to drink, Sport, or otherwise to mispend that precious time, which thing tends much to the dishonour of God, the Reproach of of Religion, greiving the soules of Gods servants, and the Prophanation of his holy Sabbath, the Santification whereof, is sometimes put for all duties, immediately respecting the Service of God conteined in the first Table.* A: 53: p: 18. It is therefore Ordered by this Court and the Authority thereof, That no *Children, Youths, Mayds* or other *Persons*, shall Transgress in the like kind on penalty of being Reputed *great provokers of the high displeasure of the Almighty GOD*, and further incurr the penalty hereafter expressed, *viz.* That the Parents and Governours of all Children above seven yeares old, (not that we approve younger Children in evill) for the first offence in that kind, upon due proof before any Magistrate, Commissioner or Select man of the Town, where such offence shall be commited, shall be *admonished*; for a second offence upon due proof as aforesaid, shall pay as a fine *five shillings*, and for a third offence upon due proof as aforesaid, *ten shillings*; and if they shall again offend in that kind, they shall be presented to the County Court, who shall augment punishment according to the merit of the fact. And for all youths and mayds above fourteen yeares old, and all elder persons whatsoever, that shall offend, and be convict as aforesaid, either for *playing, uncivel walking, drinking, travailing* from Town to Town, *going on shipboard, sporting*, or any way *mispending* that presious time, shall for the first Offence be *Admonished*, upon due proof as aforesayd; for a second Offence shall pay as a fine *five shillings*, & for the third offence *ten shillings*. and if any shall further Offend that way, they shall be bound over to the next County Court, who shall *augment punishment* according to the nature of the Offence, and if any be unable or unwilling to pay the aforesaid fines, they shall be whiped by the Cōstable Prophaness of the Sabbath. Penalty.

 not exceeding

not exceeding *Five Stripes*, for *Ten Shillings* fine and this to be understood of such Offences, as shall be Committed, during the Day Light of the Lords Day. [1653.]

A. 52. 2. *VVhereas by too sad Experience, it is observed, the Sun being set, both every Saturday, and on the Lords Day, young people and others take Liberty to walk & Sport themselves in the streets or fields in the severall Townes of this Jurisdiction, to the dishonour of God and the disturbance of others in their Religious exercises, and too frequently repair to publick houses of entertainment and there sit Drinking, all which tends not onely to the hindring of due preparation for the Sabbath, but as much as in them lyeth, renders the Ordinances of God unprofitable, and threatens the rooting out of the Power of Godlines, and procuring the wrath & Judgment of God upon us & our posterity for prevention whereof.* It is Ordered by this Court and the Authority thereof, That if any person or persons henceforth, either on the Saturday night, or on the Lords day night, after the Sun is set, shall be found sporting in the streets or fields of any town in this Jurisdiction, Drinking, or being in any house of publick entertainment (unless strangers or Sojourners in their Lodgings) and cannot give a satisfactory Reason to such Magistrate or Comissioner, in the severall Towns, as shall have the Cognizance thereof. Every such Person so found Complained of and Prooved Transgressing, shall pay *Five shillings* for every such Transgression or Suffer *Corporall Punishment*, as Authority Aforesayd shall Determine. [1658.]

Drinking in Ordinaries after Sun set

Penalty.

Sailers.

L.2.P.14 *VVHEREAS many Miscarriages are Committed by Sailers, by their immoderate Drinking and other vain expences in Ordinaries, which oftentimes occasions prejudice and damage to the Masters and Owners of the vessels, to which they belong, their men being oftentimes arrested for debts so made when their ships are ready to set sayle, for prevention whereof.* It is Ordered by this Court and the Authority thereof. That no Inkeeper, Victualer, or other seller of Wine, Beer or strong Liquors, shall after publication hereof, arrest, attach, or Recover by Law any Debt, or debts so made by any Sayler or Saylers as aforesayd, except the Master or owner of such Ship or Vessell, to whom such Sailers Belongs, have given under his hand to discharge the same, any Law, use or Custome to the Contrary not withstanding.

Salt.

UPON information given to this Court, of great damage accrewing both to Merchants and others, by reason no meet persons are appointed for to Measure Salt from such ships as Arrive in our severall Harbours. This Court Doth therefore Order & Enact That there shall be in every Maritine town within this Jurisdiction one meet person appointed by the Town from time to time who shall diligently attend this service upon due notice given by either party concerned therein, & the same truely and faithfully to discharge, for which he shall be allowed *three halfe pence* for every hogshead, the one halfe to be paid by the buyer, & the other halfe by the Seller, and what Master of Ship or other Vessels, or Merchant shall fail in the observation of this Order, he or they shall forfeit to the Country *two shillings* for every *tunn* so disposed of, unless the parties shall otherwise agree.

Salt to be measured.

Scholes.

IT being one chief project of Sathan to keep Men from the knowledg of the Scripture, as in former times keeping them in unknown tongues, so in these Latter times by perswading from the use of tongues that so at least the true sence and meaning of the Originall might be Clouded and Corrupted with false glosses of deceivers, to the end therefore that learning may not be Buried in the graves of our forefathers in Church & Commonwealth, the Lord assisting our endeavours. It is therefore Ordered by this Court and Authority thereof. That, every Township in this Jurisdiction, after

Schooles in Townes of 50 families.

after the Lord hath increased them to the number of *fifty house-holders*, shall then forth with appoint one within their towns, to teach all such Children as shall resort to him to Write & Read, whose Wages shall be payd, either by the Parents or Masters of such Children or by the inhabitants in generall, by way of supply as the major part of those that Order the prudentials of the town shall appoint. Provided that those which send their Children be not Oppresed by Paying much more, then they can have them taught for in other townes. How maintained.

2 And it is further Ordered, that where any town shall increase to the number of *one hundred families or house-holders*, they shall set up *a Grammer school*, the Master thereof, being able to instruct youth so far as they may be fitted for the Uneversety. And if any town neglect the performance hereof. above one year, then every such town shall pay *five pounds per annum* to the next such School, till they shall performe this Order. Grammer schools. Towns neglecting to pay 5 pound per anu to ẏ next schoole.

3. *Forasmuch as it greatly Concernes the welfare of the Country, that the youth thereof be educated not only in good Literature, but in sound Doctrine.* This Court doth Therefore Commend it to the serious Consideration, & special care of our Overseers of the Colledg, & the Select men in the several townes, not to admit or suffer any such to be continued in the Office or place of teaching, educating or instructing youth or children, in the Colledg or Schools, that have manifested theselves *unsound in the faith*, or *scandalous in their lives* & have not given satisfaction according to the Rules of Christ. A 54: p. 1 Heterodox Schoole Mrs not to be allowed.

Sheep.

WHEREAS *the keeping of Sheep, tends much to the benefit of the Country, & may in short time make good supply towards the cloathing of the Inhabitants, if Carefully preserved, and forasmuch as all places are not fit and Convenient for that end.* It is Ordered by this Court, That henceforth it shall be Lawfull, for any man to keep sheep, on any Common, be it for Cowes, Oxen or otherwise belonging to the Town, where he lives, or where at that time he may have Right of Common, & that without limitation, in cōmons not stinted, and in such cōmons that are stinted it shall be lawfull for any Inhabitant, to use any or all his proportion of Cōmon for sheep, acounting five sheep for one cow, steer or ox, & further it shall be lawful for the Select men of every Town from time to time, to make such Orders in their respective towns for the clearing of their cōmons of wood & brush for keeping of sheep, as also for the fines of putting rams to their flocks, as they shall judg meet. L: 2: p: 14 Liberty to keep sheepe on all cōmōs 5 sheep for one cowe. A 55 p: 12 Select men to order clearing of cōmō for sheeps pasture.

2. It is further Ordered, That if any man shall course sheep with a dog, or otherwise molest them, by driving them from their feeding, he shall pay *five shillings* for every such Offence, besides double damages, and if any dog shall kill any sheep, the owner shall either hang such dog, or pay double damages for the sheep, and if any dog hath been seen to Course or bite sheep before, not being set on, and his owner hath had notice thereof, then he shall both Hang his Dog, and pay for such sheep, as he shall either Bite or Kill, and if in such case he shall refuse to hang his dog, then the Constable of the town, upon notice thereof, shall forthwith cause it to be done. Dogs killing sheep to be hanged.

3. It is further Ordered, that all owners of sheep, who shall put their wooll to Sale, shall and hereby are enjoyned, yearly to wash their sheep, in clear water, not being either Salt, brackish or dirty, and shall take care, they be not kept in dirty or Sandy ground, between the time of Washing and Shearing, and in making up the fleeces to take care no short Locks, Lumps of dirt, or course tailes be wound up therein, upon the penalty of forfeiture of *twelve pence* a sheep for all & every defect aforesaid. [1648. 53. 56] A 53: p: 18 Sheep to be washed before shorne wool to be made up cleane

Ships, Ship-Carpenters.

WHERAS *the Building of ships is a busines of great importance, for the Common good, and therefore sutable care ought to be taken, that it be wel performed,* according

according to the Commendable course of England and other places. It is therefore Ordered by this Court and the Authority thereof. That when any ship is to be Built, within this jurisdiction, or any Vessell above thirty Tunns, the owner or builder in his absence, shall before they begin to planke, Repair to the *Governour* or *Deputy Governour* or any two *Magistrates*, upon the penalty of *ten Pounds*, who shall appoint some able man to Survey the *Work* and Workmen from time to time, as is usuall in England, and the same so appointed shall have such Liberty and power as belongs to his office: And if any Ship-Carpenter shall not upon his advice, Reforme and amend any thing which he shall find to be amiss, then upon Complaint to the *Governour* or *Deputy Governour* or any two *Magistrates*, they shall appoint two of the most sufficient Ship Carpenters of this Jurisdiction, and shall Authorize them from time to time, as need shall Require to take veiw of every such ship and all Works thereto belonging, and to see that it be Performed and carryed on according to the Rules of their art. And for this end an oath shall be Administred to them to be faithful and indifferent, between the owner and the work man, and their Charges shall be born by such as shall be found in default; And those Veiwers shall have Power to cause any bad Timbers, or other insufficient work or Materials, to be taken out and amended at the Charge of them through whose default it growes. [1641. 47.]

Surveyers appointed to view all ships in building.

Their power

Oath

Charges.

2. It is Ordered by the Authority of this Court, that all ships which come for Trading onely, from other parts, shall have free access into our Harbours, and quiet Riding there, and free Liberty to depart without any Molestation by us, they paying all such duties and Charges required by Law in the Country, as others do. [1645.]

Freedom of trade for forreign ships.

Spinning.

A. 55. P. 11.

THIS Court *taking into serious Consideration, the present Streights and necessities of the Country in respect of Cloathing, which is not like to be so plentifully supplyed from forreign parts, as in times past, and not knowing any better way or Meanes Conduceable to our subsistence, then the improoving of as many hands as may be, in Spinning Wool, Cotton, Flax &c:* Doth therefore Order and be it Ordered by the Authority of this Court. That all hands not necessarily Imployed on other occasions, as Women, Girls, and Boyes, shall and hereby are enjoyned to *Spin* according to their skill and ability, and that the Select men in every town, do consider the condition & capacity of every family, and accordingly do assess them at one or more spinners, *And because several Families are necessarily imployed the greatest part of their time, in other business, yet if opportunities were attended, some time might be spared at least by some of them for this work,* The said Select Men, shall therefore asses such families at halfe, and quarter *Spinners* according to their Capacities. And every one thus aforesaid for a whole *Spinner*, shall for time to come, *Spin* every year, for thirty weeks, *three pound a week* of *Linnen Cotton* or *Woollen* and so proportionably for *halfe & quarter Spinners*, under the penalty of *Twelve pence* a pound Short And the Select Men shall take speciall Care for the execution of the Order, which may easily be effected by dividing their Severall Townes into *Ten*, *Six*, *Five*, &c parts, and to appoint one of the *ten, six or five* &c to take an account of their divisions, and to certify the Select Men, if any be defective in what they are assessed, who shall improve the Penalties imposed in such as are negligent, for the incouragement of those that are diligent in this work. [1655.]

Select men to appoint how much each family shal spin

Strayes.

IT is Ordered by this Court and the Authority thereof. That whosoever shall take up any *Stray Beast*, or find any *goods lost*, whereof the owner is not known he shall give notice thereof to the Constable of the same Town, within *six dayes*, who shall enter the same in a book and take Order that it be Cryed at their next

Finders of goods to give notice to the Constable to cry.

Lecture

Lecture or generall Town-meeting, upon three severall dayes; And if it be above *twenty shillings Value*, at the next Market, or two next townes publick Meeting, where no *Market* is within *ten Miles*, upon pain that the party so finding, and the said Constable having such notice, and failing to do, as is here appointed, to forfeit either of them for such default, *one third part* of the value of such Stray or *lost goods*: And if the finder shall not give notice as aforesayd within one Month, or if he keep it more then Three Months, & shall not apprize it, by Indifferent men, and also Record it, with the Recorder of the *County Court* where it is found, he shall then forfeit the full value thereof. And if the owner appeareth within *one year*, after such publication, he shall have Restitution of the same, or the value thereof, paying all necessary charges, and to the Constable for his care and paines, as one of the next Magistrates, or the three Comissioners of the Town shall adjudg. And if no owner appear within the time prefixed, the said stray or lost goods, shall be to the use of the finder, paying to the Constable *ten shillings*, or the *fifth part* of the value, of such stray or lost goods, at the finders choise.

Find[illegible] to apprize and Record lost goods.

Restore the goods if the owner appear in a year

And it is Ordered, That every such finder shall put & keep from time to time a *wyth* or *wreath* about the neck of every such *stray beast*, within *one month* after such finding, upon penalty of loosing all his charges, that shall arise about it afterwards, (provided that no person shall from the *first of Aprill* to the *twentieth of December*, take up any horse, gelding or mare, for a stray, or account or use them as strayes, though the owner therof be not known, unless it be taken *damage faisant*, in inclosures) Provided also that if any owner or other, shall take off such *wyth or wreath*, or take away such beast, before he hath discharged according to this Order, he shall forfeit the full value of the thing (apprized as aforesaid) to the use of the finder. [1647]

Stray beasts to have a wyth about the neck.

Taking off y wyth or taking away y beast forfeit the value.

Strangers.

VV*Hereas we are credibly Informed, that great mischiefs have been done to other Plantations, by the resort of Commanders, Souldiers and other strangers, to prevent the like in this Jurisdiction*, It is Ordered by this Court and Authority thereof, That henceforth all Strangers of what quality soever, above the age of *sixteen yeares*, arriving in any *Ports* or parts of this Jurisdiction, in any ship or vessel, shall immediately be brought before the Governour, Deputy Governour or two other Magistrates, by the Master or Mate of the said ship or vessel, upon penalty of *twenty pound* for default thereof, there to give an account of their occasions, and busines in this Country, whereby satisfaction may be given, and order taken, with such strangers, as the said Governour, Deputy Governour, two Magistrates, or the next County Court shall see meet; who shall keep a Record of the names and qualities of all such strangers, to be Returned to the next Generall Court, *and for the publication of this Order*. It is Ordered the same be posted upon the doors or posts of the Meeting houses, & other publick places in all the port townes, of this Jurisdiction. And the Captain of the Castle, shall make known this Order to every Ship or Vessel as it passeth by, and the Constable of every port Town shall endeavour to do the like, to such ships or vessels, before they Land their Passengers. [1651]

A.51.p7

Strangers arriving to be brought before y Governour.

Capt. of the Castle to give notice of this Order.

And if any strangers or people of other nations, professing the true Christian Religion, shall fly to us, from the tyranny or oppression of their persecutors, or from famine, warrs or the like necessary & Compulsory Cause, they shall be entertained & succoured amongst us according to that power & prudence God shall give us [1641]

L.1.p.23

Strangers to be succourd

Every person within this Jurisdiction, whether Inhabitant or stranger, shall enjoy the same Law and Justice, that is generall for this Jurisdiction, which we constitute & execute one towards another in all Cases proper to our Cognizance without partiality or delay [1641.] No town or person shall receive any stranger Resorting hither with intent to Reside in this Jurisdiction, nor shall allow any Lot or Habitation to any or entertain any such above three Weeks, except such person shall have allowance, under the hand of some one Magistrate, upon Pain of

L:2 p:32

Strangers to have equal justice.

every Town, that ſhall give or ſell, any Lot or habitation, to any not ſo Licenſed, ſuch fine to the Country, as the County Court ſhall impoſe, not exceeding *fifty pounds* nor leſs then *ten pounds*; and of every perſon receiving any ſuch for longer time then is hereby allowed, except in caſe of *entertainment of friends*, reſorting from other parts of this Country in amity with us, to forfeit as aforeſaid, not exceeding *twenty pounds* nor leſs then *four pounds*, and for every month after ſo offending, ſhall forfeit as aforeſaid, not exceeding *ten pounds*, nor leſs then *fourty ſhillings*. And every Conſtable ſhall enform the Courts, of all new commers, which they know to be admitted without License from time to time. [1637, 38, 47]

No town or perſon to entertain ſtrangers w'out allowance.

Finable.

Suretyes, and goods Attached.

L.1.p.15

UPON *information of ſome inconveniencies accruing to ſeveral perſons, in that men take themſelves acquitted & free from all Legal obſervations, in caſe of appearance in Courts, according to the expreſs termes of the Bond, or at moſt if the principall there ſtay till verdict and Judgment be given (which if they be) they may then make away their eſtates, or abſent their perſons before the twelve houres be expired for granting execution, whereby the party Recovering may either be deprived of, or much dammaged in his juſt Rights.* It is therefore Ordered by this Court and the Authority thereof. That henceforth all goods attached upon any Action, ſhall not be releaſed upon the appearance of the party, or judgment given, but ſhall ſtand ingaged until the judgment, or the execution granted upon the ſaid judgment be diſcharged, nor ſhall any ſurety or ſuretyes for appearance in any Court, except in Capital or Criminal caſes, be releaſed from his or their bond, untill the execution as aforeſaid be diſcharged & ſatisfied, or the principal perſon be ſurrendred into the hands of the Marſhal or his deputy, who ſhall ſecure him till the judgment be diſcharged, any Law, Cuſtom or uſage to the contrary notwithſtanding. Provided alwayes, that henceforth in all Civil proceedings (except in caſes where the Defendant is a ſtranger) where Execution is not taken out & executed within one month, after that judgment is granted, all ſuch Attachments, whether on perſons or eſtates, with ſuretyes, ſhall be releaſed & void in Law, any Law, uſage or cuſtom to the contrary notwithſtanding, unleſs the Court that granted the judgment ſhall ſee cauſe to give further time and reſpit of Execution in any particular caſe.

Not diſcharged till the judgment be ſatisfied.

Or ye perſon delivered to ye Marſhall.

Goods and perſons attached one month after judgment releaſed.

Swearing & Curſing.

Swearing ten ſhillings

Or ſit in the ſtocks

IT is Ordered by this Court & Authority thereof, That if any perſon within this Juriſdiction, ſhall *Swear raſhly & vainly, by the Holy name of God*, or *other Oath*, he ſhall forfeit to the cōmon Treaſury for every ſuch offence *ten ſhillings*, and it ſhall be in the power of any Magiſtrate by warrant to the Conſtable, to *call ſuch perſon before him*, and upon ſufficient proof, to *ſentence ſuch offender*, and to give order to *levy the fine*, and if ſuch perſon be not able, or ſhall refuſe to pay the ſaid fine, he ſhall be *committed to the ſtocks*, there to continue not exceeding *three houres*, nor leſs then *one houre*.

L.2.p.14

More Oaths then one 20 s.

Like penalty for curſing.

2. And if any perſon ſhall *ſwear* more Oaths then *one at a time*, before he remove out of the room or company where he ſo ſweares, he ſhall then pay *twenty ſhillings*. The like penalty ſhall be inflicted for *prophane and wicked Curſing*, of any perſon or creature, and for the multiplying the ſame, as is appointed for *prophane ſwearing*, and in caſe any perſon ſo offending, by *multiplying oaths* or *curſing*, ſhall not pay his or their fines forthwith, they ſhall be *whipt* or *committed to priſon*, till they ſhall pay the ſame, at the diſcretion of the Court or Magiſtrate, that ſhall have Cognizance thereof.

Swine.

Select men to make Orders to prevent harmes by Swine.

An. 1658.

IT is Ordered by this Court and Authority thereof, That every *Town-ſhip* within this Juriſdiction, or the *Select men thereof*, are impowered and hereby required, from time to time, to make Orders, for preventing all harmes by Swine, in Corn, Meddowes, Paſtures & Gardens, as alſo all danger to Children or Elder perſons, in any reſpect by Swine, and to impoſe penaltyes according to their beſt diſcretion, and to appoint one of their Inhabitants, by warrant under the hands of the Select men, or the Conſtable, where no Select men are, to levy all ſuch fines and penalties, and if any perſon choſen to ſee the execution of this Order, ſhall neglect or refuſe the ſame, he ſhall forfeit five pounds, the one half to the Town, the other half to the party that accepts the place, and performes his duty therein.

2 And

2. *And where Townes border each upon other, whose Orders it may be are various,* Satisfaction shall be made for harmes done by Swine, according to the Orders of the towne, where the damage is done. But if the swine be ringed and yoaked, or otherwise as the Orders of the Towne, to which they belong doth Require, then where no fence is, or that it be insufficient, through which the Swine come to trespass, the owner of Land or fence shall beare all damages; And it is hereby declared, that all fences made of *Stone, Pales, Railes, Rivers, Creeks,* or *any other fences which are allowed* (by such men as are appointed in the several towns to veiw fences) to be sufficient against great Cattle, shall be held and accounted sufficient against Swine; & all Swine breaking through such fences, shall be liable to make satisfaction for all damages done.

Damage to be paid according to town orders where it is done.

No fence no damage

A. 51. p. 4

Fences sufficient

3 And if any Swine be impounded for damage done, and there be kept *three dayes,* & that no person will own them, then the party Damnified shall give notice to the two next townes (where any are within five miles Compass) that such Swine are to be sold by an *out-cry*, within three dayes after such notice by the party damnified, and in case none will buy, he shall cause them to be apprized by two indifferent men (one whereof shall be the Constable or one chosen by him) signifyed under their hands in writing, and may keep them for his own use, And in both cases, if the owner shall after appear, the overplus according to the said valuation (all damages and charges being paid) shall forthwith be Rendred to him, and if any Town or Select men shall neglect to take order for preventing harmes by Swine according to this law, more then *one Month*, after publication hereof, such town or Select Men shall forfeit to the Treasury *forty shillings* for every Month so neglecting. [1647. 51. 58.]

No owners appearing, Swine to be prized.

Tile-Earth.

IT is Ordered by this Court, That all *Tile-Earth* to make sale ware, shall be digged before the *first of the Ninth Month*, and turned over in the *Last and First Month* ensuing, a Month before it be Wrought, upon pain of forfeiting *one halfe part* of all such Tiles, as shall be otherwise made to the use of the Common Treasury. [1647.]

Tobacco.

IT is Ordered by this Court, that no man shall take any *Tobacco* within *Twenty poles of any house,* or so neer as may indanger the same or neer any Barn, Corne, or Hay Cock, as may Occasion the firing thereof, upon pain of *ten shillings* for every such Offence, besides full Recompence of all damages done by meanes thereof; Nor shall any take *Tobacco* in any *Inne or Common Victuall house*, except in a private Room there, so as neither the Master of the sayd house, nor any other guest there, shall take Offence thereat, which if any do, then such person shall forthwith forbeare upon Paine of *Two shillings six pence*, for every such Offence. And all fines Incurred by this Law, the One Halfe part shall be to the Informer, the other to the Poor of the Town where the Offence is done. [1638 47.]

Town-ship.

L. 2. p. 10

VVHEREAS *Particular Townes have many things, which concerne onely themselves and the Ordering their own affaires, and disposing of busines in their own Town.* It is therefore Ordered, that the *freemen of every town*, with such others as are allowed, or the Major part of them, shall have power to dispose of their own Lands & woods, with all the *Priviledges* and *appurtenances* of the said Townes, to grant Lots, & also to chuse their own Particular Officers, as *Constables, Serveyors* for the High-wayes, and the like annually or otherwise as need Requires; And to make such Lawes and Constitutions as may Concerne the Welfare of their Town. Provided they be not of a Criminall, but of a prudentiall Nature, & that their penalties exceed not twenty *shillings* for one Offence, and that they be not Repugnant to the publick Lawes and Orders of the Country, And if any Inhabitant shall neglect or refuse

Towns power to dispose lands

Choose Officers

To make orders

or Refuse to observe them, they shall have power to Levy the appointed penalty by distress: And if any man shall behave himselfe Offensively, at any *town-meeting*, the rest then present, shall have power to sentence him for such offence, so as the penalty exceed not *twenty shillings*.

To choose Select men. 2. And every Township hath power to chuse yearly or for less time, a convenient number of fit men to order the planting & prudential affaires of their Townes according to instruction given them in writing, provided nothing be done by them, contrary to the Laws & orders of the Country, provided also that the number of the Select men be not above *nine*.

To dispose of single persons. 3. And all townes shall take care from time to time, to Order and dispose all single Persons, & in-mates within there Townes, to service or otherwise, and if any be greived at such Order or disposall, they have Liberty to appeale to the next *County Court*.

A. 58. Who may vote in Townes. 4. And it is hereby Ordered and Enacted. That all Englishmen, that are setled Inhabitants and house-holders in any town, of the age of *twenty four yeares*, and of honest & good Conversations, being Rated at *twenty pound* estate in a single Country Rate; and that have taken the *Oath of Fidelity* to this Government, and no other (except freemen) may be Chosen Select men, *Jurers or Constables*, and have their vote, in the Choice of the Select men for the Town Affairs, Assesments of Rates and other Prudentials Proper to the Town, Provided alwayes the *Major Part* of the Companyes of Select men, be freemen from time to time, that shall make a valid Act, as also where no Select men are, to have their vote in ordering schooles, hearding of cattle, laying out highwayes, and distributing Lands, any law, use or custome to the contrary not withstanding.

A. 53. P. 18. Power to fine such as refuse the office of Constable. 5. *VVhereas Complaints have been made, that many (especially in Boston) who are meet and fit to serve the Country, in the Office of Constable, take incouragement to with-draw from that service by Reason of the Smallnes of the fines that townes have power to impose for such Refusall,* It is therefore Ordered, that henceforth it shall be Lawful for the town of *Boston* to impose the fine of *ten Pounds*, and for all other Townes, to impose the fine of *five pounds* upon every such person, (being Legally Chosen in the Respective townes) that shall Refuse to serve in the Office of a Constable in the Town where he is Chosen, if in his person he be able to execute it; And the Select men of every town are hereby impowered to order & Require the Constables to Levy the said fines by distress, which shall be to the use of the town. [30, 42, 47, 53, 58.]

Treasurers.

To keep perfect accounts. How to disburse. IT is Ordered by this Court and the Authority thereof. That the Country *Treasurer*, shall from time to time, keep exact and perfect books of accounts of all Transactions for the Country, and particularly of all debts and dues, belonging to the Country, either by *forfeits, fines, rates, gifts, legacies, rents, custom, impositions* or otherwise, as by *Whales, Shipwracks*, and things of like nature, where the owner is not known, and the Country may claim a priviledg or common right unto; as also of all his payments and disbursements for the Countryes use, which he shall not make, but by vertue of some setled Custom, Law or Order of this Court, or by special Order of this Court, or of the Council, nor shall he make any paiment to any person indebted to the Country, till such person either pay his debt or defaulke, so much as is due to the Country.

A. 54. p. 2. Count. Treas. How chosen. No Clerk of Court to be Treasurer. 2. And it is further Ordered, That henceforth there shall be *Treasurers* annually chosen in every County, by the freemen thereof, who shall give in their votes in each Town on the day of voting for nomination of Magistrates, which shall be sent sealed up, by the same person to the *Shire meeting*, and there opened before the Commissioners, who shall certifie the County Courts, under their hands, the name of the person chosen, Provided no Clerke or Recorder of any County

Court

Court shall be chosen Treasurer for the County. And the said Treasurers shall from time to time, keep exact and perfect *Books of accounts*, of all Transactions of the County, and particularly of all debts and dues belonging to the County, either by *Forfeits*, *fines*, *Rates*, *Gifts*, *Legacies*, *Rents*, *Customes*. or otherwise, as also all his *disbursments*, for the Charges of the County Courts, *shire Commissioners*, with all other Peculiar charges of the County, which he shall pay by Order of the County Court, except the *Twenty Pound* due to the *Major* of the *Regiment* for the year of Publick Exercise, which shall be Payd by the Country Treasurer as heretofore. To Pay the charges of the County

3. And it is Ordered, that all fines arising in any County Court, or by Order of one Magistrate or Commissioners impowred in *Criminall Cases*, shall from time to time be payd into the Treasurer of that County where the delinquent party doth dwel, except onely where any Person shall be taken in the Manner, and immediately Censured by Authority in any other County, where such Offence is committed. A: 58: All fines arising in ye county due to the County.

4. It is Ordered that the *Secretary* of the Generall Court, and Court of Assistants, & the *Clerke or Recorder* of every County Court, shall keep Books of account of all dues arising, within the Cognizance of the Respective Courts by entry of *Actions*, *Fines*, or otherwise, as also a true account of *all fees of the Officers*, and other *Charges of the Court*, which belongs to the Respective Treasurers to satisfy, & within *fourteen dayes* after the end of every Court, the said *Secretary*, and *Clerk*, shall deliver to the Respective *Treasurers* a true *Transcript* of all *fines* and other dues, payable to the Country or County, and the sayd *Treasurers* shall within *One Week* after the Receipt of such *Transcript*, direct his *Warrant* to the *Marshall or Constable* for the Levying thereof. And if any *Treasurer*, *Secretary*, *Marshall*, *or Constable*, make default herein, he shall suffer the penalty of *making good all Damage* that shall come thereby; And every *Treasurer for his paines and service*, is allowed *One shillings* in the *Pound* of all fines Received by him, and to be free from all Country and County Rates. And all *Treasurers* are hereby enjoyned once every Year, to give an account of all their Transactions, the Country *Treasurer* to the Generall Court, or to such as the said Court shall appoint & present the same at the Court of Election yearly. And the County *Treasurers* shall likewise yearly present their accounts to the County Courts, & if there be not enough in the *Treasurers hands* to satisfy the charges of the County, the said County Court shall give *warrants*, to levy the *arrears* upon the whole County, by Rate, to be Levied upon each Town and person (except such as are rate-free) in proportion with the Country rate, next before going, to be collected by the Constables of each town, who are hereby enjoyned to attend the same. [1648. 54, 57, 58.] Clerk of courts to keep accounts. To certify treasurer of al dues in 14 dayes. Treasurer to order warrants to call. Treasurers allowance. To give a yearly account. County court to raise taxes to defray county charges

Tryalls.

IT is Ordered that all *causes* between *Party & Party* shall first be tryed in some inferiour Court; and that if the party against whom the judgment shall pass, shall have any new evidence or other new matter to plead, he may desire a new trial in the same Court upon *a bill of review*. And if justice shall not be done him, upon that tryal he may then come to this court for Releife. [1642.] No cause to be first brought to § Gen: court

2. It is Ordered, & by this Court declared, that in all actions of Law it shall be the Liberty of the *Plantiff and Defendant* by Mutuall consent to chose whether they wil be tryed by the Bench or a Jury, unles it be where the Law upon just Reason hath otherwise determined; The like Liberty shall be granted to all persons in any criminall case. Liberty for tryals by Bench or Jury.

3 Also it shall be in the liberty of both *Plantiff and Defendant*, and likewise of every delinquent to be judged by a Jury, to chalenge any of the *Jurors* and if the chalenge be found just and Reasonable, by the Bench or the rest of the Jury, as the challenger shall chuse, it shall be allowed him, and *tales de circumstantibus* impanneled Liberty to chalenge.

neled in their Room,

4. Also *Children*, *Idiots*, *distracted persons* and all that are *strangers* or new cõmers to our plantation, shall have such allowances, and dispensations in any Case, whether Criminall or others, as religion & reason require. [1641.]

Votes.

Liberty of Voting. Or to be silent. Neuters accounted on y Negative.

IT is Ordered & by this Court declared, that all & every *freeman* & others Authorized by Law called to give any *advice*, *vote*, *verdict or sentence*, in any *Court*, *Councel* or *Civil Assembly* shall have freedom to do it according to their true judgment & Conscience, so it be done Orderly and inoffencively for the manner, and that in all cases wherein any *freeman* or other is to give his vote, be it in point of *Election*, making *Constitutions and Orders*, or *passing sentence in any case* of Judicature or the like, if he cannot see light or reason, to give it positively one way or other, he shall have *liberty to be silent*, and not pressed to a determinate vote, which yet shall be interpreted and accounted, as if he Voted for the Negative; And further that whensoever any thing is to be put to *Vote*, and Sentence to be Pronounced, or any other Matter to be *Proposed*, or Read in any Court or *Assembly*, if the *President* or *Moderator*, shall Refuse to performe it, the *Major part* of the *Members* of that Court or Assembly, shall have Power to appoint any other meet Person to doe it, and if there be just Cause to Punish him that should, and would not. [1651.]

Usury.

IT is Ordered, Decreed and by this Court declared, that no man shall be adjudged for the meer forbearance of any debt, above *eight pound* in the *hundred*, for *one year*, & not above the Rate proportionbly for all sũms whatsoever (Bils of exchange excepted) neither shall this be a colour or countenance to allow any Usury amongst us contrary to the Law of God. [1641. 43.]

L. 2. P12

Wampampeag.

IT is Ordered, that *Wampampeag*, shall pass currant in the payment of debts to the payment of *forty shillings*, the White at *Eight a penny*, the black at *four*, so as they be entire without *breaches* or *deforming spots*, except in paiment of Country Rates to the *Treasurer*, which no town or person may do, nor be accept therof from time to time. [1643. 48, 49, 50.]

Watching.

FOR *the better keeping of Watches, by the constable in the time of peace.* It is Ordered by this Court and the Authority thereof, that all *constables Watches* in every town of this Jurisdictiõ, shall begin the *first of May*, & cõtinue til the end of *September* upon the penalty of *five Pounds* to be levied on every constable neglecting the same. And it shall be the care of the constable to see that the watch be so warned, that it may not consist of all, or the greater part youths, but that able men be joyned with them that the watch may be a *sufficient watch*, unles the Select men of that town who have hereby power, shall otherwise order & dispose of the said watches, both respecting time, place, number, and quallity of persons as to them shall seem most meet. And all Inhabitants of this jurisdiction, (except such as are by Law exempted shall according as they are warned to serve the Country in the constables Watches, duely and strictly Observe the charge given them by the constables; And the constables in every Town from time to time are hereby enjoyned, to give in their charge to watch-men, that they duely examine all *Night Walkers* after *ten of the clock at Night* (unles they be known peacable Inhabitants) to enquire *whither they are going*, and what their busines is, and in case they give not *Reasonable satisfaction* to the Watchmen or constable, then the constable shall forthwith secure them till the morning, and shall carry such person or persons before the next Magistrate or Cõmissioner, to give satisfaction, for their being abroad at that time of night. And if the watch men shall find any Inhabitant or stranger, after ten of the clock at Night, behaving

A. 52. P. 12. Constable to set the watch.

A. 57. P. 25. Select men to order watches.

Constables charge to y watch.

Night walkers to be secured.

behaving themselves any wayes debauchedly, or shall be in drink, the Constable shall secure them by Commitment or otherwise till the Law be satisfied. And further the Constables to give the Watchmen in charge, to see all *Noises in the street* stilled, and lights put out (except upon necessary occasions) for the prevention of Danger by *fire* as much as may be; And every Constable shall present to one of the next Magistrates or Commissioners the name of every person, who shall upon Lawfull warning, Refuse or neglect to Watch or Ward, either in Person or by some other sufficient for that service, and if being Convented he cannot give a just excuse such Magistrate shall grant Warrant to any Constable, to Levy *five shillings* of every Offender for such default the same to be imployed for the use of the Watch of the same Town; And it is the intent of this Law, that every person of able Body (not exempted by Law) or of estate sufficient to hire an other, shall be Liable to Watch and Ward or to supply it by some Other when they shall be thereunto Required, and if there be in the same house divers such persons, whether *Sons, Servants, or sojourners*, they shall all be Compellable to Watch as aforesaid. Provided that all such as Live or keep families at their *Farme* being Remote from any Town, shall not be Compellable to Watch and Ward in Townes. [1636. 46, 52, 57.]

Watch to cause lights to be put out

L. I. p. 52

Neglect of watching forfeit 5 s.

Who compellable to watch.

Weights & Measures.

TO *the end, Measures and Weights, may be one & the same throughout this Jurisdiction.* It is Ordered by the Authority of this Court: That the *Country Treasurer* shall provide, upon the Countries Charge *Weights and Measures* of all sorts, for continuall Standards, to be sealed with the Countries Seal: *viz: One Bushell, one halfe Bushell, one Peck, one half Peck, one Ale quart, one Wine Pint & halfe Pint, one Elm, and one yard*, as also a *set of Brass Weights*, to *four Pounds* which shall be after *sixteen Ounces to the Pound*, with *fit scales*, and *steel Beam*, to Weigh and try withall. And the Constable of every Town, within this Jurisdiction shall within three Months after publication hereof. Provide upon the town Charge, all such weights at least of *Lead*, & also sufficient *Measures* as are above exprest, tryed and syzed by the Country Standards, and sealed by the said Treasurer or his Deputy in his presence, (which shall be kept and used onely, for standards for their severall Townes) who is hereby Authorized to do the same, for which he shall Receive from the Constable of each Town, *two-pence* for every *Weigh and Measure so Proved, sized, and sealed*; And the said Constable of every Town, shall commit those *Weights & Measures* unto the Custody of the Select men of their townes for the time being, who with the said Constable are hereby enjoyned to chuse one able man to be *Sealer of such weights & measures*, for their own Town from time to time, and till an other be chosen, which man so chosen they shall present, to the next *County Court*, there to be Sworn to the faithfull discharge of his duty, who shall have Power to send forth his warrants, by the Constable, to all the Inhabitants of their town to bring in all such *Measures and Weights* as they make any use of, in the *second Month from year to year*, at such time and place as he shall appoint and make Returne to the sealer in Writing of all persons so summoned, that then and there all such *Weights and Measures* may be prooved and sealed with the Town Seale, (such as in the Order for town Cattle) provided by the Constable, at Each Townes charge, who shall have for every *Weight and Measure* so sealed *One penny* from the owners thereof at the first Sealing. And all such *Measures & Weights* as cannot be brought to their just standard, he shall deface or destroy; And after the first sealing shall have nothing so long as they Continue just with the standard. *And that none may neglect their duty herein.* It is further Ordered by the Authority aforesaid. That if any *Constable, Select Men*, or *Sealer* do not execute this Order, as to every of them Appertaines, they shall forfeit to the cōmon Treasury *forty shillings for every such neglect* the space of one *Month*, and also that every person

Standards to be provided by ÿ Treasur

Constable to provide standards for townes

Sealer to be chosen by ÿ select men.

To be sworn at ÿ county Court

His duty

His fee

person neglecting to bring in their weights and Measures at the time and Place appointed they shall pay three shillings four pence for every such default, one half part whereof shall be to the Sealer, and the other halfe to the Common Treasury, which the Sealer shall have Power to Levy by Distress from time to time.
[1047]

A. 55. 2. *This Court Considering the Complaints of severall abuses, in Measuring Corne, Boards, and Cording of wood.* Doth Order that it shall be in the power of the Select men of every Town, to appoint *one, two or more*, as need shall require who shall be sworne faithfully & uprightly to *Measure* all such *Corne, Wood or Boards*, as they shall be Called unto, and that no Man shall be forced to Receive any *Corne, Wood or Boards*, (except they Agree thereunto) But such as is *Measured* by such Person or Persons, so Appointed and Sworne, the parties Receiving the *Corne*, *Wood or Boards*, paying for the *Measuring thereof*.
[1655.]

Select men to appoint measures of corn &c:

Wharfage.

IT is Ordered by this Court and the Authority thereof, that these Orders shall be Observed, by all such as shall bring goods to any wharfe, and these Rates following be Allowed; First for Wood by the *tun three-pence*, for Timber by the tun *four pence*, *for pipe staves* by the Thousand *nine-pence*, for boards by the Thousand *six pence*, for Merchants goods whether in cask or otherwise, by the tunn *six-pence*, for dry fish by the Quintall, *one penny*, for Corne by the quarter *one penny and a half peny* for great Cattle by the head *two pence*, for goats, swine or other small Cattle, except such as are sucking their dams, by the head, *a half penny*, for hay, straw & all such combustable goods by the load *six pence*, for stones by the tun *a penny*, for Cotton wooll by the bag, *two-pence*, for Sugar by the chest *three-pence*. Provided that Wharfage be taken only, where the Wharfes are Made and Maintained, and that Wood, stone and Weighty goods, shall be set up an end, or laid seven foot from the side of the Wharfe, upon penalty of double wharfage, and so for other goods, and that no goods ly on the Wharfe, *above forty eight houres* without further agreement with the wharfinger: And that it shall be Lawfull for the Wharfinger to take according to these Rates out of the Goods that are Landed, except they be satisfied otherwise.

Rates for wharfage.

2. And it is Further Ordered. that none shall Cast an *Anker*, *Graplin or Killack*, within or neer the Cove at Boston, where it may indanger any other vessels upon penalty of *ten shillings*, halfe to the Country, halfe to the wharfinger, besides paying all damages.

Casting Ankers in ye cove penalty.

3. And that it shall not be Lawfull for any person to cast any *dung, draught, dirt* or any thing to fill up the Cove, or to annoy the Neighbours, upon Penalty of *Forty shillings*, the one half to the Country, the other halfe to the Wharfinger.
[1647.]

Casting in dung penalt. 40 s.

Wills.

L.2.p.16 WHERAS *it is found by experience that some Men dying, having made their Wills, for the disposing of their estates, that the said Wills are Concealed and not prooved and Recorded, and some others dying intestate, no administration is sought for, nor Granted in any Legall way, and yet the Wives, Children, Kindred, or some freinds of the deceased, or some others do enter upon the Lands, and possess themselves of the goods of the said deceased, and the same are many times sold, or wasted, before the Creditors, to whom the deceased was indebted knew of whom to demand or how to Recover their just Debts, for prevention of such unjust and fraudulent dealings.* It is Ordered by this Court and the Authority thereof, That if any Executor Nominated in any Will, and knowing thereof, shall not at the next Court of the County, which shall be above *thirty dayes*, after the decease of the party, make probate of any will of any deceased party or shall not Cause the same to be Recorded, by the Recorder or Clerk of that County Court, where the deceased

Wills to be proved at ye next Court

deceased party last dwelt, or if any person whatsoever, shall not within the same time, take administration of all such goods, as he hath or shall enter upon of any party deceased, or if any person or persons, shall *Alienate* or *imbezell* any *Lands or goods*, before they have prooved and Recorded the will of the deceased, or taken administration, & brought in a true inventory of all the known *Lands*, goods & debts of the deceased, every such person so administring or executing, shall be liable to be Sued, and shall be bound to pay all such debts Respectively, as the deceased party owed, whether the estate of the deceased, were sufficient for the same or not, and shall also forfeit to the Country, so many summs *of five pounds* as shall be Months betwixt the next Court o that County, after the death of the party as aforesaid, and the proving of such will and Recording it, or the taking of such administration. And if any person shall *Renounce his Executor-ship*, or that none of the freinds or Kindred of the deceased party that shall dy intestate, shall seek for Administratiō of such persons estate, then the Clerk of the Writs of such town, where any such person shal dy, shall within one Month after his decease, give notice to the Court of that County to which such Town doth belong, of such *Renouncing of executor-ship* or not seeking of administration, that so the Court may take such Order therein as they shall think meet, who shall also allow such Clerk due recompence for his paines, & if any such Clerk shall fail herein, he shall forfeit *forty shillings* to the Treasury for every Months default. [1649.]

Entring the estate without administration obtained.

Able to pay all debts

Five pound per month for not proving ÿ will.

If Executor renounce ÿ Clerk to give notice to ÿ Court.

Or forfeit 40 s.

2. *And because many Merchants Sea men & other strangers resorting hither oftentimes dying & leaving their estates undisposed of, and very difficult to be preserved in the interim from one County Court to an other.* It is therefore Ordered that it shall and may be Lawfull for any two Magistrates, with the Recorder or Clerk of the County Court, Meeting together, to allow of any Will of any deceased party to the Executors or other persons in the Will Mentioned, so as the Will be testefied on the Oath of *two or more Witnesses*, and also to grant Administration to the estate of any person dying intestate within the said County, to the next *of Kin*, or to such as shall be able to secure the same, for the *next of kin* & the Recorder or Clerk of the Court, shall enform the rest of the Magistrates, of the County at the next County Court, of such Will proved or administration granted, & shall Record the same. [1652.]

A.52.P.15.

Two Magist. to take probate of wills

To grant Administration

3. And it is Ordered that when the husband or parents dy intestate, the County Court of that Jurisdiction, where the party had his last Residence, shall have power to assigne to the Widdow such a part of his estate as they shall judg just & equal as also to divide and assigne to the Children or other heires their severall parts and portions out of the said estate, Provided the Eldest Sonn shall have a Double Portion, and where there are no Sonns, the Daughters shall Inherit as Copartners unless the Court upon just Cause Alledged, shall otherwise Determine. [1641. 49.]

L.1.p.53 L.2.p.6

Count. Cour to divide ÿ estate undisposed.

Eldest Son a double portion

Witnesses

IT is Ordered decreed and by this Court declared, that no man shall be put to death, without the testimonie of *two or three Witnesses* or that which is equivolent thereunto. [1641.]

2. And it is Ordered by this Court and the Authority thereof, That any one Magistrate or Commissioner Authorized thereunto by the Generall Court may take the Testimony of any person of *fourteen yeares of age* or above, of sound understanding and Reputation in any Case Civill or Criminall, and shall keep the same in his own hands til the Court, or deliver it to the Recorder, publick Notary or Clerk of the Writts to be Recorded that so nothing may be altered in it. Provided that where any such Witness, shall have his abode within ten Miles of the Court & there Living & not disenabled by sicknes or other infirmity, the sayd Testimony so taken

Testimonies taken before one Magistr.

Witnesses to appear personally living within ten miles.

so taken out of Court shall not be Received or made use of, in the Court, except the Witnesses be also present to be further Examined about it. Provided also that in all Capitall Cases, all Witnesses shall be Present, wheresoever they dwell.

And in Capitall cases.

Witness to have allowance for his charges laid down.

3. And it is further Ordered by the Authority aforesaid, That any person summoned to appear as a Witness in any Civil Court between party and party, shall not be Compellable to travaile to any Court or place where he is to give his testimony, except he who shall so summon him shall lay down or give him satisfaction for his Travaile & Expences, outward & homeward, and for such time as he shall spend in attendance in such case, when he is at such Court or place, the Court shall a-ward due Recompence, and it is Ordered that *two shillings a day* shall be accounted due satisfaction to any witness for travaile & expences, and that when the witness dwelleth within three miles and is not at Charge to pass over any other ferry then betwixt Boston and Charlstown, then *one shilling sixpence per diem* shall be accounted sufficient and if any Witness after such paiment or satisfaction, shall faile to appear to give his Testimony, he shall be Liable to pay the parties Damages, upon an action of the Case. And all Witnesses in Criminall Cases shall have suitable satisfaction, payed by the Treasurer, upon Warrant from the Court or Judg before whom the case is tryed. *And for a generall Rule to be observed in all Criminall Cases, both where the fines are put in certaine, and also where they are otherwise.* It is further Ordered by the Authority aforesaid, that the Charges of Witnesses in al such Cases shal be born by the parties delinquent, and shall be added to the fines imposed, that so the Treasurer having upon Warrant from the Court, or other Judg satisfied such Witnesses, it may be Repayd him with the fine, that so the Witnesses may be timely satisfied & the Country not damnified. [1647.]

2 s. per diem.

1 s. 6 d. per diem.

Witness not appearing to pay damage

In Criminal cases witnes to be paid by y Treasurer, and levied on y delinquēt

Wolves.

A. 48.

WHEREAS *great loss & damage doth befall this Common-wealth by reason of* Wolves *which destroy great numbers of our cattle, notwithstanding provision formerly made by this Court for suppressing of them: therefore for the better incouragement of any to set about a work of so great concernment.* It is Ordered by this Court and the Authority thereof, that any person either English or Indian that shall kill any *Wolfe* or *Wolves*, within ten miles of any Plantation in this Jurisdiction, shall have for every *Wolfe* by him or them so killed, *ten shillings*, paid out of the Treasury of the Country Provided that due proof be made thereof unto the Plantation next adjoyning where such *wolfe* or *wolves* were killed: and also they bring a *certificate* under some Magistrates hand, or the Constable of that place unto the Treasurer. Provided also that this Order doth intend onely such Plantations as do cōtribute with us to publick charges, & for such Plantations upon the river of *Piscataway* that do not joyne with us to carry on publick Charges they shall make payment upon their own charge. [1645]

Wood.

FOR *the avoyding of injuries by Carts & boats, to seller & buyers of wood.* It is Ordered by this Court and the Authority thereof, that where wood is Brought to any towne or house by boat, it shall be thus accounted and assized. A Boat o four tunns shall be accounted three Loads; twelve tuns, nine Loads, twenty tun, fifteen Loads. Six tun, four Load and halfe, fourteen tun, ten Load and halfe, twenty-four tun, eighteen Load. Eight tun, six Load, sixteen tun, twelve Load, twenty eight tun, twenty one Load. Ten tun, seven load & half, eighteen tun, thirteen Load and halfe, thirty tun, twenty-two load and halfe.
Except such Wood as shall be sold by the Cord, which is, and is hereby Declared to be Eight foot in Length, four foot in height, and four foot Broad. [1646] 1647.]

BECAUSE

Workmen.

BECAUSE *the harvest of Hay, Corn, Hemp and Flax, comes usually so neer together that much losse can hardly be avoided.* It is therefore Ordered by the Authority of this Court; That the Constables of every town, upon Request made to them shall Require any Artificers or handy Crafts-men, Meet to Labour, to work by the day for their *Neighbours* in mowing, reaping of *corn, & inning thereof* Provided that those men whom they work for, shall duely pay them for their Work. And that if any person so Required shall Refuse, or the Constable neglect his Office herein, they shall Each of them Pay to the use of the Poor of the Town double so much as such Dayes Work Comes unto. Provided no Artificer or Handy-Crafts-Man shall be Compelled to Work as aforesayd, for others, whiles he is necessarily attending on the like Busines of his Own. [1646.]

Wrecks of the Sea.

IT is Ordered decreed and by this Court declared; That if any Ships or other Vessels, be it friend or enemy, shall suffer ship-wreck upon our Coasts, there shall be no violence or wrong offered to their persons, or goods, but their persons shall be Harboured and Releived, and their goods preserved in safety, till Authority may be certified, and shall take further Order therein. Also any Whale, or such like great fish cast upon any shore, shall be safely kept or improved where it cannot be kept, by the town or other proprietor of the land, til the Generall Court shall set Order for the same. [1641, 1647.]

Presidents and formes of things frequently used.

TO [*I. B.*] Carpenter, of [*D.*] You are Required to appear at the next Court, holden at [*B,*] on the day of the month next ensuing; to answer the complaint of [*N. C.*] for with-holding a debt of due upon a *Bond* or *Bill*: or for two heifers &c: sold you by him, or for work, or for a trespass done him in his corn or hay, by your cattle, or for a slander you have done him in his name, or for striking him, or the like, and hereof you are not to fail at your Peril. Dated the Day of the Month. [1641.] *Summons*

TO the Marshall or Constable of [*B.*] or their Deputy. You are Required to Attach the Body and goods of [*W. F.*] and to take *Bond* of him to the value of with sufficient surety or sureties for his appearance at the next Court, holden at [*S.*] on the day of the Month; then and there to answer the Complaint of [*T. M*] for &c: *as before.* And so make a true Return thereof under your hand. Dated the day &c: *Attachment.*

By the Court.
R. F.

KNOW all men by these presents, that we [*A. B.*] of [*D.*] Yeoman, & [*C. C*] of the same Carpenter, do bind our selves, our Heires and Executors to [*R. F*] Marshall, or [*M. O.*] Constable of [*D.*] aforesaid, in Pounds; upon condition that the said [*A. B.*] shall personally appear at the next Court, at [*S.*] to answer [*L. M.*] in an action of And to abide the Order of the Court therein, and not to depart without Licence. *Bond for apearance*

TO the Marshall or Constable of You are Required to *replevie* three heifers of [*T. P.*] now distreined or impounded by [*A. B.*] and to Deliver them to the said [*T. P.*] Provided he give bond to the Value of with *Replevin.*

 sufficient

Surety or sureties to prosecute his Replevin at the next Court holden at [B] & so from Court to Court till the Cause be ended, & to pay such costs and damages as the said [A. B.] shall by law Recover against him; And to make a true return thereof under your hand. Dated &c: *By the Court* *K F.*

Commissioners for the united Colonies.

VV*HERAS upon serious Consideration, wee have Concluded a Confederacie with the English Colonies of New-Plimouth, Connecticot and New-Haven as the Bond of Nature, Reason, Religion and Respect to our Nation doth Require.*

Wee have this Court chosen our trustie and well beloved Freinds [*S. B.*] and [*W. H.*] for this Colonie; for a full and Compleat Year, as any occasions and exigents may Require and particularly for the next *Meeting* at [*B.*]. And do Invest them with full power and Authority to treat and Conclude of all things, according to the true Tenor and Meaning of the Articles of Confoederation of the United Colonies, Concluded at *Boston* the ninth day of the third Month. [1643]

their powr

Oath of Fidelitie.

I [*A. B.*] being by Gods providence an Inhabitant within the Jurisdiction of this Common wealth, do freely and sincerely acknowledg my selfe to be subject to the Government therof, And do here Swear by the great and dreadfull name of the Ever-living God, that I will be true & faithfull to the same, and will accordingly yeild assistance thereunto, with my person and estate, as in equity I am bound: And will also truely endeavour to Maintain and preserve all the Liberties & Priviledges therof submitting my self unto the wholesom Laws made, and established by the same.

And farther that I will not plot or practice any evill against it, or consent to any that shall so do: but will timely discover and reveal the same to lawfull Authority now here established, for the speedy preventing thereof. So help me God in our Lord Jesus Christ.

Freemans Oath.

I [*A. B.*] being by Gods Providence an Inhabitant within the Jurisdiction of this Common-wealth, and now to be made free; doe here freely acknowledg my self to be subject to the Government thereof: And therefore do here Swear by the great and dreadfull Name of the Ever-living God, that I will be true and faithfull to the same, and will accordingly yeild assistance and support thereunto, with my person and estate, as in equity I am bound, and will also truely endeavour to maintain and preserve all the Liberties and Priviledges thereof, submitting my self unto the wholesom Laws made and established by the same. And farther, that I will not plot or practice any evill against it, or consent to any that shall so doe; but will timely discover and reveal the same to lawfull Authority now here established, for the speedy prevention thereof.

Moreover, I do solemnly bind my self in the sight of God, that when I shall be called to give my voice touching any such matter of this State, wherein Free-men are to deal; I will give my vote and suffrage as I shall in mine own conscience judg best to conduce and tend to the publick weal of the Body, without respect of persons, or favour of any man. So help me God &c:

Governours Oath

VVHERAS you [*J. VV.*] are chosen to the place of *Governour* over this Jurisdiction, for this year, and till a new be chosen and sworn: You do here Swear by the Living God, that you will in all things concerning your place, according to your best power and skill, carry and demean your self for the said time of your Government, according to the Lawes of God, and for the advancement of his Gospel, the Laws of this Land, & the good of the people of this jurisdiction. You shall do justice to all men without partialitie, as much as in you lyeth: you shall not exceed the limitations of a Governour in your place. So help you God &c:

W HER

Deputy Govern:

WHERAS you [*T. D.*] are chosen to the place of the *Deputy Governour*, &c. as in the Governours Oath, *mutatis mutandis*.

Assistants

WHERAS you [*R. B.*] are chosen to the place of *Assistant* over this Jurisdiction, for this year, and till new be chosen and sworn: you doe here swear by the Living God, that you will truly endeavour according to your best skill, to carry and demean your self in your place, for the said time, according to the Laws of God and of this land, for the advancement of the Gospel and the good of the people of this Jurisdiction. You shall dispense justice equally & impartially, according to your best skill, in all cases wherein you shall act by vertue of your place. You shall not wittingly and willingly exceed the limitations of your place. And all this to be understood, during your abode in this Jurisdiction. So help you God in our Lord Jesus Christ.

Major General.

WHEREAS you [*J. E.*] have been chosen to the Office of Sergeant Major General, of all the Military Forces of this Jurisdiction, for this present Year: You do here swear by the Ever-Living God, that by your best skill & Ability you will Faithfully discharge the Trust Committed to you, according to the Tenor & purport of the Commission given you by this Court. So help you God &c:

Treasurer

I [*R. R.*] being Chosen *Treasurer* for the Jurisdiction of the *Massachusets* for this year and untill a new be Chosen; do promise to give out *Warrants* with all Convenient diligence, for Collecting all such summs of Money as by any Court, or otherwise have been, or shall be appointed, and to pay out the same, by such sums, and in such manner as I shall be lawfully appointed by this Court, if I shall have it in my hands of the Common Treasury. And will return the names of such Constables, as shall be failing in their Office, in not collecting and bringing in to me such summs, as I shall give *Warrant* for. And will render a true account of all things concerning my said Office, when by the General Court I shall be called thereto. So help me God in our Lord *Jesus Christ*.

Publick Notary.

YOU [*W. A.*] here swear by the Name of the Living God; that in the office of a *Publick Notary* to which you have been chosen, you shall demean your selfe diligently and faithfully according to the duty of your Office. And in all Writings, Instruments and Articles that you are to give testimony unto, when you shall be Required, you shall perform the same truely and sincerely according to the nature thereof, without delay or *Covin*. And you shal enter and keep a true Register of all such things as belong to your Office. So help &c:

Marshal.

YOU [*E. M.*] shall diligently, faithfully, and with what speed you may, Collect and gather up all such fines, and summs of Money, in such goods as you can find of every person, for which you shall have *Warrant* so to do by the Treasurer for the time being. And with like faithfulnes, speed & diligence, Levie the goods of every person, for which you shall have *Warrant* so to do, by vertue of any *Execution* granted by the Secretarie, or other Clerk authorized thereunto, for the time being. And the same goods so collected or levied, you shall with all convenient speed deliver in to the Treasurer, or the persons to whom the same shall belong. And you shall with like care and faithfulnes, serve all *Attachments*, directed to you, which shall come to your hands; and return the same to the Court where they are returnable, at the times of the return thereof.

And you shall perform, do and execute, all such lawfull Commands, directions and warrants, as by lawfull authority here established shall be committed to your care and charge, according to your Office. All these things in the presence

Presence of the Living God you bind your self unto, by this your Oath to performe during all the time you continue in your Office, without favour, fear, or partialitie of any person. (And if you meet with any case of difficultie, which you cannot Resolve by your self, you may suspend till you may have advice from authority)
So help &c:

Associates

YOU [*M. N.*] being Chosen Associate for the Court for this year, and till new be Chosen, or other Order taken, Do here Swear, that you will do equall right and justice in all Cases that shall come before you, after your best skill and knowledg, according to the Laws here established. So help you God &c:

VVheresoever any three men are deputed to end small Causes, the Constable of the place within one Month after, shall returne their names to the next Magistrate, who shall give Summons for them forthwith to appear before him; who shall administer to them this Oath.

Three men

YOU [*A. B.*] being Chosen and appointed to end small Causes not exceeding fourty shillings Value, according to the Lawes of this jurisdiction, for this Year ensuing, do heer Swear by the Living God that without Favour or affection, according to your best light, you will true judgment give & make for all the Causes that Come before you. So help you God &c:

Grand-Jury.

YOU Swear by the Living God that you will Diligently inquire & faithfully present to this Court, whatsoever you know to be a breach of any Law established in this jurisdiction according to the Mind of God; And whatsoever Criminall Offences you apprehend fit to be here presented, unless some necessary and Religious tye of Conscience truely grounded upon the Word of God bind you to Secresie. And whatsoever shall be Legally Committed by this Court to your judgment, you will Returne a true and just Verdict therein according to the Evidence given you, and the Laws Established amongst us. So help you God &c.

Pettie-Jurie.

YOU Swear by the Living God, that in the Cause or Causes now Legally to be Committed to you by this Court, you will true tryal make, & just verdict give therein, according to the Evidence given you, and the Laws of this jurisdiction. So help you God &c:

Life and death.

YOU do Swear by the great Name of Almighty God, that you will well and truly try, & true deliverance make of such Prisoners at the *barr*, as you shall have in charge, according to your evidence. So help you God &c:

Witnesses.

YOU Swear by the Living God, that the evidence you shall give to this Court concerning the Cause now in question, shall be the truth, the whole truth and nothing but the truth. So help you God &c:

Untimely death.

YOU Swear by the Living God, that you will truely present the Cause and manner of the Death of [*J. B.*] according to evidence, or the light of your knowledg and Conscience. So help you God &c:

The forme of the Oath to be administred to the Sergeant Majors of the Severall Regiments and so Mutatis Mutandis, to the other Military Officers.

Sergeant Major & other chief Officers,

VVHereas you [*R. S.*] have been Chosen to the Office of Sergeant Major, of the Regiment in the County of [*M.*] for this present Year, and untill another be Chosen in your place; You do here swear by the *Living* God, that by your best skill and ability, you will faithfully discharge the trust Committed to you, according to such Commands & directions as you shall from time to time upon all occasions receive from the Sergeant Major Generall, by vertue of his Commission from the Court, & according to the Laws and Orders by this Court made and established in this behalfe. So help you God &c:

YOU [R. B.] swear truly to Performe the Office of a Clerk of a Trained Band, to the utmost of your ability, or Endeavours, according to the particulars specified, (and peculiar to your Office) in the Military laws. So help &c: *Clerk of the Band.*

YOU shall faithfully Endeavour with all good Conscience to Discharge this trust committed to you, as you shall Apprehend to Conduce most to the safety of this Common Wealth. You shall not by any sinister devices or for any partiall respects or private ends, do any thing to the hinderance of the effects of any good and seasonable Counsels. You shall appoint or remoove no Officer by any partiality, or for personall respects, or other prejudice: but according to the Merit of the person in your apprehentions. You shall faithfully endeavour to see that Martiall disciplin may be strictly upholden, not easing or burthening any, otherwise then you shall judge to be just & equal. You shall use your power over mens lives as the last and onely meanes which in your best apprehentions shall be most for the publick safety in such Case. So help you God in our Lord Jesus Christ. *Commissi: of martial disciplin.*

VVHERAS you [E. G.] are chosen Constable within the Town of [C.] for one year now following, and untill other be sworne in the place: you do here swear by the Name of Almighty God, that you will carefully intend the preservation of the peace, the discovery and preventing all attempts against the same. You shall duely execute all *Warrants* which shall be sent unto you from lawfull Authority here established and shall faithfully execute all such Orders of Court as are committed to your Care: and in all these things you shall deal seriously & faithfully while ye shall be in Office, without any sinister Respects of favour or displeasure. So help you God &c *Constable.*

VVHERAS you [J. G.] are chosen an officer for the searching and sealing of Leather within the town where you now dwell, for the space of a year and till an other be Chosen and sworne in your Room. you do here swear by the ever living God, that you will Carefully and duely attend the execution of your said Office with all faithfullnes for the good of the Common wealth, according to the true intent of the laws in such case provided. So help you God: *Leather Sealer.*

YOU [C. D.] heer Swear by the Living God that you will from time to time faithfully execute your Office of *Clerk of the Market*, in the Limits whereto you are appointed, for the Ensuing year and till an other be Chosen and sworn in your place: And that you will do therein impartially according to the Laws here established, in all things to which your Office hath Relation. So help you God &c: *Clerk of Market.*

YOU [S. S.] doe here swear by the Ever-Living God, that you will to your power faithfully execute the Office of a *Searcher* for this year ensuing, & till another be Chosen and sworne in your place, concerning all goods prohibited; & in speciall for *Gun-powder, shot, Lead & Ammunition*: and that you will diligently search all Vessels, Carriages and persons that you shall know, suspect or be informed, are about to transport or carry any thing out of this Jurisdiction contrary to Law. And that you will impartially seize, take and keep the same in your own custody: one halfe part whereof shall be for your service in the said Place; The other You *Searcher.*

shall

shall forthwith deliver to the Treasurer. All which goods so seized and disposed you shall Certify under your hand to the Auditor-generall within one month from time to time. So help you God &c:

Apprizer

WHEREAS you [*T D.*] are chosen *Apprizer* of such *land* or goods as are now to be presented to you, you do here Swear by the Living God, that all partiality, prejudice and other sinister Respects laid aside, you shall apprize the same and every part thereof, according to the true & just value thereof at this present by common account by your best judgement and conscience. So help you God &c:

Viewers of Pipestaves

WHEREAS you [*J. B.*] are Chosen veiwer of pipe-staves within the town of [*B.*] you do here swear by the Everliving God, that at all convenient times while you shall be in place, when you shall be Required to execute your office, you shall diligently attend the same, and shall faithfully without any sinister Respects, try and sort all *pipe-staves* presented to you, & to make a true entry thereof according to law. So help you God in our Lord Jesus Christ.

Customers Oath.

WHEREAS you [*A. B.*] are Chosen Customer for the year ensuing, you do here Swear by the Eve-Living God, that you will from time to time faithfully execute your Office, to your best skil according to the Orders of this Court for the Custome of all such goods, as are imported or exported, due by Law unto the Country and all other things belonging to your Office, & to give a true account to the Treasurer at the end of every three Months from time to time, or when you shall by Law be thereunto Required. So help you God &: [1649.]

Viewers of Fish Oath

YOU Swear &c: that you shall impartially veiw such fish as are presented before you, and determine what part thereof is Merchantable & which is Refuse fish & unmerchantable, according to your best skill, knowledg and judgement. So help you God [1652.]

Packers Oath.

WHEREAS you [*A. B.*] are chosen a packer of beef, pork and other things for the town of [*B.*] you do here swear by the Living-God that you will well and truly pack all beef, Pork and other things when you shall be thereunto Required, you shall pack no kind of goods, but such as are good & sound nor any goods in any Cask that is not of a just & full gage, you shall also set your particular mark upon all cask packed by you, and in all things proper to the place of a packer, you shall faithfully discharge the same from time to time according to your best judgement & conscience. So help you God. [1652.]

FINIS.

AN
ALPHABETICAL TABLE
SHEWING
The generall Titles and chief Heads of this Book of LAWS; (and more particularly, the Office of Constables.) In which, S. signifies *Section*, and P. *Page*.

THE TABLE.

Constables,

THE TABLE.

THE TABLE.

Dowries,

THE TABLE.

THE TABLE.

Pipe

THE TABLE.

Sodo-

THE TABLE

FINIS.

SUPPLEMENTS,

1661 - 1668.

From Secretary Rawson's Copy.
By permission of the American Antiquarian Society,
of Worcester, Mass.

TABLE OF CONTENTS.

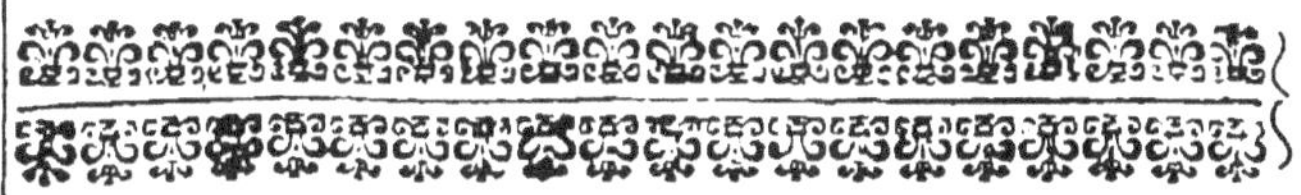

SEVERALL

LAVVS AND ORDERS

Made at Severall

GENERAL COURTS

In the Years 1661. 1662. 1663.

Printed and Published by Order of the General Court *held at* Boston *the* 20th *of* October, 1663.

By EDWARD RAWSON *Secr.*

MAY the 22. 1661.

THis Court, *being desirous to try all means, with as much lenity as may consist with our Safety, to prevent the Intrusions of the* Quakers, *who besides their absurd and Blasphemous Doctrines, do like Rogues and Vagabonds come in upon us, and have not been Restrained by the Laws already provided*; Have Ordered, That every such Vagabond Quaker, found within any part of this Jurisdiction, shall be Apprehended by any person or persons, or by the Constable of the Town wherein he or she is taken; and by the Constable, or in his absence by any other person or persons, conveyed before the next Magistrate of that Shire wherein they are taken, or Commissioner invested with Magistratical Power: And being by the said Magistrate or Magistrates, Commissioner or Commissioners, adjudged to be a *Wandering Quaker*, viz. One that hath not any Dwelling, or orderly allowance as an Inhabitant of this Jurisdiction; and not giving civil Respect, by the usuall Gestures thereof, or by any other way or means manifesting himself to be a Quaker, shall by Warrant under the Hand of the said Magistrate or Magistrates, Commissioner or Commissioners, directed to the Constable of the Town wherein he or she is taken, or in absence of the Constable, to any other meet person, Be stripped naked from the Middle upwards, and tyed to a Carts tayle, and Whipped through the Town, and from thence immediately conveyed to the Constable of the next Town towards the Borders of our Juris

Order against Quakers and Vagabond Rogues.

Jurisdiction, as their Warrant shall direct; and so from Constable to Constable, till they be conveyed through any the outwardmost Towns of our Jurisdiction.

And if such Vagabond Quaker shall return again, then to be in like manner Apprehended, and conveyed as often as they shall be found within the Limits of our Jurisdiction. Provided, every such Wandring Quaker, having been thrice Convicted and sent away as abovesaid, and returning again into this Jurisdiction, shall be Apprehended, and Committed by any Magistrate or Commissioner as abovesaid, unto the House of Correction within that County wherein he or she is found, untill the next Court of that County; where if the Court judge not meet to Release them, they shall be Branded with the Letter *R.* on their left Shoulder, and be severely Whipt, and sent away in manner as before. And if after this, he or she shall return again; then to be proceeded against as Incorrigible Rogues, and Enemies to the Common Peace, and shall immediately be Apprehended, and Committed to the Common Goal of the Country, and at the next Court of Assistants shall be brought to their Tryal, and Proceeded against according to the Law made *Anno* 1658. *pag.* 36. for their Punishment on Pain of Death. And for such Quakers as shall arise from amongst our selves, they shall be Proceeded against as the former Law of *Anno* 1658. *pag.*36. doth provide, until they have been Convicted by a Court of Assistants; and being so Convicted, he or she shall then be Banished this Jurisdiction; and if after that they shall be found in any part of this Jurisdiction, then he or she so Sentenced to Banishment, shall be Proceeded against as those that are strangers and Vagabond Quakers, in manner as is above expressed.

And it is further Ordered, That whatsoever Charge shall arise about Apprehending, Whipping, Conveying, or otherwise about the Quakers, to be laid out by the Constables of such Towns where it is expended and to be repaid by the Treasurer out of the next Country Levy. And further, That the Constables of the several Towns are hereby Impowered from time to time, as necessity shall require, to Impress Cart, Oxen, and other Assistance for the execution of this Order.

AUGUST the 7th. 1661.

Laws about Shipping & Fishing Repealed.

THe Court judgeth it meet to Declare, That the Law *tit. Ships, second Section, That all Ships which comes for Trading onely from other parts, shall have free access into our Harbours, &c.* shall and is hereby Repealed.

And also that the first Section of the Law *tit. Fish, Fishermen, pag.*32. shall and is hereby Repealed.

MAY the 7th. 1662.

As an Addition to the Laws about Apparel.

W*Hereas excess in Apparel amongst us, unbecoming a Wilderness-condition, and the Profession of the Gospel, whereby the Rising Generation are in danger to be Corrupted and Effeminated; which Practises are witnessed against by the Laws of God and sundry Civil and Christian Nations:* It is therefore Ordered and Enacted by this Court, and the Authority thereof, That all persons within this Jurisdiction, whether the Children, or Servants that are under government in Families

milies, that shall wear any Apparel exceeding the quality and condition of their Persons or Estate, or that is apparently contrary to the ends of Apparel; and either of these to be so judged by the Grand-Jury and County Court of that Shire where such Complaint or Presentment is made: All such persons being Convicted, shall for the first Offence be Admonished; for the second Offence pay a Fine of Twenty shillings; for the third Offence, Forty shillings; and so following, as the Offences are multiplied, to pay Forty shillings a time to the Treasury of that County. Also if any Taylor shall make or fashion any Garment for such Children or Servants under government as aforesaid, contrary to the minde and order of their Parents, or Governours, Every such Taylor shall for the first Offence be Admonished; and for the second Offence forfeit double the Value of such Apparel or Garment as he shall fashion or make, contrary to the minde and order of their Parents or Governours: Half to the Owner, and half to the Country. And all Grand-jury men are hereby Enjoyned to Present all those whom they do judge breakers of this Order.

How to Rate Sheep.

WHereas in the Law tit. Publick Charges, pag. 14. *Sheep are to be assessed at Twenty five shillings a head, and that they are now fallen to about a fourth part of the Price they then were ordinarily sold for, whereby many are discouraged for keeping such useful Creatures:* It is therefore Ordered by this Court, and the Authority thereof, That henceforth the Rate for Sheep shall be at ten shillings a Head, Any thing in the said recited Law to the contrary notwithstanding.

The Keepers discharge of Prisoners in Case.

IT is Ordered That when any persons are Committed to Prison in any Civil Action, the Keepers of the Prison shall not stand charged with their Supply of Victuals or other Necessaries. And in case the Prisoner hath no Estate, and will be deposed before any Magistrate, that he is not worth Five pounds, the Plaintiff shall provide for his Relief, or otherwise the Keeper shall not stand charged with him: and all such Charges the Plaintiff shall have power to levy with the Execution, before the party be delivered from Prison.

Order about Vagabond and Wandring persons.

T*His Court being sensible of the encrease of Prophaneness and Irreligiousness, by reason of the Vagrant and Vagabond life of sundry persons, as well Inhabitants as Forreigners, that wander from their Families, Relations and Dwelling places, from Town to Town, thereby drawing away Children, Servants, and other persons, both younger and elder, from their lawful Callings and Imployments, and hardning the hearts of one another against all Subjection to the Rules of Gods Holy Word, and the Established Laws of this Colony: All which to prevent,* This Court doth hereby Order and Enact, That all such persons, where ever they may be found in any place of this Jurisdiction, be Apprehended by the Constable of the said place, with or without further Warrant, and brought before the next Magistrate; who if upon Examination shall finde them to be such as do not give a good and satisfactory account of such their Wandring up and down, they shall proceed with and against them as Rogues and Vagabonds, and cause them to be Corporally punished, and sent from Constable to Constable, until they come to the place of their abode: Or in case they will not confess where their abode is within this Colony, nor yet voluntarily depart out of the same; then to be sent to the House of Correction, there to remain until the next Court of that County.

OCTOBER the 8th. 1662.

Complaint being made to this Court, of abuse offered to Justice, through liberty granted, by the Keepers of the Prisons, to such persons as stand Committed for Payment of Fines, and on Execution granted in Civil Cases: This Court do Order, That no person or persons Committed as abovesaid, shall be permitted by the Keeper of the Prison to go at liberty without the Precincts of the Prison, but by the License of the Court that Committed him, or of the Creditor for whom Execution is granted; On Penalty of Paying the Fine imposed, and satisfaction of the Execution in any Civil case.

Keepers of Prisoners danger.

Whereas it hath been commonly practised, that Attachments have been directed to the Marshall to be served in any Town under the Jurisdiction of that Court whereof the Marshall is Officer, notwithstanding the Law doth Order, That all Attachments shall be directed to the Constable in such Towns where no Marshall dwells: It is hereby Ordered and Declared, That the said Custome shall be accounted Legal, and shall not abate the Proceeding to Tryal of any Cause. Provided no more Costs be charged on the Defendant, then by Law are due to Constables for serving Attachments.

Marshals may serve Attachments.

This Court heretofore, for some Reasons inducing, did judge meet to suspend the execution of the Laws against Quakers, *as such, so farre as they respect Corporal Punishment or Death, during the Courts pleasure. Now forasmuch as new Complaints are made to this Court of such persons abounding, especially in the Eastern parts, indeavouring to draw away others to that wicked Opinion:* It is therefore Ordered, That the last Law *tit. Vagabond Quakers,* May 1661. be henceforth in force in all respects. Provided that their Whipping be but through three Towns: And the Magistrate or Commissioners signing such Warrant, shall appoint both the Towns, and Number of Stripes in each Town to be given.

Order against Vagabond Quakers *May* 1661. in force.

Whereas it appears, that notwithstanding such wholesome Orders as have been hitherunto by the Select men *of* Boston, *provided for the Restraint of all persons from violent Riding in the streets of the said Town: Yet neverthelesse, many take the liberty and boldness to Gallop frequently therein, to the great endangering the Bodies and Limbs of many persons, especially Children, who are ordinarily abroad in the streets, and not of age or discretion suddenly to escape such danger.* This Court having seriously considered the Premises, being careful to prevent a Practice that is like to be of such dangerous consequence, Do Order, That no person whatsoever shall after the Publication hereof, Gallop any Horse within any the streets of the said Town, upon Penalty of forfeiting Three shillings and four pence for every such Offence, upon conviction before any one Magistrate or Commissioner of *Boston*, to be paid to the Treasurer of the County of *Suffolk*; unless it appear on extreme necessity.

Penalty for Galloping in *Boston* streets.

OCTOBER the 20th, 1663.

For the better Regulating of Elections upon the Day of Election, and avoiding the inconveniences which may attend the same: It is Ordered by this Court, That henceforth the General Court, both Magistrates and Deputies, shall meet together in the Court Chamber at seven of the clock that morning, and become a

Court

Court, and begin and consider of such things as are necessary in reference to the Work of the Day.

2. That for time to come all Votes of the Freemen in each Town within this Jurisdiction, be sent in Proxies sealed up as the Law requireth: And that none be admitted to give Votes personally at the Day of Election, except the Members of the General Court.

Order for Regulation of Elections.

3 That the Constable of each Town shall some convenient time before the Day of Election, give due notice to all the Freemen of that town, to meet together to give their Votes for Elections: And that none shall be admitted to give their Votes for any other, unless the person Voting be also present, or send his Vote sealed up in a Note directed to the Deputy or Townsmen, met together for that Work.

4. That the Constable shall cause a List of the Number of Names of such as give their Votes, fairly Written, and Sealed with the Votes.

5. That no person be made Free upon the Day of Election. And a Copy hereof to be Published immediately after the breaking up of this Court.

THis *Court having perused and considered the Letter received from His Majesties most Honourable Privy Council, dated the* 24th *of* June *last, relating to an Act of Parliament, Entituled,* An Act for the Encouraging and Increasing of Shipping and Navigation. *As an Addition and Explanation of former Orders made by this Court concerning these Affairs;* It is hereby Ordered and Enacted, That the several Officers hereafter mentioned, are hereby Deputed and Authorized to see that the said Act be performed, so farre as it concerns the Government of this Plantation, both in Seizing Ships or Vessels inhibited by the said Act to trade here; taking Bonds of all Ships and Vessels that Lades in our Ports any Commodity expressed in the said Act, of the Growth, Product or Manufactory of the English Plantations, who shall not produce Certificate that they have given Bond already, as the said Act requireth. And in case of Neglects or Contempt, to Seize such Vessels or Ships that Lades the aforesaid Goods without giving Bond, or shewing Certificates: And to keep accounts of all such Ships and Vessels, with the Names of the Masters, that Lades here as aforesaid, and Return an Account twice every year, with Copies of the said Bonds and Certificates, unto the Governour for the time being, by him to be transmitted to *London*, directed to the Chief Officer there.

Officers authorized about Shipping.

The Officers appointed, are as followeth:

For the Ports of *Boston* and *Charles-Town*, Mr. *Edward Rawson*.

For *Salem*, *Marble-head*, and *Glocester*, Mr. *Hilliard Veren*.

For the River of *Piscataq*, and *Isle of Shoals*, and Ports adjacent, Captain *Brian Pendleton*.

Their Names,

The Fees they are Authorized to take of every Shipmaster, are

For taking Bond, and transcribing the Copy, Five shillings.

For Receiving and Entring a Certificate, Two shillings six pence.

For giving Certificate, and Recording it, Two shillings six pence.

Their part of Seizures, as the said Act directeth.

And Fees.

And that all imployed in this trust, do from time to time make Return of all Bonds and Certificates by them passed, to Mr. *Rawson*, who by the Governours Advice shall make Return thereof for *England*, as the Act of Parliament requireth. And that Mr. *Rawson* do from time to time present the Council of this

Order requiring Bond of Shipmasters, &c.

this Common-weal, or in default thereof the Court of Assistants, with true Accounts of all Bonds and Certificates, and Copies of all Letters that he shall send for *England*, in any wise referring to this matter.

Moreover it is Ordered, That the Secretary take special care forthwith to send by the first opportunity, Four Copies of the Councils, and one of the Copies of the Act of Parliament relating thereunto, to the Four General Goveroments of *New-England*, viz. *Plimouth*, *Conecticot*, *New-Haven*, and *Road-Island*.

Common Attorney no Deputy.

IT is Ordered by this Court, and the Authority thereof, That no person who is an usual and Common Attorney in any Inferiour Court, shall be admitted to sit as a Deputy in this Court.

Persons exempt from Voting in Elections.

WHereas it is found by experience, that there are many who are Inhabitants of this Jurisdiction, who are Enemies to all Government, Civil and Ecclesiastical, who will not yield obedience to Authority, but make it much of their Religion to be in opposition thereto; and refuse to bear Arms under others, who notwithstanding combine together in some Towns, and make Parties suitable to their Designs, in Election of such persons according to their Ends: It is therefore Ordered by this Court, and the Authority thereof, That all persons, Quakers or others, which refuse to attend upon the Publick Worship of God here Established; that all such persons, whether Freemen or others, acting as aforesaid, shall and hereby are made Uncapable of Voting in all Civil Assemblies, during their obstinate persisting in such wicked wayes and courses, and untill Certificate be given of their Reformation.

And it is further Ordered, That all those Fines and Mulcts of any such Delinquents as aforesaid, which are not gathered nor paid to the several Treasurers of the Countries, as also what Fines shall be laid on them for the future, shall be delivered by the Order of the County-Treasurers respectively, to the Select men of the several Towns whereunto they belong, to be by them improved for the Poor of the Town.

Officers Commissions.

FOr a more full and clear understanding of the intent of this Court in reference to Commissions granted to Military Officers: It is Ordered and hereby Declared, That all Commissions of Inferiour Officers be and do stand good and in force, notwithstanding the Death or Removal of their Superiour Officers.

Disorder in Souldiers to be punished by the Officers.

It is also further Ordered, That all trained Souldiers, whether Horse or Foot, shall repair to their several Quarters, and lodge their Arms immediately after their dismission upon Training dayes: And whosoever shall either singly or in companies remain in Arms, and vainly spend their time and Powder by inordinate shooting in the day or night after their Release; such Souldiers upon conviction shall be punished by their Superiour Officers Order, upon the next Training-day at the Head of the Company, by sharp Admonition, or otherwise with any usual Military Punishment, at the discretion of the chief Officer: Provided the Magistrate have not taken notice of the matter before.

It is also further Ordered, That all Souldiers, whether Horse or Foot, who shall disobey the lawful Commands of their Superiour Officers upon any Training-day, either in time of Exercise in the Body, or otherwise Refusing to perform any Service which their Officers in their discretion shall judge expedient, in order to the furtherance and promoting Military Work; such refractory Souldiers shall b punished either by Admonition, or otherwise, at the Head of of the Company, with any usual Military Punishments, at the discretion of the Chief Officers.

It is also further Ordered, and be it hereby Enacted, That the Law limiting Troops not to exceed Seventy persons in a Troop, as also for Allowance of Five shillings *per Annum*, is hereby Repealed, in reference to any that shall be Listed after the Publication of this Order. And that henceforth none shall be admitted to be a Listed Trooper, but such whom themselves or Parents under whose government they are do pay in a single Country Rate for One hundred pounds Estate, and in other respects qualified as the Law provides: And the same certified under the Hand of the Constable of the Town where they live.

Troopers allowance of 5 s *per Annum* repealed.

BE it also Enacted by the Authority of this Court, That no Masters of Ships or Seamen, having their Vessels Riding within any of our Harbours in this Jurisdiction, shall presume to Drink Healths, or suffer any Healths to be drunk within their Vessels by day or night; or to shoot off any Gun after the day-light is past, or on the Sabbath-day, on Penalty for every Health twenty shillings, and for every Gun so shot, twenty shillings. And the Captain of the Castle is hereby Enjoyned to give notice of this Order to all Ships that pass by the Castle.

Penalty for drinking Healths &c. in Ships or Vessels.

FINIS.

SEVERAL

LAVVS AND ORDERS

Made at Severall

GENERAL COURTS

In the Years 1661. 1662. 1664.

PRinted and Published by Order of the General Court held at Boston the 19th of October, 1664.

By EDWARD RAWSON Secr.

OCTOBER 14. 1654.

IT is Ordered, That the Keeper of the Prison for the time being, shall henceforth have the same liberty that the Marshall hath in all Civill Cases; to take sufficient Bayle after Commitment, as the Marshall might before Commitment. Keepers liberty to take Baile.

MAY the 22d. 1661.

THe Court understanding there is much Inequality, in that divers are freed from those watches, whereof all do receive equal benefit; for an explication of the Law concerning Constables Watches, Do Order, That the Magistrates, Deputies of this Court, for the time being, Elders of Churches, the Publick sworn Officers of the Country, with the Commission Officers in each Trained Band, be freed from all ordinary Watches and Wards of the Constables, and no other Persons; excepting such persons as shall have speciall and personal freedome, by Order of this Court, any former Order, Graunt or Custome notwithstanding. Persons exempted from Constables Watches.

DECEMBER 31. 1661.

UPon Complaint of the great abuses that are daily committed by Retailers of Strong-waters, Rhums &c. both by the stillers thereof, and such as have it from forreign

None to still or retail strong liquors without licence.

forreign parts: This Court do therefore Order, that henceforth no Person or Persons shall practize the craft of stilling strong-waters, nor shall sell or retail any by less quantyties then a quarter cask, and the same to be delivered not at several times, or in several parcels, but at one time, without covin or fraud, excepting onely such as shall be allowed annually by the County Courts respectively, on penalty of five Pounds forfeiture, for every time that any Person, or Persons shall be legally convicted thereof, any Law, Usage or Custome, or former licences to the contrary notwithstanding, provided alwayes this Law shall not prohibit such Merchants as have strong liquors from forreign parts in Cases from selling the same by the whole Case, either to such as are going to Sea, or to Masters of families of good report.

MAY 7th 1662.

Encouragement to kill woolves.

THis Court doth Order, *as an encouragement to persons to destroy Woolves*, That henceforth every person killing any Woolf, shall be allowed out of the Treasury of that County where such woolf was slain, Twenty shillings, and by the Town Ten shillings, and by the Country Treasurer Ten shillings: which the Constable of each Town (on the sight of the ears of such Woolves being cut off) shall pay out of the next Country rate, which the Treasurer shall allow.

Owners of fence to pay damage in cases, &c.

WHereas the Laws published concerning Fences, and Cattle, being in this second Edition transported from their first order and method, much difficulty doth many times arise concerning the true meaning thereof, whereby great damages do acrue to many of the Inhabitants, and Consequently to the Country, for prevention whereof, This Court doth Order and Enact, that where any cattle shall trespass on any Propriety, not appearing to be sufficiently fenced against swine sufficiently yoaked and ringed, or Cowes, and such cattle as will be restreined by a sufficient fence in the judgement of the viewers of fences as *pag* the 11th. *Sect*. 6th. in all such cases the owners of the fence or of the land, shall bear all such damages As to them thereby susteyned, any thing in the said Order or any other Law, Custome or Usage to the contrary notwithstanding.

OCTOBER 8. 1662.

Country and County Treasurers direction alike, &c.

WHereas the Law title Treasurers doth not so fully explain it self as it intended in Order to the execution of the same, in reference to County Treasurers, This Court declares, that the same power and direction given to the Country Treasurer in his Place, is likewise intended to the County Treasurer in his place and limits, for the better discharge of his duty, and that every Constable be trusted with the Collecting of any County Rate, which doth not within his year pay in his respective County Rate, and make up his accounts with the Treasurer from which he had his Warrant so to do, such Constable shall forfeit to the County forty shillings for his defect, and be liable to clear his accounts within two months; and that every County Treasurer shall present the names of such Constables as shall neglect their duty, to the next County Court, and that Corn or other goods paid into the County Treasurers, shall be at the same prizes that this Court shall from time set for the Country Rate from year to year, any custome or usage to the contrary notwithstanding.

MAY 18th 1664.

THis Court being sensible of the great encrease of Prophaness amongst us, especially in the younger sort, taking their opportunity by meeting together in places of publick entertainment, to corrupt one another by their uncivil and wanton carriages, rudely

rudely singing and making a noise, to the disturbance of the family, and other guests if any be in the house, This Court do therefore Order, and hereby Enact, that no Person or Persons whatsoever, do presume either in word or deed, to carry it uncivilly or wantonly, singing rudely or making a noise to the disturbance of the family or any other guests, in any place of publick entertainment, on penalty of paying five shillings for every offence against this Law, being thereof legally convicted before any Court, Magistrate, or Commissioner, and where sundry persons are in the same company where any such rude and uncivil carriages are acted, and the particular person or persons unknown, every of the said persons shall be liable to the like penalty, unless they can attest their innocency, and do freely give in their testimony against the nocent: and if any person allowed to keep a house of publick entertainment shall suffer such carriages by any person or persons, and not legally prosecute the same before Authority on legal conviction thereof before the County Court of whom they had their licence, they shall be debarred of any further reneual thereof.

Penalty for rude singing in Taverns, &c.

AUGUST 3d 1664.

IN *Answer to that part of His Majestyes Letter*, of June 28 1662, *Concerning Admission of Freemen.* This Court doth Declare, That the Law prohibiting all Persons, except Members of Churches, and that also for allowance of them in any County Court, are hereby Repealed, And do hereby also Order and Enact That from henceforth all English men presenting a Certificate under the hand of the Ministers, or Minister of the Place where they dwell, that they are Orthodox in Religion, and not Vicious in their Lives, and also a certificate under the hands of the Select men of the place, or of the major Part of them, that they are Free-holders: and are for their own propper Estate (without heads of Persons) Rateable to the Country in a single Country Rate, after the usuall manner of valuation in the place where they live, to the full vallue of *Ten shillings*, or that they are in full Communion with some Church amongst us; It shall be in the Liberty of all and every such Person or Persons, being *twenty four* yeares of age, Householders, and settled Inhabitants in this Jurisdiction, from time to time to present themselves and their desires to this Court, for their addmittance to the freedome of this common-wealth, and shall be allowed the priviledge, to have such their desire Propounded and put to Vote in the General Court, for acceptance to the freedome of the body pollitick, by the sufferage of the major parte according to the Rules of our Patent.

Order relating to the manner of admission to freedome.

WHereas *in the Law Booke* title *Millitary*, Sect. 11. *the three Cheife Military officers in each Town, except Boston, together with the Magistrates or Deputies thereof, are appointed a Committee of Militia for such Towns, without mentioning the Officers of Horse to be of the said Committee.* This Cour doth Declare, that the Commission Officers of Horse, in the Towns where they dwell, shall be added thereto and hereby are appointed and impowred, to be of the Committee of Militia, for such towns where they dwell, any Law or Custome to the contrary notwithstanding.

Officers of horse to be added to the Committee of Militia, in the towns where they live.

OCTOBER 19. 1664

FOrasmuch *as several Persons who from time to time are to be made freemen, live remote and are not able without great trouble and charge to appear before this*

County Courts Power to give the Oath of Freedome.

Court to take their respective Oaths; It is therefore Ordered, that henceforth it shall be in the power of any County Court, to administer the Oath of Freedome to any persons approved of by the General Court, who shall desire the same, any Law or Custome to the contrary notwithstanding.

Order regulating Elections Repealed, and Elections to be In *Statu quo*

T*He Court understanding, that the late Law made in* October 1663. *For the regulating of Elections, is not so satisfactory to the Freemen as was expected; and for some other reasons which have been alledged*; Do judge meet to Order, that the said Law shall and is hereby Repealed, and that Elections shall henceforth run in the ordinary course as formerly.

Such as are liable to Constables Watches are alike liable to Military Watches, &c.

F*Or as much as complaints have been made to this Court of very great Inequality in keeping and maintaining of Military Watches, the burden of that service lying mainly if not altogether upon such as bear arms, when several persons of good estate are free, all which considered*; It is Ordered, That henceforth all persons whatsoever, within this Jurisdiction, who are liable to serve in Constables watches, shall also be liable to the like service in all Military watches, either in their own persons or by a sufficient supply to be made by all such persons as aforesaid, or shall pay twelve pence in mony, and that under the penalty of five shillings for every such neglect, to be levyed by the Clark of each Company, by warrant under the hand of the chief Officer of the same.

F I N I S.

SEVERAL

LAVVS and ORDERS

Made at the

GENERAL COURTS

IN

May 3. *August* 1. & *October* 11. 1665.

PRinted *and Published by Order of the* General Court *held at* Boston *the* 11th *of* October, 1665.

By *Edward Rawson* Secr'.

MAY the 3. 1665.

Addition to the Law of Fornication.

T*Here being a seeming contradiction between the Laws tit.* Fornication, pag.33. *and title* Punishment, *pag.*67. This Court doth Declare, That the former referring to a particular Crime, a shameful Sin, much increasing amongst us, to the great dishonour of God, and our Profession of his Holy Name, the punishment of that Sin shall be as is prescribed in the said Law, Any thing that may seem to restrain or limit the same, contained in the other Law *tit. Punishment*, notwithstanding. And in case any person legally convicted of that or any other shameful and vicious Crime, be a Freeman; It shall be in the liberty and power of the Court that hath the proper cognizance thereof, besides any other Penalty or Punishment, to adde Disfranchisement thereto.

Order for Rating strangers: Or, Order for Assessments on strangers.

T*His Court understanding that several Gentlemen Merchants strangers, in the beginning of every year frequently coming into these parts, and bringing great store of English and other Goods of all sorts to great value; and usually making up their Markets to their great advantage before the* Sixth Moneth, *when the Rates, or Order for the Collecting of them, by Law is to issue out, (not without a considerable disadvantage to the Merchants and Shop-keepers, Residents and Inhabitants of this Colony, who have born the heat of the day, and are fain to be at all the Charge for supporting of the Government) and the said Merchants strangers taking the chief of the benefit of the Trade, and make their escapes without any* *payment to support the Government of this place, under, and by which they reap so great advantage to themselves:* It is therefore Ordered, That it shall be henceforth lawful for the Select men of each Town, where such Strangers are, or shall be, to assess all such Strangers, according to the *Cargo's* they shall bring into this Country: Or in case of their refusal to give a true Account of their Estate to the Select-men; then the said Select-men shall, and hereby are impowered to make their Assessment on all such Strangers in any Moneth of the Year, yearly, in proportion to a single Rate by will and doom, as the Inhabitants of this Country are used to be rated; and for non-payment, by the Constables to levy their said Assessments, as in other cases, by Warrant from the said Select-men.

Directions to Court-officers to grant Copies, &c.

R*Esolved upon the Question*, That the words *Rolls, Records, or Register of any Court or Office*, contained in the Printed Laws *tit. Records, &c. Sect.* 3. *pag.*69. are to be interpreted and understood onely of such acts of Court as concern particular persons in matters of Justice, License, Grant or Approbation; or of such Laws as are of publick concernment.

AUGUST 1. 1665.

All Fines for Prophanation of the Sabbath as formerly to be to the Counties, &c.

T*His Court being sensible, that through the wicked practices of many persons, who do prophane Gods holy Sabbaths, and contemn the publick Worship of his House, the Name of God is greatly dishonoured, and the Profession of his People here greatly scandalized, as tending to all Prophaneness and Irreligion; As also that by reason of the late Order of* October 20. 1663. *remitting the Fines imposed on such to the use of the several Towns, the Laws made for reclaiming such Enormities are become ineffectuall:* Do therefore Order and Enact, That henceforth all Fines imposed according to Law for Prophanation of the Sabbath, Contempt or Neglect of Gods Publick Worship, Reproaching of the Laws, and Authority here Established according to His Majesties Charter, shall be to the use of the several Counties, as formerly; Any thing in the abovesaid Law to the contrary notwithstanding. And in case any person or persons so sentenced, do neglect or refuse to pay such Fine or Mulct as shall be legally imposed on them, or give Security in Court to the Treasurer for payment thereof, every such person or persons so refusing or neglecting to submit to the Courts Sentence, shall for such his contempt be Corporally punished, according as the Court that hath cognizance of the case shall determine: And where any are Corporally punished, their Fines shall be remitted.

OCTOBER 11. 1665.

Rule for Entry of Actions.

VV*Hereas sundry Inconveniences do arise, by reason that Plaintiffs in Civil Cases do delay to Enter their Actions, to the great expence of much precious time, and damage to the Publick:* This Court doth therefore Order, That henceforth no Action shall be Entred after the first day of the Court is ended. And in case any Plaintiff shall delay his Entry longer then the first Forenoon of the Courts sitting, every such person or persons shall pay double Entry-money. And all persons, whether Parties or Witnesses, are enjoyned to attend their respective Concerns in every Court of Justice, as well the first Forenoon of the Court, as afterwards; and shall present the whole Plea and Evidence before the Case be committed to the Jury, and no after-

after-Plea or Evidence ſhall be admitted to any perſon, Any Law, Uſage or Cuſtome to the contrary notwithſtanding. And for that end, all Marſhals and Conſtables are enjoyned to make their Returns of Attachments by them ſerved, ſome time the firſt Forenoon of the Court that is to take cognizance of the Caſe concerned therein. Provided, That the double Entry-money be paid by him that ſo neglects his Entry, and not put the Defendant to unneceſſary charge through his default.

Addition to the Law of Inne-keepers.

AS *an Addition to the Law tit.* Inne-keepers: It is Ordered by this Court, and the Authority thereof, That where any perſon or perſons whatſoever ſhall preſume to keep an houſe of Publick Entertainment, Ordinary, Cooks ſhop, or ſhall by Retail ſell Wine, Strong Beer, Liquors or Cider, without Licenſe firſt had and orderly obtained; or having had Licenſe, and not renewed as the Law requireth, or being diſcharged for any Miſdemeanour committed, or ſuffered to be done in their houſes, or in or about the ſame: It ſhall be lawful for any Court or Magiſtrate on complaint made to them of such Miſdemeanour, to ſend for ſuch perſon or perſons before them, and being legally convicted of any the aboveſaid Offences, to require Bond, with ſufficient Sureties for the good Abbearance of ſuch perſon or perſons, and in ſpeciall for their Obſervance of the ſaid Law: And in caſe of Refuſall to give ſuch Bond with Sureties as is required; The Court or Magiſtrate that hath cognizance of ſuch Complaint, ſhall commit ſuch perſon or perſons convicted as aboveſaid to Priſon, untill the next Court of that County.

FINIS.

SEVERALL

LAVVS AND ORDERS

Made at the

GENERAL COURT

Held at Boston, the 23[d] of *May*, 1666. And on the 11th of *October* following.

PRinted and Published by Order of the General Court, the said 11th of October, 1666.

By EDWARD RAWSON Secr.

WHereas this Court hath already provided for the well Ordering and setling the Militia of this Common-wealth, as in the Law tit. Military, yet, forasmuch as many Complaints are presented to this Court, that the said Orders are not so attended as is to be desired, considering the present Juncture of affaires between our English Nation and forreign Enemies, who are now engaged in a bloody warre, which calls for a prudential endeavour of our own safety, against any forreign Invasion or suddain Surprizal; This Court doth therefore Order, and Enact, that the said Military Laws be by all persons therein mentioned, forthwith attended in all respects, and for the better effecting the same, the *Major General* is required forthwith by warrant under his hand to the *Majors* of the several Regiments, require them to make diligent inquiry into the state of the several Companies under their charge, and to be certified under the hands of the Commission Officers, or Chief Officers where no Commission Officers are, of each Company, of all defects of Armes, Amunition, or otherwise in every respect, and the said *Majors* respectively are required to give speedy advice to the *Major General* what posture their said Regiments are in, and wherein the said *Majors* cannot of themselves forthwith make redress of any defects in the said Companies, the said Majors with the advice of the Major General have hereby power to use all lawfull means to effect the same. And all inferiour Officers are hereby required to yield ready obedience to all such warrants sent to them by the said

Major General & Majors power to see that all the Armes of the Country be readily fixt.

Penalty for defects of Inferiour Officers.

Majors,

Majors respectively, or Major General, upon the penalty of five pounds for every defect to be levied by distress by such person as the said Major General and Majors of the Regiments shall depute, which said fines shall be for a stock of Powder for the said Company where the defects arise from time to time.

All the fines to goto procure a stock of Powder for the company where the defects arise.

And *whereas several Towns in this Jurisdiction, are not under the Command of any Serjeant Major, as* Dover, Portsmouth, *&c, as also the Towns of the County of* Hampshire; It is Ordered that the Major General take care for regulating of the Military affaires of such Towns, till they are brought under a Major as in other Counties and all Military Officers of such places are required Obedience to the Orders of the Major General from time to time, upon the penalty above mentioned, for every defect.

The several Towns that are not under Majors of Regiments to be Regulated & Ordered by the Major General.

Order to prevent Drunkenness in Indians.

Their strong Liquors &c to be seized by any person.

On refusal to confess &c. to be committed to Prison.

Their accusation against persons to be evidence unless ye party clear himself on Oath, &c.

If Drunk to pay ten shillings or be whipt with ten stripes, &c.

W*Hereas the sin of Drunkenness amongst the Indians doth much increase, notwithstanding the Laws provided against that crying sin;* This Court doth therefore Order that any person or persons that shall see, know or finde, any Indian with any strong Liquors, Wine, or strong Drink that such Indians have any way gotten without order as the Law directs, shall have power to seize the same, and to deliver the said strong drink to the Constables of the Town or Place where such Indians are found, with their persons to be conveyed before some Magistrate, or Commissioner, who have power to deal in such cases, and such Indians as are found drunk, being apprehended, and will not confess how, or where they had the said Wine, Liquors or strong Drink, shall be secured or imprisoned, until they make a just acknowledgement where they had their Drink aforesaid, or committed to the house of Correction, and there labour to discharge the charge of their provision.

And if any such indian do accuse any person for selling or delivering strong drink unto them, such Indian accusation shall be accounted valid, against any such persons accused, except such persons shall clear themselves by taking their Oath to the contrary, any Law, or Custome to the contrary notwithstanding.

And it is also further Ordered that whatsoever Indian shall hereafter be taken Drunk, shall pay the sum of *ten shillings* or else be whipt, by laying on *ten stripes*, according to the discretion of the Judge, whether Magistrate or Commissioner, who shall have cognizance of the case: and in all Towns where no Magistrate or Commissioners are, such cases shall be judged by the select men, or major part of them.

Pikemen to provide Buffe Coats or Quilted coats in stead.

W*Hereas the Law* tit. *Military*, Sect. 7. *Requires every Pikeman to be compleatly furnished (amongst other weapons with a sufficient Corslet) This Court considering that Corslets are wanting to many Souldiers in several Companies and that supplies therein are not easily to be attained;* It is therefore now Ordered, and by the Authority of this Court Enacted; that every Pikeman within this Jurisdiction, shall be compleatly furnished, either with a sufficient Corslet, Buffe Coat, or Quilted Coat, such as shall be allowed by the Chief Officer, under whose command they from time to time shall serve, upon the penalty in the recited Law already expressed, any Law, Custome or Usage to the contrary notwithstanding.

AS an Addition & explanation of the Law tit. *Strayes, This Court finding that several inconveniences and troubles do arise about Strayes, Cattle and Horses &c, and that the temptation may be too great on some persons in remote Towns and Farms to take up cattle. &c. and make Strays of them, the whole benefit redounding to themselves;* This Court doth Order for the time to come, that all Strayes shall be first cryed in that Town of which they have the Brand-mark, and that all such Strayes and other lost Goods conteined in the said Law, shall be entred with the County Recorder in each County, and by him transferred to the Country Treasurer within one Moneth, and in case the said Goods and Strayes are not owned within one year, as is therein expressed, then the one halfe, or the value of one halfe shall be to the use of the Countrey, and the other halfe to the finder, the charges being first payd out of the whole.

Addition to the Law of Strayes.

To be cryed in the Town on which they have the Brand mark.

To be entred with the Recorder of the County.

Halfe to the Countrey & the other halfe to the finder.

WHereas this Court hath encouraged and authorized some Persons to make Gun-powder and have promised to enable them thereunto, by such publick and necessary Orders as may conduce to the effecting the same, The consideration whereof hath mooved the Court hereby to Order and Enact, that the Select men of every Town (where the Powder makers Authorized, by this Court shall desire it) be Authorized and required hereby, to make and execute such Orders in their respective Towns, as they shall judge meet (with the advice of skilfull persons) for increasing and procuring of *Salt Peeter*, and to impose such penalties as the Select men shall see meet not exceeding ten shillings for one offence, upon all persons that shall neglect or refuse to perform such Order or Orders, for the propagating and increasing of *Salt Peeter*, in their respective Towns: and moreover the said select men are further impowred to choose and appoint an Officer or Officers, and to allow him a convenient stipend annually, for his paines out of the fines, or otherwise to look to the executing such Orders as they shall make in that behalfe.

Order impowring the Select men to make Orders with penalty to propagate salt Peeter, &c.

And it is further Ordered that such Select men who shall neglect or refuse to make and effectually execute such necessary Orders, as shall conduce to the ends aforesaid, they shall be presented at the Court of that County, and there be fined for their neglect at the discretion of the Court, not exceeding five pounds for one offence, and this Law to be put in execution forthwith after the publication thereof, and this to continue during the Courts pleasure.

F I N I S.

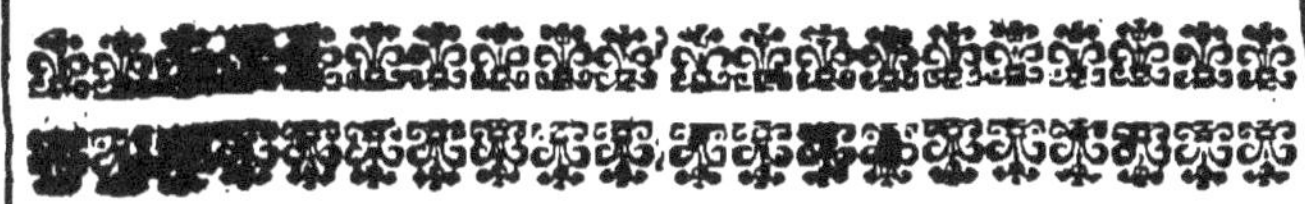

SEVEVAL LAVVS AND ORDERS Made at the GENERAL COURT OF ELECTION· Held at Boston in NEW-ENGLAND the 29th. of *April* 1668.

PRinted and Published by their Order.

EDWARD RAWSON. *Secr.*

WHereas sundry Complaints have been made of much inequality in the annual Assessments to publick charges the several Towns, and Counties not paying in a just proportion one to another, as is the true intent of the Law Title Charges; It is therefore Ordered by this Court and the Authority hereof, that henceforth from time to time, there shall be some meet, able, faithful and judicious men chosen and Authorized by this Court, *viz.* two in the County of Essex, two in Suffolk; two in Middlesex, and two in Norfolk, who meeting together with the Commissioners of the several Towns, they or the major part of them so met together, shall have the absolute and final determination of the just proportion of each Town, and of each person and estate therein, so as that there may be a just and equal proportion between County and County, Town, and Town. Merchants and Husbandmen, with all other Handicrafts as much as in them lye; *And whereas there are several Merchants and others, Traders, that do bring in considerable quantities of Goods among us, do gain great Estates thereby, yet they pass* Addition to the Rule for equal Assessments·

away

away without paying their dues to the Publick, It is therefore Ordered by this Court and the Authority thereof, that henceforth from time to time there shall be appointed and impowred by this Court, two or more meet able and judicious persons in the several Sea port Towns of this Colony, *viz.* in *Salem*, *Charlstown*, *Boston*, and *Portsmouth*, who from time to time, in their several Towns, shall repair to all Warehouses or other places where any forraign Goods or Commodities are put on shoare in any of our Harbours, or are sold or retailed on board of any Ship, Shallop or other Vessel, and require of the Merchant, Owner or other retailer thereof, the sight of his Invoyces, or other just and true accompt of all Goods by them imported, as abovesaid, and in case any Merchant, Retailer, or other Trader as abovesaid, shall refuse to shew their Invoyces, or other just accompt of their Goods by them imported, and that on Oath to be taken, before a Magistrate if required, in all such cases it shall be in the liberty of the two Commissioners impowred in that Town as above is expressed, and by this Court they are Authorized and Impowred, to assess such Merchant, or other Trader or Traders as to them shall deem meet, according to their own will and doom, and accordingly shall give warrant to the Constable of the Town, to levy of them *1 d. per li.* to be paid in to the Publick Treasury as the Law requires.

And it is also Ordered by the Authority aforesaid, that the meeting of the Commissioners in the several Towns, with those appointed by this Court this present year at Boston, the first third day of the week in the *7th.* Month, the fourth day at Cambridge, the sixth day at Salem, and the second day of the week next following at Salisbury, at eight of the clock in the morning, to perform the service and trust hereby committed to them, to which meetings the Commissioners, for the several Towns shall bring with them a list fairly writen of all persons and estates, every mans estate distinctly, and not in the gross sum only and the several parcels thereof, with the value put upon it, that so a full and exact Examination may be made, and an equal imposition put upon the inhabitants of this Colony, and the cause of those Complaints, that one is eased, whilst another is burthened, may hereafter be removed.

County Commissioners

And for County Commissioners, This Court do Nominate and appoint *Capt. Hopefull Foster* and *Ensign Daniel Fisher* for Suffolk, *Capt. Edward Johnson* and *Capt. John Wayt* for Middlesex, *Lieutenant Samuel Apleton* and *Lieutenant Oliver Purchis* for Essex, *Capt. Thomas Bradbury* and Mr. *Samuel Dalton* for Norfolk.

Commissioners for Sea ports

And for Sea port Towns, Mr. *Anthony Stodard*, and Capt *William Davis* for Boston, Capt. *John Allen*, and Mr. *Jacob Green* for Charlstown, Mr *Edmund Batter*, and Mr. *Henry Bartholmew* for Salem, Mr. *Elias Stileman*, and Mr. *Nathaniel Fryer* for Portsmouth.

Trade with Indians.

Trade with Indians for Peltry & Amunition regulated.

IT is Ordered by this Court and the Authority thereof, that henceforth every Person, that is or shall be allowed by the Treasurer of the Country to trade Peltry or Skins with the Indians, shall have liberty to sell unto any Indian

Indian or Indians, not in hostility with us or any of the English in New-England, Powder, Shot, Lead, Guns, (*i.e.*) hand Guns, Rapier or Sword blades Provided he or they pay unto the Country Treasurer every half Year in mony six pence a pound for every pound of Powder, six pence for every ten pounds of Shot or Lead, three shillings for every Gun, three shillings for every dozen of Rapier or Sword blades; and so proportionably for any quantity that he or they shall sell to any Indian or Indians and every such Person allowed to trade as aforesaid, shall upon Oath deliver to the Trasurer a true and just accompt of the particulars of the abovementioned Commodities, by him or them sold unto any Indian or Indians. And it is further Ordered that any person allowed as before that shall be convicted before any two Magistrates, or County Court of selling or bartering, any of the forementioned Commodities, unto any Indian whereof he or they have not given a true and just accompt, and made due payment unto the Treasurer as is above expressed, every such person or persons shall forfeit to the publick Treasury, five pounds sterling for every pound of powder, five pounds for every ten pounds of shot or lead, ten pounds for every Gun great or small, and ten pounds for every dozen of Rapier or Sword blades, and so proportionably for any quantity of the aforesaid Commodities, sold or bartered by him or them unto any Indian or Indians, and all persons except such as are allowed are hereby prohibited from selling any of the forementioned Commodities, unto any Indian or Indians, upon the penalty expressed, in the Law *title* Indians Sect. 2 And this Order to continue in force during the Courts pleasure, any Law or Order to the contrary notwithstanding.

Every allowed Trader paying to the Country Treasurer several sums appointed, &c.

Impost on Wine and Strong Liquors.

WHereas the General Court hath formerly for good and weighty reasons laid an Impost upon Wines and strong Waters imported, It is thought Expedient by this Court for good causes and considerations to set a rate, upon all *Cyder*, *Mum*, *Ale* and *Beer*, sold in publick houses licensed to sell such things, that is to say *two shillings sixpence* per *Hogshead* upon all *Cyder*, *Ale* and *Beer*, and *five shillings* per *Hogshead* upon all *Mum*, and so in proportion thereto, to each of them in greater or lesser quantities And this Court doth further Order that these Rates or Sums abovesaid be paid to the Treasurer of the Country or to his assignes in money by every person licensed to keep an *Inne*, *Ordinary* or *House of publick entertainment*, within this Jurisdiction whatsoever; And to that end every person so licensed and selling are Ordered and Required to keep a true and just accompt of what he or they shall sell from time to time, and that at the end of every Month or Week being thereto required, after the publication hereof, they shall present the said accompt to the Treasurer abovesaid upon Oath if required, or to his assign and pay all the Money due hereby, and in case any of the persons licensed as abovesaid, shall refuse or neglect to do what is above Ordered upon conviction before any two Magistrates, or Court of that County, where the offence is committed, shall pay treble damage to the Country, or forfeit his or their license, at the discretion of that Authority that shall take cognizance thereof.

Impost on Wine strong Liquors

Impost on Ale and Beer 2 s. 6 d. per Hogshead.

Mum 5 s. per Hogshead

Treasurer and his Assistants to farm the Imposts.

Treasurer and his Assistants to let and let to farm the Imposts &c.

IT is Ordered and by this Court Enacted that the Treasurer of the Country, with the assistance of Capt. *Daniel Gookin*, Mr. *Anthony Stoddard*, and Mr. *John Rickards*, be, and is hereby impowred and authorized, to Rent, Set or to Farm, let, for the use and in the behalf of the Country, for one or more years not exceeding three years, all these particulars following,

Viz. 1. The Impost of Wine, Brande, and Rhum.

2. The benefit of Beaver, Furrs, and Peltry with the Indians.

3. The Rates of drawing of Wines from Vintners.

4. The Rates upon Beer, Cyder, Ale, Mum, from publick Sellers.

5. The benefit of selling Ammunition to Indians.

Wines and strong liquors imported to be entred with the Officer.

Wines & strong Liquors imported to be entred with the Officer.

FOr the better Explanation and effectual Execution of the Law tit. Impost, pag. 39. It is Ordered and Enacted by this Court and the Authority thereof that all wines and strong waters imported into this Jurisdiction, according to that Law, be entred with the Officer in particulars, both for quantity and quality before any of it be landed, upon the penalty of the forfeiture of all that is landed before it be entred; It is Ordered that the Impost required by Law, be paid to the Officer in Money or the best of the specie at Money prices

It is further Ordered that the Committee Authorized by this Court, to make improvement of this Impost or any three of them, are hereby Authorized to appoint and constitute Officers, make Orders, and give such directions as shall be necessary, for the effectual receiving the said Impost, and the Rate imposed by this Court, upon the Retaylers of Wine, Beer, Ale, Mum, and Cider, and the business of giving liberty to trade for Peltry, and selling Powder, Shot, Lead and Guns, and other Armes to the Indians.

Seasonable transcribing and delivery of matters of publick concern by the Secretary.

Order for the seasonable transcribing and delivery of matters of publick concern by the Se.

W*Hereas by reason that the Orders of this Court referring to the Commissionating, Appointing, and Impowring any particular person or persons for any special trust, negotiation or other matter as from time to time do arise are not duely & seasonably transcribed and delivered to those concerned therein, the ex-*

pectation

pectation of this Court is many times disappointed, and dammage to the Publick doth inevitably accrue,

It is therefore Ordered by this Court, that the Secretary, from time to time within ten dayes after the end of every Sessions of the General Court, shall copy out all such special Orders of this Court as abovesaid, and deliver the same to the Marshall General, who shall receive the same at the Secretaries house, and take Order for the speedy and certain conveyance thereof, to those whom they are especially directed unto, and for such Orders as do require a more speedy dispatch then the time above limited, the Officers above named shall accordingly hasten the same, — To the Marshal General.

Also the Marshal General shall from time to time receive all warrants, that are to be sent to the several Towns, from the Country Treasurer, as also the Laws that are at any time to be published, either printed or written, and cause them to be delivered according to the direction given him from the Treasurer or Secretary. — Marshal General to attend the Treasurers and Secretaries direction, &c.

The best improvement of Stone Horses.

W*Hereas the breed of Horses in the Country is utterly spoyled, whereby that useful Creature will become a burthen, which otherwise might be beneficial, and the occasion thereof is conceived to be through the smalness and badness of Stone Horses and Colts that run in Commons and Woods;* For prevention whereof this Court doth Order and Enact, and be it Ordered and Enacted by the Authority hereof, that no Stone Horse above two years old shall be suffered to go in Commons and Woods at liberty, unless he be of comely proportion, and sufficient stature, not less then fourteen hands high, reckoning four inches to a handful, and such a Horse to be viewed and allowed, by the major part of the Select men of the Town where the owner lives; and if any person or persons turn any Stone Horse upon the Commons or at Liberty, or in the Woods, — Order for the best improvment of Stone Horses

being

being not viewed and allowed as before, he or they shall forfeit Twenty shillings a Month, for every Stone horse running at liberty, after he is a two years old, which penalty is to be taken by warrant, of the Select men and imployed to the Towns use, and if the Select men of any Town do neglect their duty in taking their fines, and viewing such as are brought in according to this Law, they shall forfeit Twenty shillings to the County Treasurey; and this Law to be in force the first of *October* next.

The prises of Horses for the Country Rate.

Order regulateing prises of Horses in the Country Rate.

WHereas the prizes of Horses and Mares in the Country Rate, hath been recconed at Ten pounds *per* Horse *and* Mare, *which hath been for a good space much more then upon an equal consideration, above their worth for the general, for the more equal and just proceeding in Country Rates for the future;* It is therefore Enacted by the Authority of this Court, that all Horses and Mares of 3 years old, and upward, shall be recconed at five pounds *per* Horse and Mare, and all under that age, as two years old, &c. at three pounds *per* Colt, and all of a year old, &c. at Thirty shillings *per* Colt, *&c.*

Order to build a dry Dock.

Order and encouragement to build a dry Dock

WHereas this Court in October 1667. *granted liberty to any person to build a dry Dock in Boston or Charlstown, reference unto the said Order being had;* It is Ordered, by this Court that if any person see cause to set upon building such a dry Dock, and shall finish the same within one year after the next session of this General Court, such person shall have the sole advantage of such Dock to himself, heires, and assignes after the said Dock shall be finished and it is Declared that no other person shall be allowed to undertake the building of a dry Dock in this Jurisdiction for the space of twenty one years, after the finishing of the first Dock undertaken, provided such undertaker keep and maintain the said Dock in such repair at all times as may attend the end proposed.

FOR

Fishermens liberty to cut flakes regulated

FO the Explanation of an Order bearing date, 1646. and the Repealing of the same 1667. for giving a liberty to Fishermen according to a reservation in the Patten:, to cut down wood for flakes or stage and other uses, about their fishing imploy, that it is intended only in that Order to give liberty to such as are strangers, and come only to make Fishing Voyages, and not to Fishermen that are Inhabitants, who are not to trespass upon any person in their propriety, but are liable to make satisfaction with dammages, as in any other Action of Trespass no way restraining Fishermen in Common Lands, any Law, Custom, or Usage to the contrary notwithstanding.

FINIS.

AT A GENERAL COURT

HELD AT BOSTON,

April 29. 1668.

VV Hereas *Thomas Gold*, *VVilliam Turner*, and *John Farnham Senior*, Obstinate and Turbulent *Anabaptists*: Have some time since Combined themselves with others in a pretended Church Estate, without the knowledge or approbation of the Authority here Establ shed, as the Law requires, to the great griefe and offence of the godly Orthodox; some of themselves being persons Excommunicated from the Churches to which they formerly belonging; have also Constituted among themselves, Officer or Officers, to carry on all Administrations in their pretended Church Society, Contrary also to the Law in that case provided, *viz.* that such Officers should be Able, Pious and Orthodox: For which irregularities they have been Convented before severall Courts, and about two yeares since were enjoyned by this Court to desist from the said practice, and to returne to our allowed Church-Assemblies, which they have not in the least attended.

The Councill in *March* last, desirous (after long forbearance) to use the utmost meanes to convince and reduce them, intreated the assistance of divers Elders, who in the meeting house at *Boston* did publickly endeavour the same. this Court considering with how great Pertenacy and presumption the said *Thomas Gold* and company had continued their Scismatical assembling together, the Order of this Court notwithstanding, judged it necessary to Convent the said *Thomas Gold*, *William Turner* and *John Farnham Senior*, before them, that from themselves the Court might understand what Effect the endeavours of the said Elders had taken with them: where the said persons did in open Court assert their former practice to have been according to the mind of God, and that nothing that they had heard convinced them to the contrary; which practice, being also otherwise circumstanced, with makeing Infant Baptisme a Nullity, and thereby makeing us all to be unbaptized persons, and so consequently no Regular Churches, Ministry or Ordinances and also renouncing all our Churches as being so bad and corrupt, that they are not fit to be held Communion with, denying to submit to the Government of Christ in the Church, and entertaining of those that are under Church Censure, thereby

thereby making the discipline of Christ in his Churches to be of none effect, and manifestly tending to the disturbance and distruction of these Churches; the which practise of theirs upon examination before the Court they profess themselves still resolved to adhere unto all which to allow, would be the setting up a free-scool for seduction into wayes of Error, and casting off the Government of Christ Jesus in his own appointments, with a high hand, and opening a door for all sorts of abominations to come in among us, to the disturbance not only of our Ecclesiastical enjoyments, but also contempt of our Civil Order, and the Authority here established, doth manifestly threaten the dissolution and ruine, both of the peace and order of the Churches and the Authority of this Government: which our duty to God and the Country doth oblige us to prevent, by using the most compassionate effectual means to attain the same; all which considering, together with the danger of disseminating their errors and incouraging presumptuous irregularities, by their example should they continue in this Jurisdiction, this Court doth judge it necessary that they be removed to some other part of this Country or else where: And accordingly doth order that the said *Thomas Gold, William Turner*, and *John Farnham* senior; do before the twentieth of *July* next remove themselves out of this Jurisdiction, and that if after the the twentieth of *July*, the said *Thomas Gold, William Turner*, and *John Farnham* senior, or either of them be found in any part of this Jurisdiction, without License first had and obtained from this Court or the Council, he or they shall forthwith be apprehended and committed to prison, by warrant from any Magistrate; there to remain without baile or mainprize until he or they shall give sufficient security to the Governour or any Magistrate, immediately to depart the Jurisdiction and not to return as abovesaid: And all Constables and other Officers are required to be faithful and diligent in the execution of this Sentence And it is further Ordered that the keepers of all prisons whereto the said *Thomas Gold, William Turner* and *John Farnham* senior, or any of them shall be Committed, shall not permit any resort of company of more then two at one time, to any of the said persons. And although we might expect that our indulgence till the *twentieth of July*, might prevaile with them to restraine their offencive practices, during the time permitted them to continue amongst us, yet our experience of their high Obstinate and Presumptuous carriages doth gage us to prohibit them any further meeting together on the Lords-day, or upon any other dayes, upon pretence of their Church estate or for the administration or exercises of any pretended Ecclesiastical function as dispensation of the Seals or preaching; wherein if they shall be taken offending, they shall be imprisoned till the tenth of *July* next and then left at their liberty, within ten dayes to depart the Jurisdiction upon penalty as abovesaid.

Edward Rawson Secret.

FINIS.

SEVERAL LAVVS AND ORDERS

Made at the

General Court,

Held at Boston in New-England,

October 14. 1668.

PRinted and Publifhed by their Order.

Edward Rawfon Secr.

Cambridge Printed in the Year, 1668.

Several Laws and Orders,

Made at the General Court held at *Boston* in *NEW-ENGLAND*, October 14. 1668.

Maritime Affaires.

WHereas through the blessing of God upon this Jurisdiction, the Navigation and Maritime affairs thereof, is grown to be a considerable interest, the well management whereof, is of great concernment to the publick weale; for the better ordering the same for the future, and that there may be known Laws and Rules for all sorts of persons imployed therein, according to their several stations and capacities, and that there may be one Rule for the guidance of all Courts in their proceedings, in distributive justice; This Court doth Order, and be It Ordered by the Authority thereof,

SECT. 1.

That whereas there is many times differences between owners of Ships, Ketches, Barques and other vessels, in setting forth their several parts, whereby damage doth accrew to the particular concernment of owners, and if not prevented, may be a great obstruction of Trade, where there are several owners concerned, as owners in Ship, Ketch, Barque or other Vessel whatsoever, used for Traffick, Commerce, Fishing, Log, Board, Wood or Stone, carriage upon salt or fresh Water, all such owners of lesser part, shall be concluded for the setting forth of his part, by the major part of the whole concerned, such owners so concluded, having notice given them of the meeting for such conclusion, if they be nigh hand; and in case of any owner refusing, or by reason of neglect or absence, or not able to provide for the setting forth his part, the Master of such Ship or Vessel may take up upon the bottom, for the setting forth of the said part; the which being defrayed, the remainder of the income of such part to be paid by the Master to the said owner.

Sect. 2.

And in case of Fraightment, where any owner shall refuse to assent to the letting out of Ship or Vessel, where he is interessed, such dissenter shall manifest it by some publick act of protest, before the signing of charter party, except the master or the rest of the owners or both, conceal from him or them their actings, then his or their protest after charter party, signed by themselves or agents, shall be taken for legal dissent, yet not to hinder the proceed of the Ship or Vessel, but that those so sending her forth, shall be liable to respond his part upon ensurance according to the custome of Merchants, which ensurance is to be defalked out of that part of hire, due for such owners which dissented.

Sect. 3.

Whereas Masters of Ships or other Vessels, have their owners live part in one Country and part in another, whereby they have in themselves not only oportunity; and some have made use thereof in their own persons, to represent the major part of the owners in the place where he comes; It is therefore Ordered that such Master shall not be taken to have vote in the ordering of such vessel further then his own interest, except he make it appear to the rest of the owners, where he is, that he is authorized under the hands of such owners absent, and then he is to have votes according to the proportion of parts he so stands for, and the majority of parts are to carry it as before; nevertheless it is to be understood, that any owner hath power to make sale of his part, either to the rest of the owners, or others, as may be most to his own advantage, and if any Master shall presume to act contrary hereunto, what damage shall be sustained by the rest of the owners, the Master shall be liable to make good, it being duely proved against him.

Sect. 4.

All Masters taking charge, as Masters of ship or other vessel, & not being sufficient to discharge his place, or that through negligence, or otherwise, shall imbezel the owners or imployers stock, or time, or that shall suffer his men to neglect their due attendance on board, both by day and night, especially when or whilest Merchants Goods are on board, and that Himself or Mate be not on board every night, to see good orders kept, upon defect therein, such Master shall be liable to pay the damage that shall accrew by such neglect, it being duely proved against him.

Sect. 5.

For the Masters better securing their men to them, and to prevent

all

all Coven, they shall make clear agreements with their Marriners, and Officers, for their wages, and those agreements enter into a Book, and take the several mens hands thereto, a copy whereof the Master as a portlige bill shall leave with their owners if required of them, before their setting saile upon the voyage, and all such agreements, the Master shall make good to the seamen, and such ship or vessel as they saile in, shall be liable for to make good the same.

Sect. 6.

All Masters of greater or lesser vessels, shall make due and meet provisions of victuals and drink for their seamen, or passengers, according to the laudable custome of our English Nation, as the custome and capacity of the places they saile from will admit, upon penalty of paying damages sustained for neglect thereof.

Sect. 7.

That no Master shall ship any seaman or marriner that is shipt before by another Master or Imployer upon a voyage, nor shall any seaman ship himself to any other man, until he be discharged from him that shipt him first, upon penalty of him that entertains him to pay one months pay, that such seaman agrees for, as also of such seaman shipping himself to pay one months pay that he agrees for: the half thereof to be paid to the use of the poor of the Town or place where the offence is committed, the other half to the complainer or informer.

Sect. 8.

No Master of ship or vessel shall saile into any Haven or Port, except necessitated thereunto by wind or weather, or for want of provision, or for security from Pirates, but such port as by charter party, or his bill of Lading, he is bound unto, until he hath delivered his goods according to his engagement; and in case any Master shall take in goods for more ports and places then one, he shall declare himself so to do, to those that fraight upon him, and in case he shall voluntarily go to any other Port or Harbor, then he is obliged to as above: if damage to the Merchants goods happen thereby, such Master shall make good the same, it being duely proved against him.

Sect. 9.

Any Master hired out or imployed by his owners upon any voyage, receiving advice from his imployers, that the alteration of the voyage when they are abroad, may be much for their security and advantage, by going to some other port, the Master seeing meet to close with that advice, the marriners shall not hinder his proceed. unless where any of the seamen shall have made a particular contract with the Master to the contrary, provided that they be not carried to ſtay out above one year, nor be carried to a·y place where they may be liable to be preſſed into a ſervice they are not willing unto

Sect. 10.

Maſters ſhall ſee that their Officers, and Marriners be duely paid their wages according to agreement made with them, upon the finiſhing of their voyage, without delay or trouble, upon penalty of paying damages for neglect, and all coſts that the ſeamen ſhall be at for recovering the ſame.

Sect. 11.

Whereas many times Maſters take in Merchants goods on board their ſhips or veſſels upon fraight, when yet they are not meetly fitted with ſuitable tackling and ſeamen for the ſecurity of ſuch ſhips or veſſels and goods: It is Ordered, that in caſe any Maſter of ſhip or veſſel after he hath laden upon his ſhip or veſſel any Merchants goods to be tranſported, ſhall for want of ſufficient ground tackle (if to be had) or becauſe of want of ſufficient men being on board, come a ſhore to the damage of ſuch Merchants or fraighters in their goods, the ſhip ſhall be liable to make good ſuch damages; and in caſe the defect appear to be in the Maſter and men both, or either, the owners ſhall recover ſuch damage from them.

Sect. 12.

Where any Ship Maſter hath mored his ſhip or veſſel, none other ſhall come ſo near to him firſt mored as to do him damage or receive damage by him, upon the penalty of him ſo coming to make good all the damage, and to be farther puniſhed if wilfulneſs or perverſeneſs in the action be proved againſt him.

Sect. 13.

In caſe any Maſter of ſhip or veſſel under ſaile ſhall run on board any other ſhip or veſſel at an Anchor, and damnifie him, the party offending ſhall pay the damage, and ſuch ſhip or veſſel as he ſailes in ſhall be liable to arreſt for the making good the damage, the damage to be judged by indifferent men, appointed by the Judges thereof, unleſs the parties agree among themſelves.

Sect. 14.

In caſe of loſs of goods by reaſon of throwing ſome over board to eaſe the veſſel to ſave the reſt, the goods thrown over board, ſhall not be done without the Maſter and major part of the companies conſent, or at leaſt of the officers with the Maſter, which goods ſhall be brought into an Avarage, and the whole loſs to be born by ſhip, and goods, and wages in proportion that are ſaved; the like courſe ſhall be for cutting of Maſts, and loſs thereof, or boats, cables or anchors, as alſo of riggin and ſailes, for the ſafety of the whole, the Merchants goods are to bear a part of the loſs.

In

Sect. 15.

In case a ship or vessel, at setting forth proves deficient, and gives over the voyage, the charges the Merchant hath sustained in shipping and landing his goods, shall be born by the Master & owners of such vessel, that presumes to take goods into an insufficient bottom.

Sect. 16.

Any ship or vessel at sea receiving damage by the Masters or marriners negligence, yet bringeth the Merchants goods home, and delivereth them according to bills of lading, he shall receive his fraight, but if the Goods be damnified the Master or marriners shall make good the damage.

Sect. 17.

If any ship or vessel in storm shall break loose and fall upon another, and do her damage for want of ground tackle, the ship breaking loose shall make good the damage; but if it appear the Master, or marriners, or both, are negligent of freshing their hoase, or clearing their Cables, they shall pay the damage for such neglect.

Sect. 18.

All marriners being shipt upon a voyage, and in pay, they shall duely attend the service of the Masters ship or vessel for the voyage, and not absent themselves day or night without leave from the Master, upon forfeit for every offence five shillings.

Sect. 19.

No officers or marriners shall be disorderly or unruly, to occasion disturbance in the ship or other vessel he is shipped upon, to hinder or damnifie the voyage, to be proved by the Master or other marriners, or both, upon penalty of paying the damage if able, and in case of inability to pay, to suffer corporal punishment as the nature of the offence may appear to the Judges; and in case Master or marriners shall conceale the offences of such, and refuse to give in evidences therein, they shall be amerced or imprisoned, as the Judges shall see meet.

Sect. 20.

If any shall undertake the charge of Pilot, boat-swain, gunner, or any other office, in ship or other vessel, and not be able to discharge the duty of the place, such shall lose their wages in part or in whole, and be further punished for their presumption, as the Judges shall see meet.

Sect. 21.

All marriners shall keep true watch at sea or in harbor, as the Master shall appoint, upon pain of forfeit of twelve pence for every default, to be defalked out of their wages.

Sect.

Sect. 22.

Any marriner that hath entred upon a voyage, and shall depart and leave the voyage, shall forfeit all his wages, one half to the poor, the other half to the Master and owners, and be further punished by imprisonment or otherwise as the case may be circumstanced, to be judged by the Magistrate or Magistrates they are complained to, except such seaman shall shew just cause for his so leaving the voyage, and shall procure an order therefore from Authority.

Sect. 23.

If any marriner shall have received any considerable part of his wages, and shall run away from the ship or vessel he belongs to, and decline the service of the Master in the prosecution of the voyage, he shall be pursued as a disobedient runaway servant, and proceeded with as such a one.

Sect. 24.

If any marriner shall entertain any person or persons on board the ship or vessel he sailes in, without the masters leave, or Masters or marriners shall do it at unseasonable times, he or they shall forfeit twenty shillings, one half to the poor, the other half to the owners.

Sect. 25.

No seaman, or seamen, or officer shall commit any outrage upon the Master of any ship or vessel, but those so offending shall be severely punished, by fine or other corporal punishment, as the fact shall appear to be circumstanced to the Judges that shall hear it, and as they shall judge meet; if any officers or marriners, shall combine against the Master, whereby the voyage shall be diverted or hindred, or that damage thereby shall accrue to the ship and goods, they shall be punished with loss of wages, as otherwise as mutiniers, as the case may require.

Sect. 26.

In case any ship or vessel be in distress at sea, by tempest or other accident, the marriners shall do their utmost endeavour to assist the Master in saving ship and goods, and not desert him without apparent hazard appear, that by their staying they may lose their lives.

Sect. 27.

And in case of suffering shipwrack, the marriners are without dispute upon their getting on shore, to do their utmost endeavours to save the ship or vessel, tackle and apparel, as also the Merchants goods as much as may; out of which they shall have a meet compensation for their hazard and paines; and any upon conviction of negligence herein shall be punished.

Bastards.

Bastards.

WHereas there is a Law provided by this Court for punishing of Fornicators, but nothing as yet for the easing of Towns, where Bastards are born, in regard of the poverty of the Parent or Parents of such Children sometimes appearing, nor any rule held forth touching the reputed Father of a Bastard for legal conviction.

It is therefore Ordered, and by this Court Declared, that where any man is legally convicted to be the Father of a Bastard childe, he shall be at the care and charge to maintain and bring up the same, by such assistance of the Mother as nature requireth, and as the Court from time to time (according to circumstances) shall see meet to Order: and in case the Father of a Bastard, by confession or other manifest proof, upon trial of the case, do not appear to the Courts satisfaction, then the Man charged by the Woman to be the Father, shee holding constant in it, (especially being put upon the real discovery of the truth of it in the time of her Travail) shall be the reputed Father, and accordingly be liable to the charge of maintenance as aforesaid (though not to other punishment) notwithstanding his denial, unless the circumstances of the case and pleas be such, on the behalf of the man charged, as that the Court that have the cognizance thereon shall see reason to acquit him, and otherwise dispose of the Childe and education thereof. Provided alwayes, in case there be no person accused in the time of her travail, it shall not be available to abate the conviction of a reputed Father, any Law, Custome or usage to the contrary notwithstanding.

Tolling of Cattle.

F*or the prevention of felonious practices growing upon us, by stealing of Horse-kinde, and other Neat Cattle, and selling them as their own.*

It is Ordered by this Court and the Authority thereof, that there shall be a Toll-Book kept in every Town by the Clerk of the Writs, wherein all Horse kinde and other Cattle, as aforesaid, bought of any person, shall be entred, with their age, colour and marks, at the peril of the buyer, with the name of the seller, and such seller shall have two Vouchers, to testifie the said seller to be the proper owner of such Horse kinde, or other Cattle so sold; or in case of Horse kinde or Cattle so sold, shall be challenged by any other person, the Vouchers in case of the escape of the seller, shall be liable to all damages that shall arise thereupon; and the Clerk of the Writs shall have three pence of the buyer, for entring every such Horse kinde, or Neat Cattle, and if any Horse kinde, or other Cattle as aforesaid, so bought by any person be not Toll'd, nor Sellers, nor Vouchers found, upon challenge of any such Cattel, the said buyer shall be liable to all damages, as the Felon himself should be were he present, and any person or persons having lost any Horse kinde, or other such Cattle, shall have free liberty to search any Toll-Book in any Town in any such case.

Signing of Warrants.

IT is Ordered by this Court and the Authority thereof, that the Secretary for the time being, shall from time to time, sign all warrants for the execution of persons sentenced to death, either in the General Court or Court of Assistants: and that the Secretary or Clerk of every Court, shall signe Warrants for executions in all other judgements of Courts civil or criminal; any custome or usage to the contrary notwithstanding.

Idle

Idle Persons.

W*hereas, in*] *the Law tit. House of Correction, Idle persons are particular*]*ly named as such, as the Law intendeth should* [*be committed*]*to that House for Correction and reformation: This Court taking notice, upon good information and sad complaints, that there are some persons in this Jurisdiction, that have families to provide for, who greatly neglect their callings, or mispend what they earn, whereby their families are in much want, and are thereby exposed to suffer, and to need relief from others.*

This Court for remedy of these great and unsufferable evils, do declare, that by idle persons (mentioned in the recited Law) such neglectors of their families, are comprehended amongst the rest, and that in a special manner.

Sabbath breakers.

F*Or the better prevention of the breach of the Sabbath.* It is enacted by this Court and the Authority hereof, that no servile work shall be done on that day, *namely*, such as are not works of *Piety*, of *Charity*, or of *Necessity*, aud when other works are done on that day, the persons so doing, upon complaint, or presentment, being legally convicted thereof, before any Magistrate, or County Court, shall pay for the first offence *Ten shillings* fine, and for every offence after to be doubled; and in case the offence herein be circumstanced with prophaness, or high-handed presumption, the penalty is to be augmented at the discretion of the Judges.

As an Adition to the Law, for preventing prophaning the Sabbath day, by doing servile work; this Court doth Order, that whatsoever Person in this Jurisdiction, shall travel upon the Lords day, either on horse back or on foot, or by boats, from, or out of their own Town, to any unlawful assembly or meeting, not allowed by Law; are hereby declared to be prophaners of the Sabbath, and shall be proceeded against as the persons that prophane the Lords day, by doing servile work.

Single Persons.

F[I]t is Ordered by this Court and the Authority hereof, that the following Order shall be directed and sent by the *Clerks* of the several shire *Courts*, to the *Constables* of the *Towns* within their shire, who are enjoyned faithfully to execute the same, and if upon the return made, it doth appear that the Select [men are negligent in] executing the Laws therein mentioned; th[e Court shall proceed] against them by Admonition, or fine, as the [merit of the case may] require, and shall also dispose of single person[s or stubborn Chil-] dren or servants, to the House of Correction, ac[cording to the in-] tent of the Law, any Law, Custome or Usage to[the contrary not-] withstanding.

To the Constable of A.

W*Hereas the Law published by the honoured General Court,* lib. 1 pag. 76. sect. 3. *do require all Towns, from time to time, to dispose of all single Persons and Inmates within their Towns to service, or otherwise,* and in pag. 16. tit. Children and Youth, It is required of the Select men, that they see that all *Children* and *Youth*, under family Government, be taught to reade perfectly the English Tongue, have knowledge in the Capital Laws, and be taught some Orthodox Catechism, and that they be brought up to some honest imployment, profitable to themselves and the Common Wealth; and in case of neglect on the part of the Family Governours, after admonition given them, the said Select Men are required, with the help of two Magistrates, or next Court of that shire, to take such Children or Apprentices from them, and place them forth with such as will look more straitly to them.

The neglect whereof, as by sad experience from Court to Court abundantly appears, doth occasion much sin and prophaness to increase among us, to the dishonour of God, and the ensnaring of many Children and Servants, by the dissolute lives and practices of such as do live from under Family Government, and is a great discouragement to those Family Governours, who conscientiously endeavour to bring up their Youth in all Christian nurture, as the Laws of God and this Common wealth doth require:

THese are therefore in his Majesties Name to require you to acquaint the Select men of your Town, that the Court doth expect and will require, that the said Laws be accordingly attended, the prevalency of the former neglect notwithstanding: and you are also required to take a list of the names of those young persons within the bounds of your Town, and all adjacent Farms though out of all Town bounds, who do live from under Family Government, *viz.* do not serve their Parents or Masters, as Children, Apprentices, hired Servants, or Journey men ought to do, and usually did in our Native Country, being subject to their com-

mands

[mands and discipline; and the same you are to return to the next Court to be held at on the day of ; and hereof you are to make a true return, under your hand, and not to faile.]

[NOTE 62. — I have completed this section from the corresponding section in Code of 1672, pp. 149, 150. There is evidence in Rawson's copy that there was a printed page, which would be number 19, and the *verso* would be 20. It seems highly probable that these two pages contained certain laws which we find in the Code of 1672, either dated in 1668, or clearly passed in the October session of that year. These five laws are as follows: —

Code of 1672, p.	2.	Age of Plaintiffs and Defendants (dated 1668)	10 lines.
" "	11.	Breach of the Peace (Rec. iv, pt. ii, p. 397.)	14 "
" "	11.	Judgment for Title of House do.	16 "
" "	46.	Ecclesiastical (Rec. iv, pt. ii, p. 396.)	18 "
" "	53.	Fish (Rec. iv, pt. ii, p. 368.)	10 "
" "	"	" (Rec. iv, pt. ii, p. 400.)	15 "
		Total	83

As the Supplement is in pages of 42 lines, there would be room to print these laws on the two pages, 19 and 20, which we know existed. Moreover, we find that all of the laws which were in this Supplement of 1668 are reprinted in the Code of 1672, excepting five, and the reason of these omissions is evident. They are

1st. "Charges Public" (my page 239). This law was repealed May 19, 1669. (Rec. iv, pt. ii, p. 420.)

2d. "Imposts" (p. 242). The first part of this law was not put in the Code, as it was a temporary law.

3d. "Horses rated for Taxation" (p. 244). In the Code of 1672, the law is given according to this act, but the marginal citation is Anno 1657. The law of *that* year, however, as cited in the Code of 1660, fixed the rates at £10, 7, and 5, respectively; and we see that the marginal references cannot be implicitly believed in small details. The law was again amended in 1677.

4th. "Dry Dock in Boston" (p. 244). Evidently a special law, and therefore omitted in 1672.

5th. "Anabaptists" (pp. 246–247). Not reprinted, it being termed "a sentence of the Court," when the Secretary was ordered to print it. (Rec. iv, pt. ii, p. 404.)

Lastly. On p. 116 of the Code of 1672 there is a law title "Military," dated in 1668, which is a misprint for 1669. (See Rec. iv, pt. ii, p. 422, May 19, 1669.)

As to the undated paragraphs in the Code of 1672, besides those already noted as passed in 1668, I can affix the true dates as follows: —

	Page	Title		Date	Reference
Code of 1672.	Page 9,	Title,	Benevolences, law of	May 31, 1671.	(Rec. iv, pt. ii, p. 488.)
	" 17,	"	Coopers, "	May 19, 1669.	(Rec. iv, pt. ii, p. 421.)
	" 39,	"	Debt, "	"	(do. p. 422.)
	" 41,	"	Deputies, "	Oct. 21, 1663.	(do. p. 87.)
	" 48,	"	Quakers, "	"	(do. p. 88.)
	" 53,	"	Fish, "	Oct. 12, 1670.	(do. p. 462.)
	" 54,	"	" "	"	(do. do.)
	" 57,	"	Galloping, "	Oct. 8, 1662.	(do. p. 59.)
	" 70,	"	Impost, "	May 19, 1669.	(do. p. 366.)
	" 106,	"	Malt, "	May 30, 1660.	(Rec. iv, pt. i, p. 418.)

W. H. W.]

INDEX OF NAMES AND SUBJECTS.

INDEX TO THE LAWS.

300

www.ingramcontent.com/pod-product-compliance
Lightning Source LLC
Chambersburg PA
CBHW021126270326
41929CB00009B/1059

* 9 7 8 3 3 3 7 1 5 4 6 4 6 *